LAND
OF THE
LUSTROUS
7

HARUKO ICHIKAWA

D1255605

CHARACTER INTRODUCTIONS

Yellow Diamond
HARDNESS: 10
The eldest. Has had many hobbies, but forgot them all.

Cairngorm
HARDNESS: 7
Has enjoyed reading just a little ever since the Ghost Quartz days. Would actually prefer the reading be done aloud by Lapis.

Rutile
HARDNESS: 6
The gem doctor. Is a workaholic, and therefore has no hobbies.

Phosphophyllite
HARDNESS: 3.5
The hero of our story, Phosphophyllite... Phosphophyllite? Today we'll be introducing everyone's hobbies.

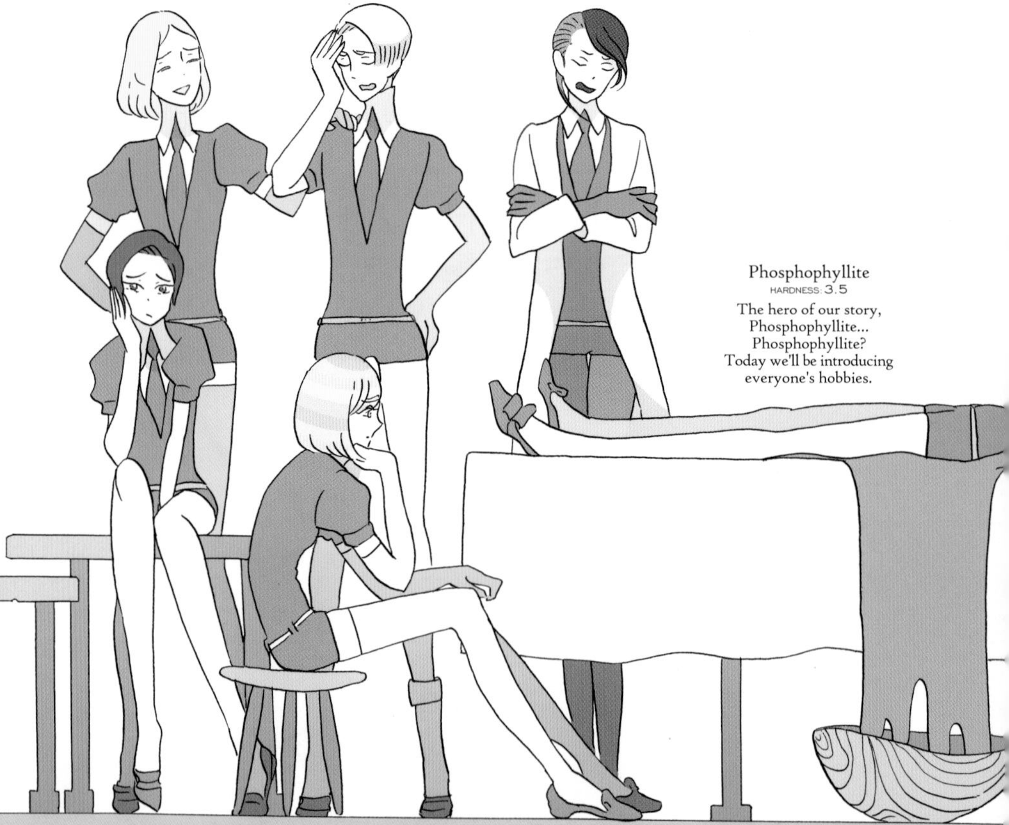

Benitoite
HARDNESS: 6.5
Enjoys cloud-gazing. Also likes playing card games at night with the other gems, despite being terrible at them.

Diamond
HARDNESS: 10
Likes cute and pretty things.

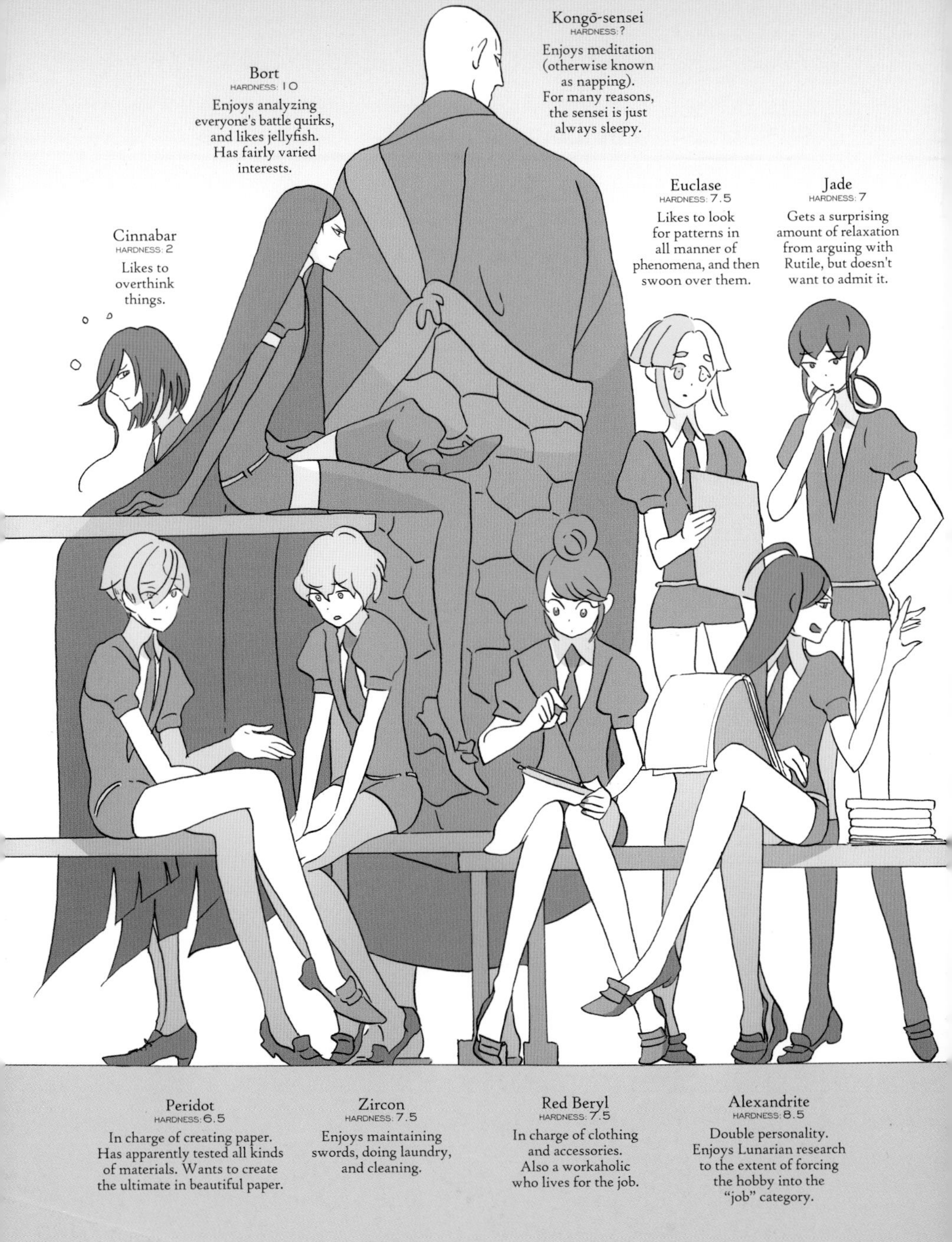
Kongō-sensei
HARDNESS: ?
Enjoys meditation (otherwise known as napping). For many reasons, the sensei is just always sleepy.
Bort
HARDNESS: 10
Enjoys analyzing everyone's battle quirks, and likes jellyfish. Has fairly varied interests.
Jade
HARDNESS: 7
Gets a surprising amount of relaxation from arguing with Rutile, but doesn't want to admit it.
Euclase
HARDNESS: 7.5
Likes to look for patterns in all manner of phenomena, and then swoon over them.
Cinnabar
HARDNESS: 2
Likes to overthink things.
Alexandrite
HARDNESS: 8.5
Double personality. Enjoys Lunarian research to the extent of forcing the hobby into the "job" category.
Red Beryl
HARDNESS: 7.5
In charge of clothing and accessories. Also a workaholic who lives for the job.
Zircon
HARDNESS: 7.5
Enjoys maintaining swords, doing laundry, and cleaning.
Peridot
HARDNESS: 6.5
In charge of creating paper. Has apparently tested all kinds of materials. Wants to create the ultimate in beautiful paper.

CONTENTS

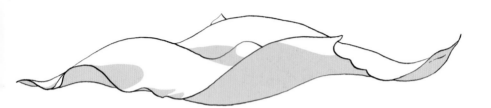

CHAPTER 45:

The Long Winter

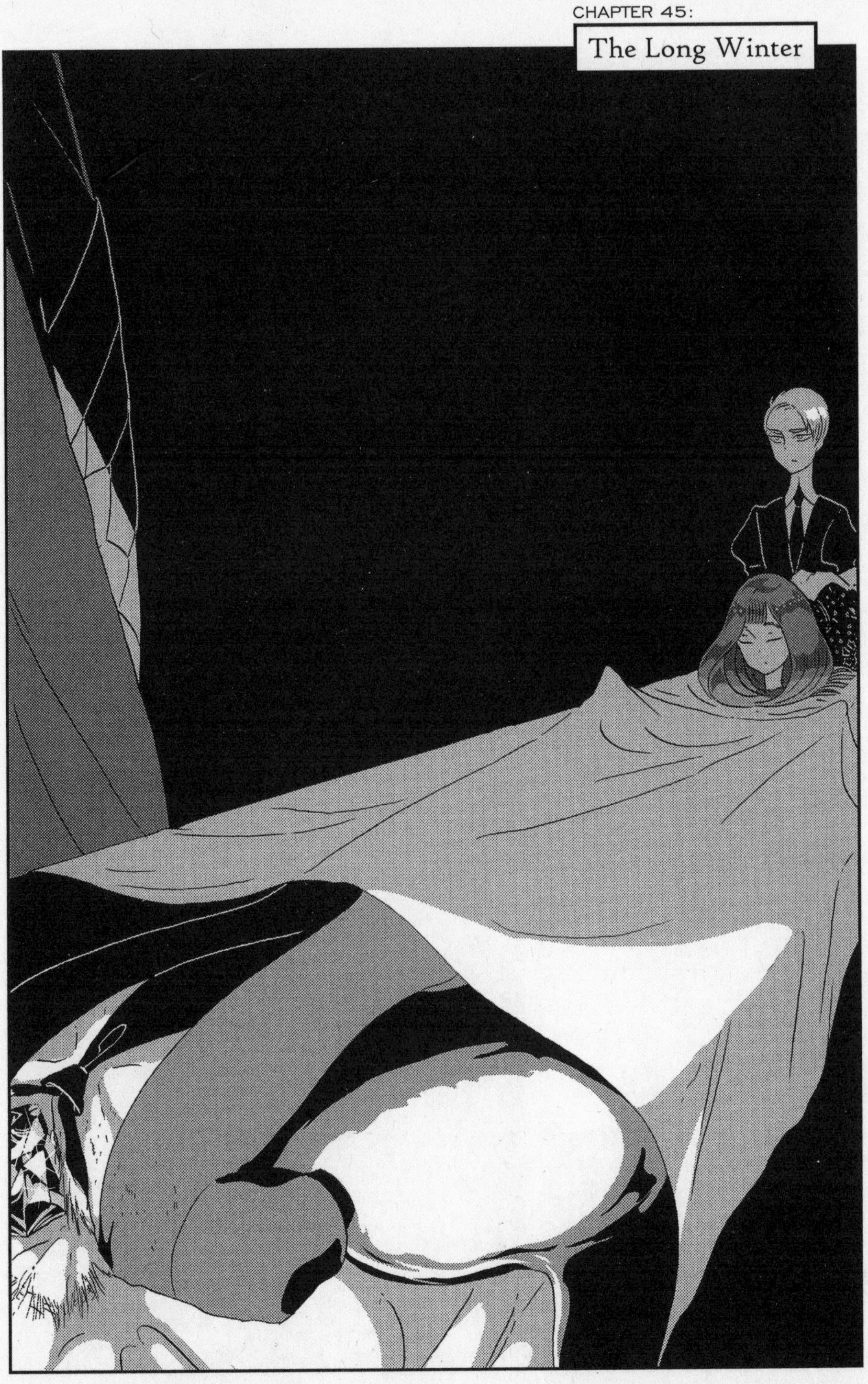

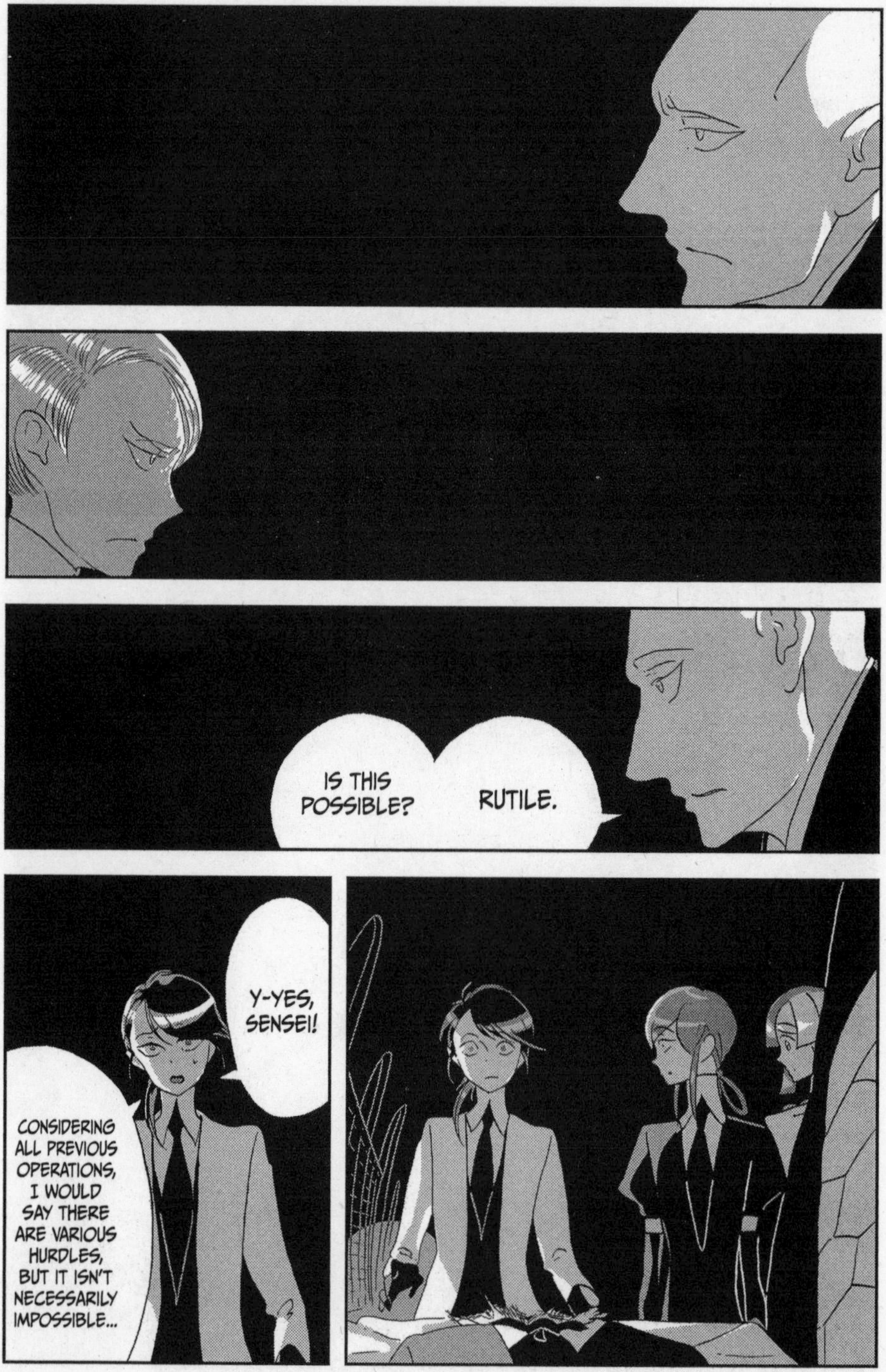
RUTILE.
IS THIS POSSIBLE?
Y-YES, SENSEI!
CONSIDERING ALL PREVIOUS OPERATIONS, I WOULD SAY THERE ARE VARIOUS HURDLES, BUT IT ISN'T NECESSARILY IMPOSSIBLE...

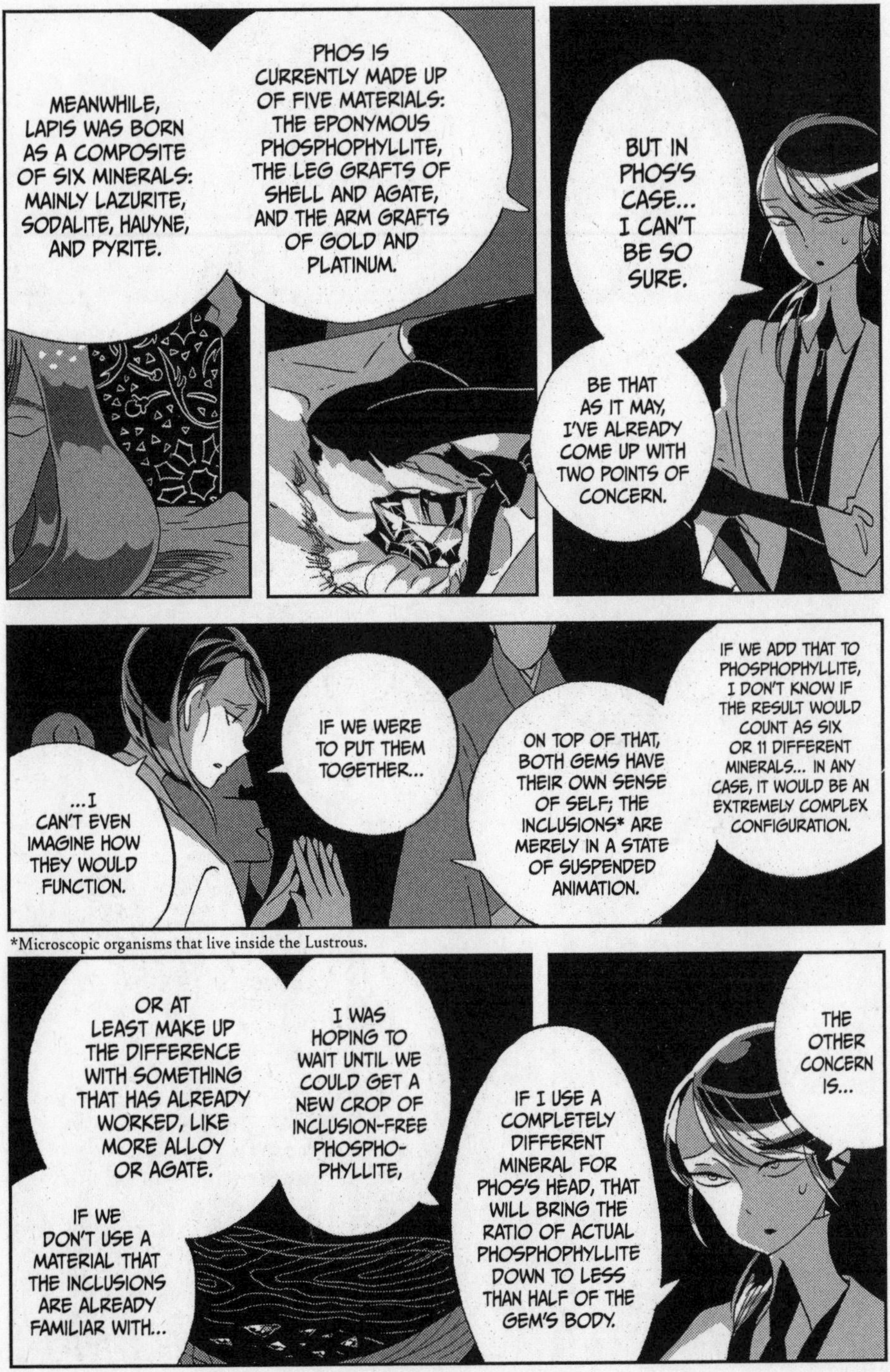
BUT IN PHOS'S CASE... I CAN'T BE SO SURE.
BE THAT AS IT MAY, I'VE ALREADY COME UP WITH TWO POINTS OF CONCERN.
PHOS IS CURRENTLY MADE UP OF FIVE MATERIALS: THE EPONYMOUS PHOSPHOPHYLLITE, THE LEG GRAFTS OF SHELL AND AGATE, AND THE ARM GRAFTS OF GOLD AND PLATINUM.
MEANWHILE, LAPIS WAS BORN AS A COMPOSITE OF SIX MINERALS: MAINLY LAZURITE, SODALITE, HAUYNE, AND PYRITE.
IF WE ADD THAT TO PHOSPHOPHYLLITE, I DON'T KNOW IF THE RESULT WOULD COUNT AS SIX OR 11 DIFFERENT MINERALS... IN ANY CASE, IT WOULD BE AN EXTREMELY COMPLEX CONFIGURATION.
ON TOP OF THAT, BOTH GEMS HAVE THEIR OWN SENSE OF SELF; THE INCLUSIONS* ARE MERELY IN A STATE OF SUSPENDED ANIMATION.
IF WE WERE TO PUT THEM TOGETHER...
...I CAN'T EVEN IMAGINE HOW THEY WOULD FUNCTION.
THE OTHER CONCERN IS...
IF I USE A COMPLETELY DIFFERENT MINERAL FOR PHOS'S HEAD, THAT WILL BRING THE RATIO OF ACTUAL PHOSPHOPHYLLITE DOWN TO LESS THAN HALF OF THE GEM'S BODY.
I WAS HOPING TO WAIT UNTIL WE COULD GET A NEW CROP OF INCLUSION-FREE PHOSPHO-PHYLLITE,
OR AT LEAST MAKE UP THE DIFFERENCE WITH SOMETHING THAT HAS ALREADY WORKED, LIKE MORE ALLOY OR AGATE.
IF WE DON'T USE A MATERIAL THAT THE INCLUSIONS ARE ALREADY FAMILIAR WITH...

*Microscopic organisms that live inside the Lustrous.

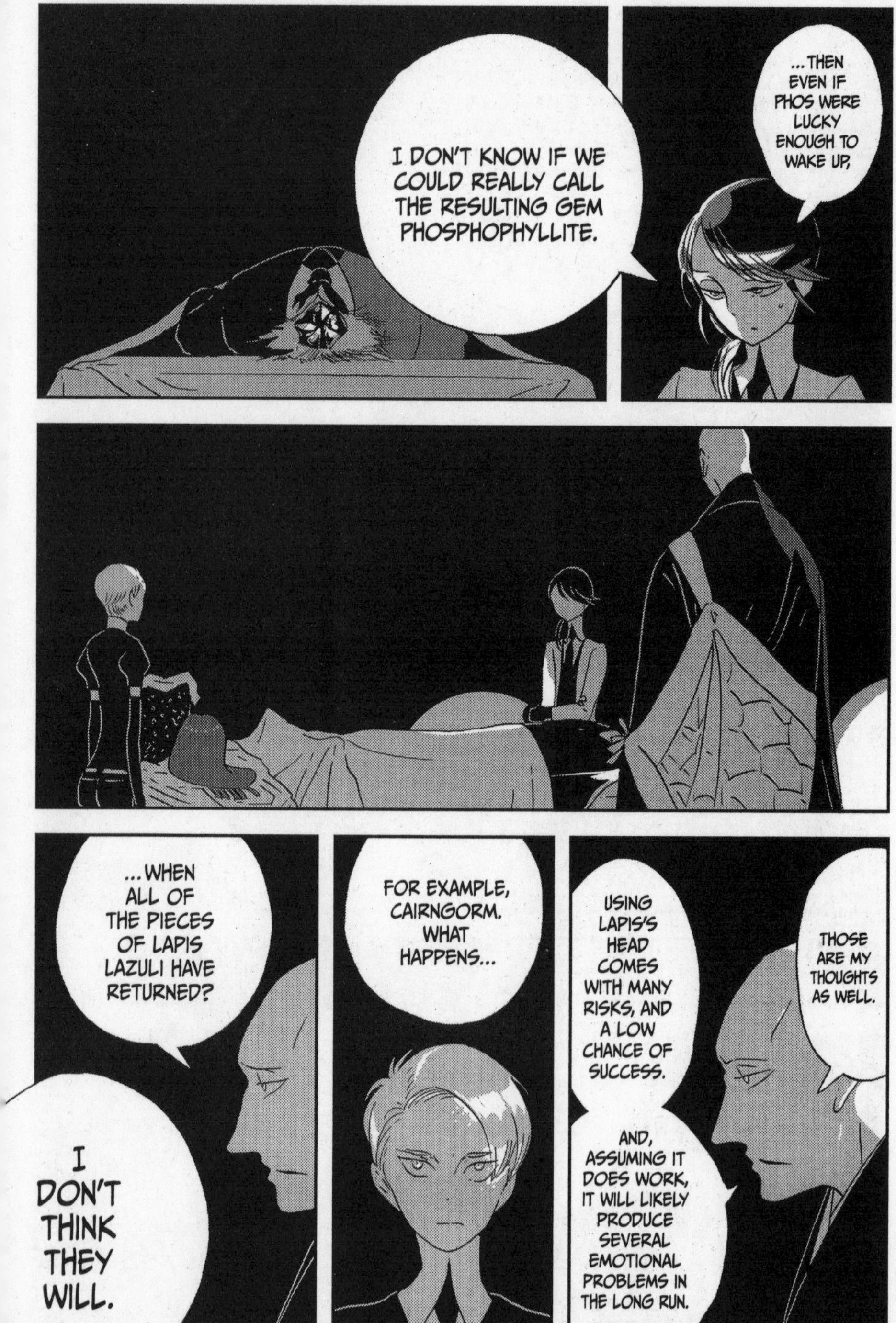
...THEN EVEN IF PHOS WERE LUCKY ENOUGH TO WAKE UP,
I DON'T KNOW IF WE COULD REALLY CALL THE RESULTING GEM PHOSPHOPHYLLITE.
THOSE ARE MY THOUGHTS AS WELL.
USING LAPIS'S HEAD COMES WITH MANY RISKS, AND A LOW CHANCE OF SUCCESS.
AND, ASSUMING IT DOES WORK, IT WILL LIKELY PRODUCE SEVERAL EMOTIONAL PROBLEMS IN THE LONG RUN.
FOR EXAMPLE, CAIRNGORM. WHAT HAPPENS...
...WHEN ALL OF THE PIECES OF LAPIS LAZULI HAVE RETURNED?
I DON'T THINK THEY WILL.

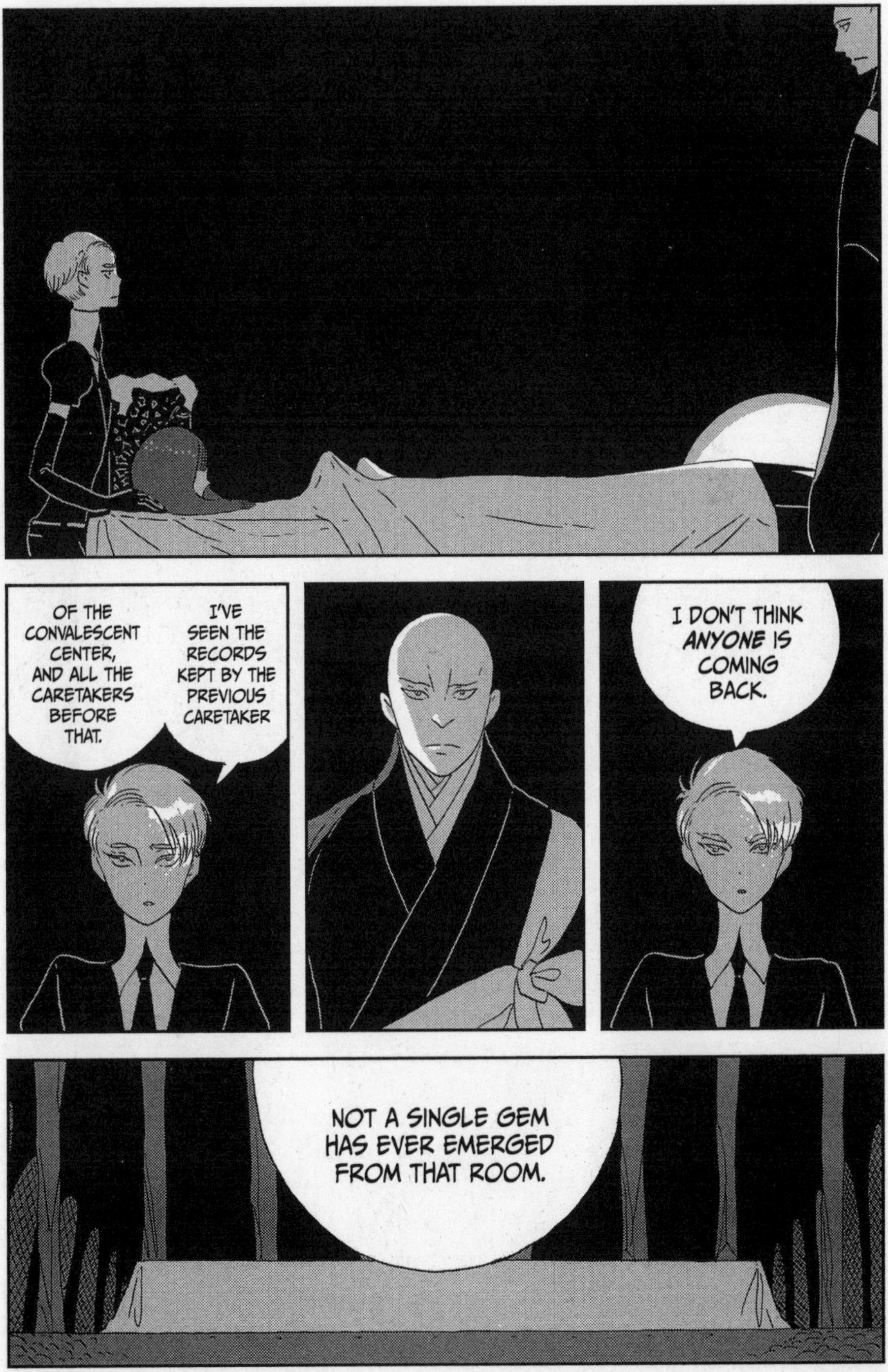
I DON'T THINK *ANYONE* IS COMING BACK.
I'VE SEEN THE RECORDS KEPT BY THE PREVIOUS CARETAKER
OF THE CONVALESCENT CENTER, AND ALL THE CARETAKERS BEFORE THAT.
NOT A SINGLE GEM HAS EVER EMERGED FROM THAT ROOM.

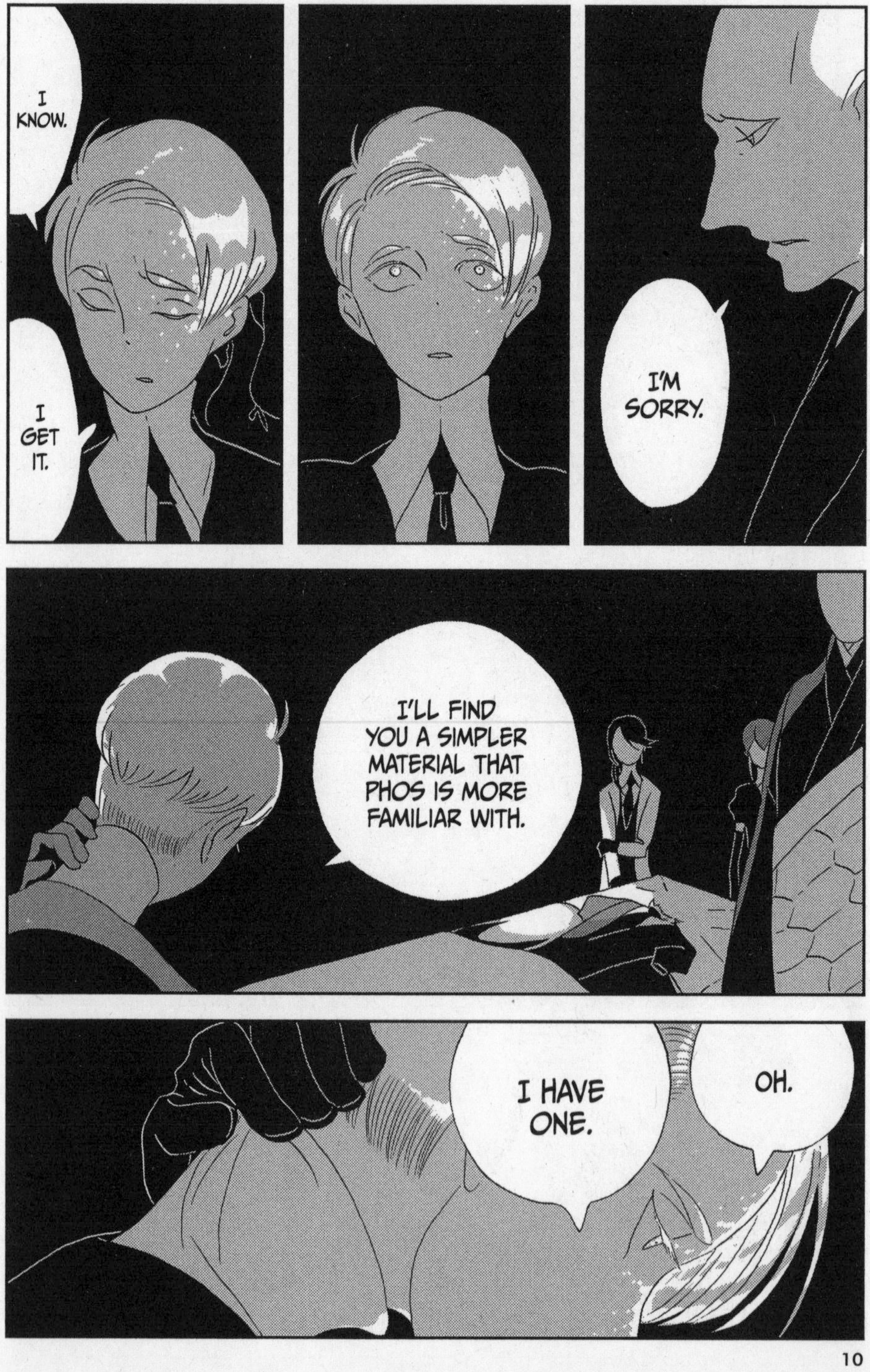
I'M SORRY.
I KNOW.
I GET IT.
I'LL FIND YOU A SIMPLER MATERIAL THAT PHOS IS MORE FAMILIAR WITH.
OH.
I HAVE ONE.

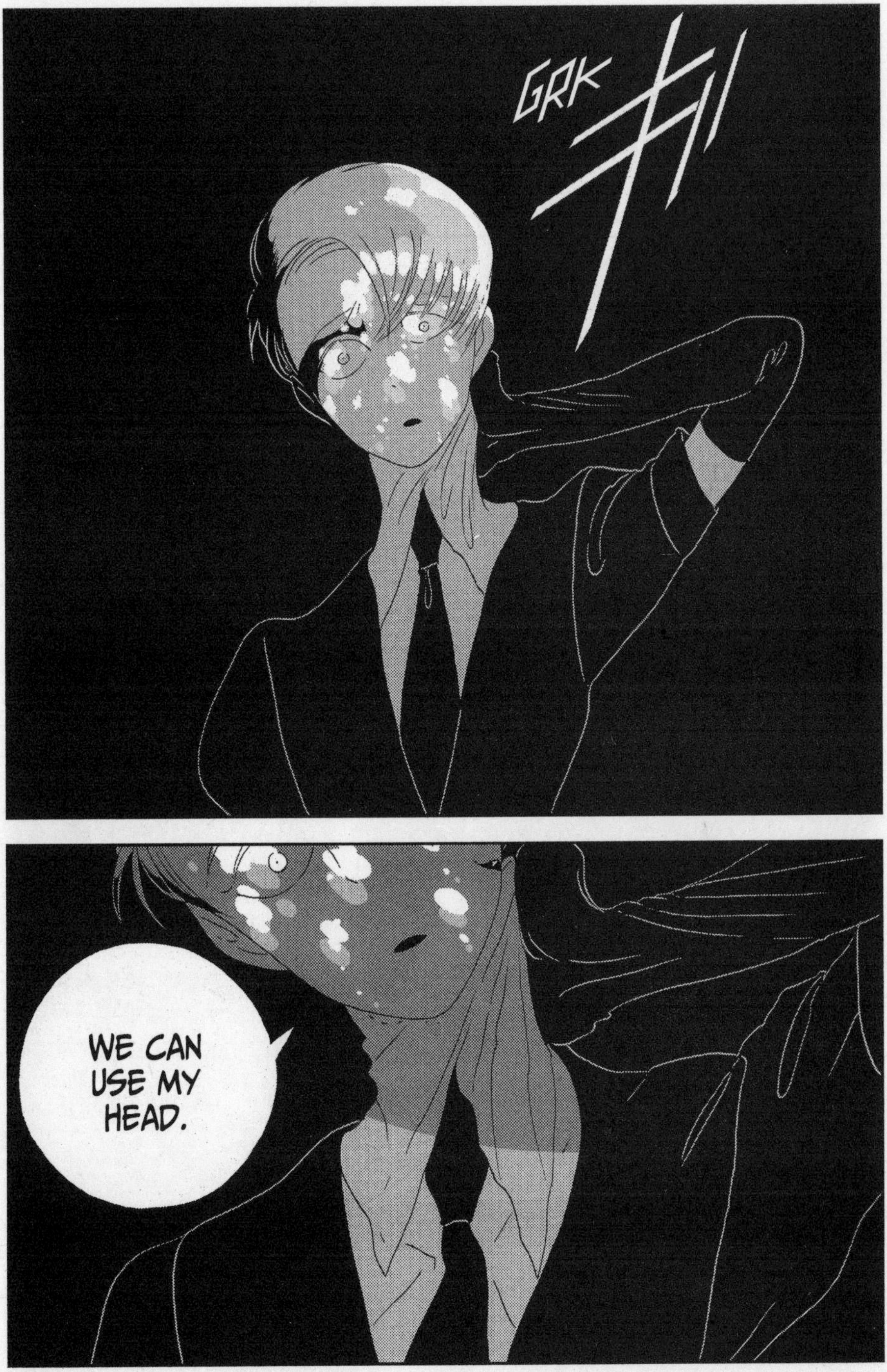
GRK ギリ
WE CAN USE MY HEAD.

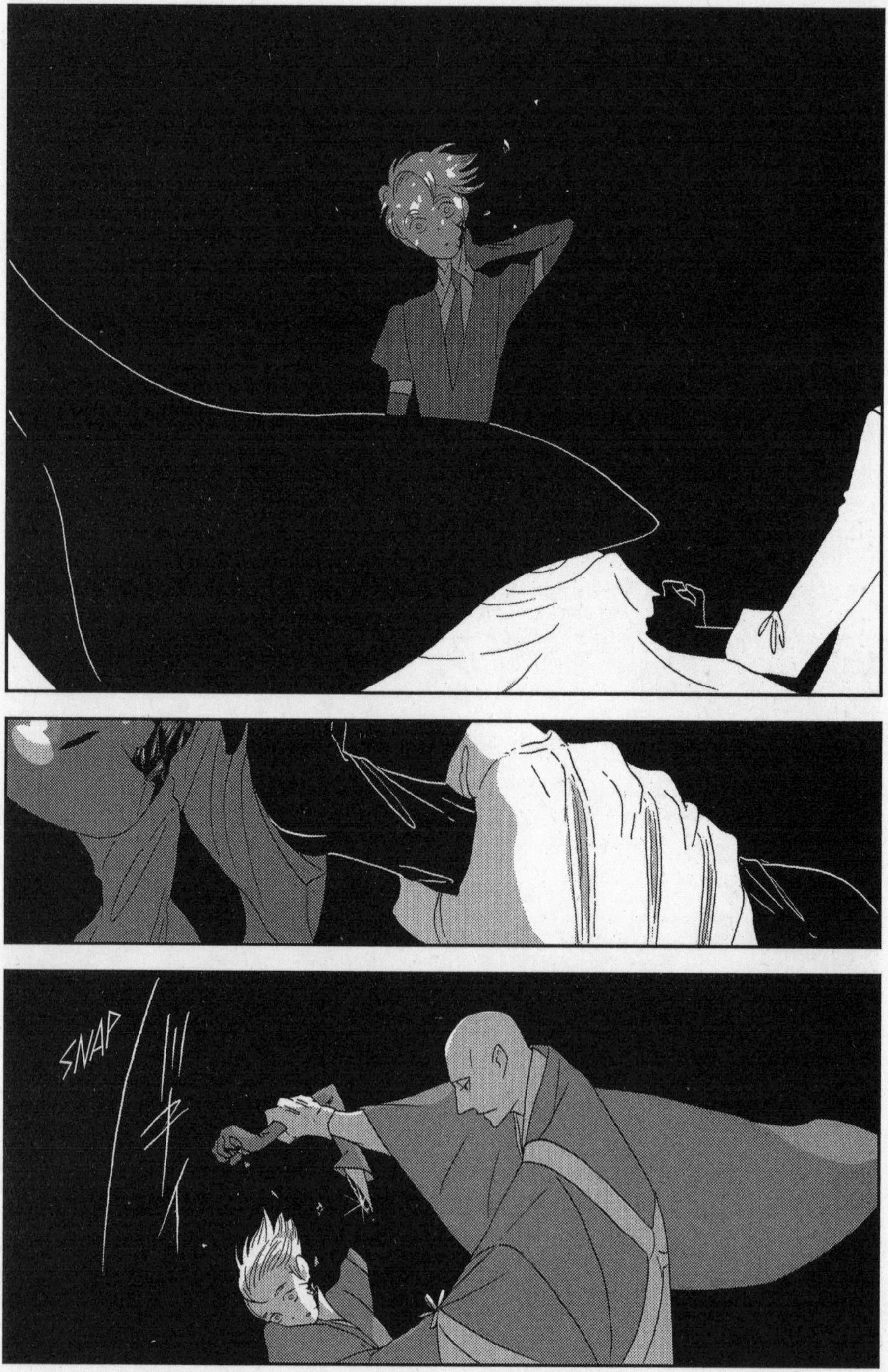
SNAP

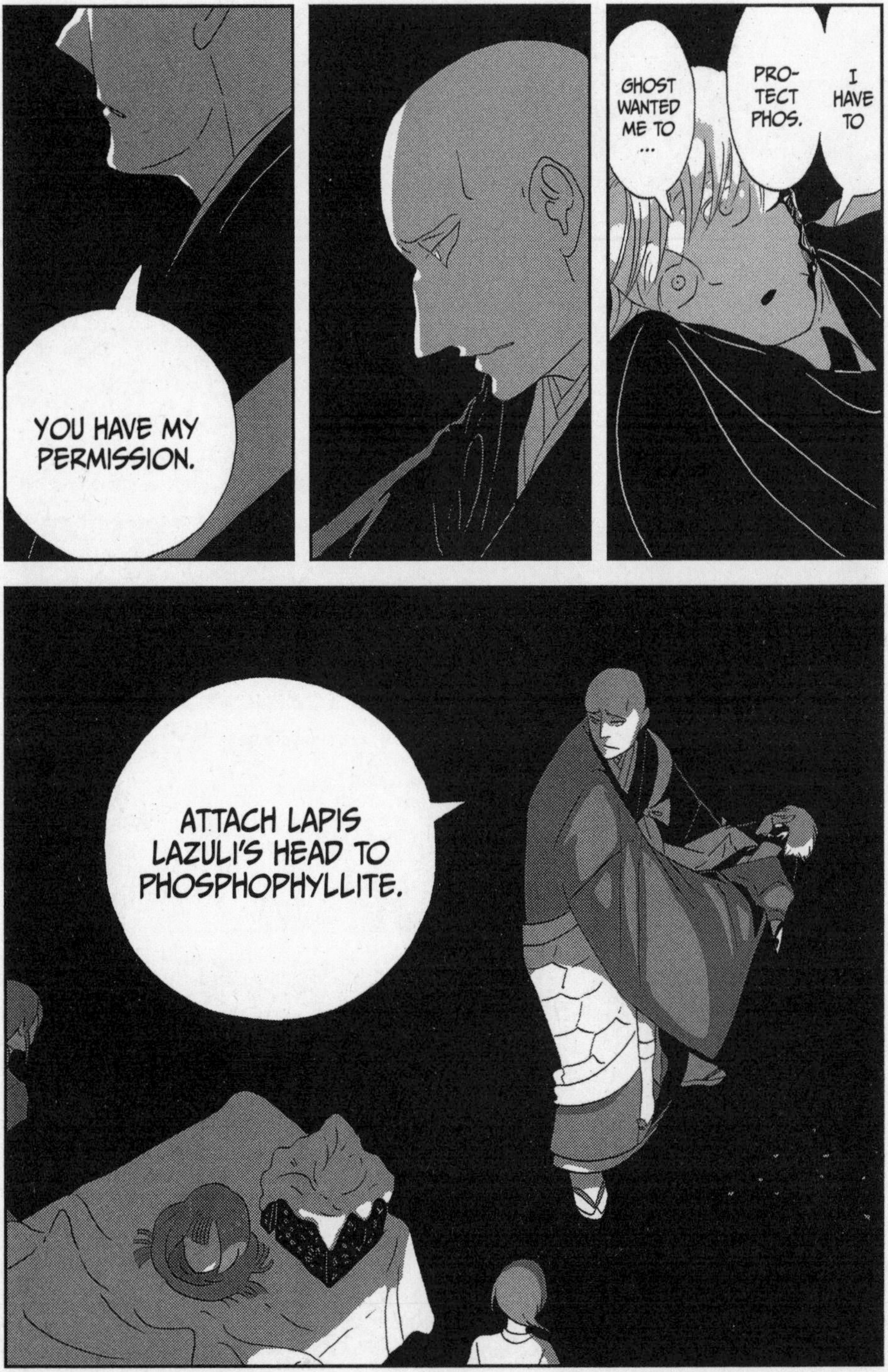
I HAVE TO
PROTECT PHOS.
GHOST WANTED ME TO ...
YOU HAVE MY PERMISSION.
ATTACH LAPIS LAZULI'S HEAD TO PHOSPHOPHYLLITE.

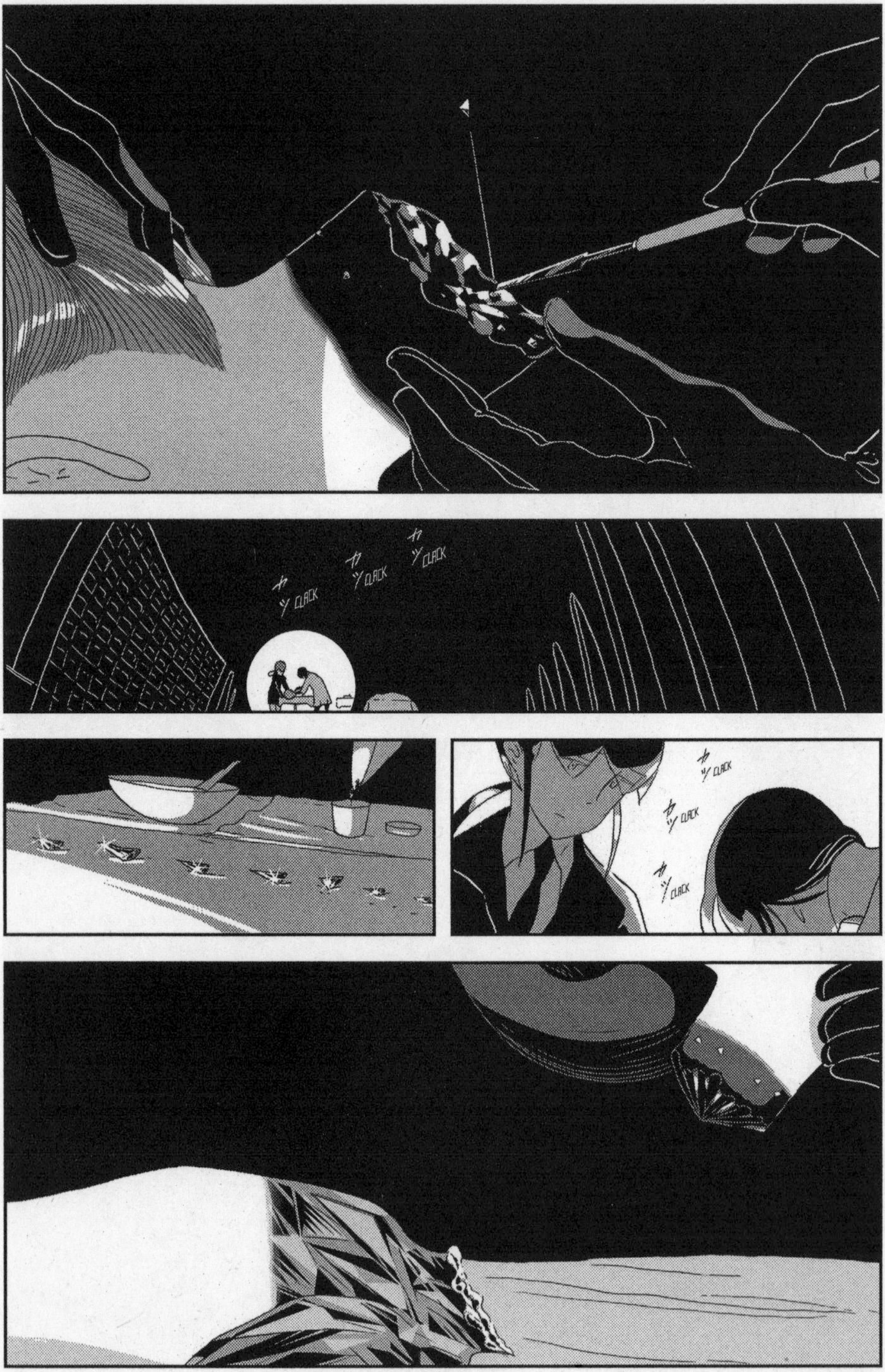

カツ CLACK
カツ CLACK
カツ CLACK
カツ CLACK
カツ CLACK
カツ CLACK

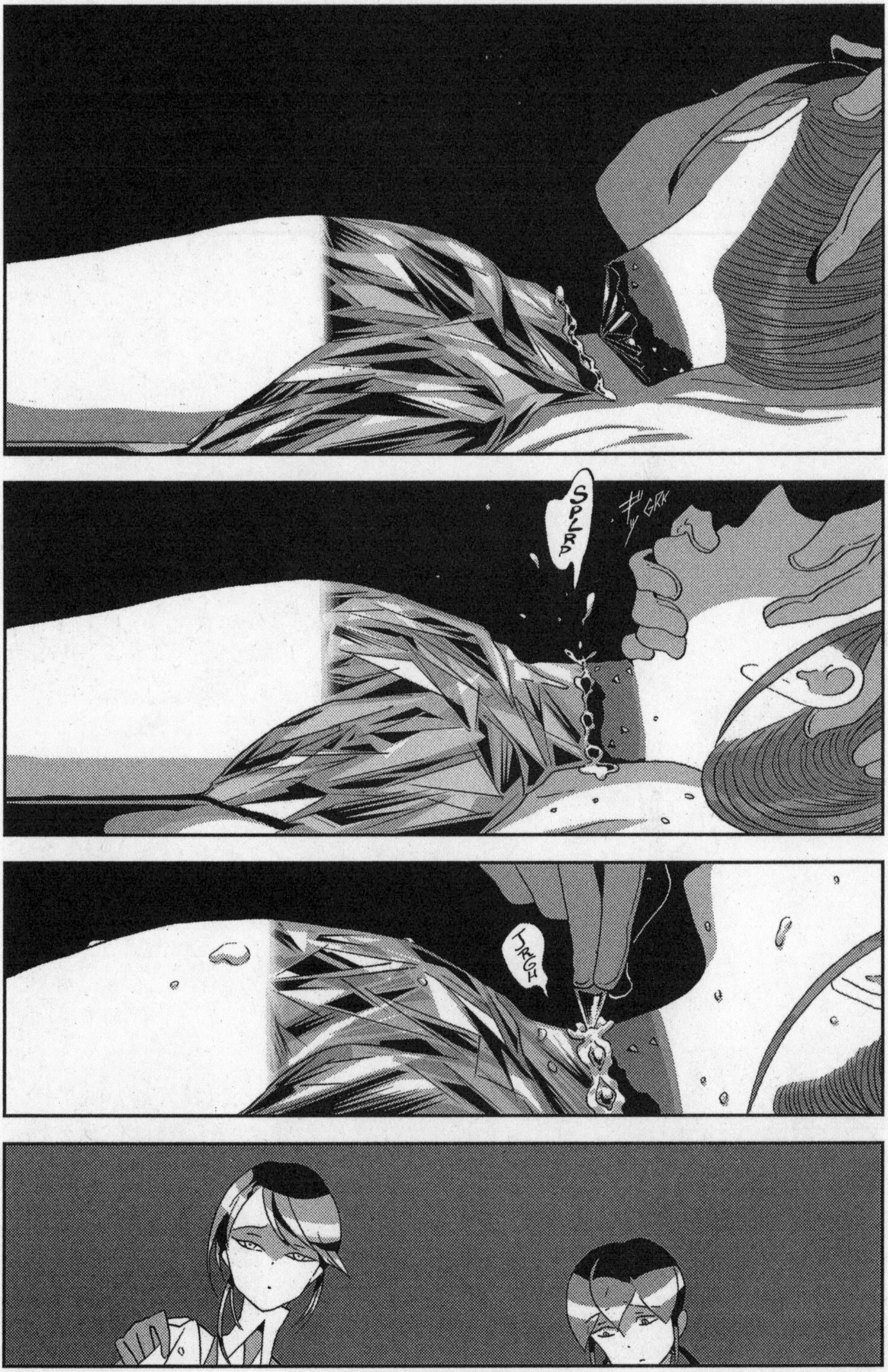
GRK
SPLRP
JRGH

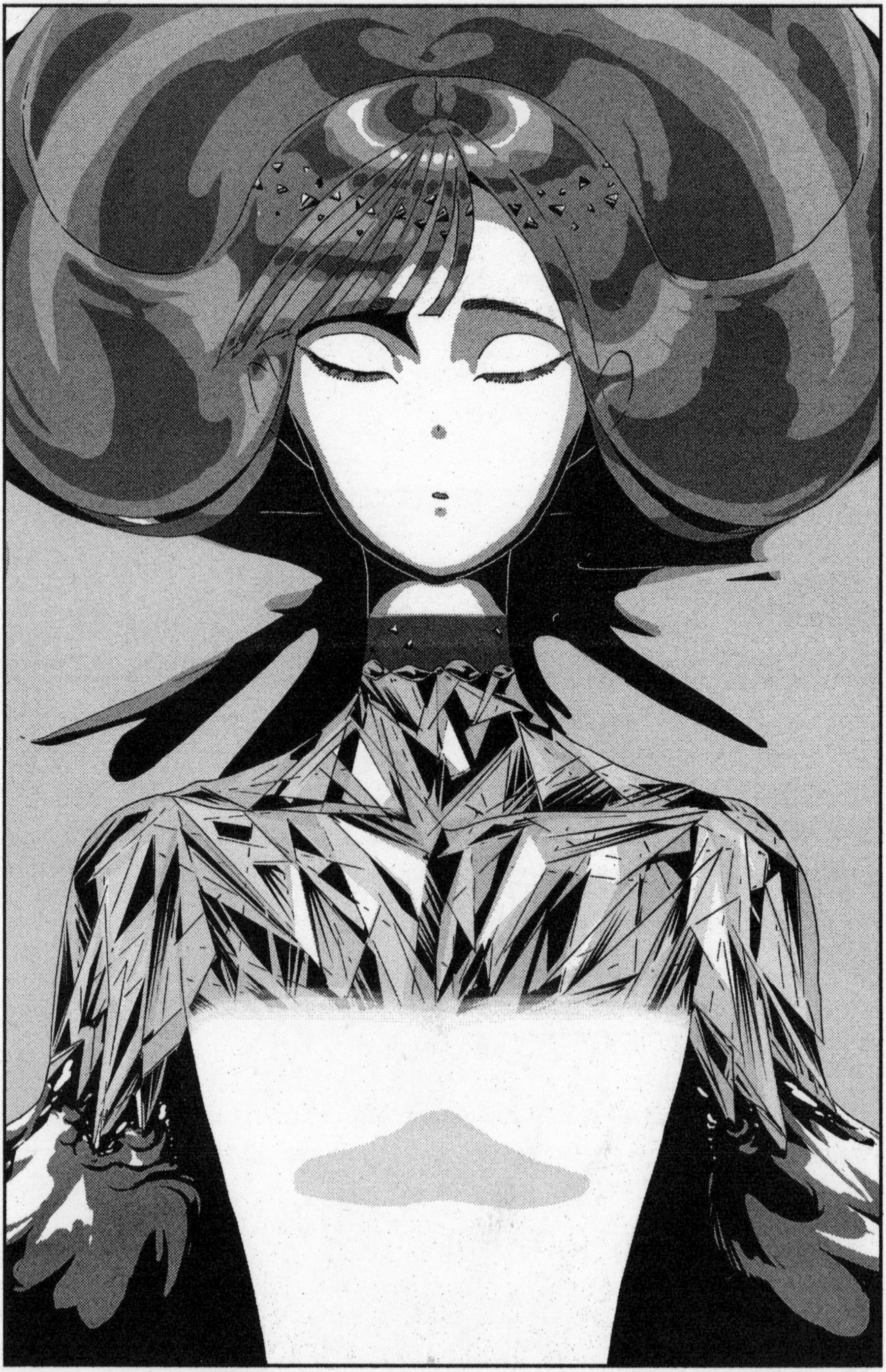

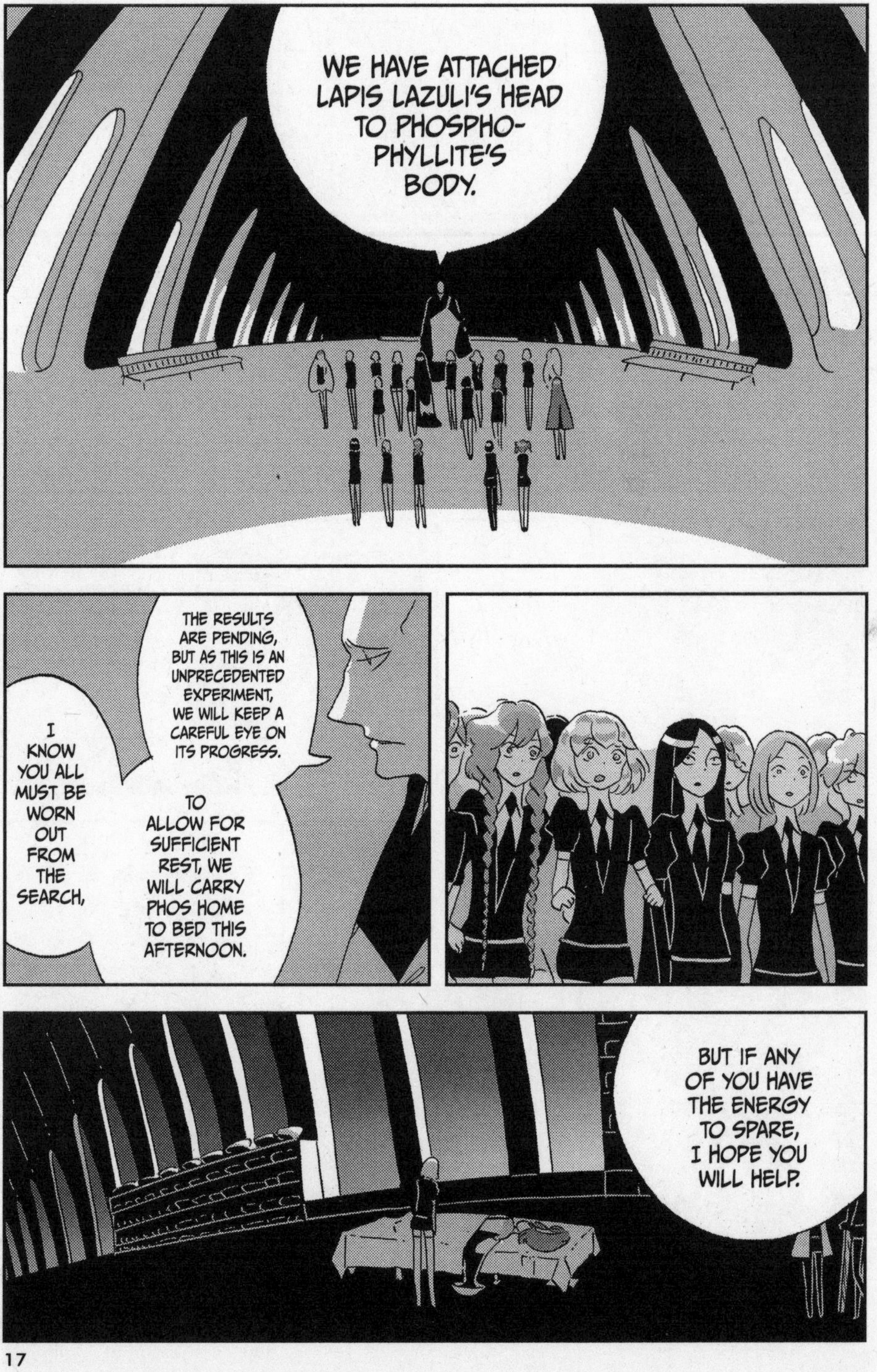
WE HAVE ATTACHED LAPIS LAZULI'S HEAD TO PHOSPHO-PHYLLITE'S BODY.
THE RESULTS ARE PENDING, BUT AS THIS IS AN UNPRECEDENTED EXPERIMENT, WE WILL KEEP A CAREFUL EYE ON ITS PROGRESS.
I KNOW YOU ALL MUST BE WORN OUT FROM THE SEARCH,
TO ALLOW FOR SUFFICIENT REST, WE WILL CARRY PHOS HOME TO BED THIS AFTERNOON.
BUT IF ANY OF YOU HAVE THE ENERGY TO SPARE, I HOPE YOU WILL HELP.

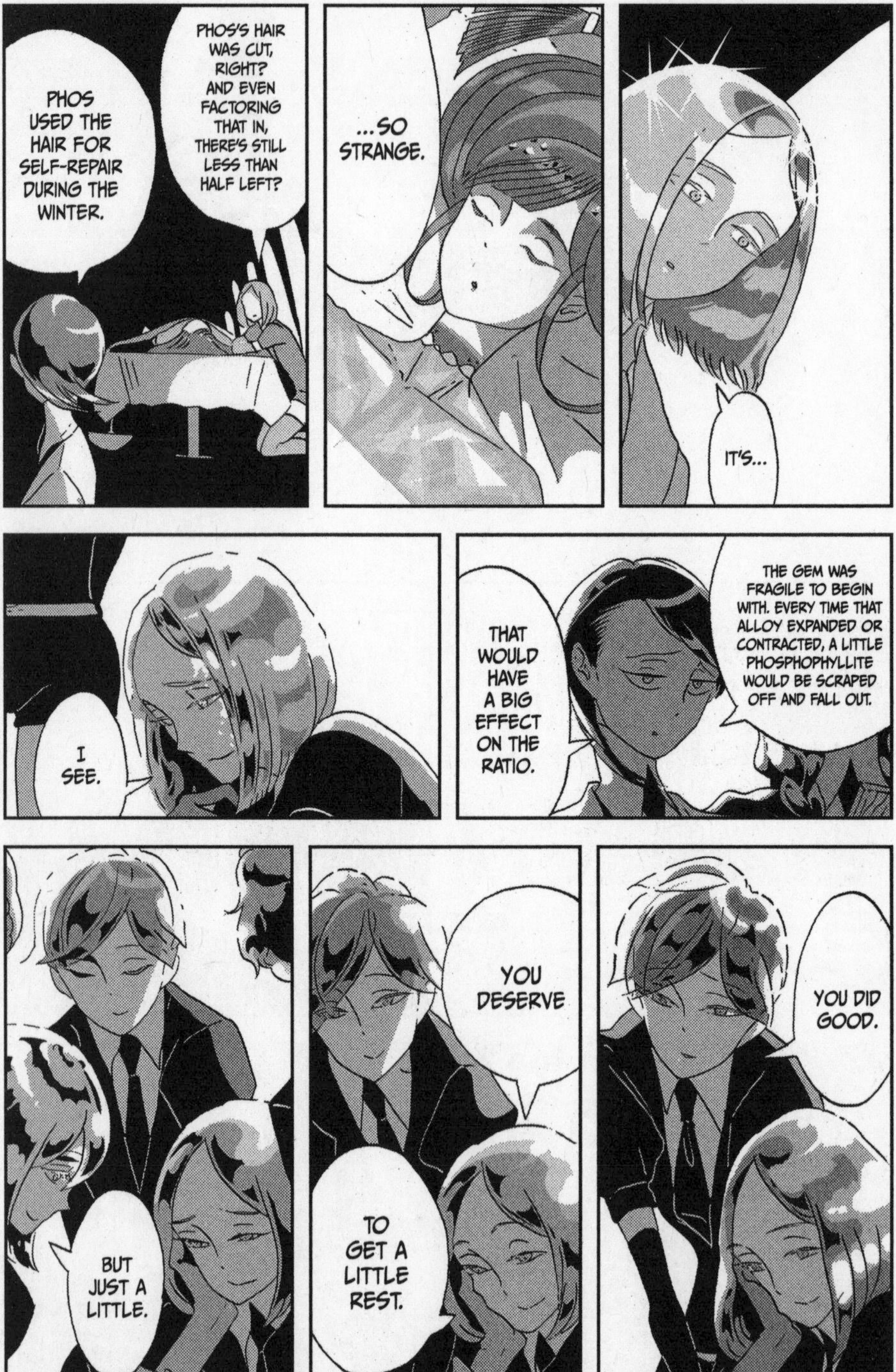
IT'S...
...SO STRANGE.
PHOS'S HAIR WAS CUT, RIGHT? AND EVEN FACTORING THAT IN, THERE'S STILL LESS THAN HALF LEFT?
PHOS USED THE HAIR FOR SELF-REPAIR DURING THE WINTER.
THE GEM WAS FRAGILE TO BEGIN WITH. EVERY TIME THAT ALLOY EXPANDED OR CONTRACTED, A LITTLE PHOSPHOPHYLLITE WOULD BE SCRAPED OFF AND FALL OUT.
THAT WOULD HAVE A BIG EFFECT ON THE RATIO.
I SEE.
YOU DID GOOD.
YOU DESERVE
TO GET A LITTLE REST.
BUT JUST A LITTLE.

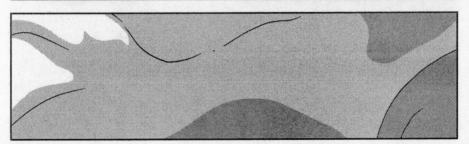

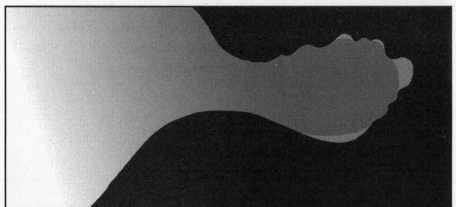

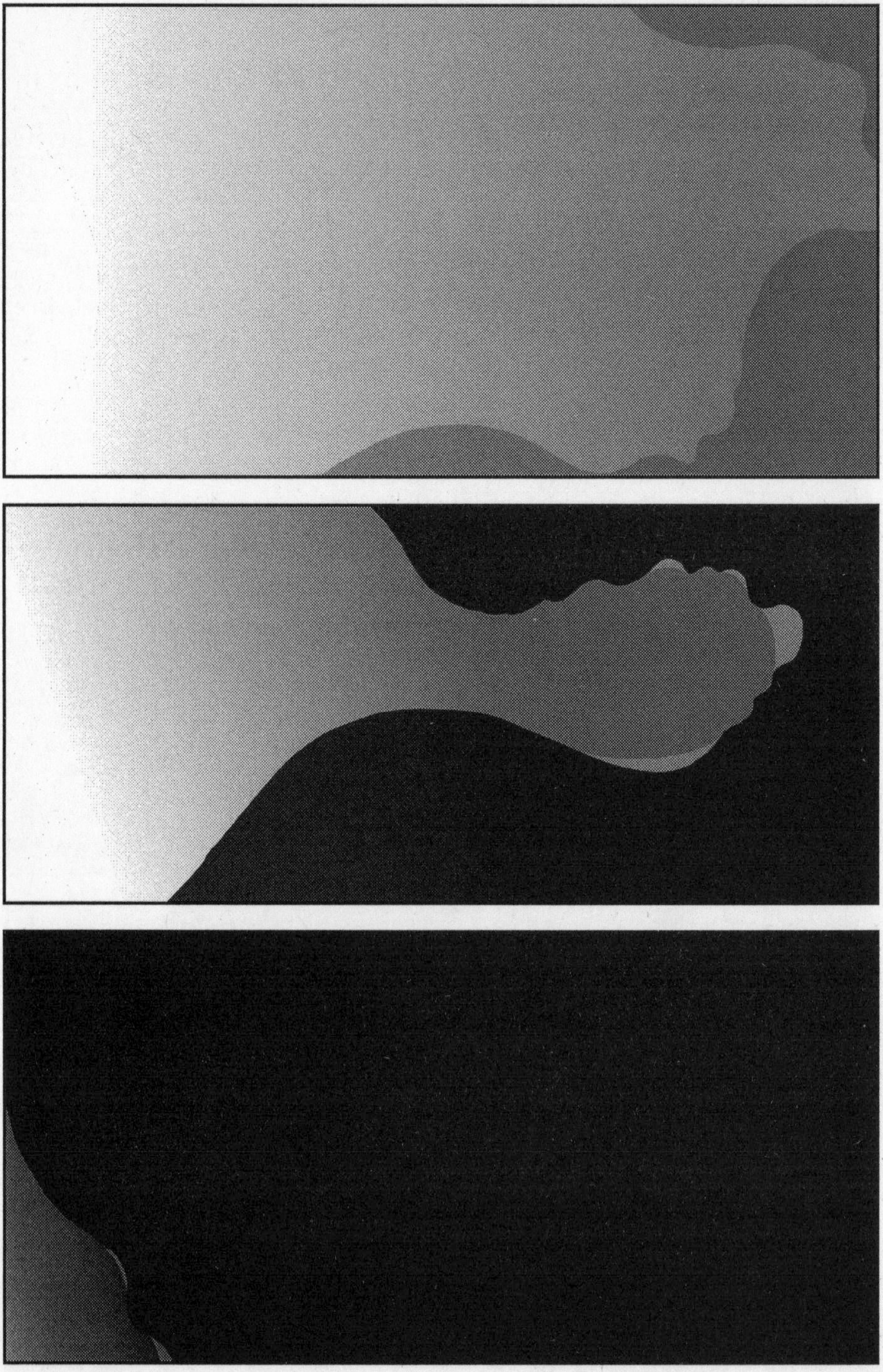

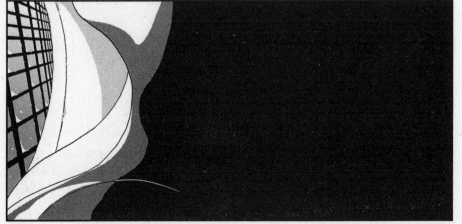

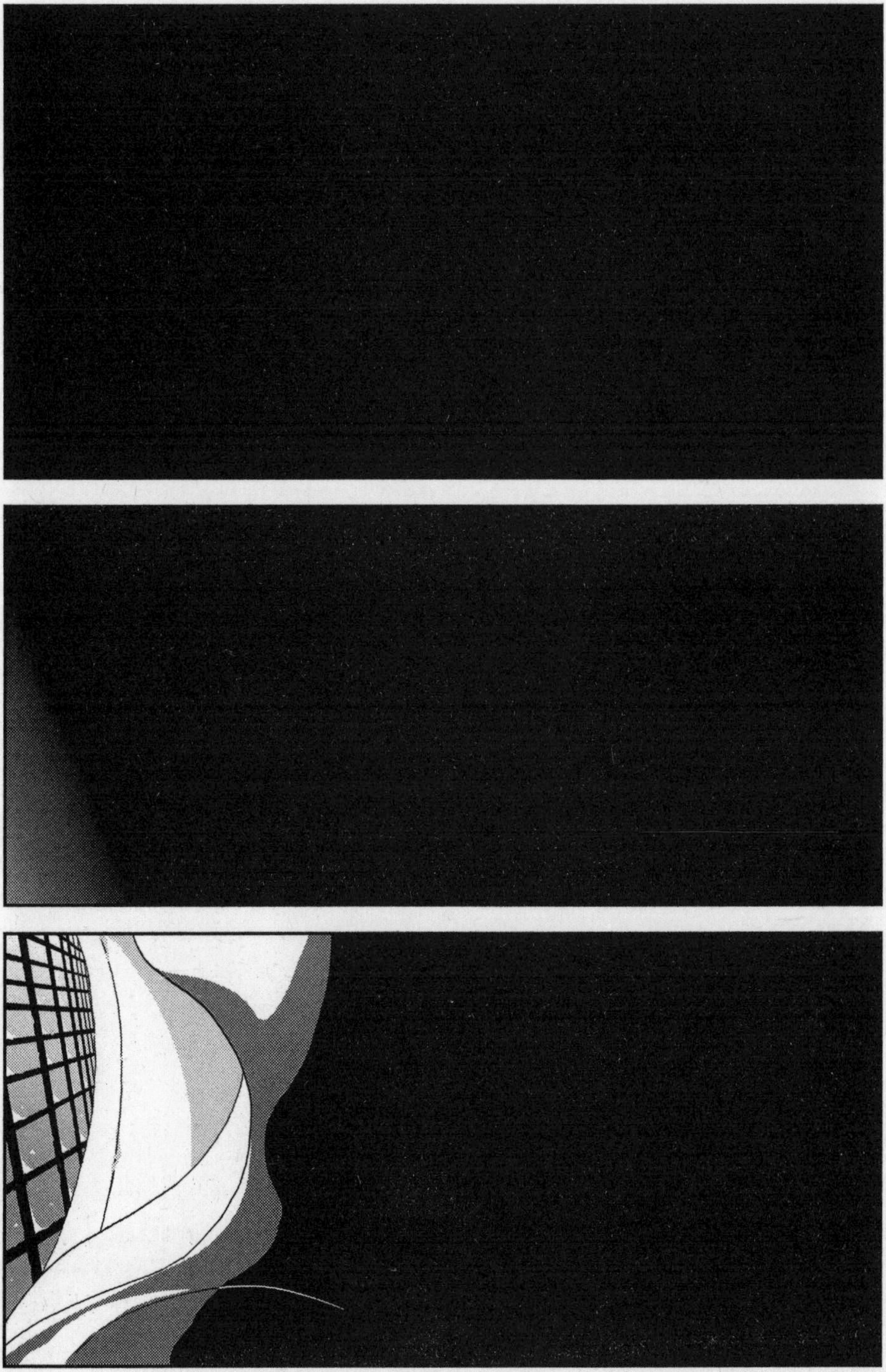

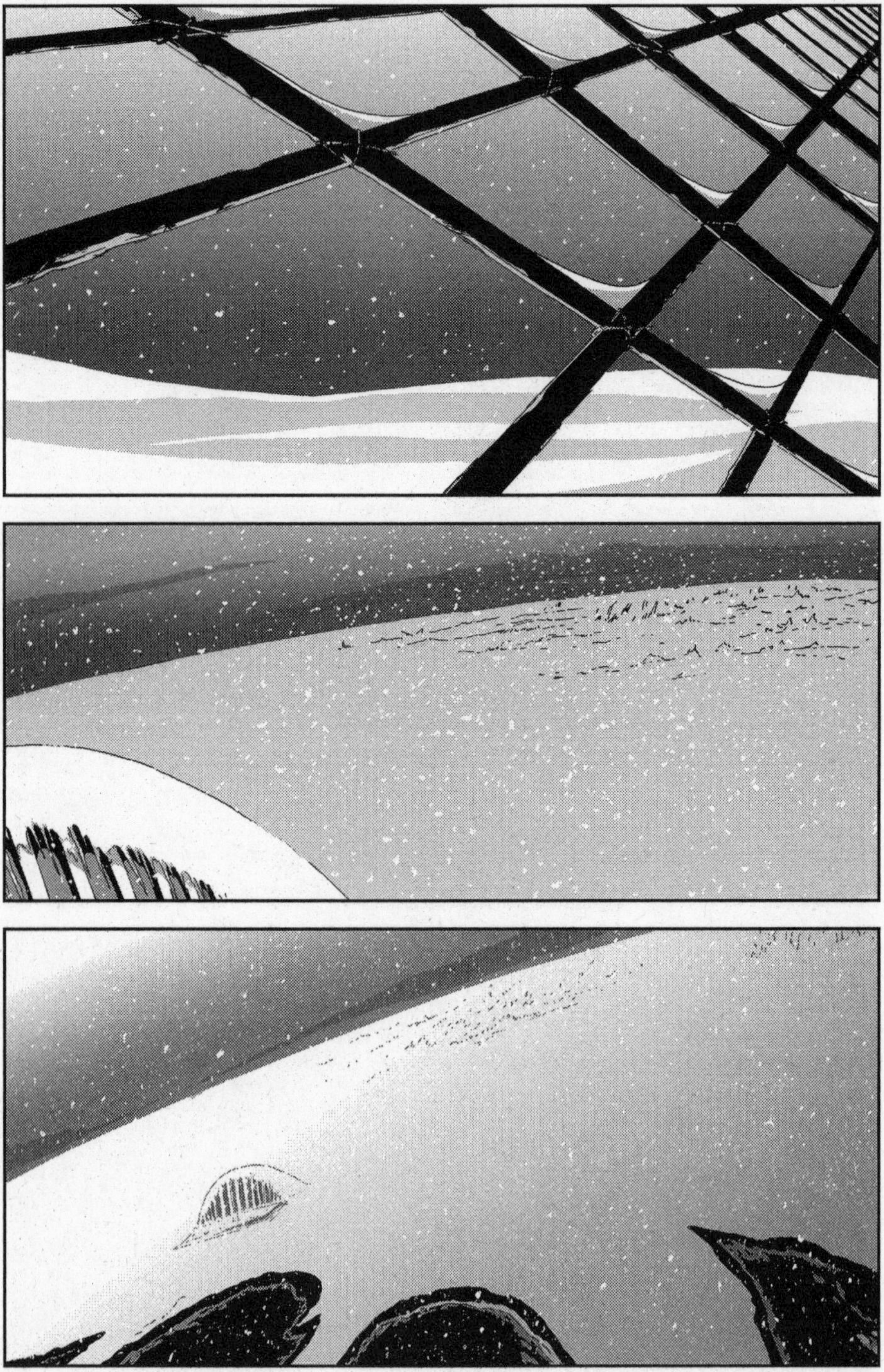

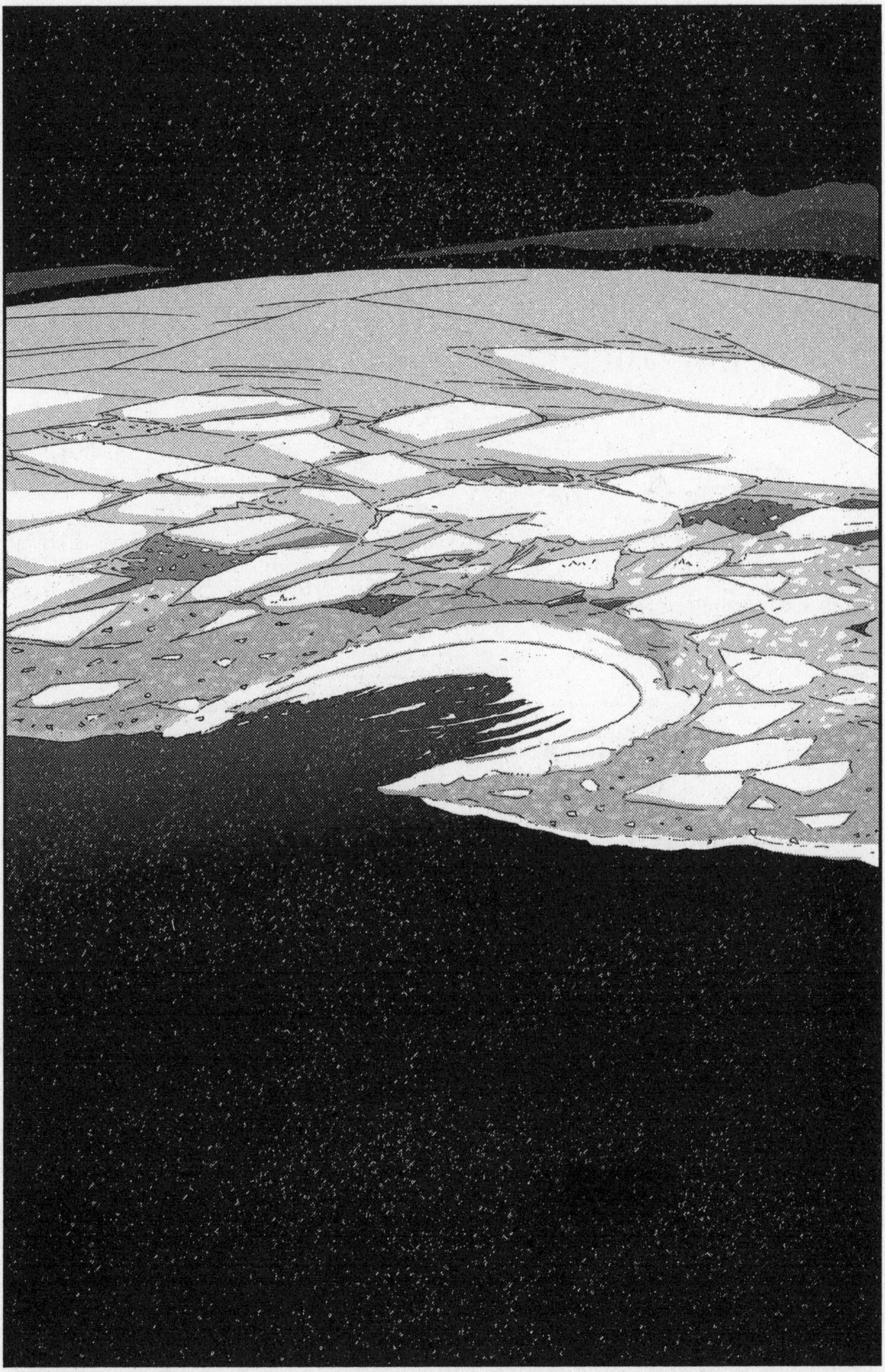

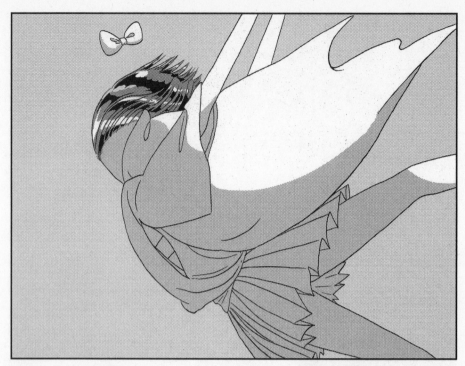

GO!

ARRRGH, IT'S BORT! AIM FOR THE SPOT WHERE BORT'S GONNA LAND!

31 TO EIGHT!

BENITO!

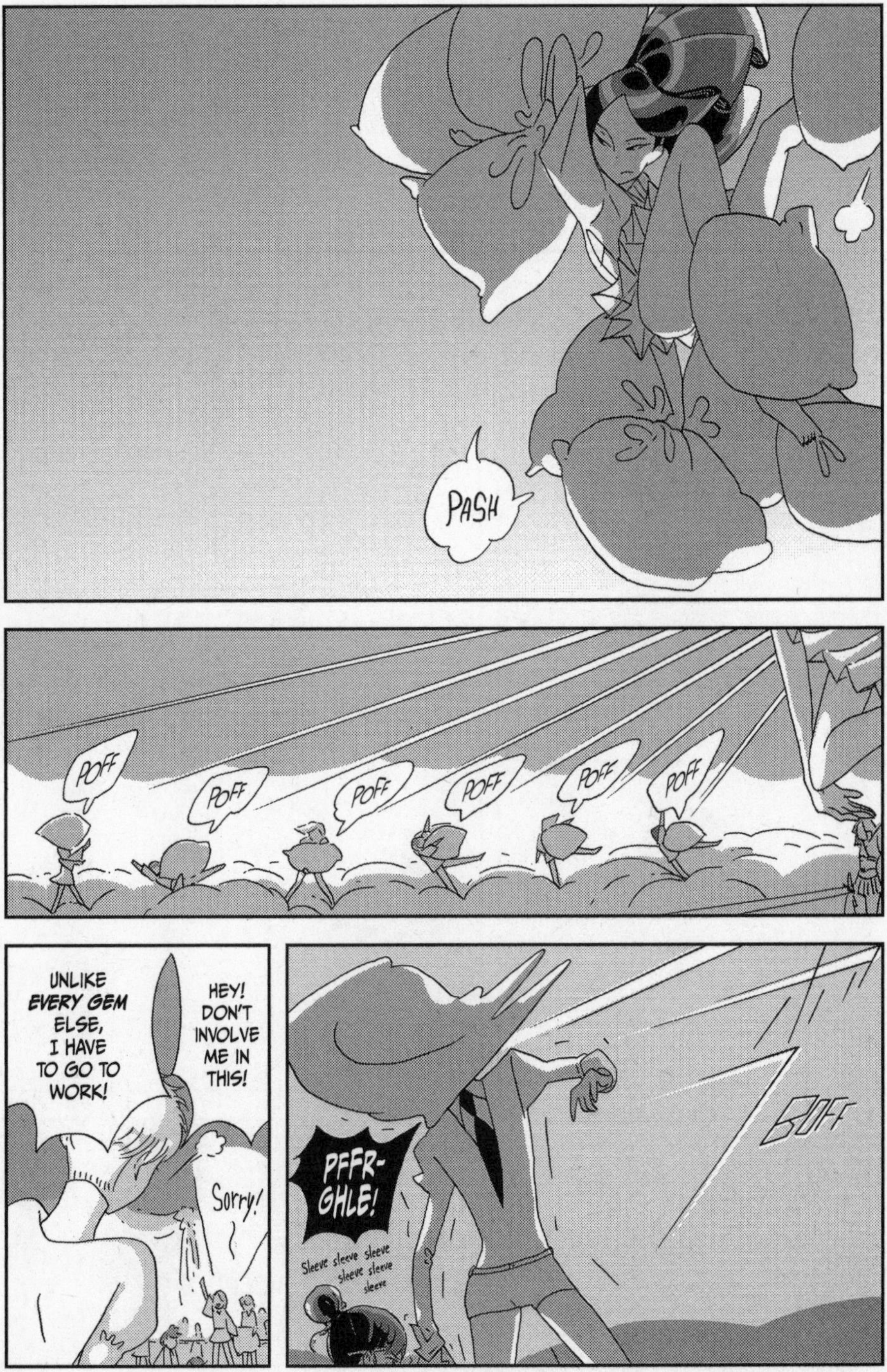
PASH
POFF
POFF
POFF
POFF
POFF
POFF
BOFF
PFFR-GHLE!
Sleeve sleeve sleeve sleeve sleeve sleeve
HEY! DON'T INVOLVE ME IN THIS!
UNLIKE EVERY GEM ELSE, I HAVE TO GO TO WORK!
Sorry!

GET
EM!

WAAAH!!!

AAAH!

YEARGH!

FOR
CRYING
OUT
LOUD.

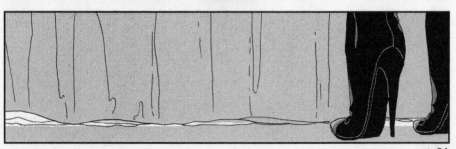

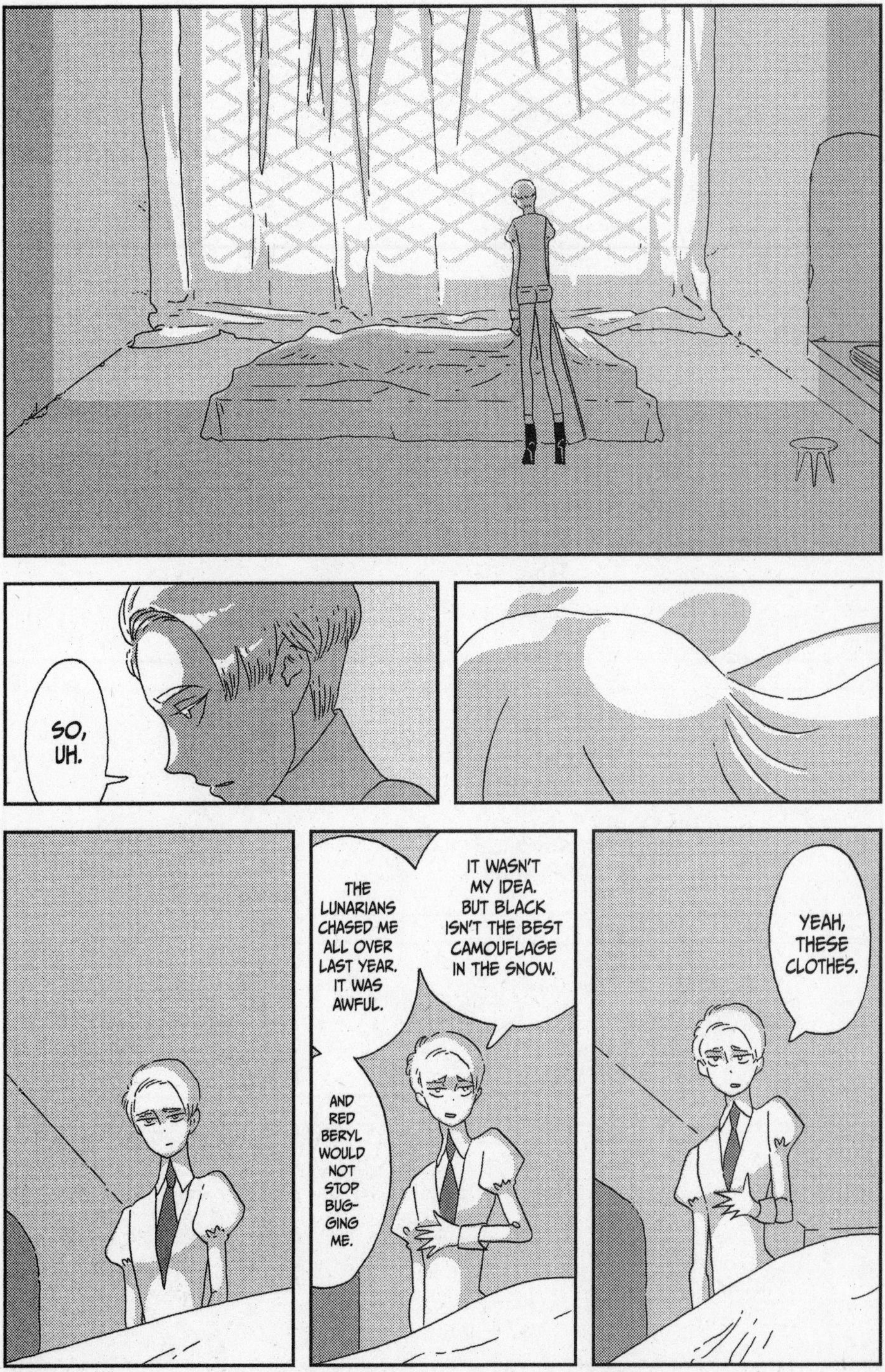
SO, UH.
YEAH, THESE CLOTHES.
IT WASN'T MY IDEA. BUT BLACK ISN'T THE BEST CAMOUFLAGE IN THE SNOW.
THE LUNARIANS CHASED ME ALL OVER LAST YEAR. IT WAS AWFUL.
AND RED BERYL WOULD NOT STOP BUG-GING ME.

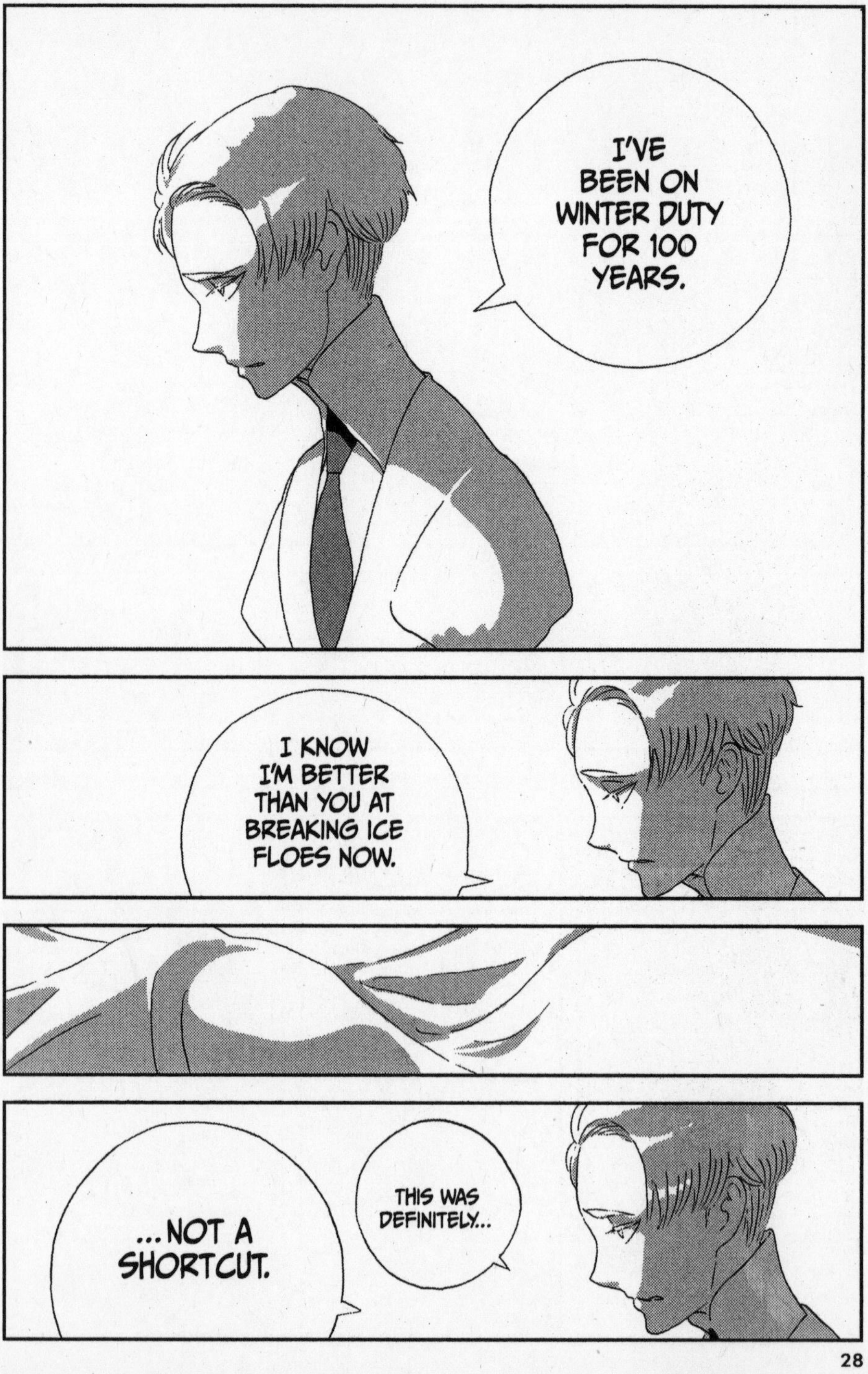
I'VE BEEN ON WINTER DUTY FOR 100 YEARS.
I KNOW I'M BETTER THAN YOU AT BREAKING ICE FLOES NOW.
THIS WAS DEFINITELY...
...NOT A SHORTCUT.

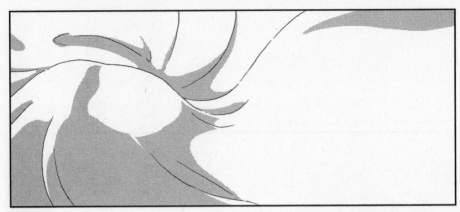

I'LL SEE YOU AGAIN TONIGHT.

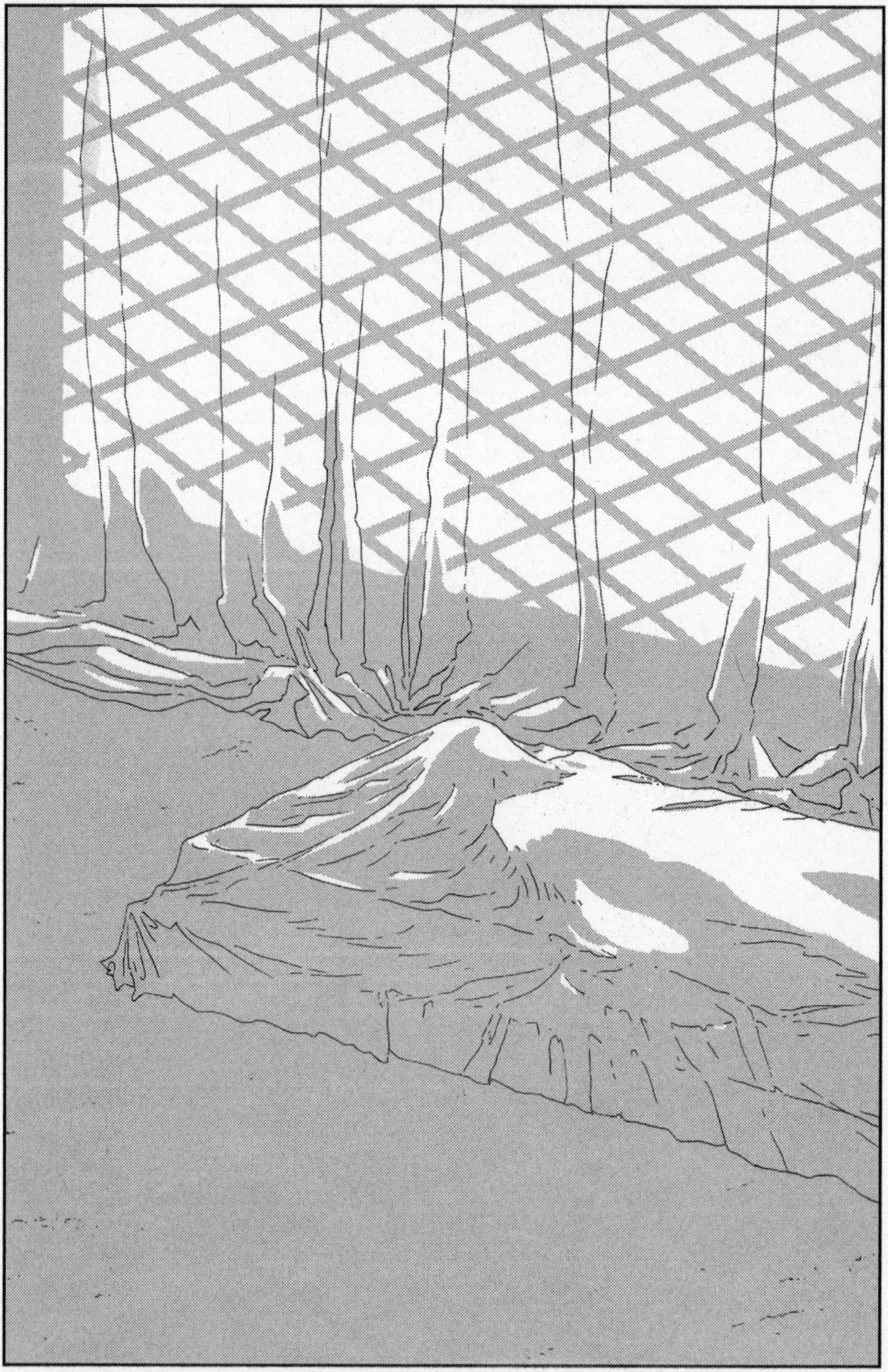

CHAPTER 45: The Long Winter END

CHAPTER 46:

Lapis Lazuli

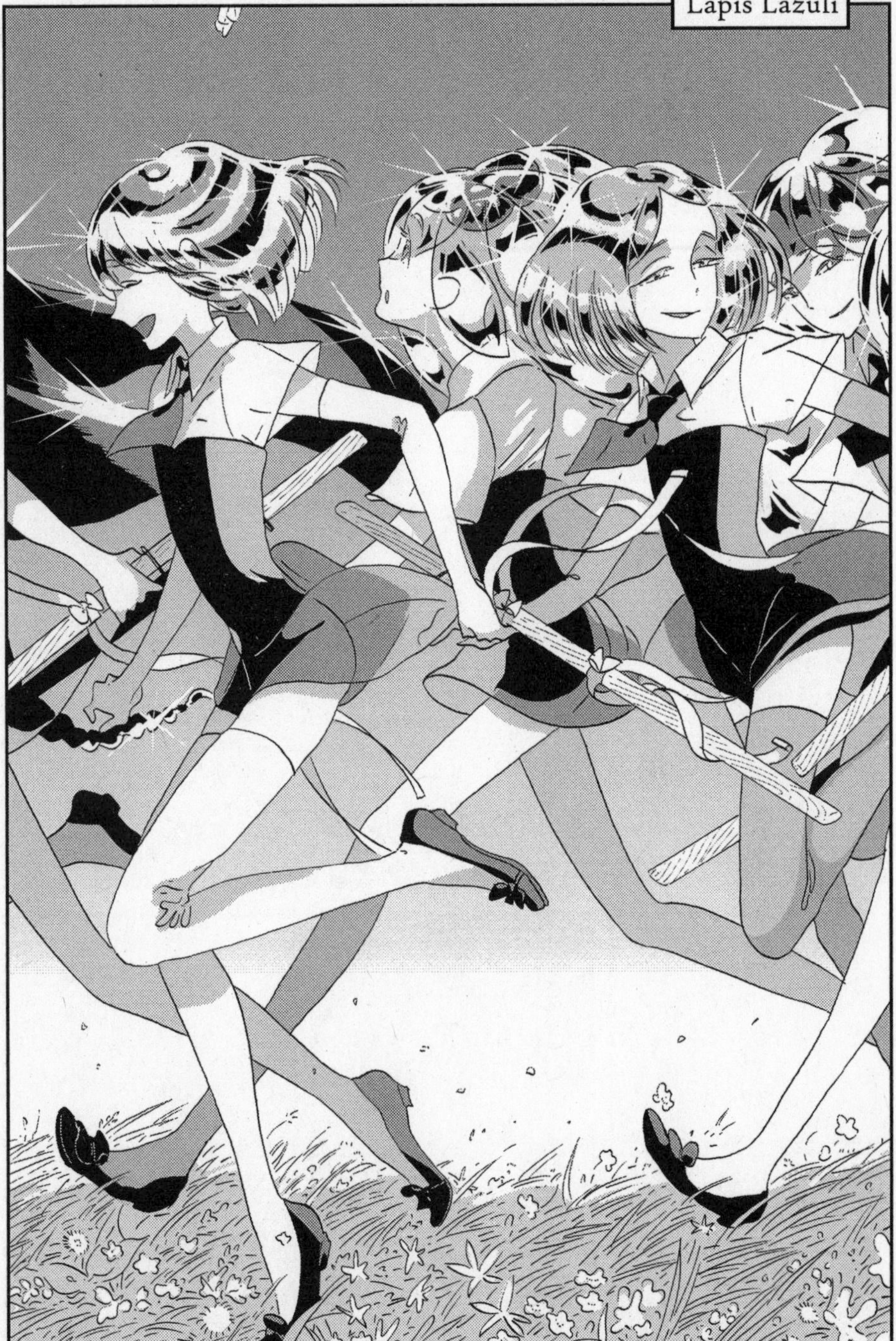

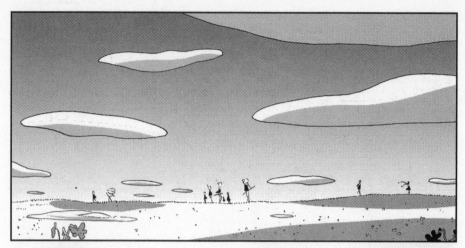

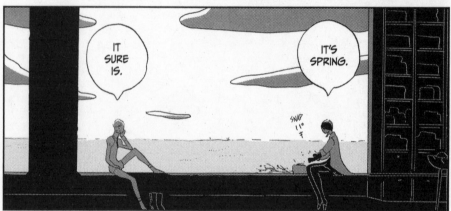

IT'S SPRING.
SNAP
IT SURE IS.
THE MOMENT YOU'VE ALL BEEN WAITING FOR!
YAWN
TA-DA!
I MADE A SPECIAL NEW AESTIVATION OUTFIT JUST FOR YOU, CAIRNGORM! YOU SPOILED GEM, YOU!
NOW GET CHANGED SO I CAN TAILOR IT! GO ON, GET!
I ASK EVERY YEAR,
BUT IS THERE A POINT TO WEARING THIS JUST TO SLEEP IN?

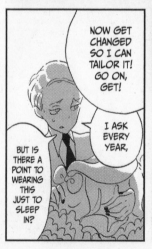

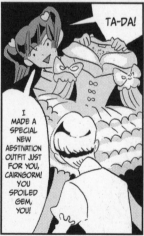

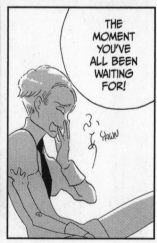

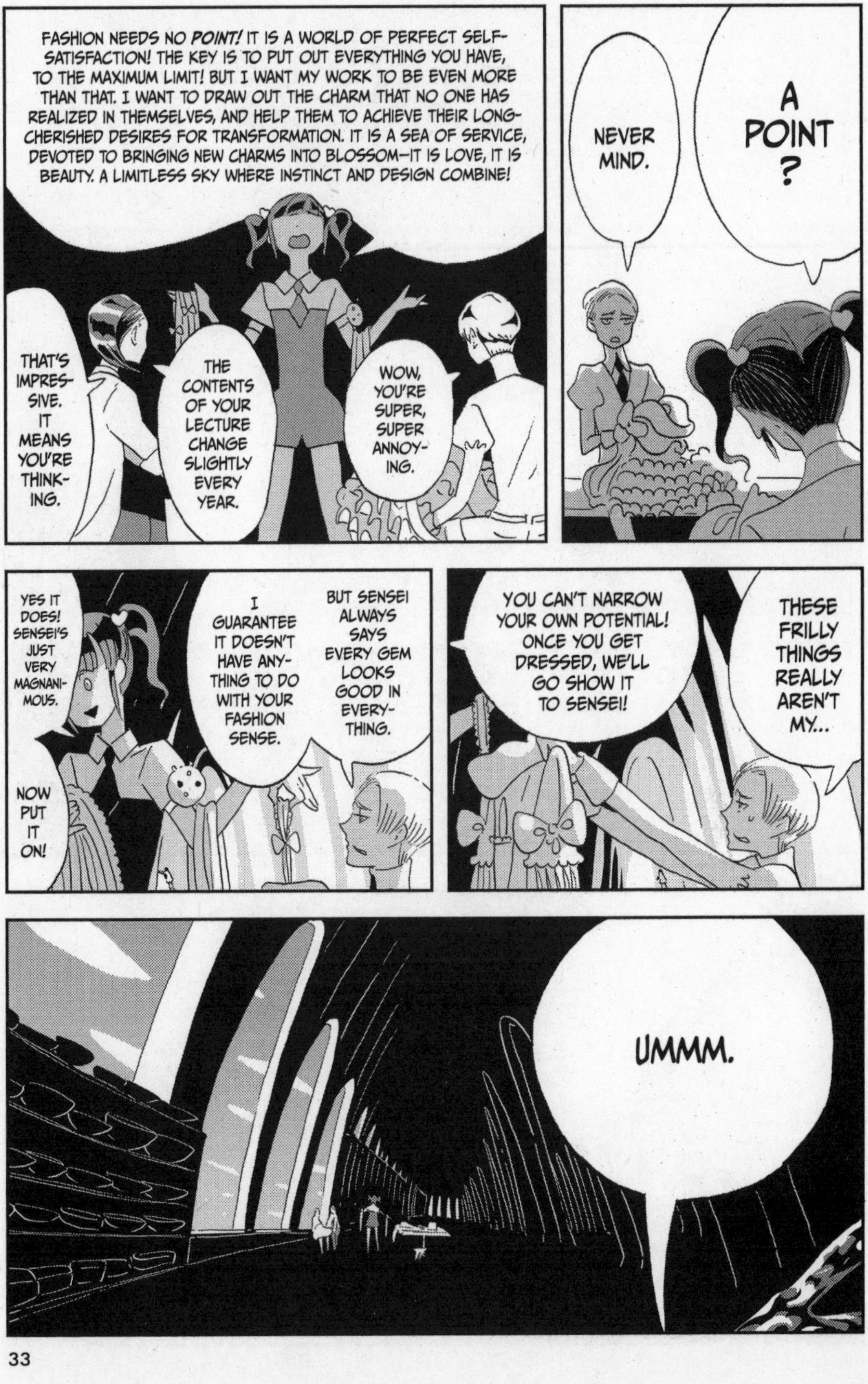
A POINT?
NEVER MIND.
FASHION NEEDS NO *POINT!* IT IS A WORLD OF PERFECT SELF-SATISFACTION! THE KEY IS TO PUT OUT EVERYTHING YOU HAVE, TO THE MAXIMUM LIMIT! BUT I WANT MY WORK TO BE EVEN MORE THAN THAT. I WANT TO DRAW OUT THE CHARM THAT NO ONE HAS REALIZED IN THEMSELVES, AND HELP THEM TO ACHIEVE THEIR LONG-CHERISHED DESIRES FOR TRANSFORMATION. IT IS A SEA OF SERVICE, DEVOTED TO BRINGING NEW CHARMS INTO BLOSSOM—IT IS LOVE, IT IS BEAUTY. A LIMITLESS SKY WHERE INSTINCT AND DESIGN COMBINE!
WOW, YOU'RE SUPER, SUPER ANNOYING.
THE CONTENTS OF YOUR LECTURE CHANGE SLIGHTLY EVERY YEAR.
THAT'S IMPRESSIVE. IT MEANS YOU'RE THINKING.
THESE FRILLY THINGS REALLY AREN'T MY...
YOU CAN'T NARROW YOUR OWN POTENTIAL! ONCE YOU GET DRESSED, WE'LL GO SHOW IT TO SENSEI!
BUT SENSEI ALWAYS SAYS EVERY GEM LOOKS GOOD IN EVERYTHING.
I GUARANTEE IT DOESN'T HAVE ANYTHING TO DO WITH YOUR FASHION SENSE.
YES IT DOES! SENSEI'S JUST VERY MAGNANIMOUS.
NOW PUT IT ON!
UMMM.

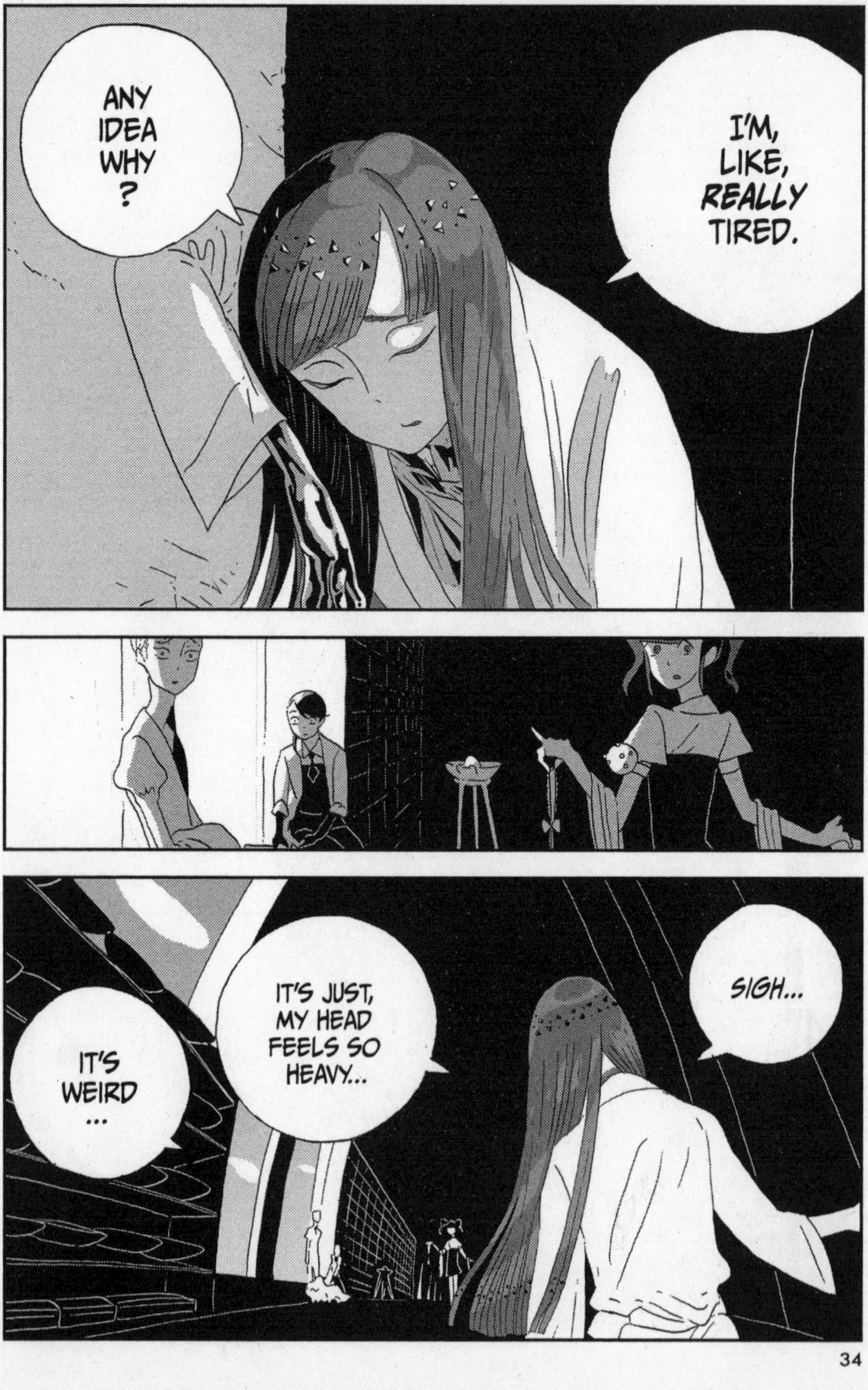
I'M, LIKE, REALLY TIRED.
ANY IDEA WHY?
SIGH...
IT'S JUST, MY HEAD FEELS SO HEAVY...
IT'S WEIRD ...

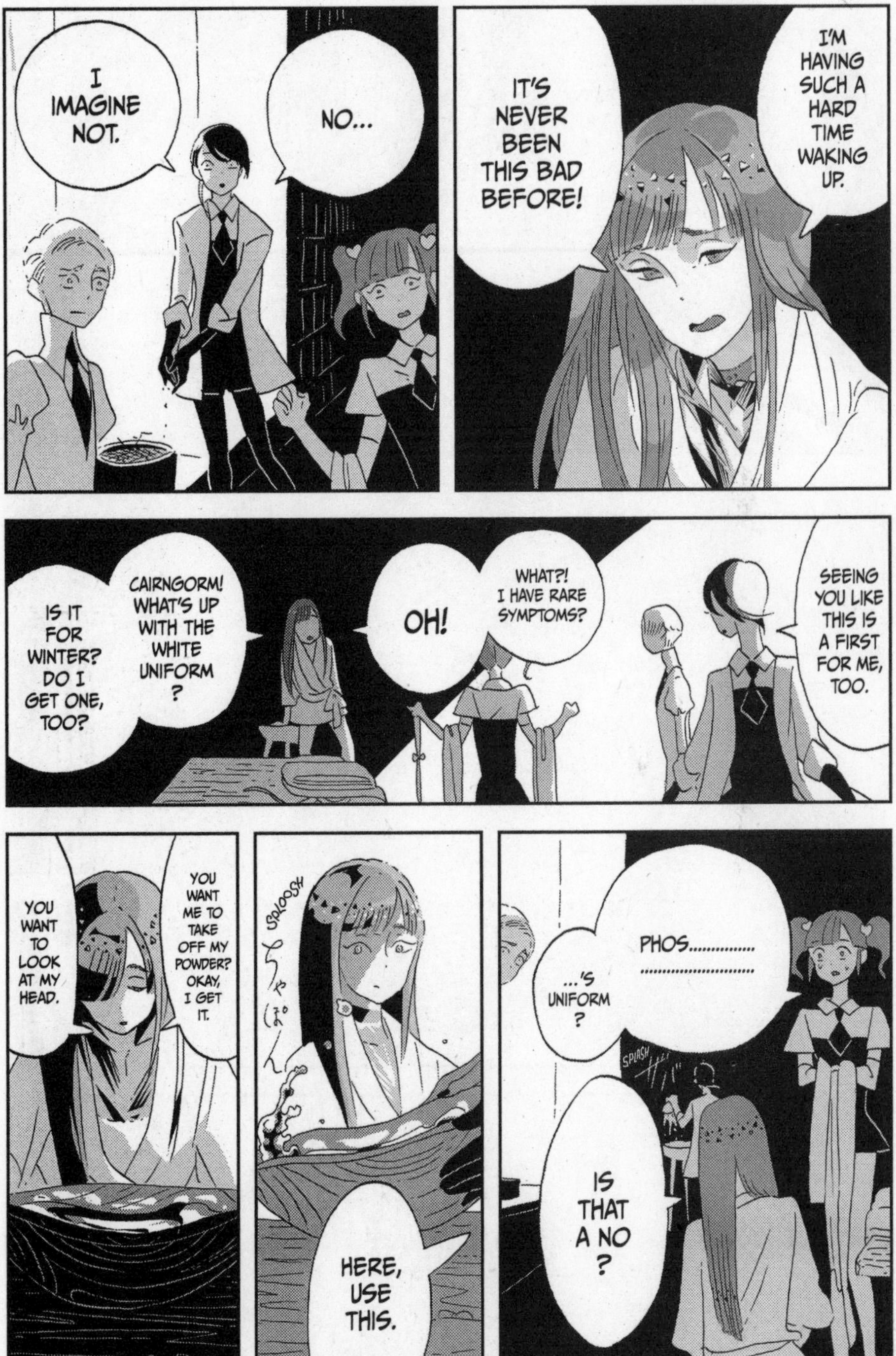
I'M HAVING SUCH A HARD TIME WAKING UP.
IT'S NEVER BEEN THIS BAD BEFORE!
NO...
I IMAGINE NOT.
SEEING YOU LIKE THIS IS A FIRST FOR ME, TOO.
WHAT?! I HAVE RARE SYMPTOMS?
OH!
CAIRNGORM! WHAT'S UP WITH THE WHITE UNIFORM?
IS IT FOR WINTER? DO I GET ONE, TOO?
PHOS..
...'S UNIFORM?
SPLASH
IS THAT A NO?
SPLOOSH
ちゃぽん
HERE, USE THIS.
YOU WANT ME TO TAKE OFF MY POWDER? OKAY, I GET IT.
YOU WANT TO LOOK AT MY HEAD.

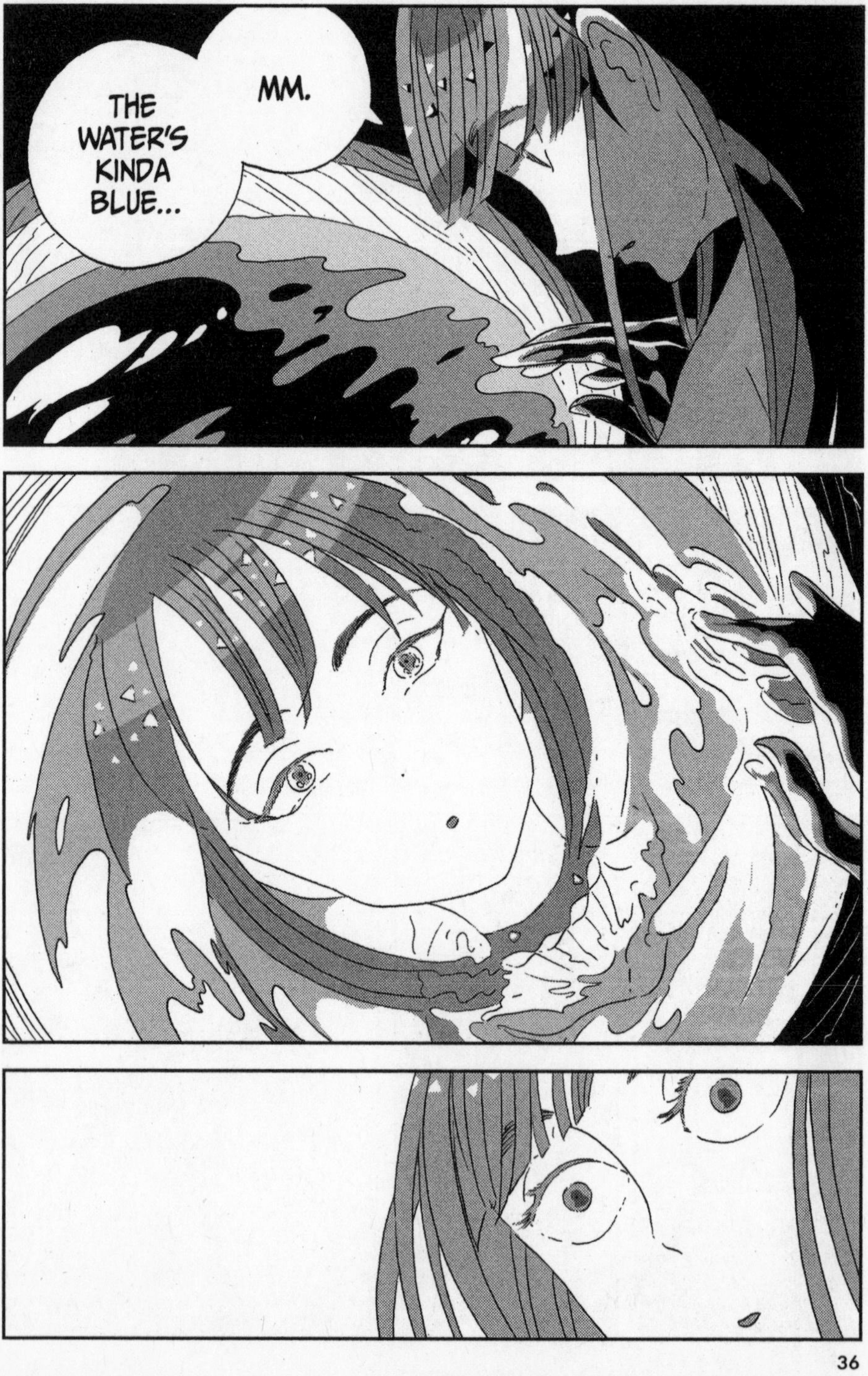
MM.
THE WATER'S KINDA BLUE...

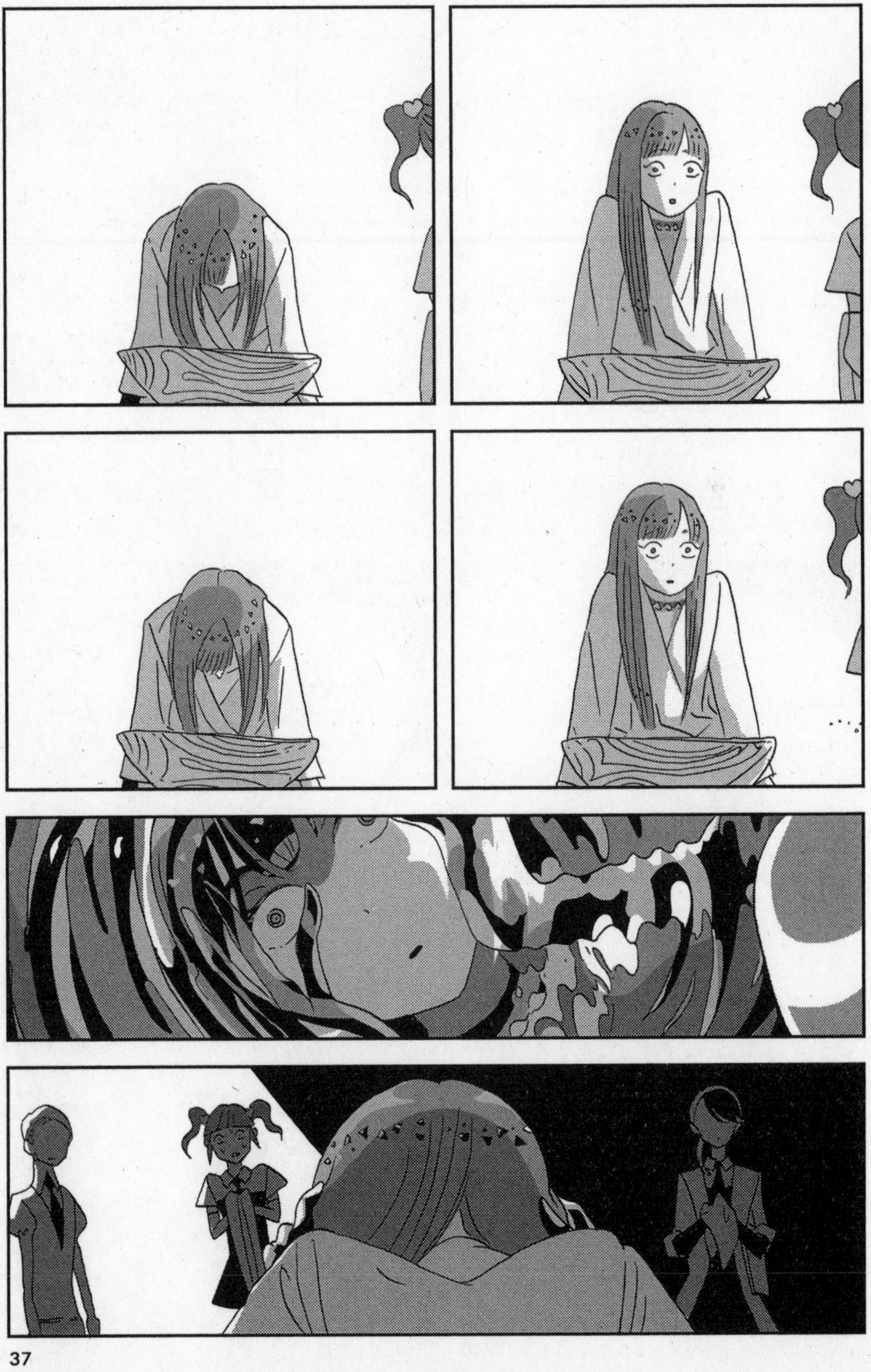

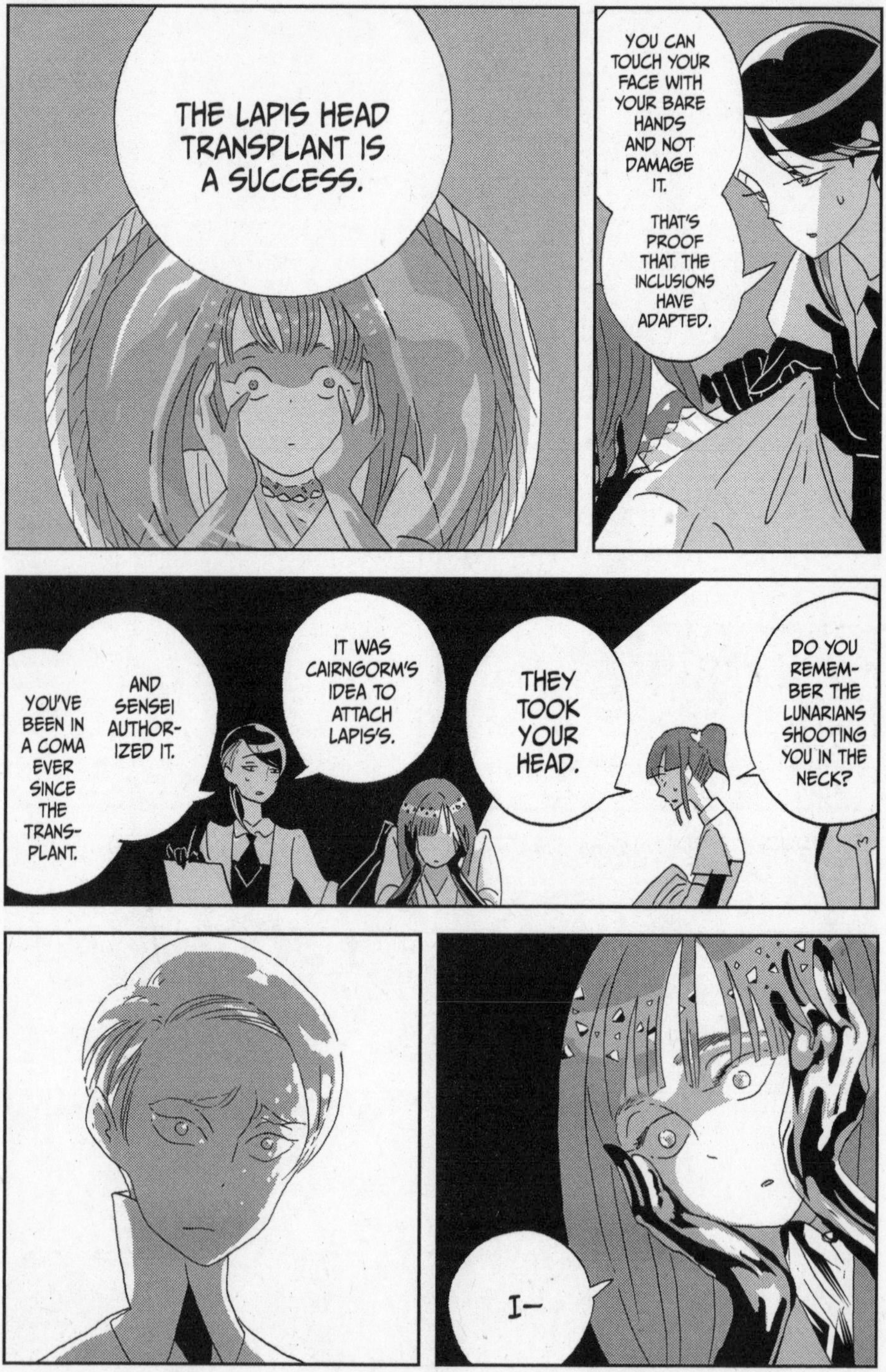
YOU CAN TOUCH YOUR FACE WITH YOUR BARE HANDS AND NOT DAMAGE IT.
THAT'S PROOF THAT THE INCLUSIONS HAVE ADAPTED.
THE LAPIS HEAD TRANSPLANT IS A SUCCESS.
DO YOU REMEMBER THE LUNARIANS SHOOTING YOU IN THE NECK?
THEY TOOK YOUR HEAD.
IT WAS CAIRNGORM'S IDEA TO ATTACH LAPIS'S.
AND SENSEI AUTHORIZED IT.
YOU'VE BEEN IN A COMA EVER SINCE THE TRANSPLANT.
I—

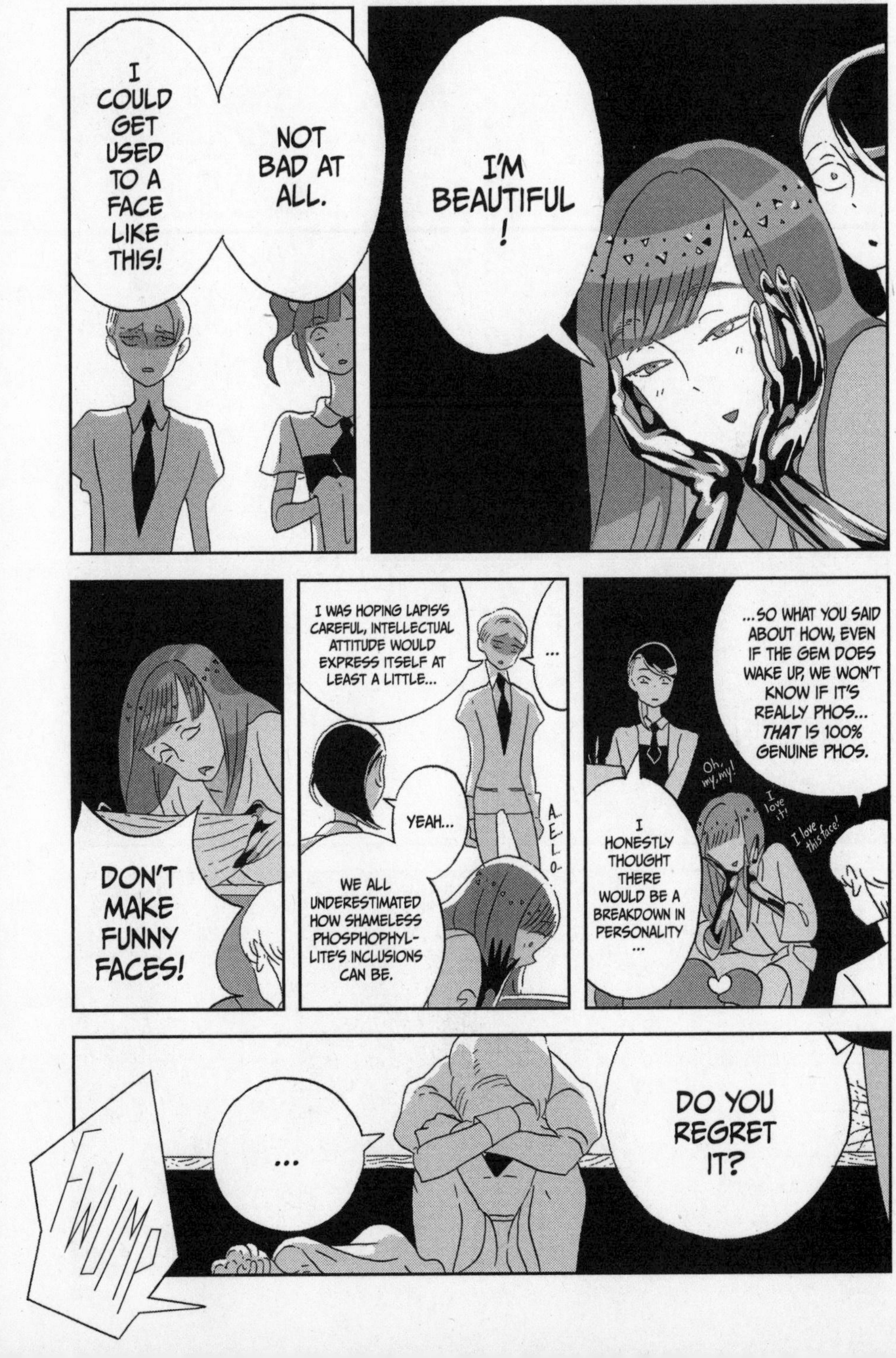
I'M BEAUTIFUL!
NOT BAD AT ALL.
I COULD GET USED TO A FACE LIKE THIS!
...SO WHAT YOU SAID ABOUT HOW, EVEN IF THE GEM DOES WAKE UP, WE WON'T KNOW IF IT'S REALLY PHOS... *THAT* IS 100% GENUINE PHOS.
Oh, my, my!
I love it!
I love this face!
I HONESTLY THOUGHT THERE WOULD BE A BREAKDOWN IN PERSONALITY...
...
I WAS HOPING LAPIS'S CAREFUL, INTELLECTUAL ATTITUDE WOULD EXPRESS ITSELF AT LEAST A LITTLE...
YEAH...
A... E... I... O...
WE ALL UNDERESTIMATED HOW SHAMELESS PHOSPHOPHYLLITE'S INCLUSIONS CAN BE.
DON'T MAKE FUNNY FACES!
DO YOU REGRET IT?
...
FWUMP

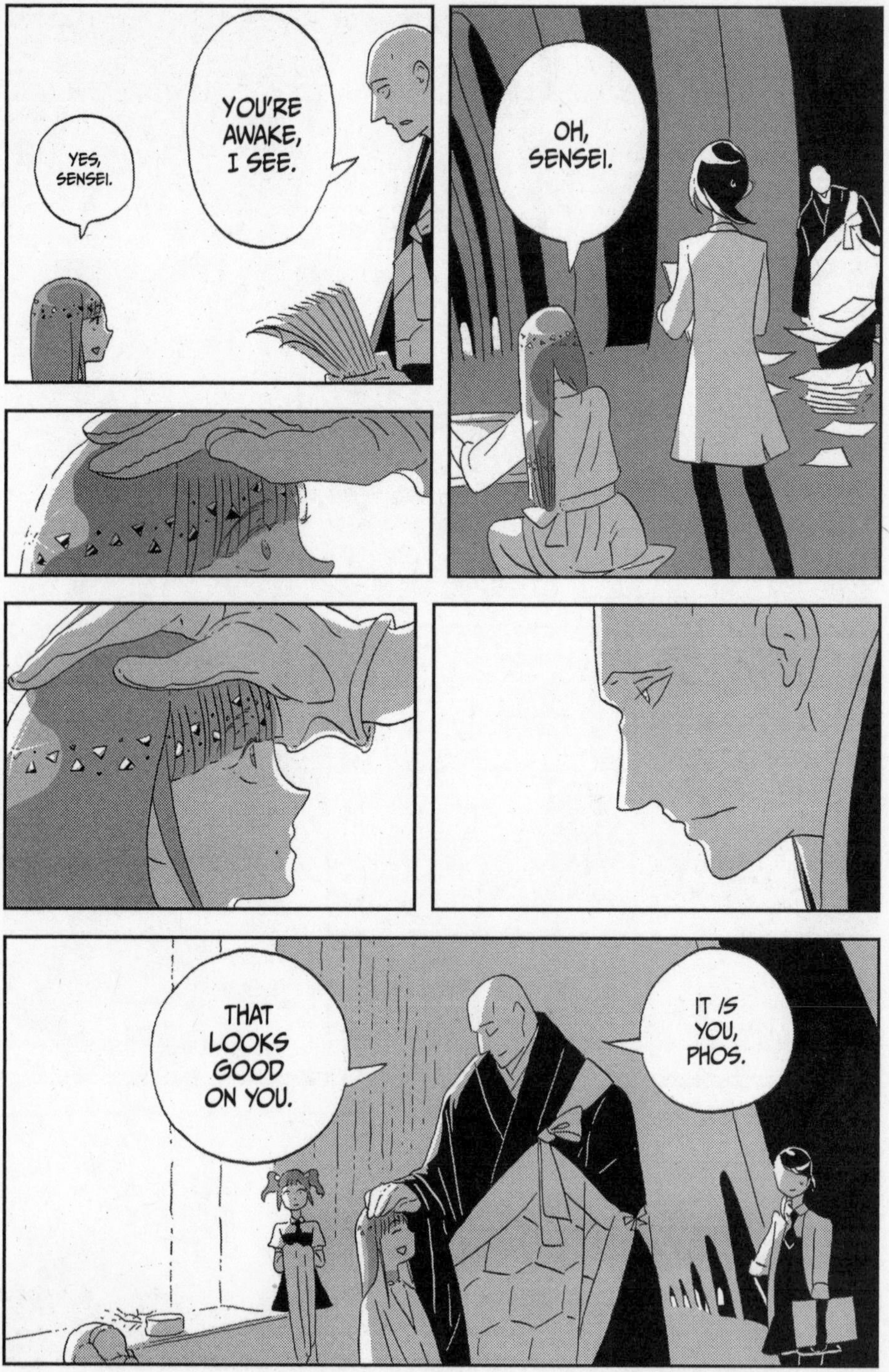
OH, SENSEI.
YOU'RE AWAKE, I SEE.
YES, SENSEI.
IT IS YOU, PHOS.
THAT LOOKS GOOD ON YOU.

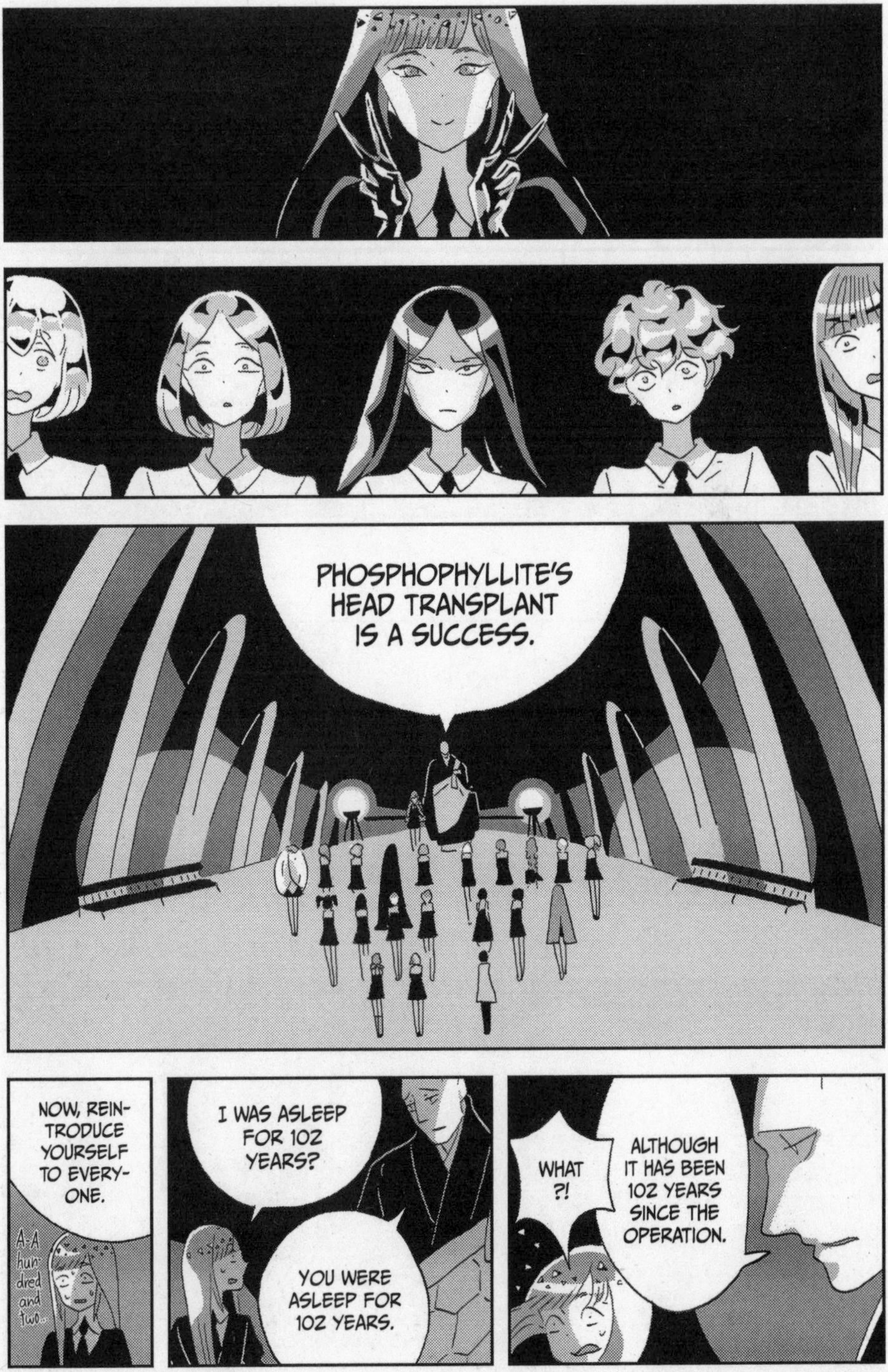
PHOSPHOPHYLLITE'S HEAD TRANSPLANT IS A SUCCESS.
ALTHOUGH IT HAS BEEN 102 YEARS SINCE THE OPERATION.
WHAT?!
I WAS ASLEEP FOR 102 YEARS?
YOU WERE ASLEEP FOR 102 YEARS.
NOW, REINTRODUCE YOURSELF TO EVERYONE.
A-A hundred and two...

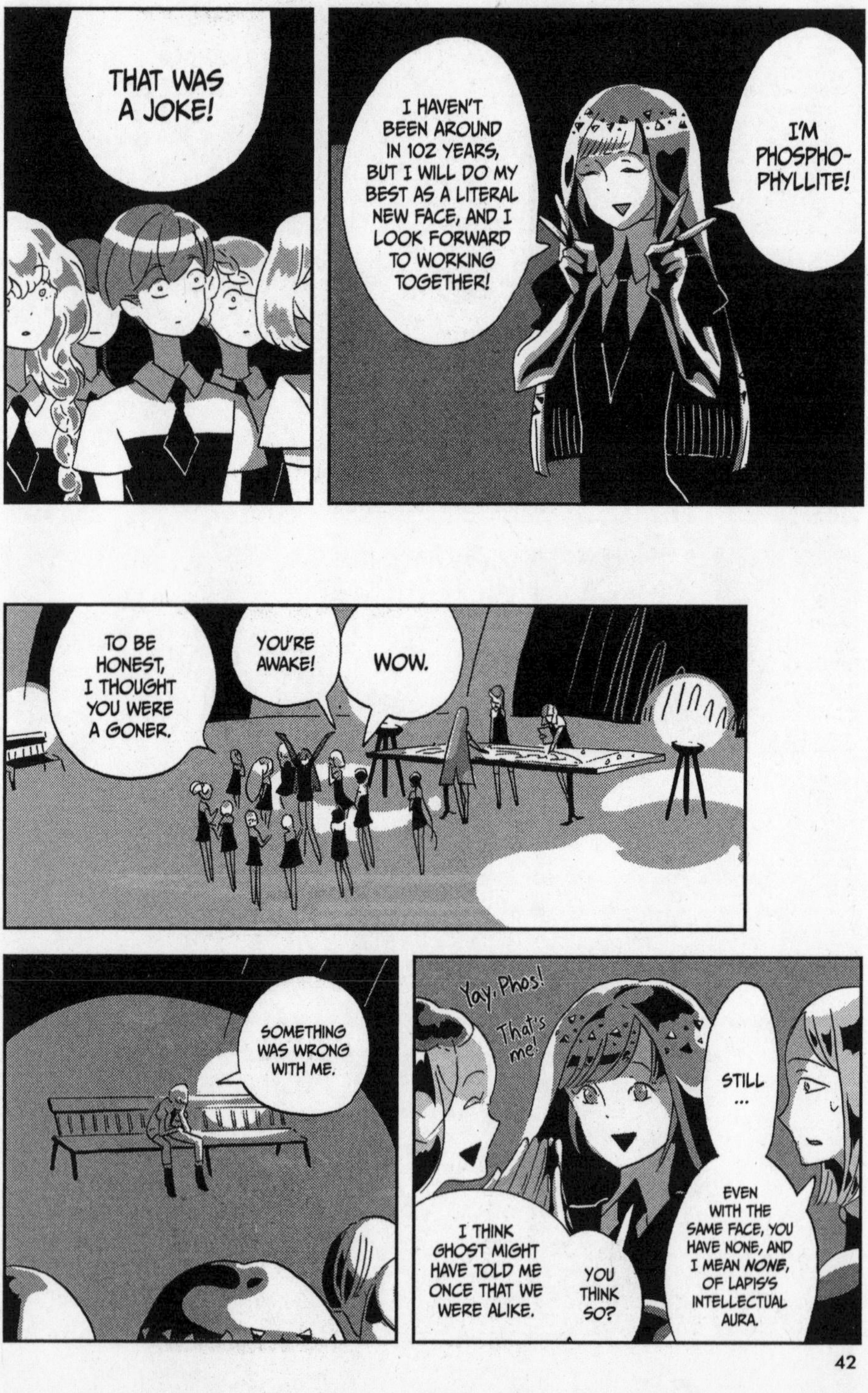

I'M PHOSPHO-PHYLLITE!
I HAVEN'T BEEN AROUND IN 102 YEARS, BUT I WILL DO MY BEST AS A LITERAL NEW FACE, AND I LOOK FORWARD TO WORKING TOGETHER!
THAT WAS A JOKE!
WOW.
YOU'RE AWAKE!
TO BE HONEST, I THOUGHT YOU WERE A GONER.
Yay, Phos!
That's me!
STILL ...
EVEN WITH THE SAME FACE, YOU HAVE NONE, AND I MEAN *NONE*, OF LAPIS'S INTELLECTUAL AURA.
YOU THINK SO?
I THINK GHOST MIGHT HAVE TOLD ME ONCE THAT WE WERE ALIKE.
SOMETHING WAS WRONG WITH ME.

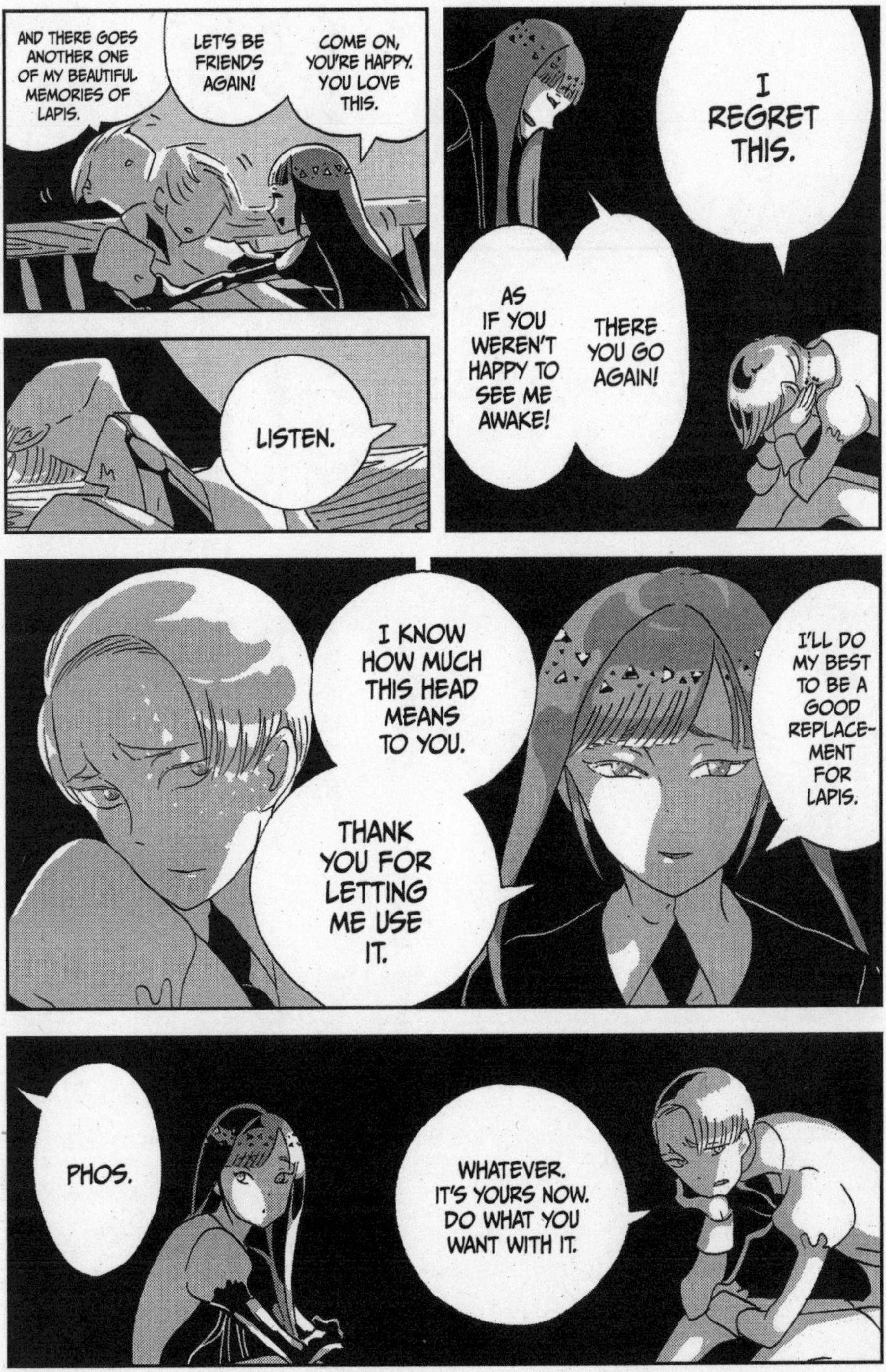
I REGRET THIS.
THERE YOU GO AGAIN!
AS IF YOU WEREN'T HAPPY TO SEE ME AWAKE!
COME ON, YOU'RE HAPPY. YOU LOVE THIS.
LET'S BE FRIENDS AGAIN!
AND THERE GOES ANOTHER ONE OF MY BEAUTIFUL MEMORIES OF LAPIS.
LISTEN.
I'LL DO MY BEST TO BE A GOOD REPLACE-MENT FOR LAPIS.
I KNOW HOW MUCH THIS HEAD MEANS TO YOU.
THANK YOU FOR LETTING ME USE IT.
WHATEVER. IT'S YOURS NOW. DO WHAT YOU WANT WITH IT.
PHOS.

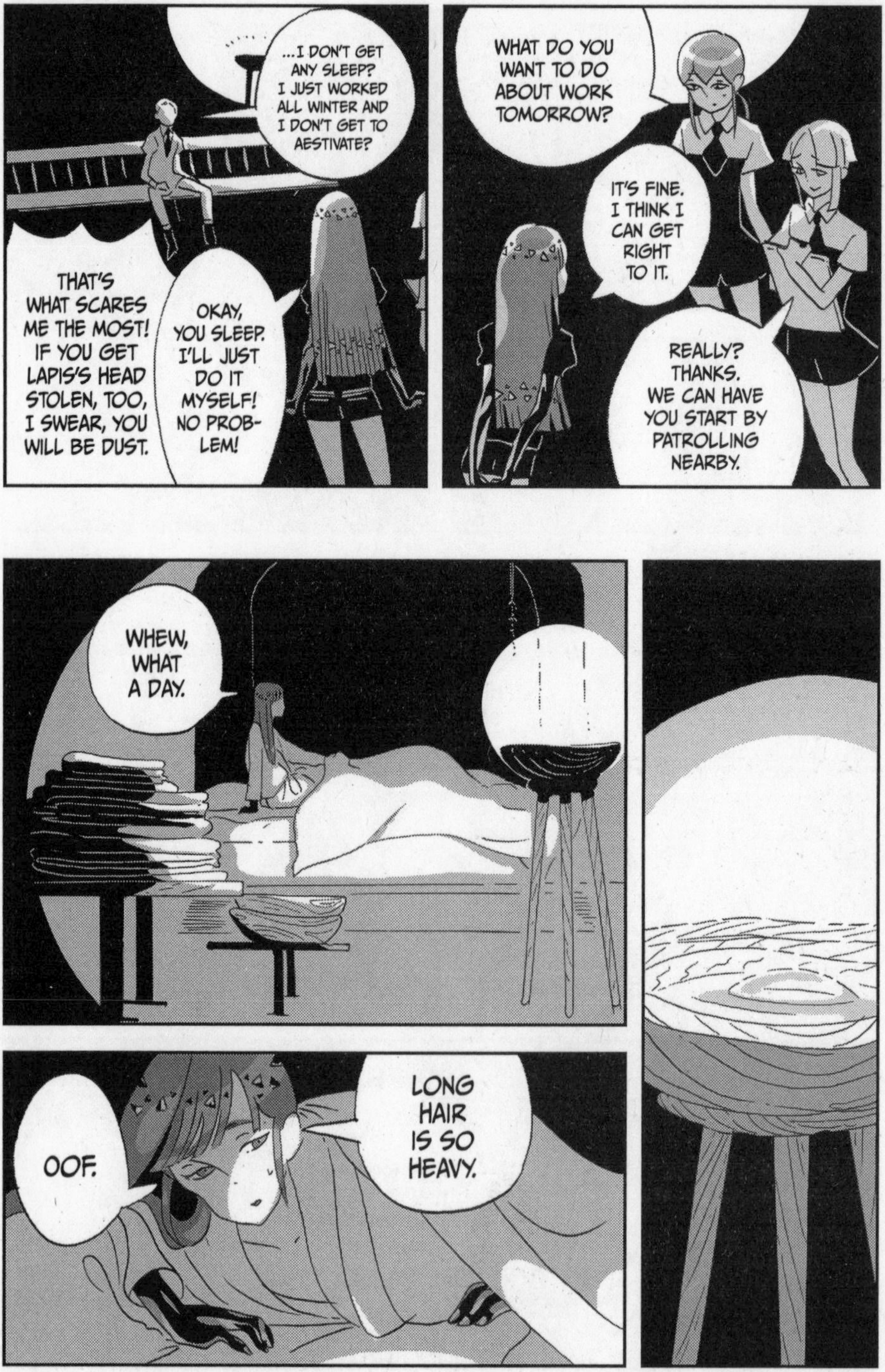
WHAT DO YOU WANT TO DO ABOUT WORK TOMORROW?
IT'S FINE. I THINK I CAN GET RIGHT TO IT.
REALLY? THANKS. WE CAN HAVE YOU START BY PATROLLING NEARBY.
...I DON'T GET ANY SLEEP? I JUST WORKED ALL WINTER AND I DON'T GET TO AESTIVATE?
OKAY, YOU SLEEP. I'LL JUST DO IT MYSELF! NO PROB-LEM!
THAT'S WHAT SCARES ME THE MOST! IF YOU GET LAPIS'S HEAD STOLEN, TOO, I SWEAR, YOU WILL BE DUST.
WHEW, WHAT A DAY.
LONG HAIR IS SO HEAVY.
OOF.

STARTING TOMORROW,

I THINK I'M GOING TO HAVE TO START REMEMBERING A LOT OF STUFF...

WELL, I'M SURE IT'LL WORK OUT.

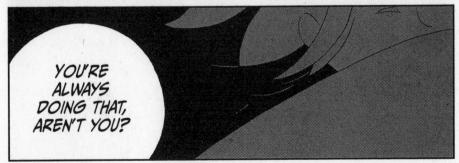

YOU'RE ALWAYS DOING THAT, AREN'T YOU?

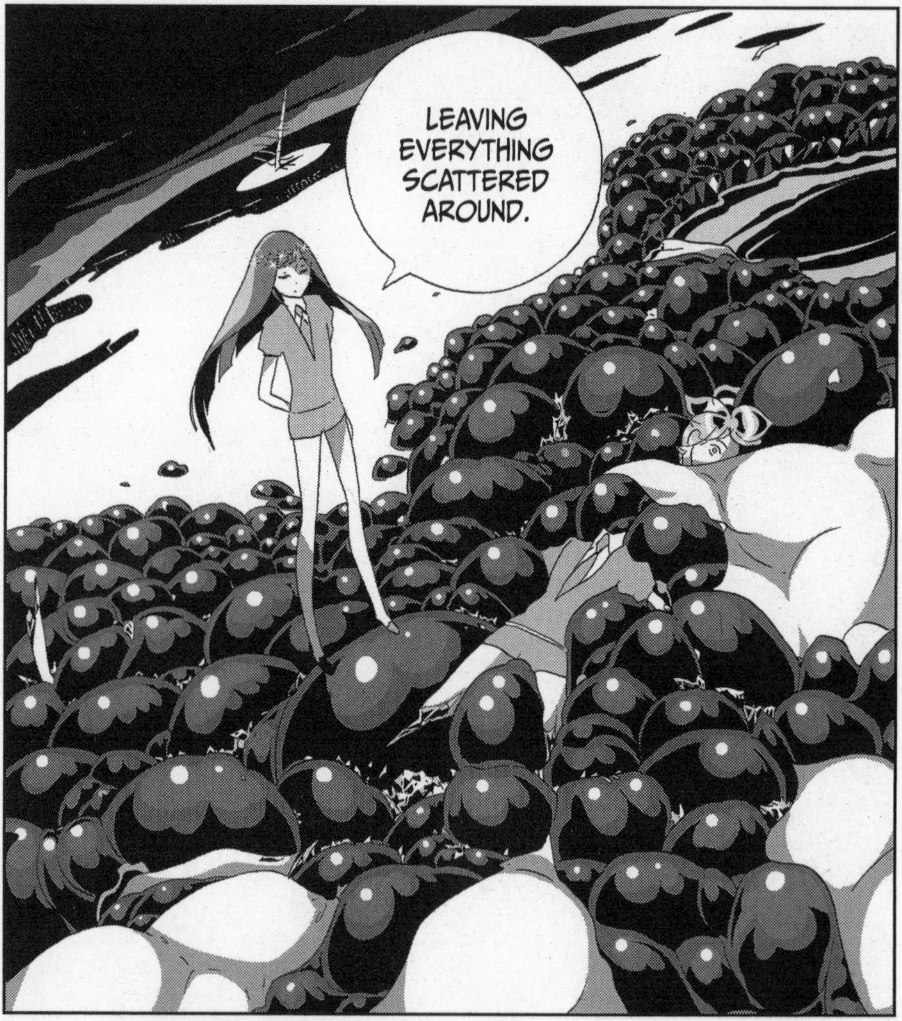
LEAVING EVERYTHING SCATTERED AROUND.
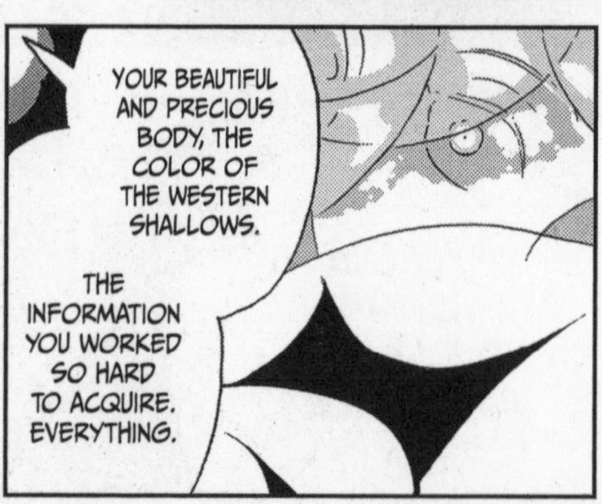
YOUR BEAUTIFUL AND PRECIOUS BODY, THE COLOR OF THE WESTERN SHALLOWS.
THE INFORMATION YOU WORKED SO HARD TO ACQUIRE. EVERYTHING.
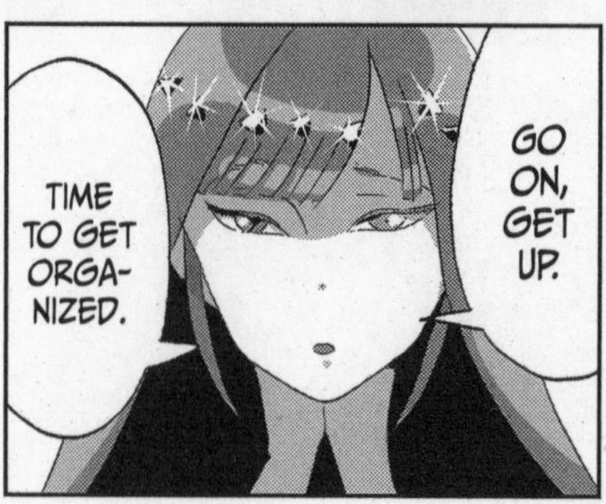
GO ON, GET UP.
TIME TO GET ORGA-NIZED.

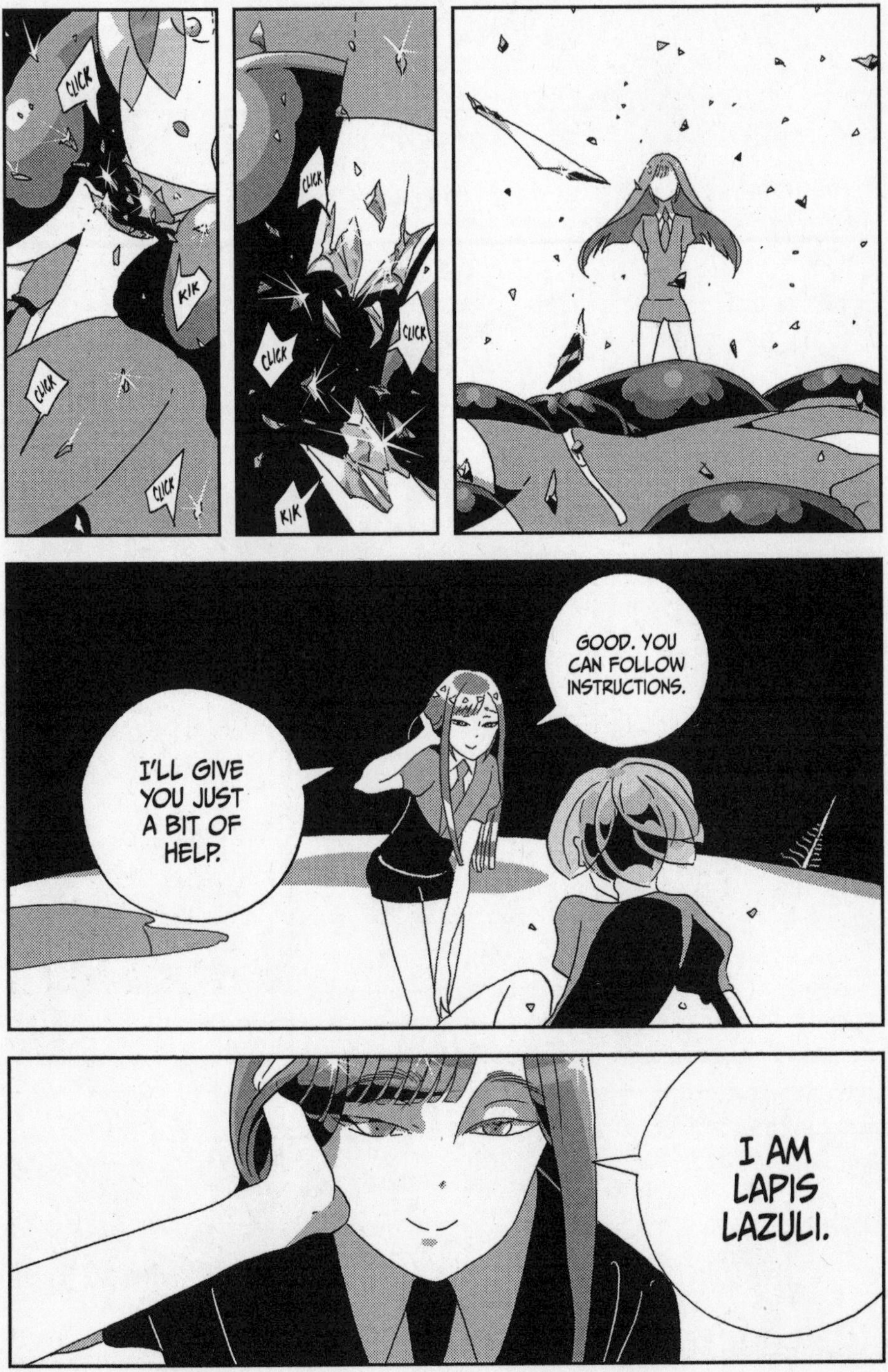
CLICK
CLICK
CLICK
KIK
CLICK
KIK
CLICK
CLICK
GOOD. YOU CAN FOLLOW INSTRUCTIONS.
I'LL GIVE YOU JUST A BIT OF HELP.
I AM LAPIS LAZULI.

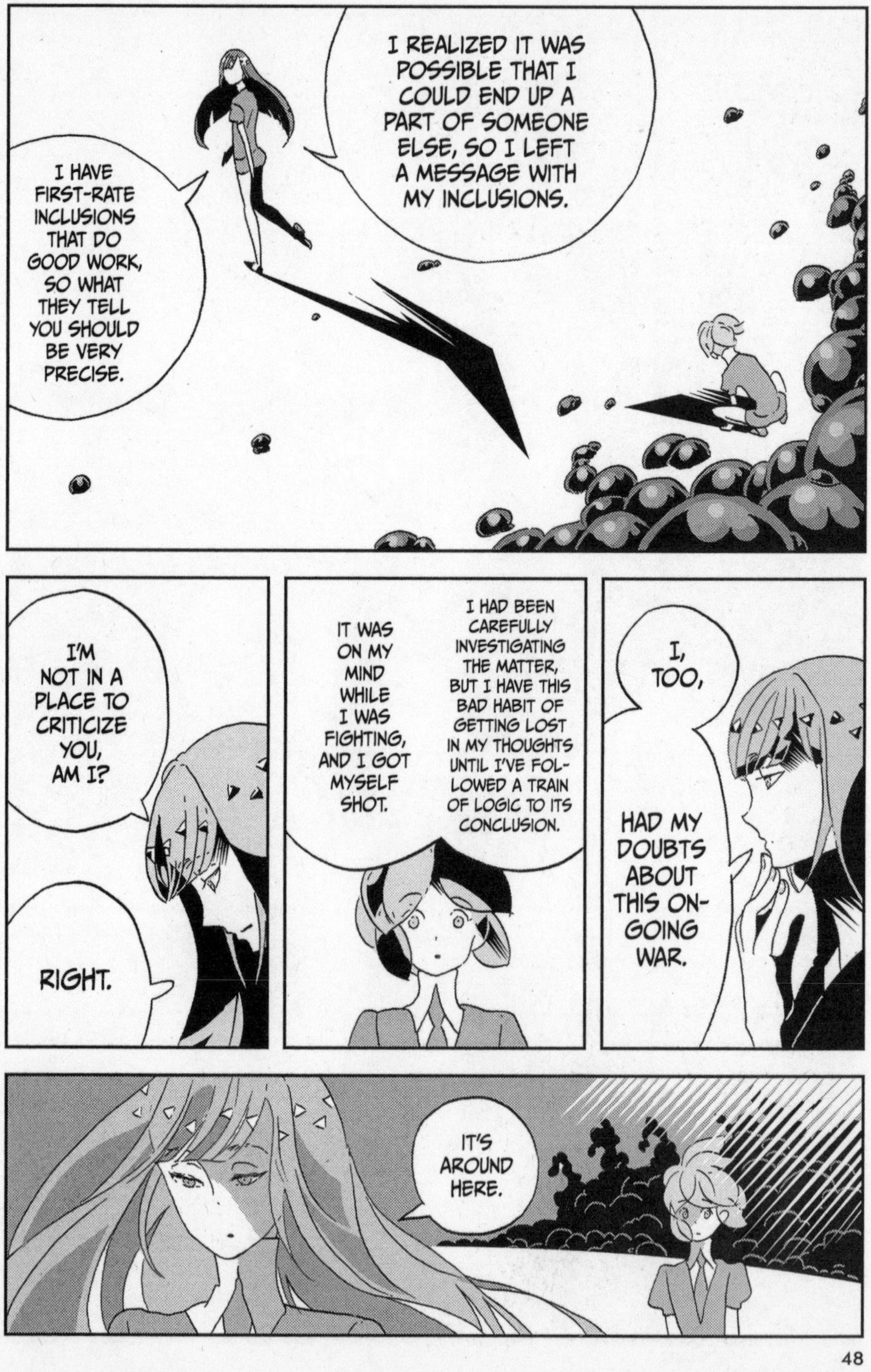
I REALIZED IT WAS POSSIBLE THAT I COULD END UP A PART OF SOMEONE ELSE, SO I LEFT A MESSAGE WITH MY INCLUSIONS.
I HAVE FIRST-RATE INCLUSIONS THAT DO GOOD WORK, SO WHAT THEY TELL YOU SHOULD BE VERY PRECISE.
I, TOO,
HAD MY DOUBTS ABOUT THIS ON-GOING WAR.
I HAD BEEN CAREFULLY INVESTIGATING THE MATTER, BUT I HAVE THIS BAD HABIT OF GETTING LOST IN MY THOUGHTS UNTIL I'VE FOL-LOWED A TRAIN OF LOGIC TO ITS CONCLUSION.
IT WAS ON MY MIND WHILE I WAS FIGHTING, AND I GOT MYSELF SHOT.
I'M NOT IN A PLACE TO CRITICIZE YOU, AM I?
RIGHT.
IT'S AROUND HERE.

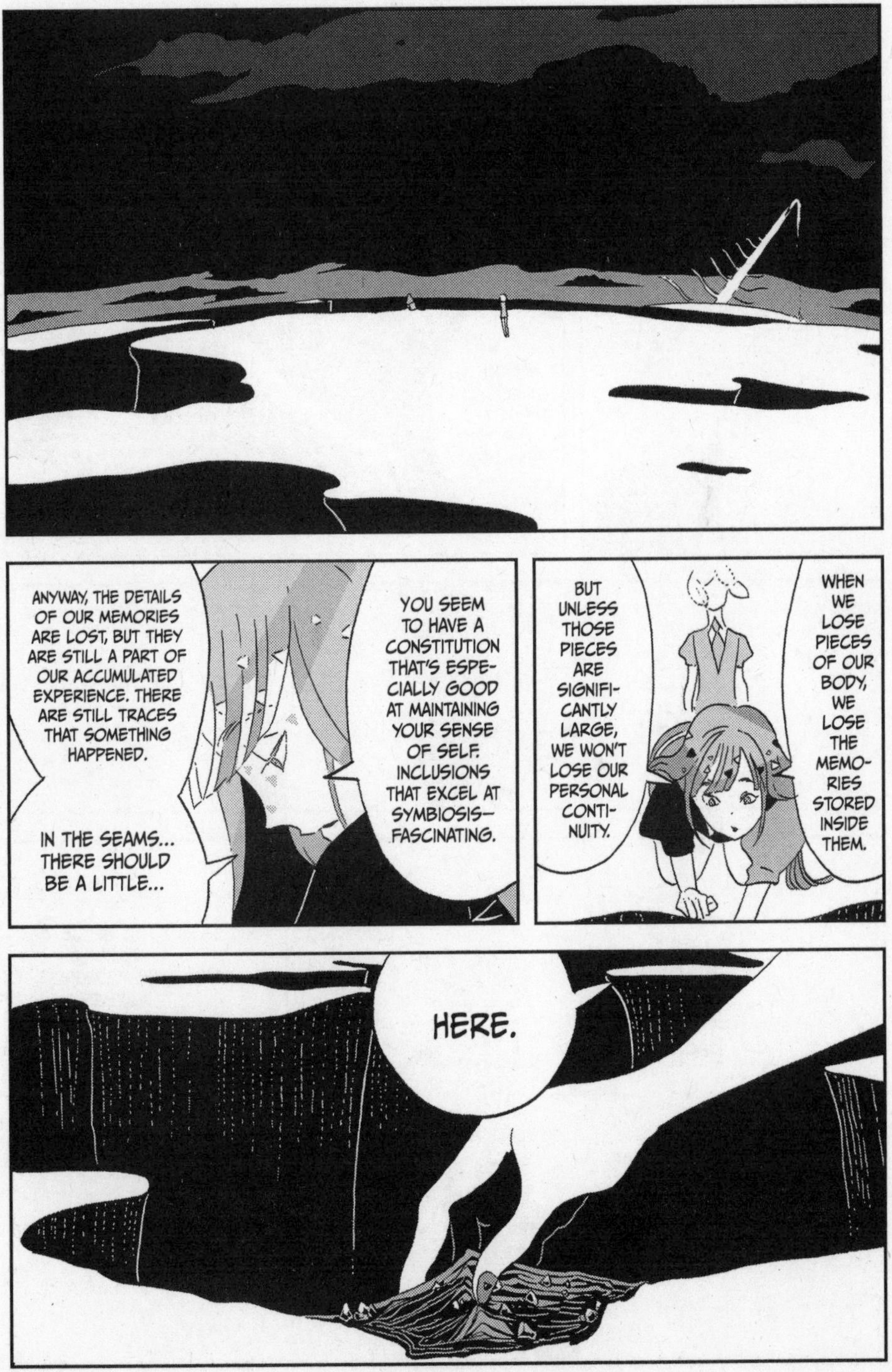
WHEN WE LOSE PIECES OF OUR BODY, WE LOSE THE MEMORIES STORED INSIDE THEM.
BUT UNLESS THOSE PIECES ARE SIGNIFICANTLY LARGE, WE WON'T LOSE OUR PERSONAL CONTINUITY.
YOU SEEM TO HAVE A CONSTITUTION THAT'S ESPECIALLY GOOD AT MAINTAINING YOUR SENSE OF SELF. INCLUSIONS THAT EXCEL AT SYMBIOSIS— FASCINATING.
ANYWAY, THE DETAILS OF OUR MEMORIES ARE LOST, BUT THEY ARE STILL A PART OF OUR ACCUMULATED EXPERIENCE. THERE ARE STILL TRACES THAT SOMETHING HAPPENED.
IN THE SEAMS... THERE SHOULD BE A LITTLE...
HERE.

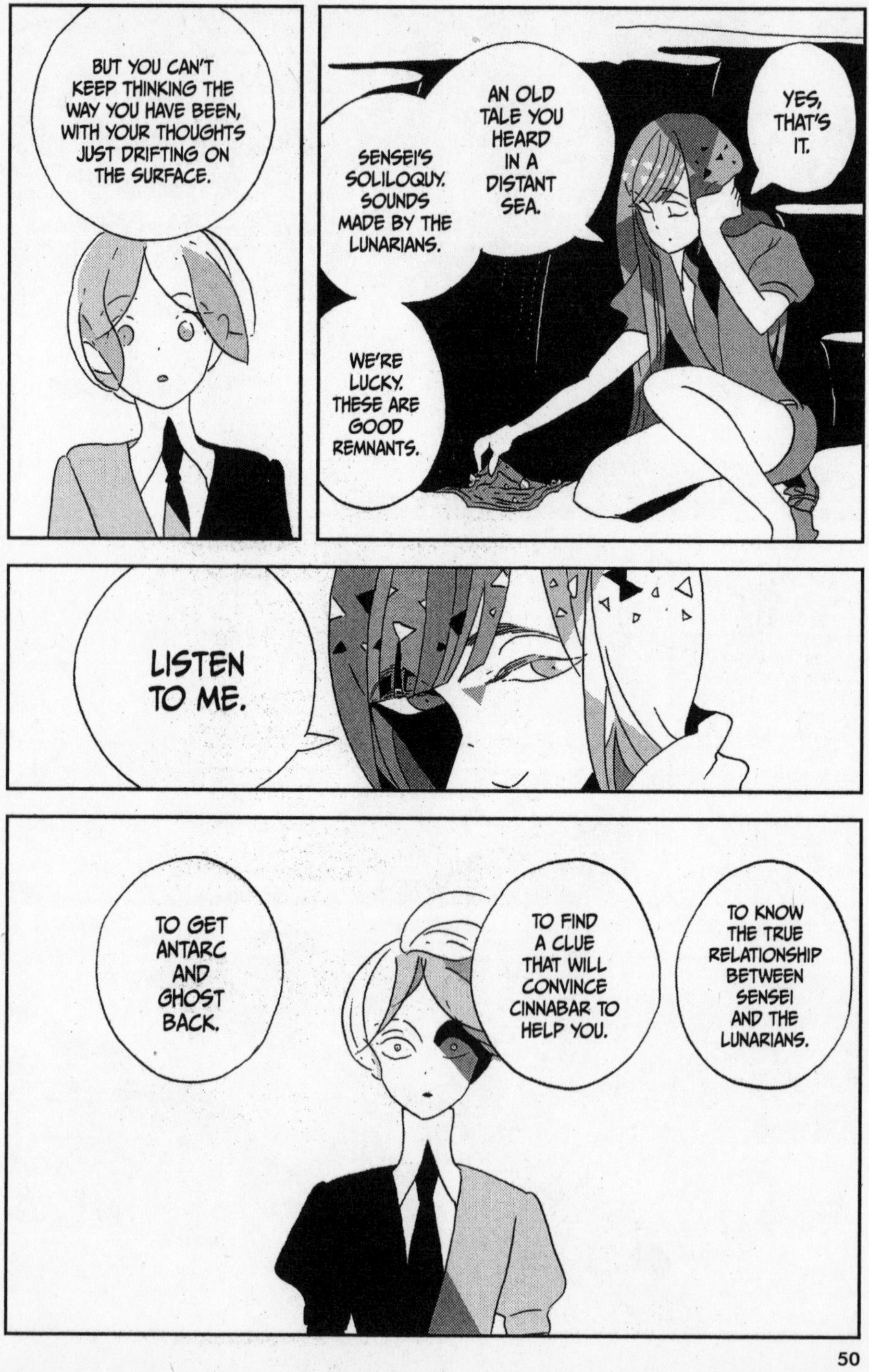
YES, THAT'S IT.
AN OLD TALE YOU HEARD IN A DISTANT SEA.
SENSEI'S SOLILOQUY. SOUNDS MADE BY THE LUNARIANS.
WE'RE LUCKY. THESE ARE GOOD REMNANTS.
BUT YOU CAN'T KEEP THINKING THE WAY YOU HAVE BEEN, WITH YOUR THOUGHTS JUST DRIFTING ON THE SURFACE.
LISTEN TO ME.
TO KNOW THE TRUE RELATIONSHIP BETWEEN SENSEI AND THE LUNARIANS.
TO FIND A CLUE THAT WILL CONVINCE CINNABAR TO HELP YOU.
TO GET ANTARC AND GHOST BACK.

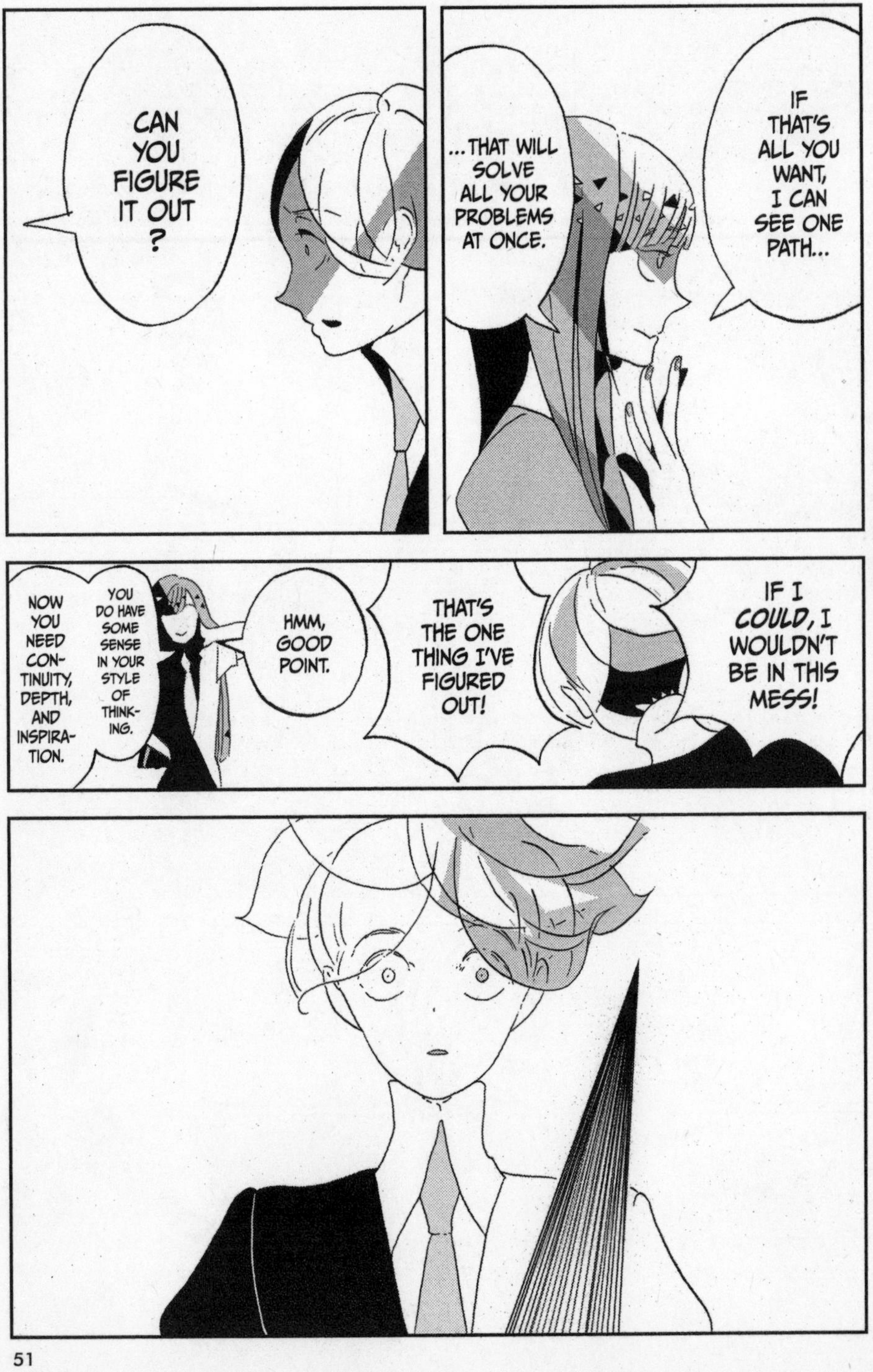
IF THAT'S ALL YOU WANT, I CAN SEE ONE PATH...
...THAT WILL SOLVE ALL YOUR PROBLEMS AT ONCE.
CAN YOU FIGURE IT OUT?
IF I *COULD*, I WOULDN'T BE IN THIS MESS!
THAT'S THE ONE THING I'VE FIGURED OUT!
HMM, GOOD POINT.
YOU DO HAVE SOME SENSE IN YOUR STYLE OF THINK-ING.
NOW YOU NEED CON-TINUITY, DEPTH, AND INSPIRA-TION.

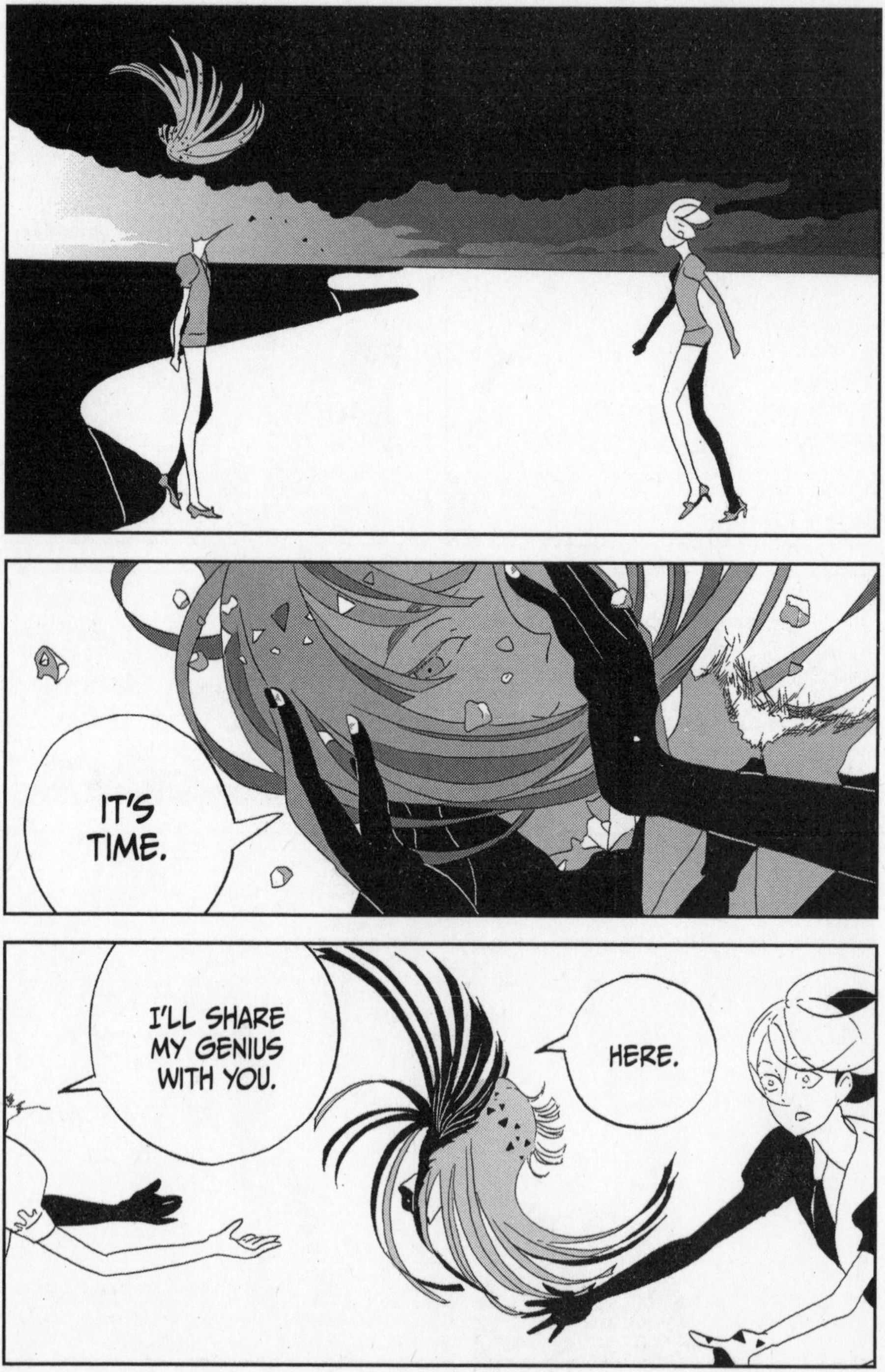
IT'S TIME.
HERE.
I'LL SHARE MY GENIUS WITH YOU.

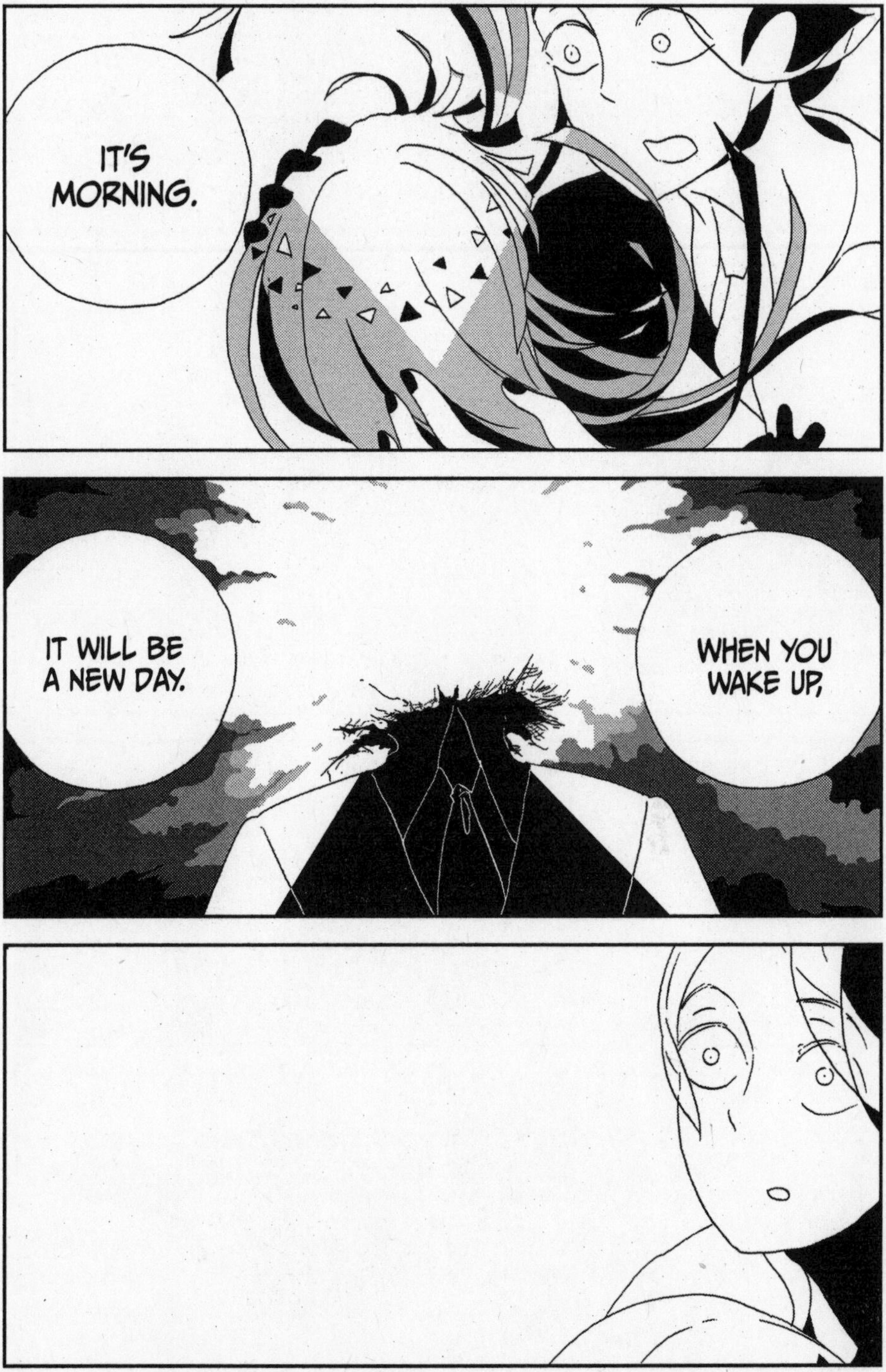
IT'S MORNING.
WHEN YOU WAKE UP,
IT WILL BE A NEW DAY.

...WAS AN EXHAUSTING DREAM.

THAT...

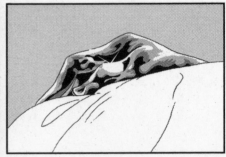

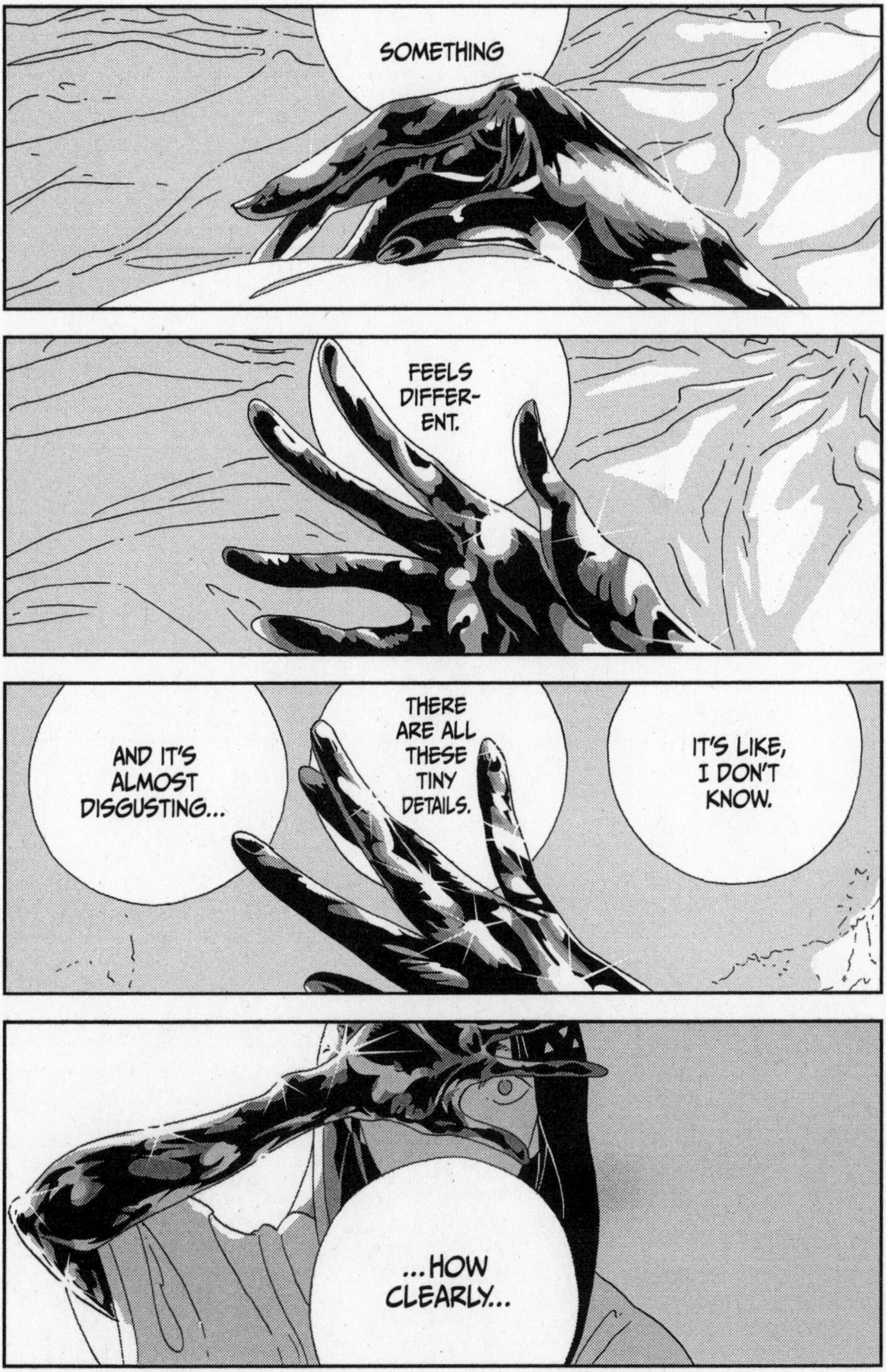
SOMETHING
FEELS DIFFER-ENT.
IT'S LIKE, I DON'T KNOW.
THERE ARE ALL THESE TINY DETAILS.
AND IT'S ALMOST DISGUSTING...
...HOW CLEARLY...

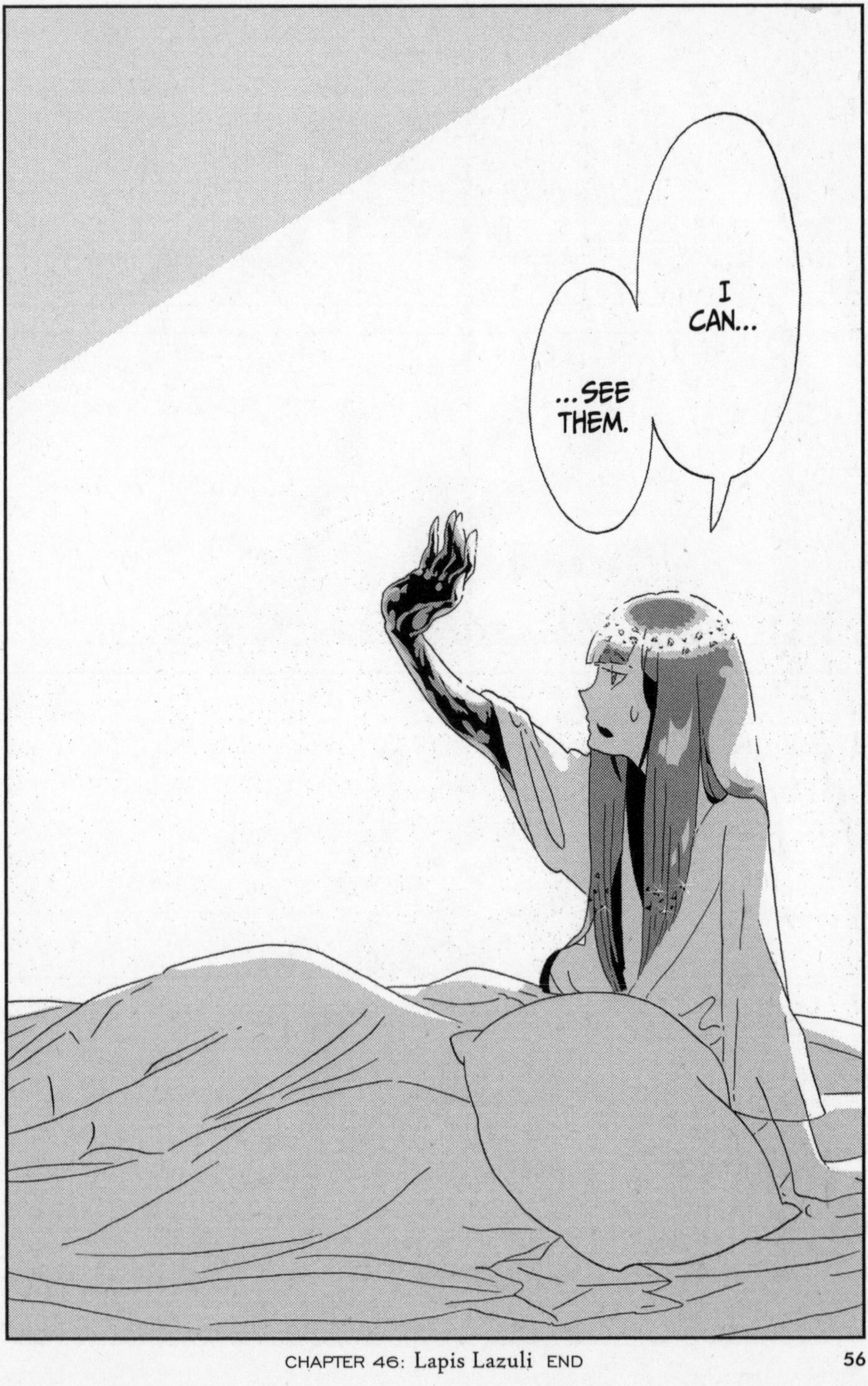
I CAN...
...SEE THEM.

CHAPTER 46: Lapis Lazuli END

CHAPTER 47:

102 Years

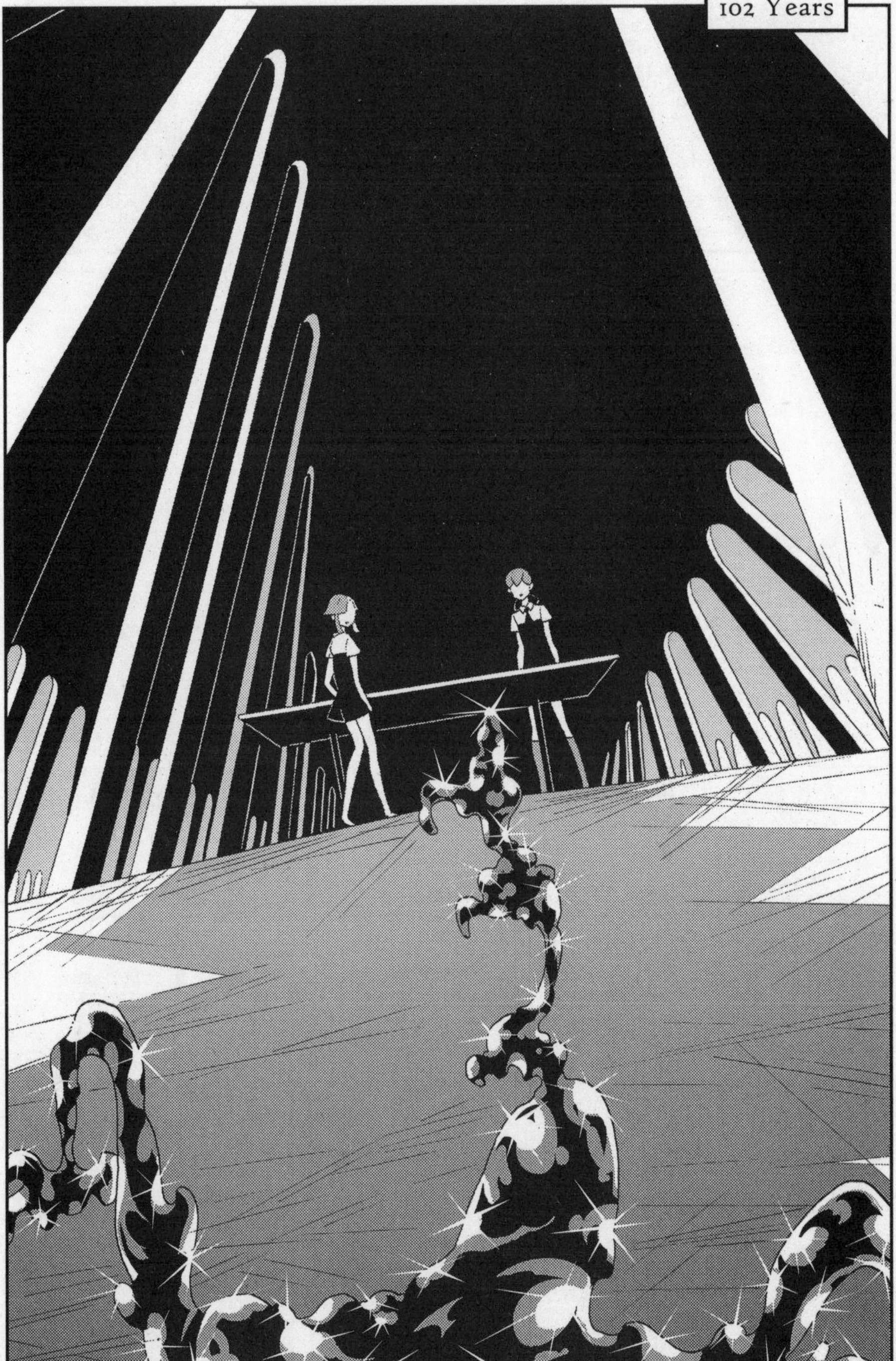

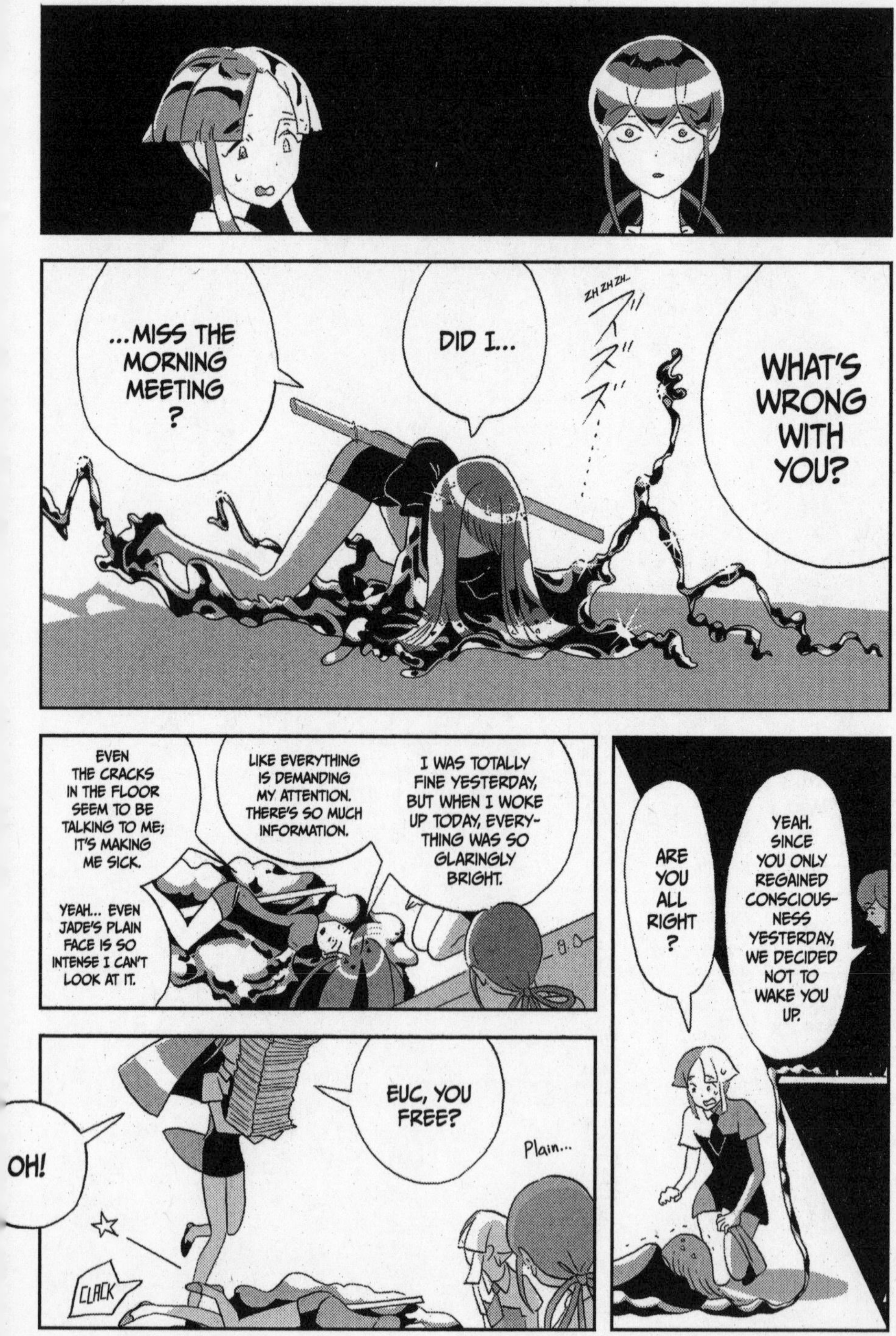
WHAT'S WRONG WITH YOU?
ZH ZH ZH...
DID I...
...MISS THE MORNING MEETING ?
YEAH. SINCE YOU ONLY REGAINED CONSCIOUS-NESS YESTERDAY, WE DECIDED NOT TO WAKE YOU UP.
ARE YOU ALL RIGHT ?
I WAS TOTALLY FINE YESTERDAY, BUT WHEN I WOKE UP TODAY, EVERY-THING WAS SO GLARINGLY BRIGHT.
LIKE EVERYTHING IS DEMANDING MY ATTENTION. THERE'S SO MUCH INFORMATION.
EVEN THE CRACKS IN THE FLOOR SEEM TO BE TALKING TO ME; IT'S MAKING ME SICK.
YEAH... EVEN JADE'S PLAIN FACE IS SO INTENSE I CAN'T LOOK AT IT.
EUC, YOU FREE?
Plain...
OH!
CLACK

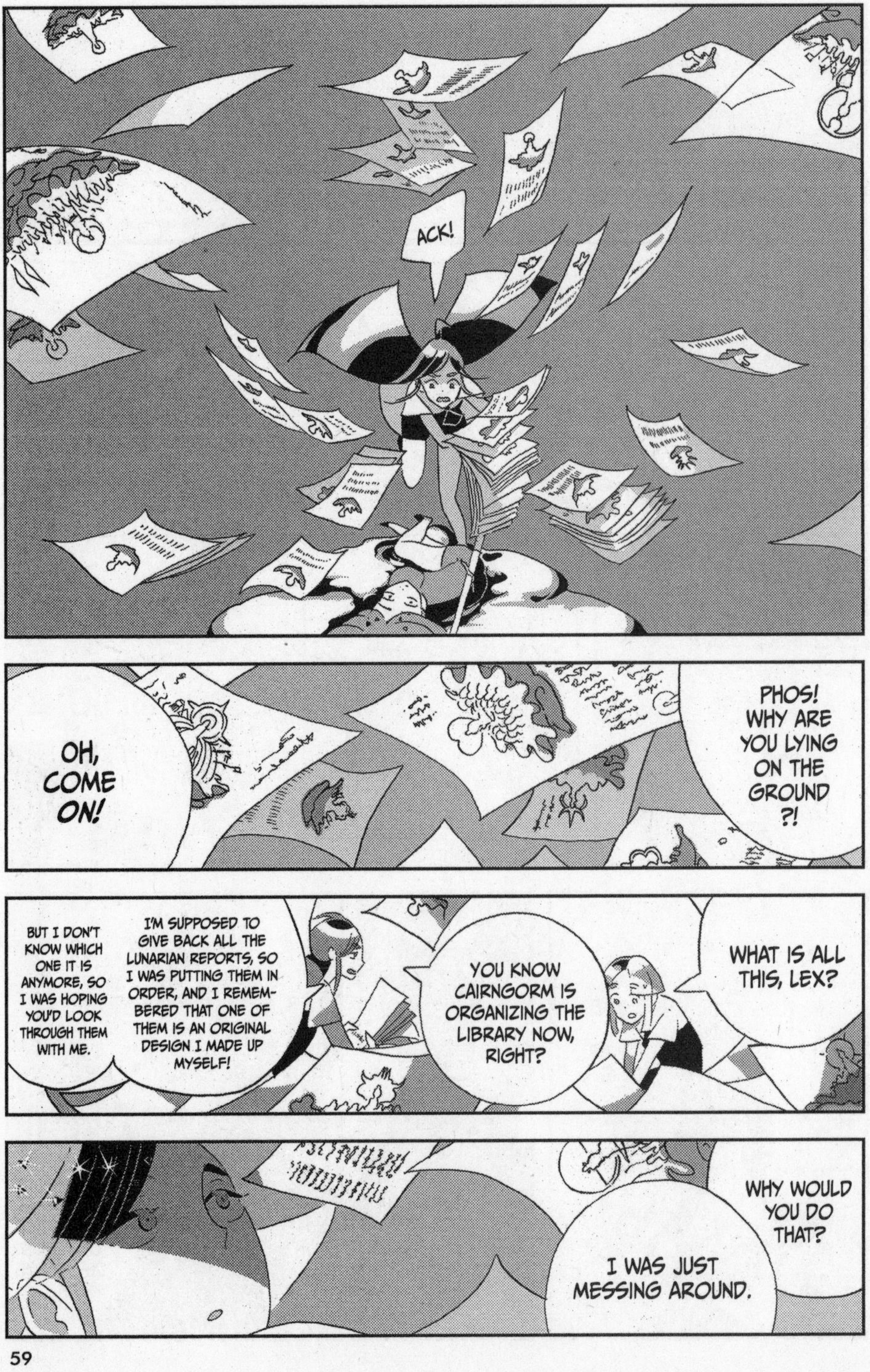
ACK!
PHOS! WHY ARE YOU LYING ON THE GROUND ?!
OH, COME ON!
WHAT IS ALL THIS, LEX?
YOU KNOW CAIRNGORM IS ORGANIZING THE LIBRARY NOW, RIGHT?
I'M SUPPOSED TO GIVE BACK ALL THE LUNARIAN REPORTS, SO I WAS PUTTING THEM IN ORDER, AND I REMEMBERED THAT ONE OF THEM IS AN ORIGINAL DESIGN I MADE UP MYSELF!
BUT I DON'T KNOW WHICH ONE IT IS ANYMORE, SO I WAS HOPING YOU'D LOOK THROUGH THEM WITH ME.
WHY WOULD YOU DO THAT?
I WAS JUST MESSING AROUND.

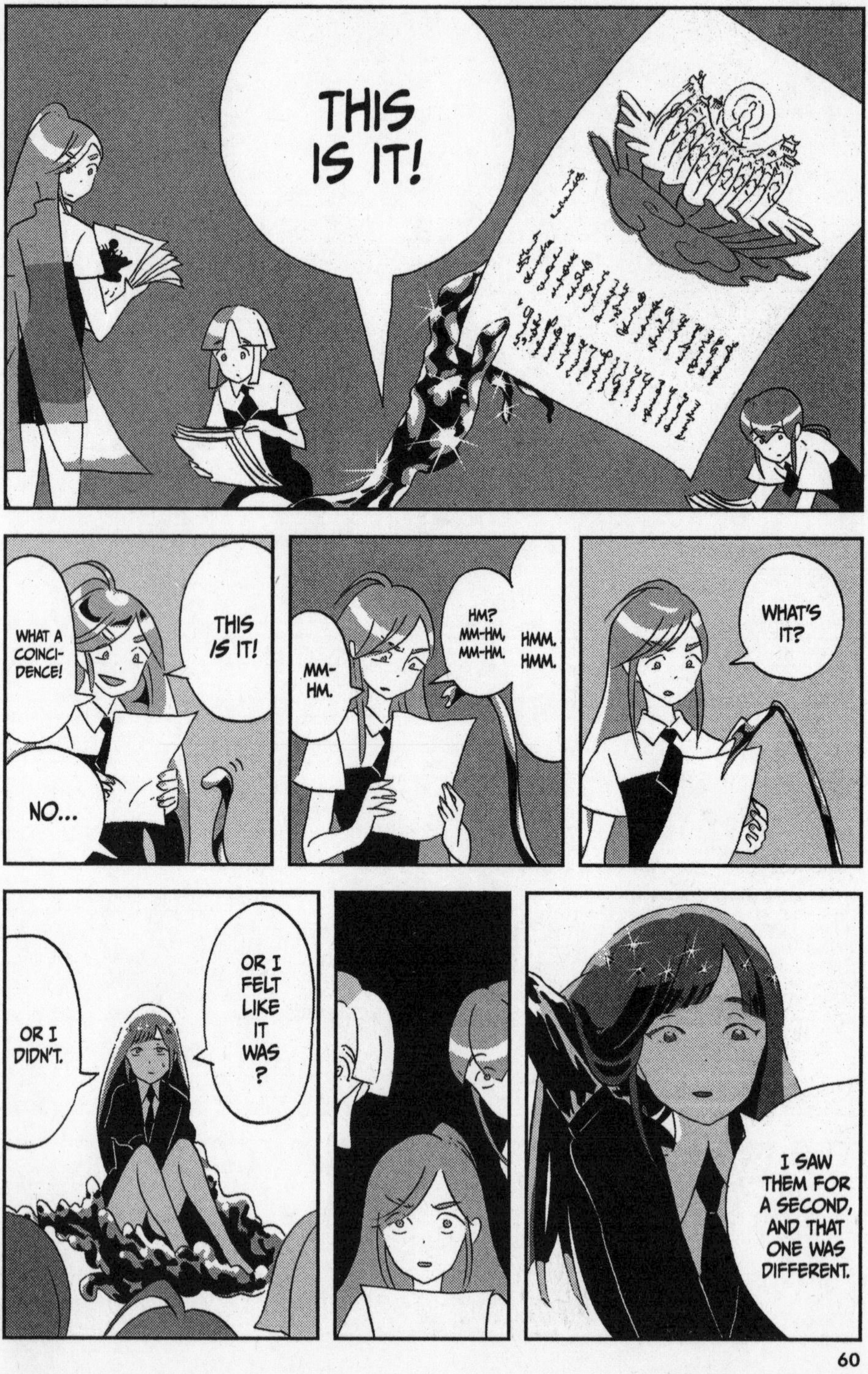
THIS IS IT!
WHAT'S IT?
HMM. HMM.
HM? MM-HM, MM-HM.
MM-HM.
THIS *IS* IT!
WHAT A COINCIDENCE!
NO...
I SAW THEM FOR A SECOND, AND THAT ONE WAS DIFFERENT.
OR I FELT LIKE IT WAS?
OR I DIDN'T.

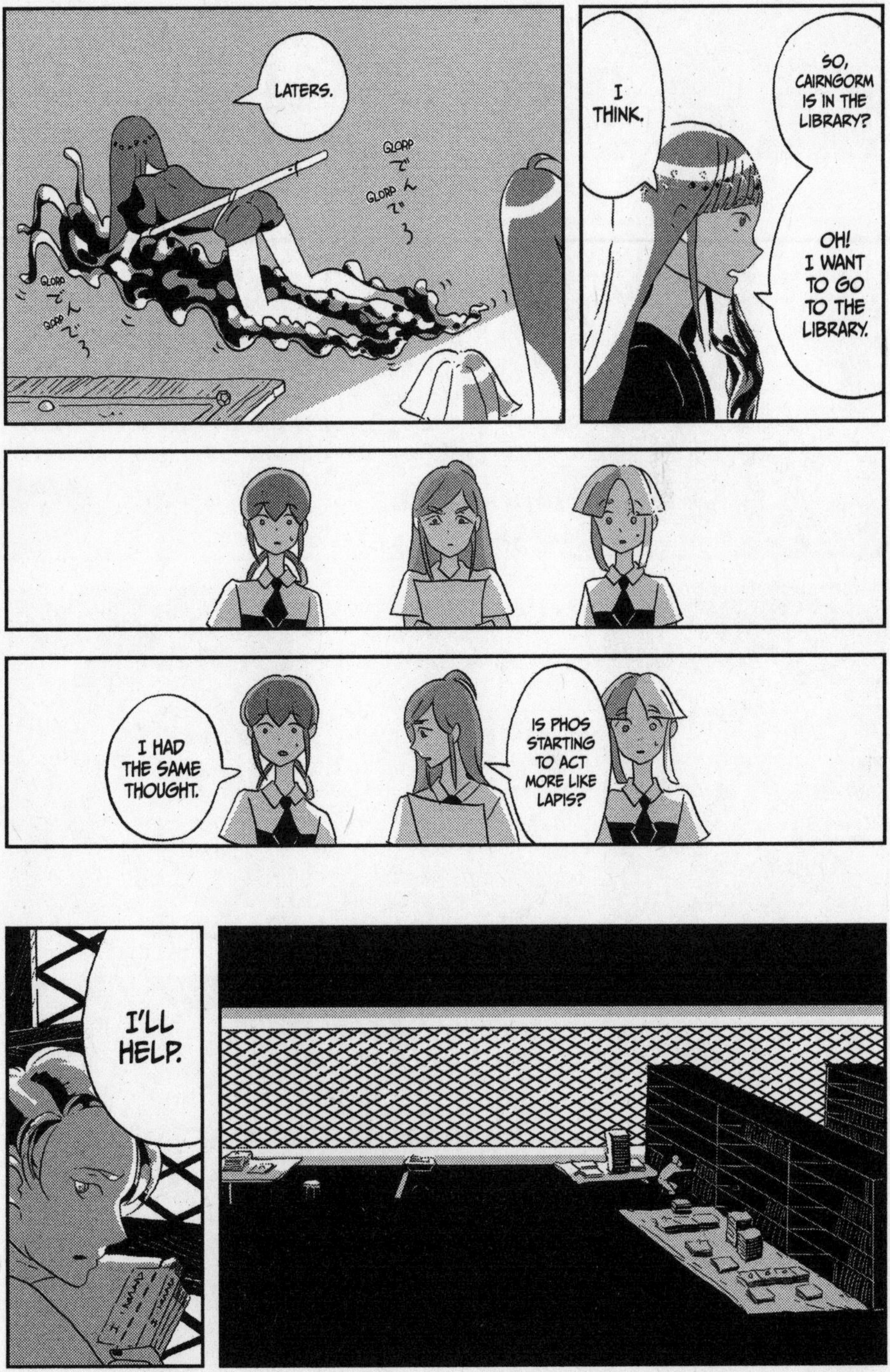
SO, CAIRNGORM IS IN THE LIBRARY?
OH! I WANT TO GO TO THE LIBRARY.
I THINK.
LATERS.
GLORP でん GLORP でろ
GLORP でん GLORP でろ
IS PHOS STARTING TO ACT MORE LIKE LAPIS?
I HAD THE SAME THOUGHT.
I'LL HELP.

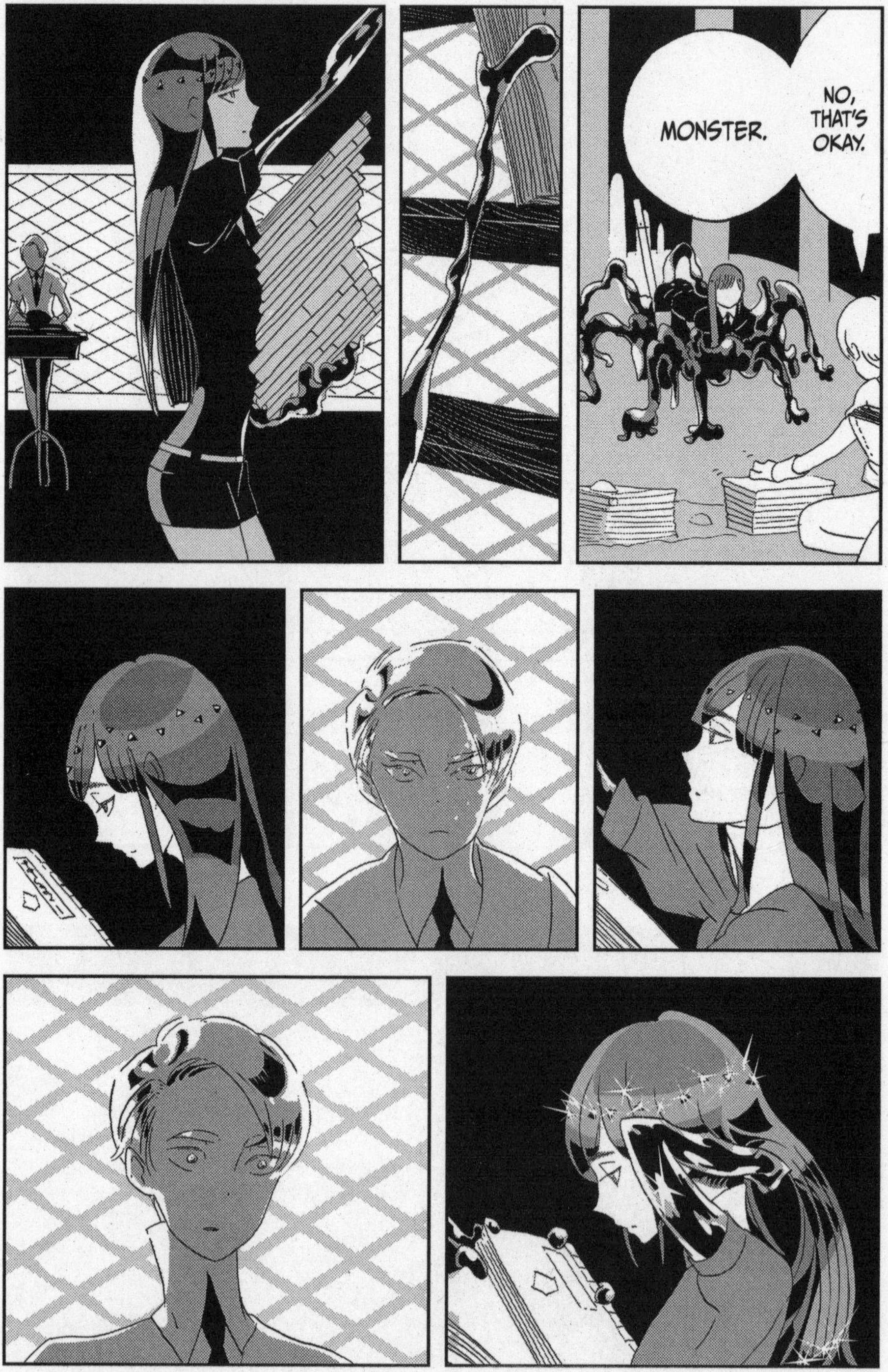
NO, THAT'S OKAY.
MONSTER.

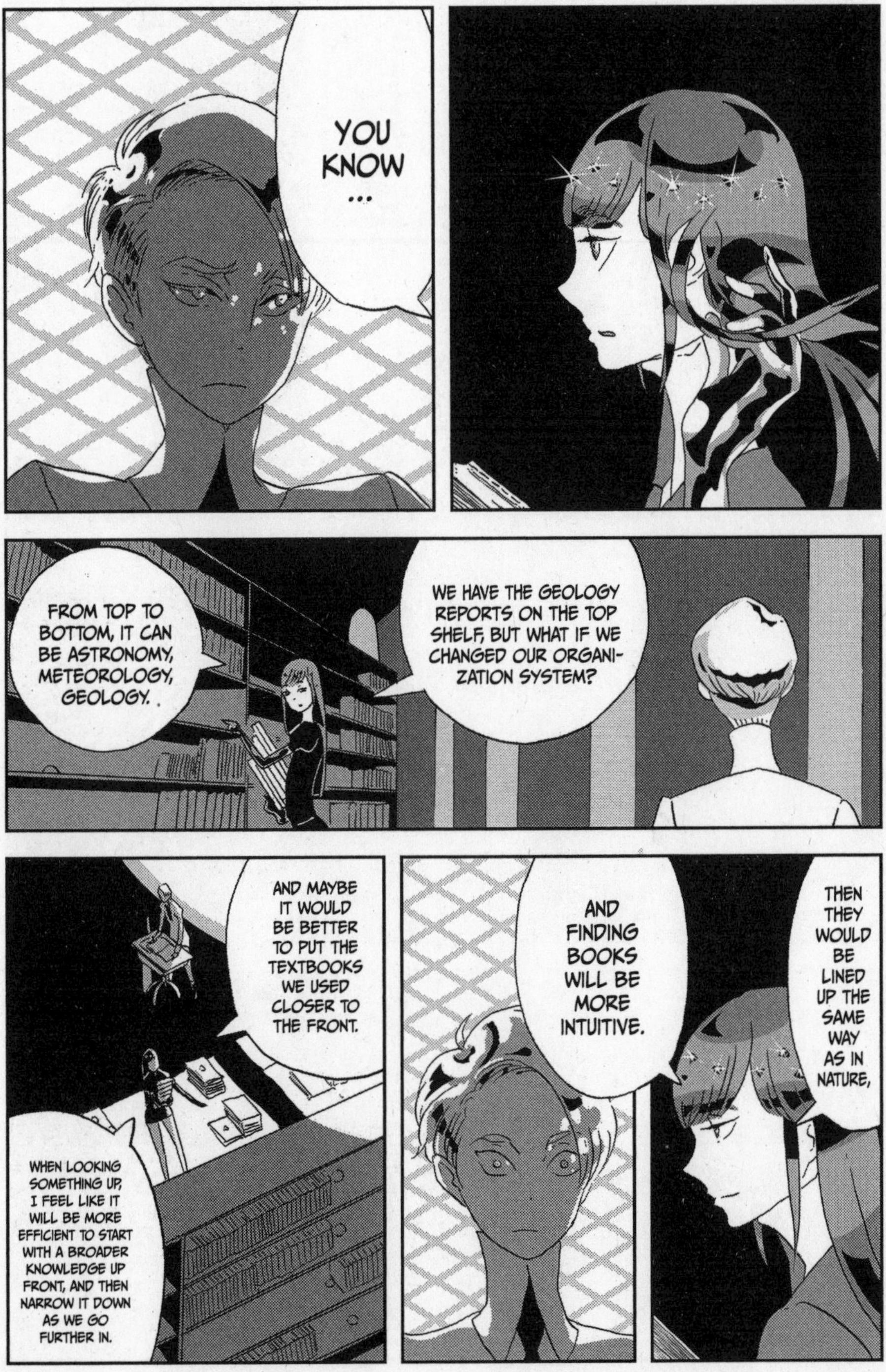
YOU KNOW ...
WE HAVE THE GEOLOGY REPORTS ON THE TOP SHELF, BUT WHAT IF WE CHANGED OUR ORGANI-ZATION SYSTEM?
FROM TOP TO BOTTOM, IT CAN BE ASTRONOMY, METEOROLOGY, GEOLOGY.
THEN THEY WOULD BE LINED UP THE SAME WAY AS IN NATURE,
AND FINDING BOOKS WILL BE MORE INTUITIVE.
AND MAYBE IT WOULD BE BETTER TO PUT THE TEXTBOOKS WE USED CLOSER TO THE FRONT.
WHEN LOOKING SOMETHING UP, I FEEL LIKE IT WILL BE MORE EFFICIENT TO START WITH A BROADER KNOWLEDGE UP FRONT, AND THEN NARROW IT DOWN AS WE GO FURTHER IN.

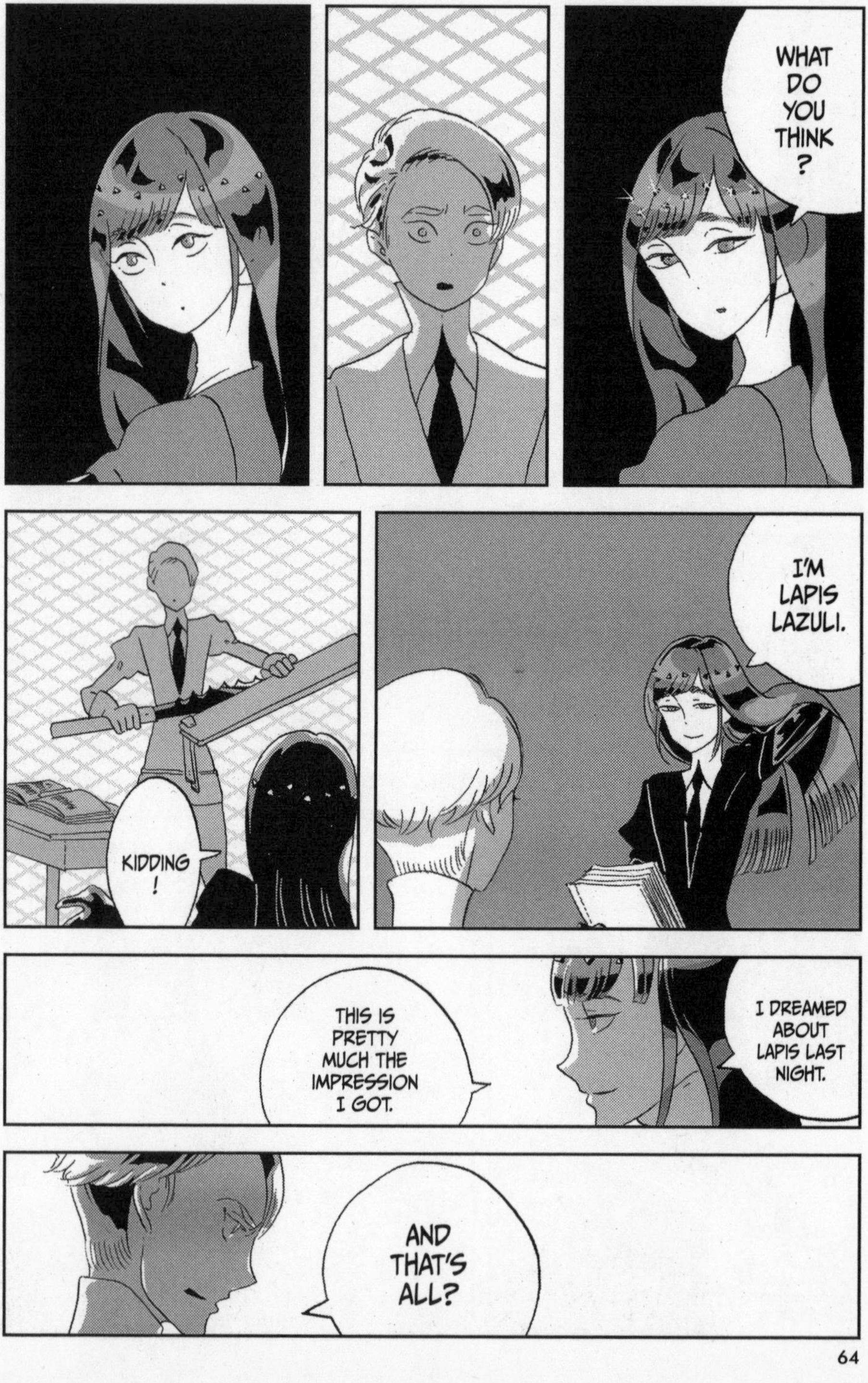
WHAT DO YOU THINK?
I'M LAPIS LAZULI.
KIDDING!
I DREAMED ABOUT LAPIS LAST NIGHT.
THIS IS PRETTY MUCH THE IMPRESSION I GOT.
AND THAT'S ALL?

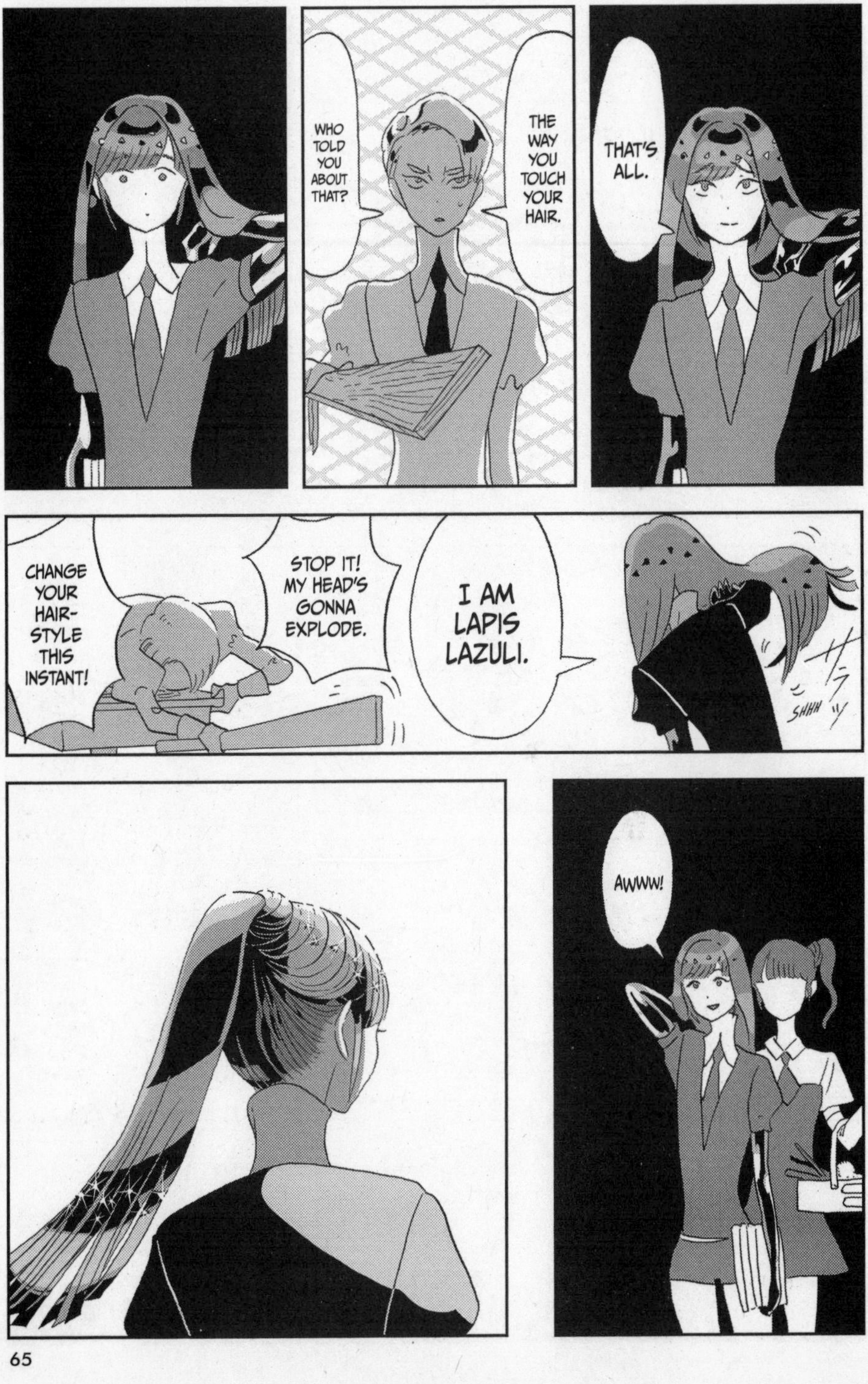
THAT'S ALL.
THE WAY YOU TOUCH YOUR HAIR.
WHO TOLD YOU ABOUT THAT?
SHHH
I AM LAPIS LAZULI.
STOP IT! MY HEAD'S GONNA EXPLODE.
CHANGE YOUR HAIR-STYLE THIS INSTANT!
AWWW!

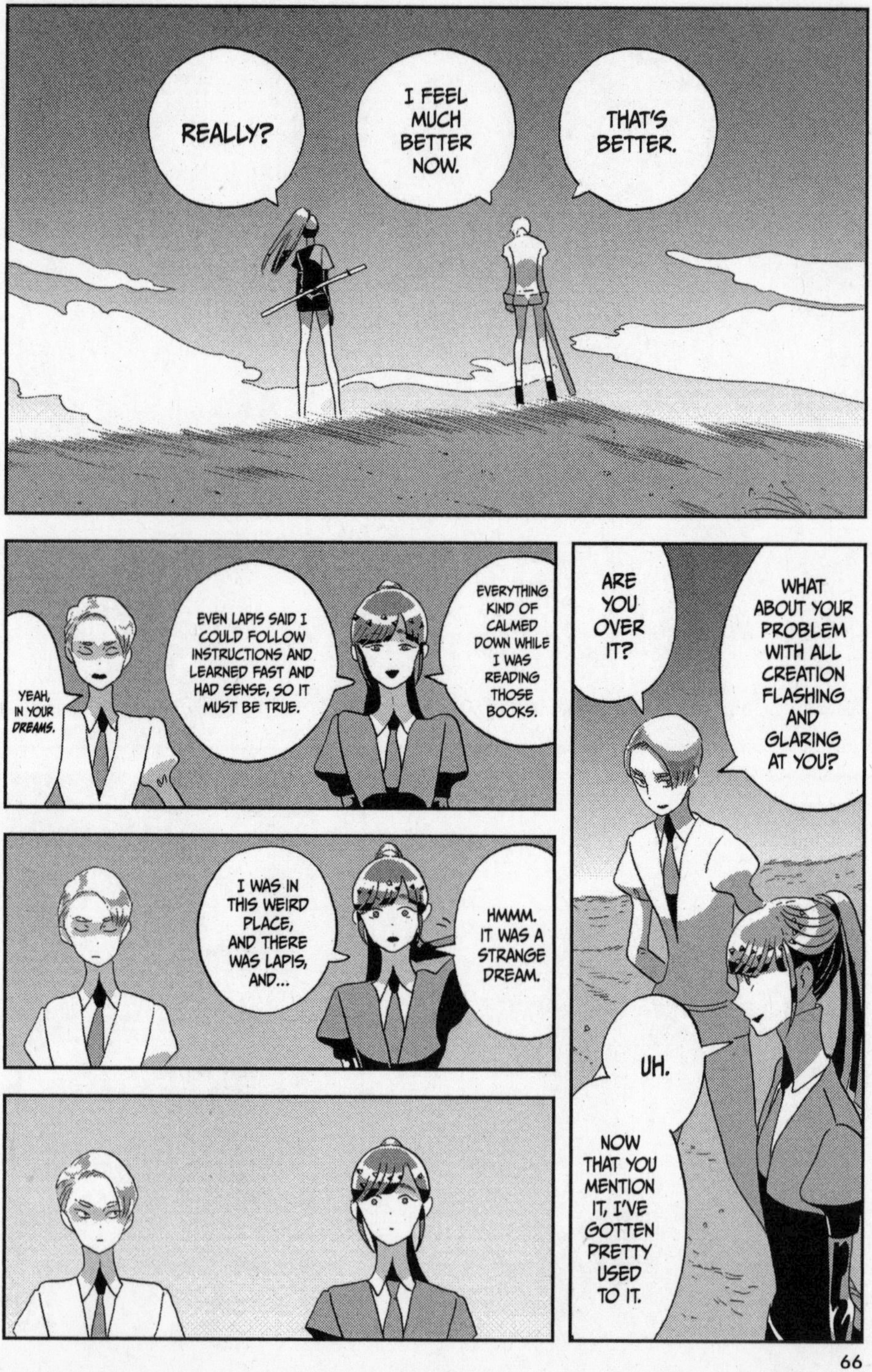
THAT'S BETTER.
I FEEL MUCH BETTER NOW.
REALLY?
WHAT ABOUT YOUR PROBLEM WITH ALL CREATION FLASHING AND GLARING AT YOU?
ARE YOU OVER IT?
UH.
NOW THAT YOU MENTION IT, I'VE GOTTEN PRETTY USED TO IT.
EVERYTHING KIND OF CALMED DOWN WHILE I WAS READING THOSE BOOKS.
EVEN LAPIS SAID I COULD FOLLOW INSTRUCTIONS AND LEARNED FAST AND HAD SENSE, SO IT MUST BE TRUE.
YEAH, IN YOUR DREAMS.
HMMM. IT WAS A STRANGE DREAM.
I WAS IN THIS WEIRD PLACE, AND THERE WAS LAPIS, AND...

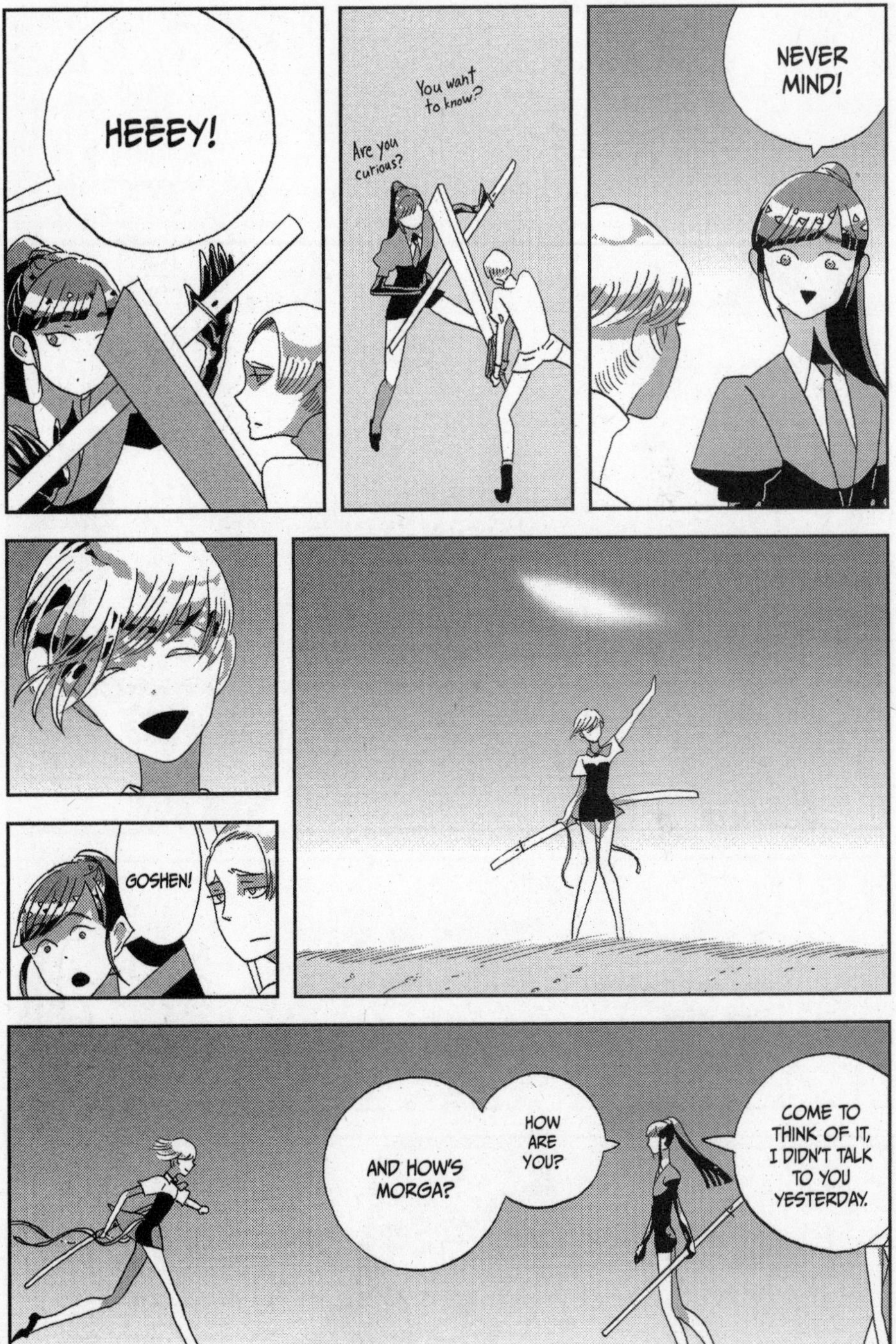
NEVER MIND!
You want to know?
Are you curious?
HEEEY!
GOSHEN!
COME TO THINK OF IT, I DIDN'T TALK TO YOU YESTERDAY.
HOW ARE YOU?
AND HOW'S MORGA?

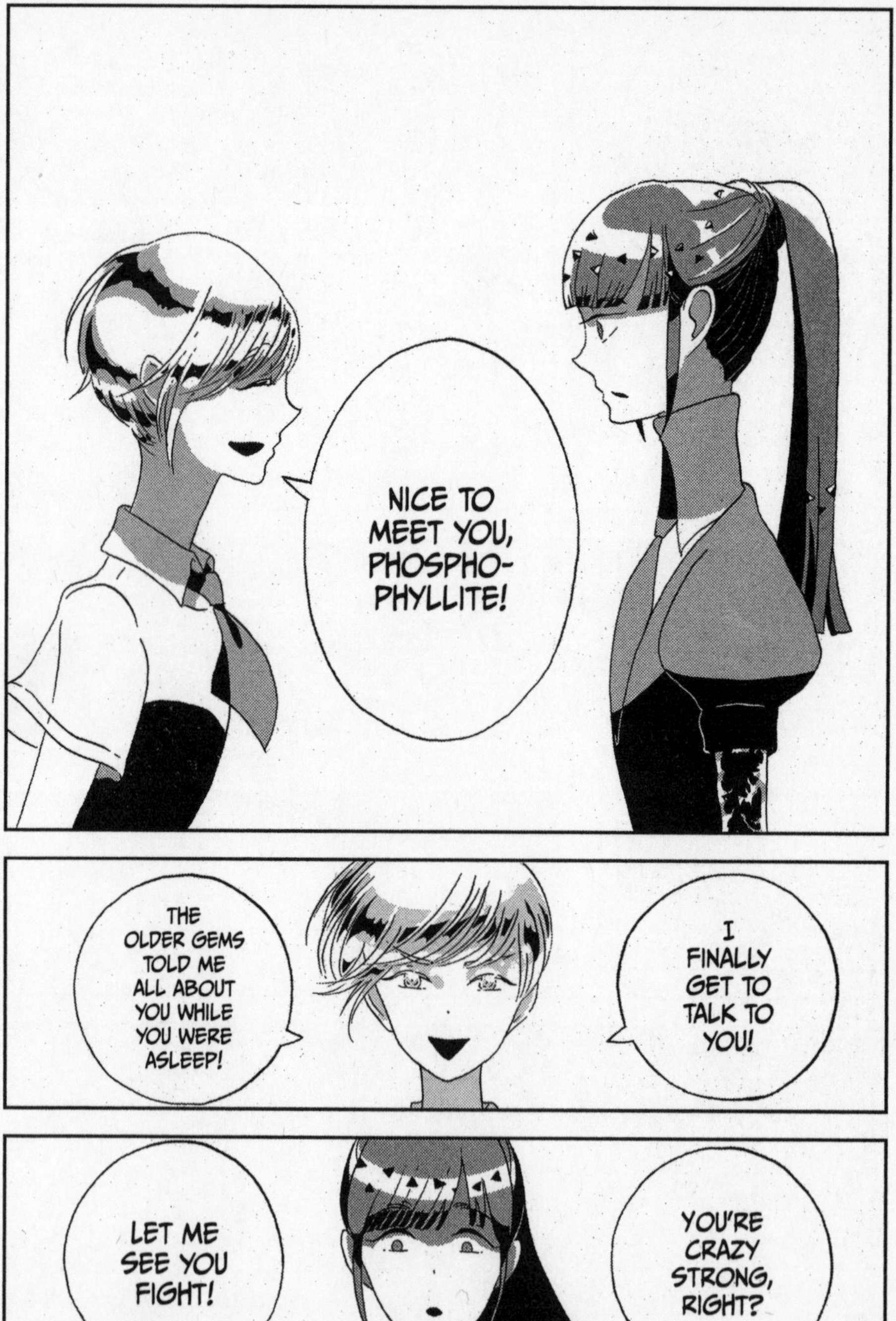
NICE TO MEET YOU, PHOSPHO-PHYLLITE!
I FINALLY GET TO TALK TO YOU!
THE OLDER GEMS TOLD ME ALL ABOUT YOU WHILE YOU WERE ASLEEP!
YOU'RE CRAZY STRONG, RIGHT?
LET ME SEE YOU FIGHT!

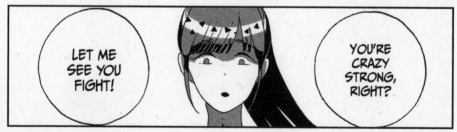

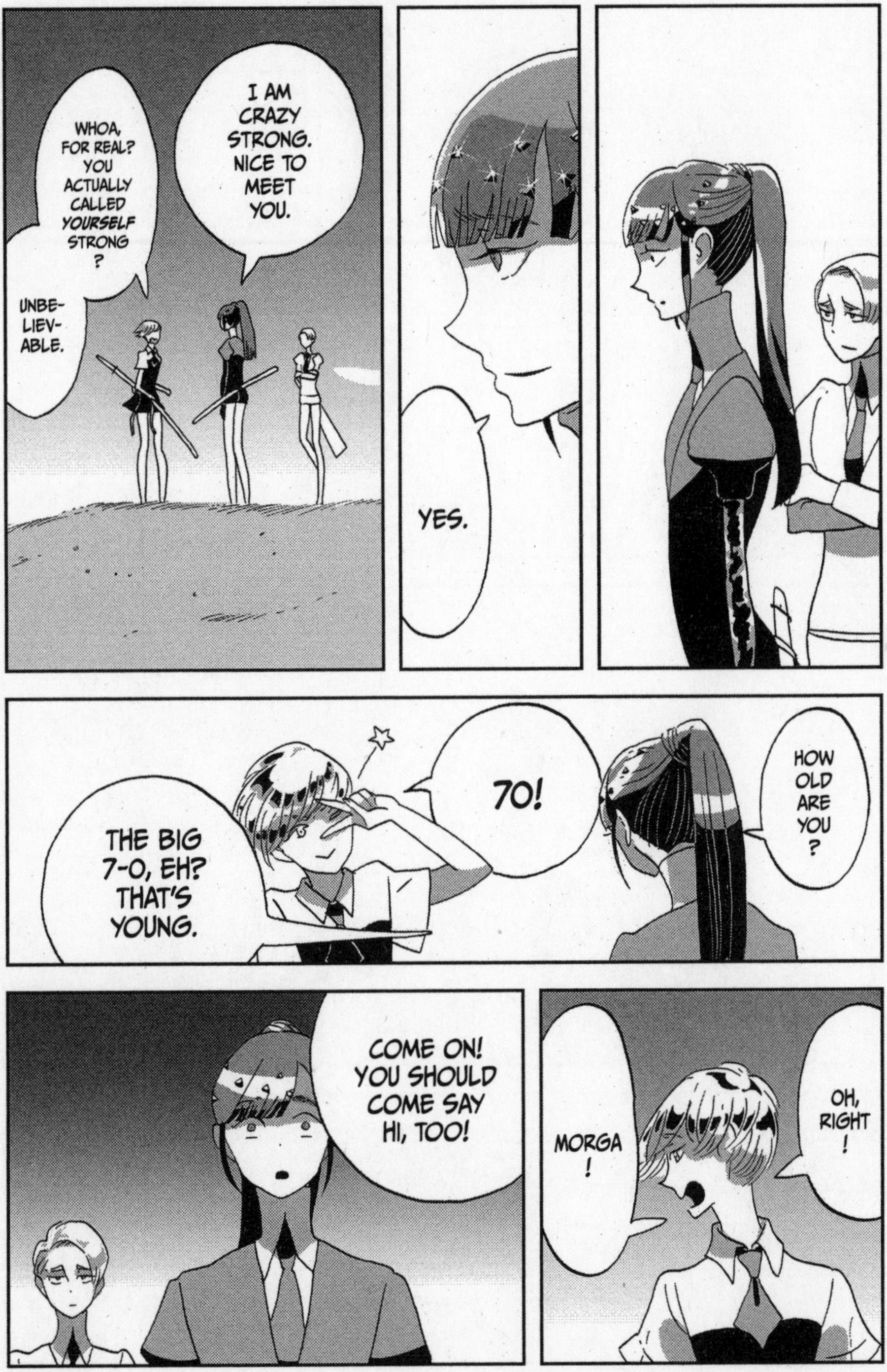
YES.
I AM CRAZY STRONG. NICE TO MEET YOU.
WHOA, FOR REAL? YOU ACTUALLY CALLED YOURSELF STRONG?
UNBE-LIEV-ABLE.
HOW OLD ARE YOU?
70!
THE BIG 7-0, EH? THAT'S YOUNG.
OH, RIGHT!
MORGA!
COME ON! YOU SHOULD COME SAY HI, TOO!

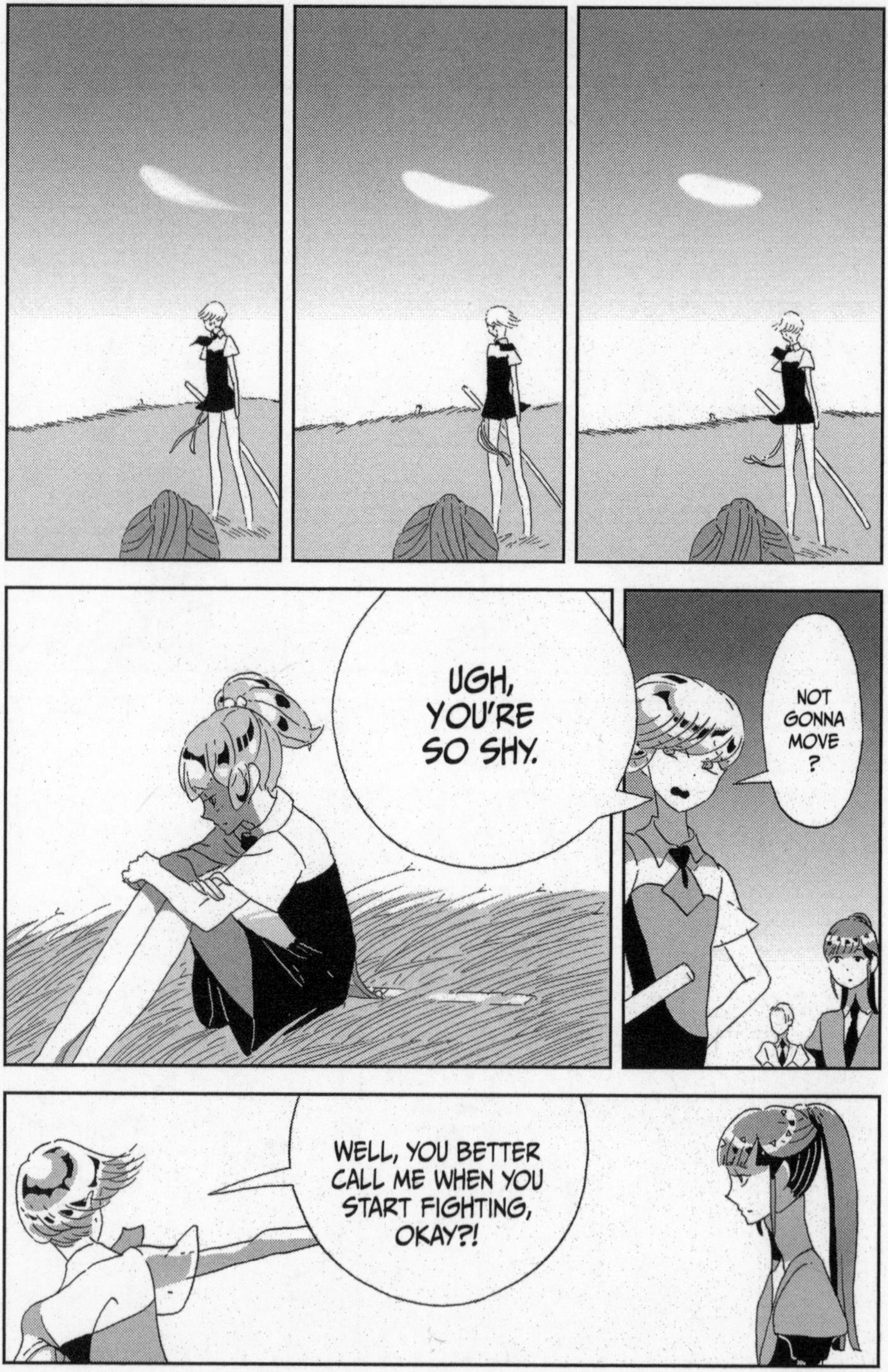
NOT GONNA MOVE?
UGH, YOU'RE SO SHY.
WELL, YOU BETTER CALL ME WHEN YOU START FIGHTING, OKAY?!

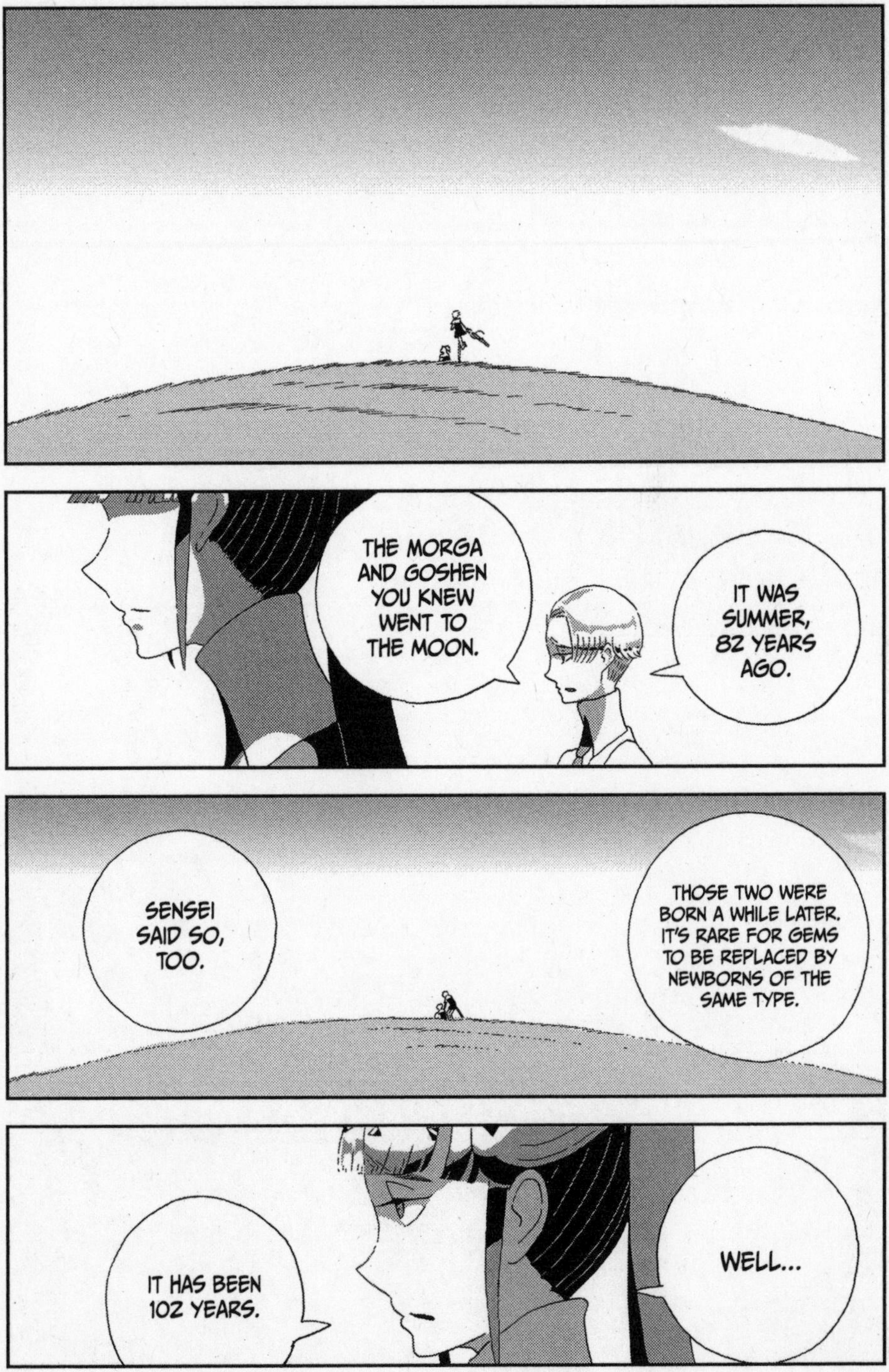
IT WAS SUMMER, 82 YEARS AGO.
THE MORGA AND GOSHEN YOU KNEW WENT TO THE MOON.
THOSE TWO WERE BORN A WHILE LATER. IT'S RARE FOR GEMS TO BE REPLACED BY NEWBORNS OF THE SAME TYPE.
SENSEI SAID SO, TOO.
WELL...
IT HAS BEEN 102 YEARS.

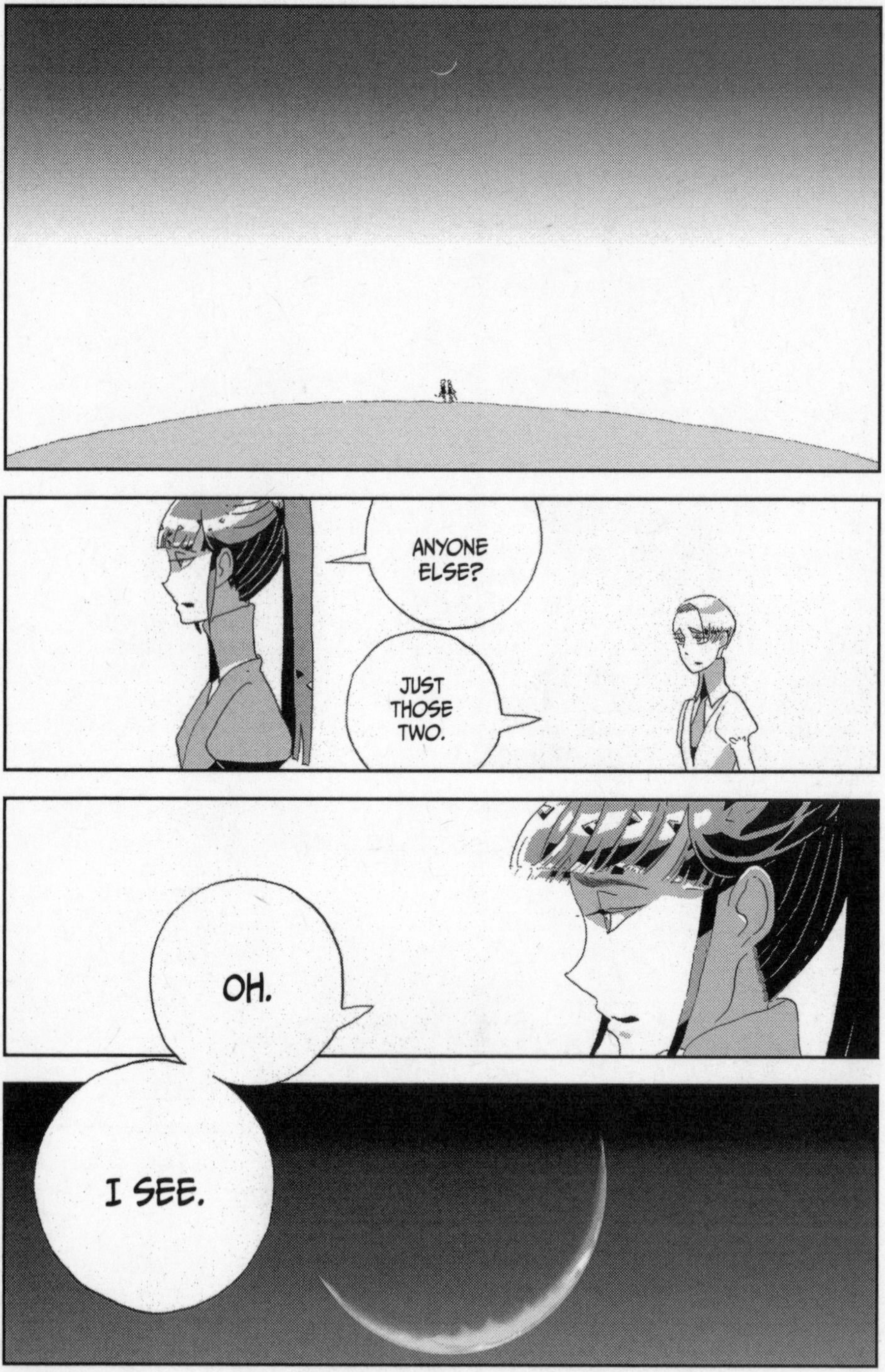
ANYONE ELSE?
JUST THOSE TWO.
OH.
I SEE.

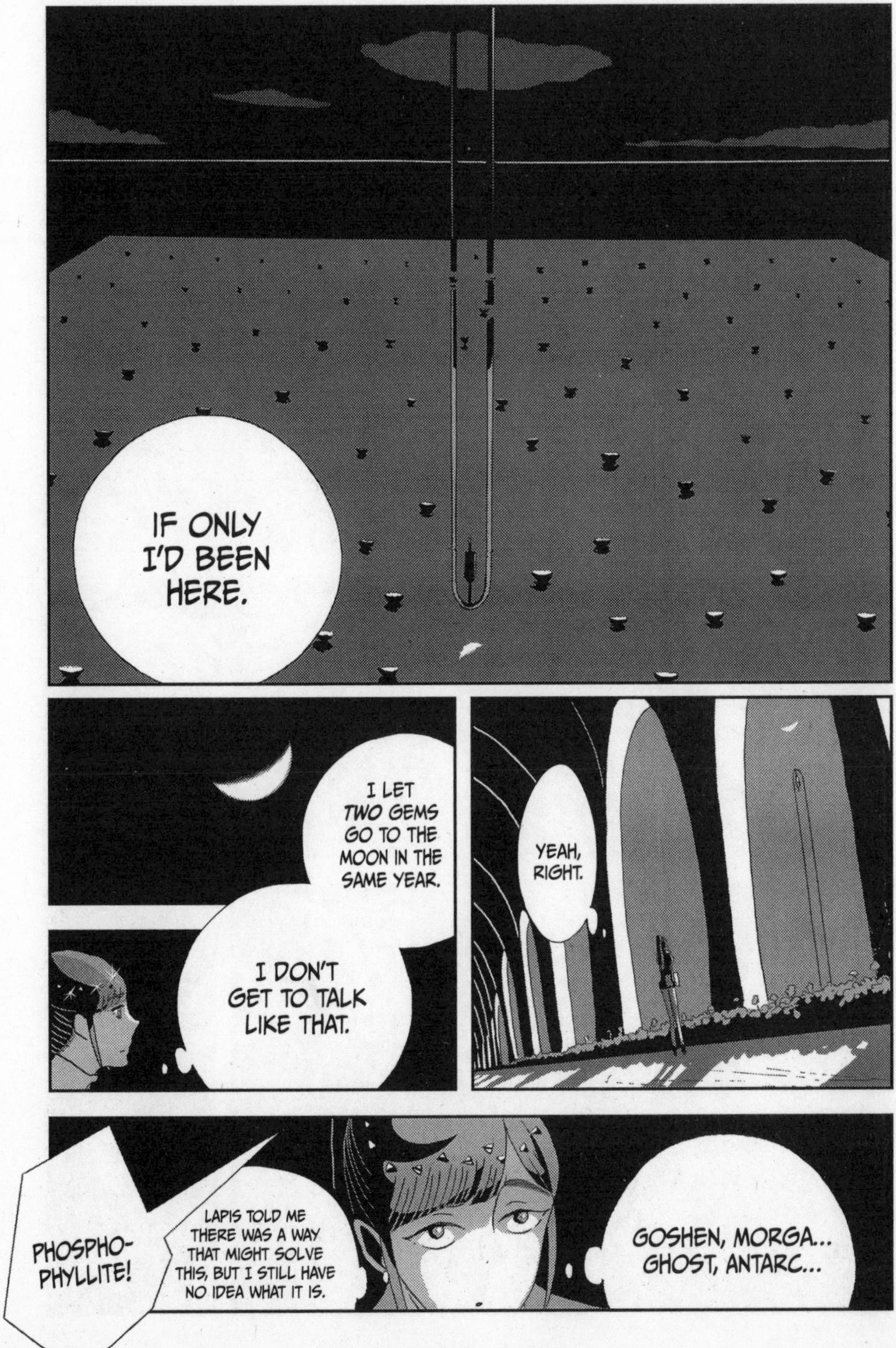
IF ONLY I'D BEEN HERE.
YEAH, RIGHT.
I LET *TWO* GEMS GO TO THE MOON IN THE SAME YEAR.
I DON'T GET TO TALK LIKE THAT.
GOSHEN, MORGA... GHOST, ANTARC...
LAPIS TOLD ME THERE WAS A WAY THAT MIGHT SOLVE THIS, BUT I STILL HAVE NO IDEA WHAT IT IS.
PHOSPHO-PHYLLITE!

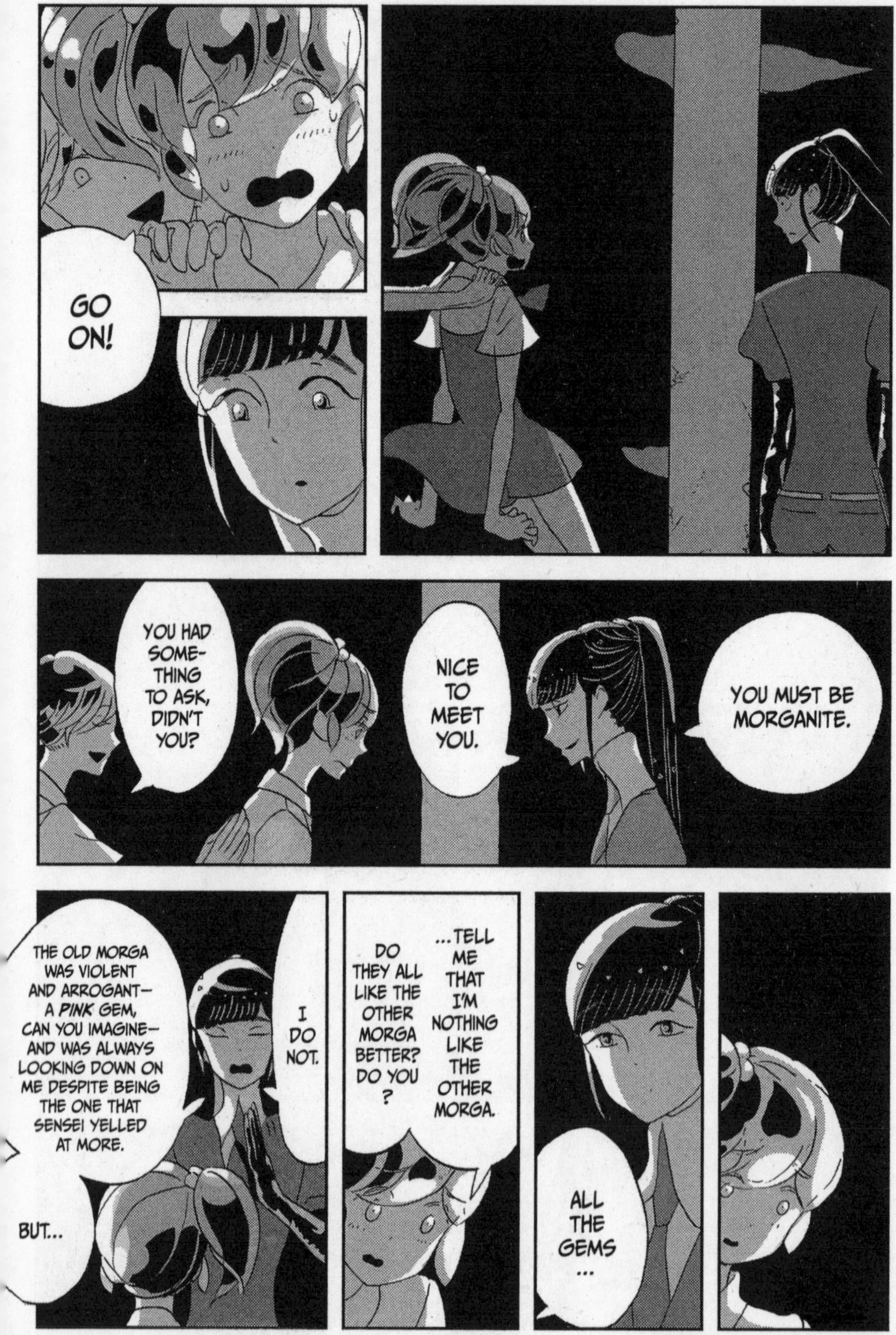
GO ON!
YOU MUST BE MORGANITE.
NICE TO MEET YOU.
YOU HAD SOME-THING TO ASK, DIDN'T YOU?
ALL THE GEMS ...
...TELL ME THAT I'M NOTHING LIKE THE OTHER MORGA.
DO THEY ALL LIKE THE OTHER MORGA BETTER? DO YOU ?
I DO NOT.
THE OLD MORGA WAS VIOLENT AND ARROGANT— A *PINK* GEM, CAN YOU IMAGINE— AND WAS ALWAYS LOOKING DOWN ON ME DESPITE BEING THE ONE THAT SENSEI YELLED AT MORE.
BUT...

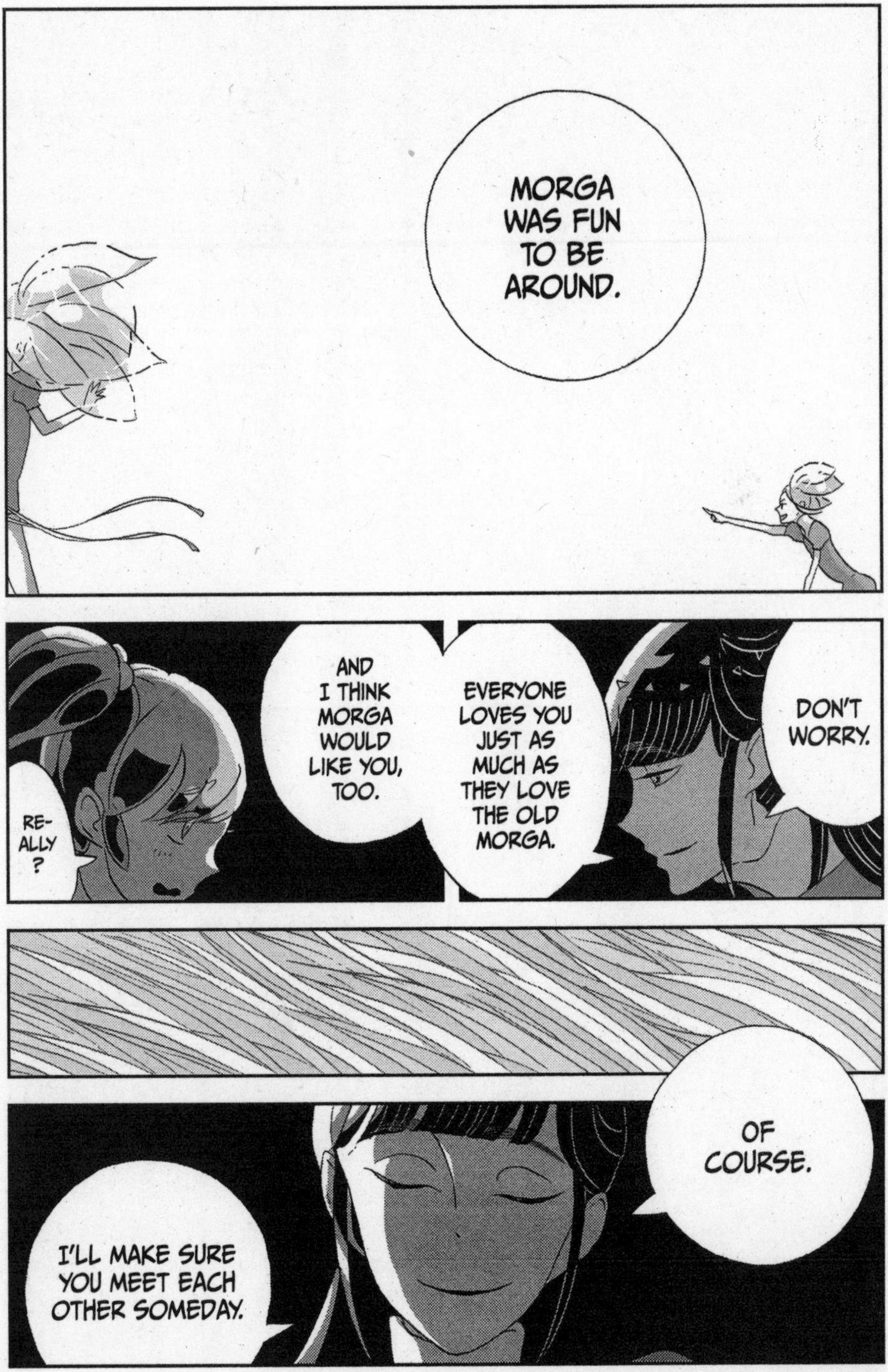
MORGA WAS FUN TO BE AROUND.
DON'T WORRY.
EVERYONE LOVES YOU JUST AS MUCH AS THEY LOVE THE OLD MORGA.
AND I THINK MORGA WOULD LIKE YOU, TOO.
RE-ALLY?
OF COURSE.
I'LL MAKE SURE YOU MEET EACH OTHER SOMEDAY.

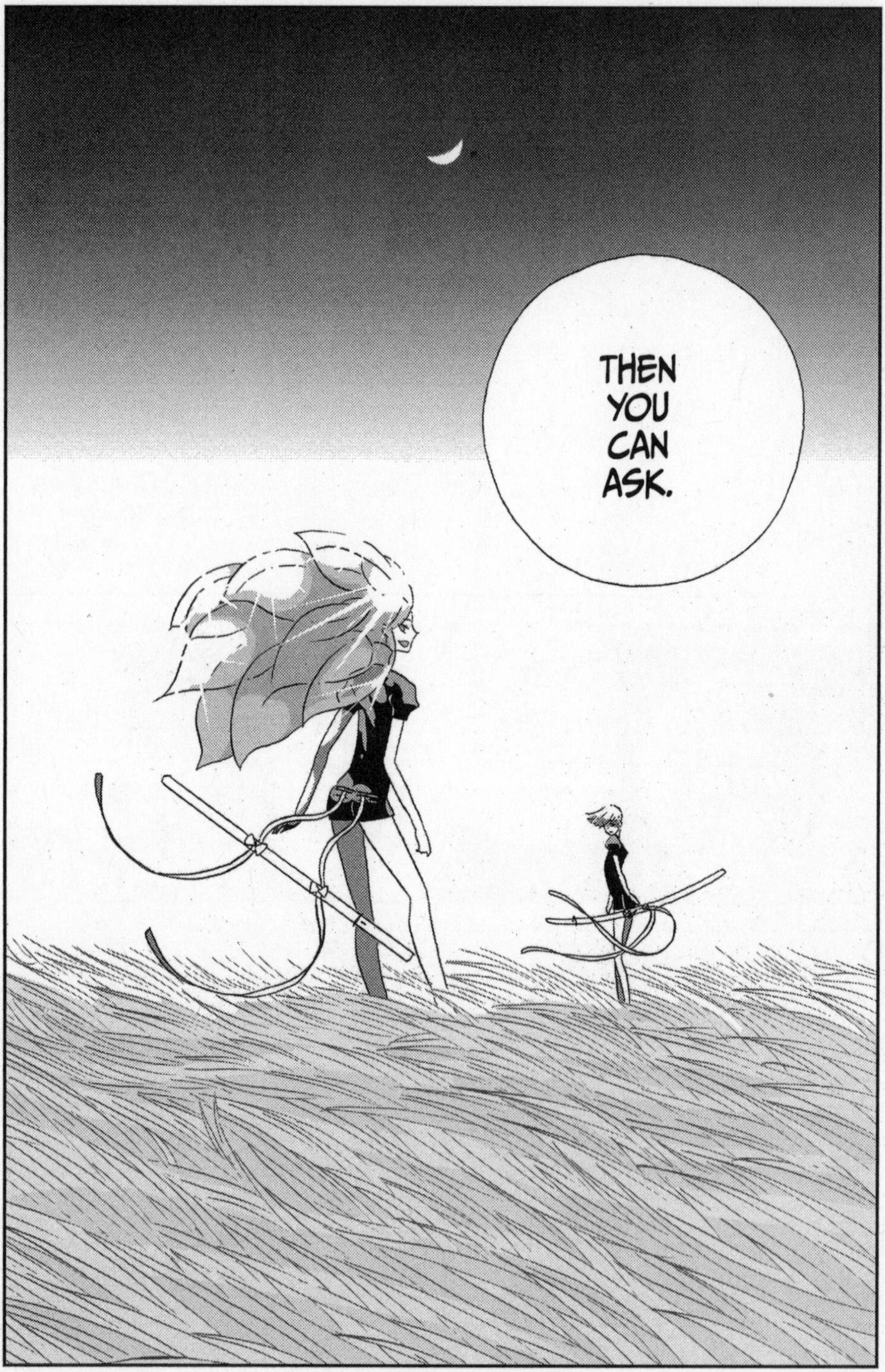
THEN YOU CAN ASK.

CHAPTER 48:

An Old Tale Heard in the Sea

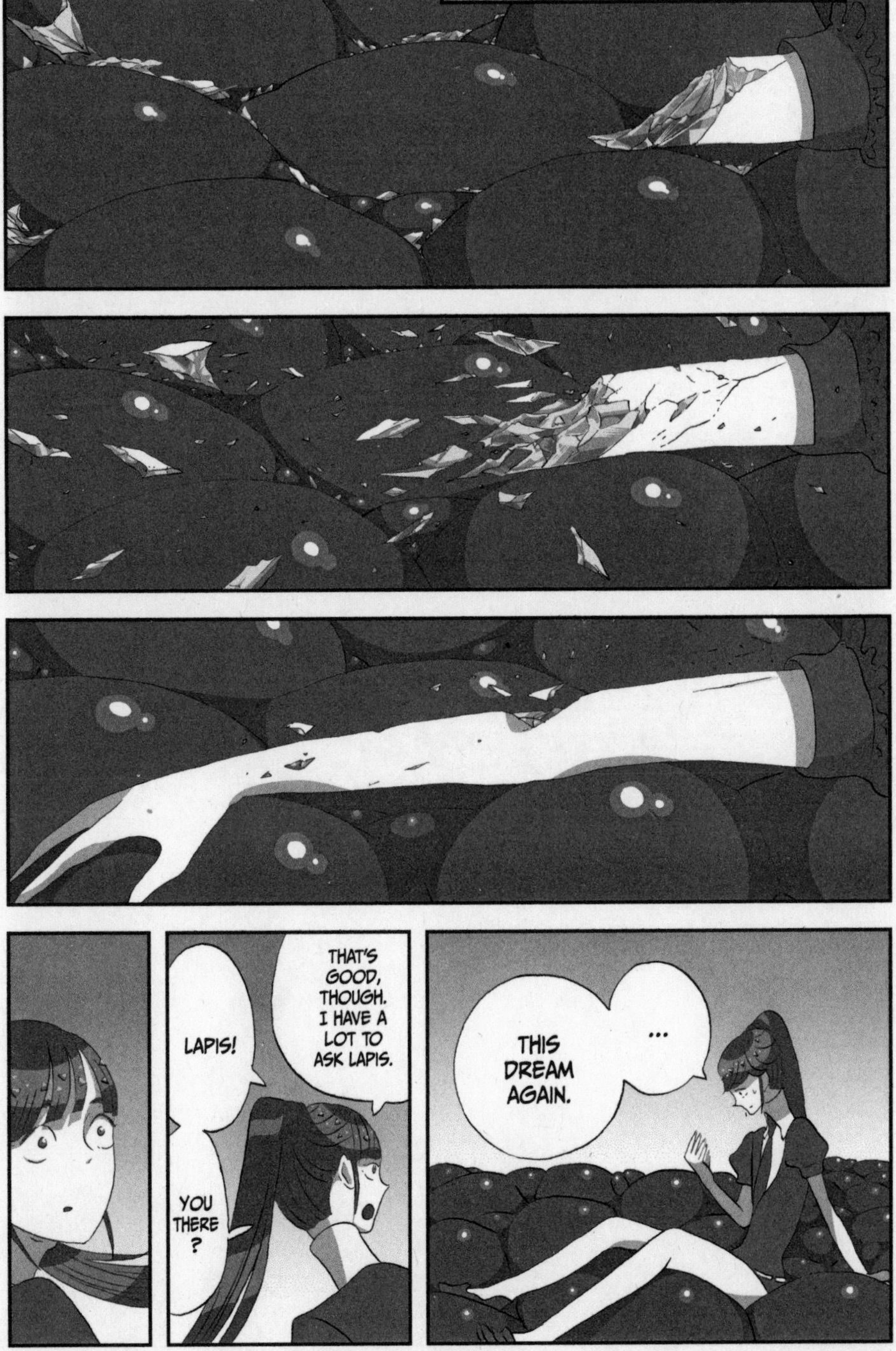
...
THIS DREAM AGAIN.
THAT'S GOOD, THOUGH. I HAVE A LOT TO ASK LAPIS.
LAPIS!
YOU THERE ?

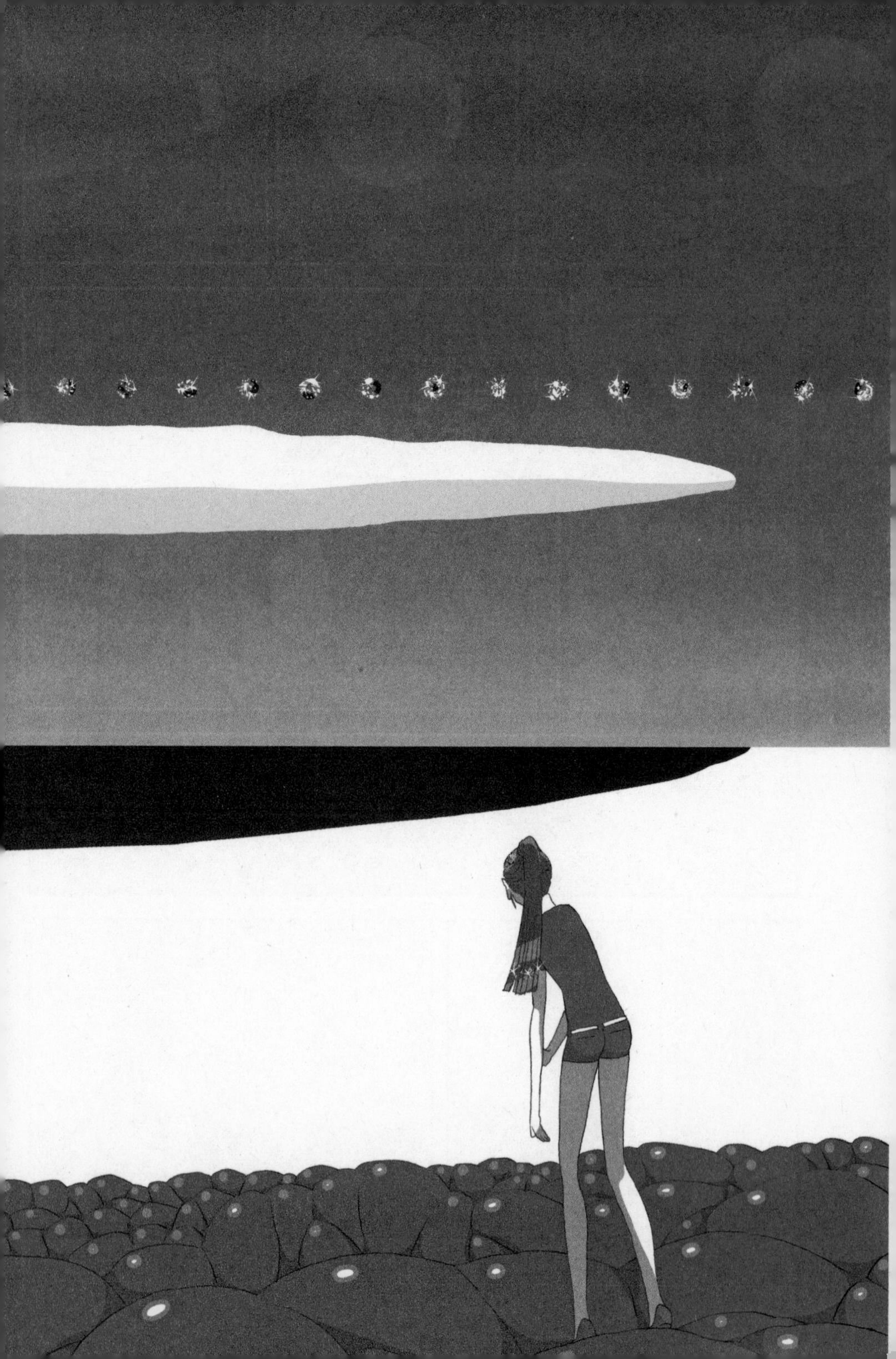

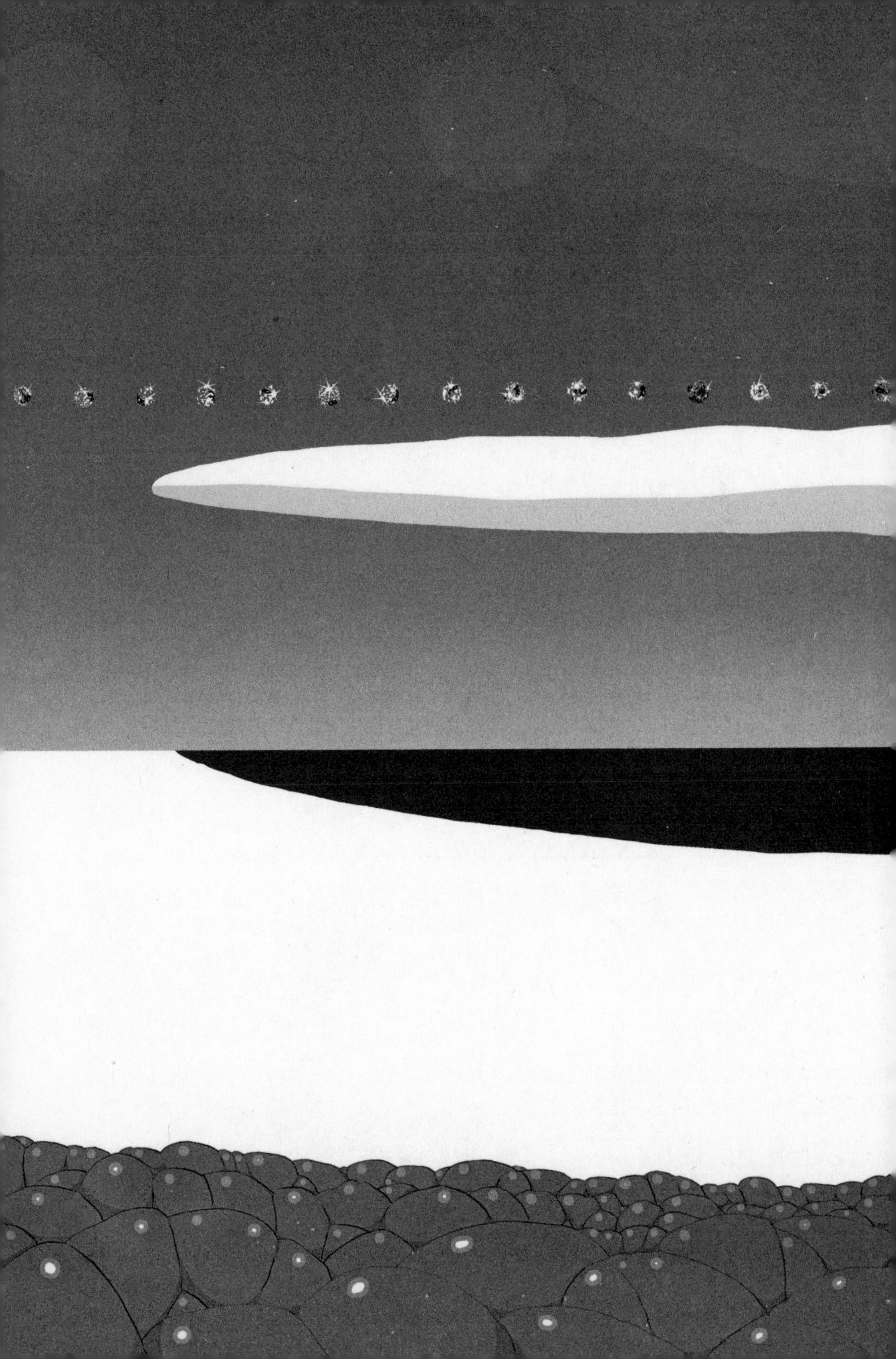

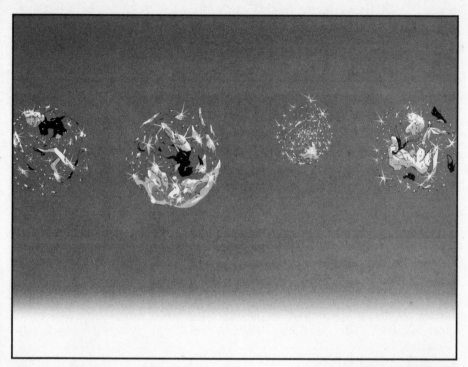

GOSHEN... MORGA. GHOST. ANTARC.

AH!

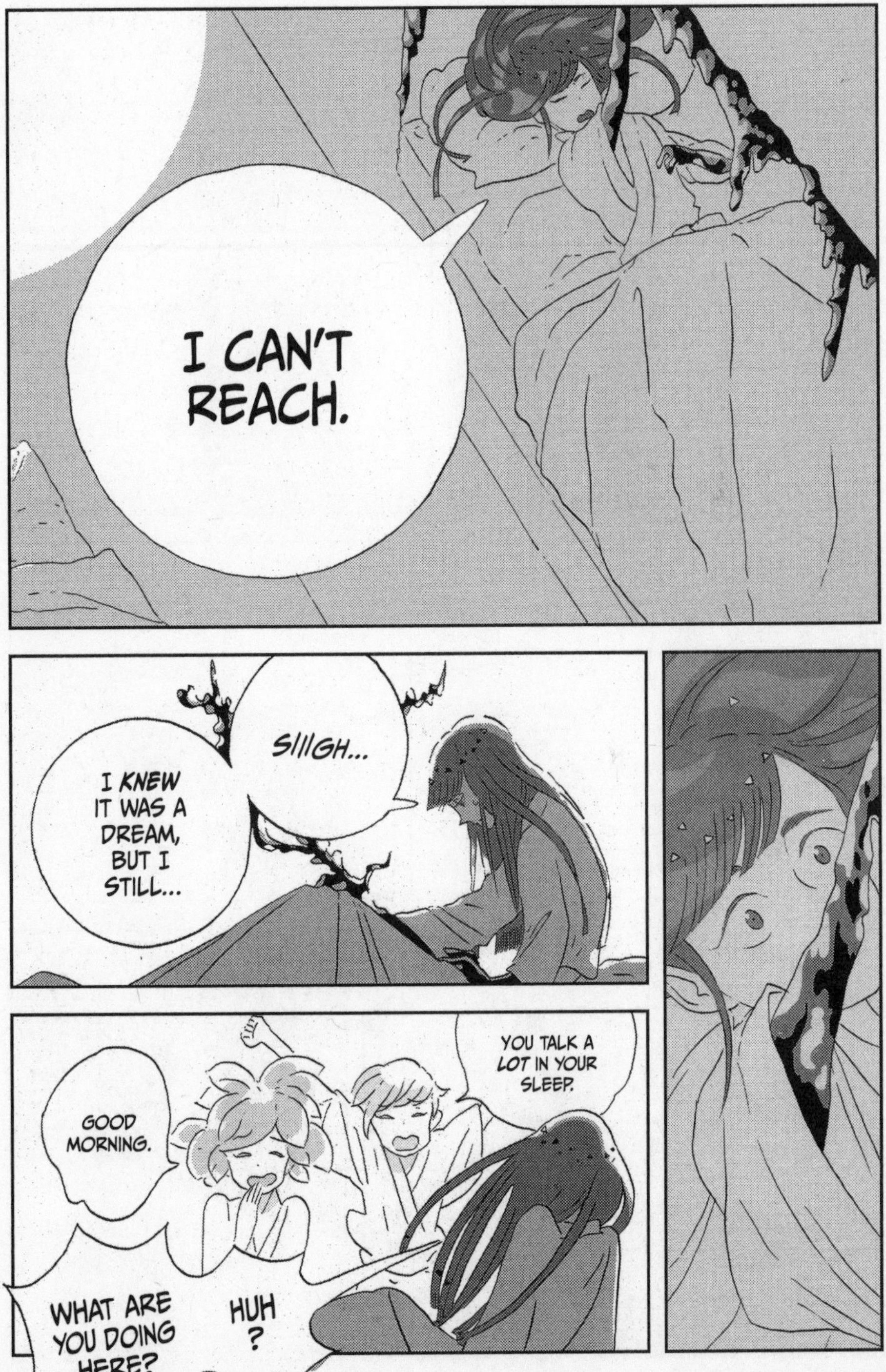
I CAN'T REACH.
SIIIGH...
I *KNEW* IT WAS A DREAM, BUT I STILL...
YOU TALK A *LOT* IN YOUR SLEEP.
GOOD MORNING.
HUH?
WHAT ARE YOU DOING HERE?

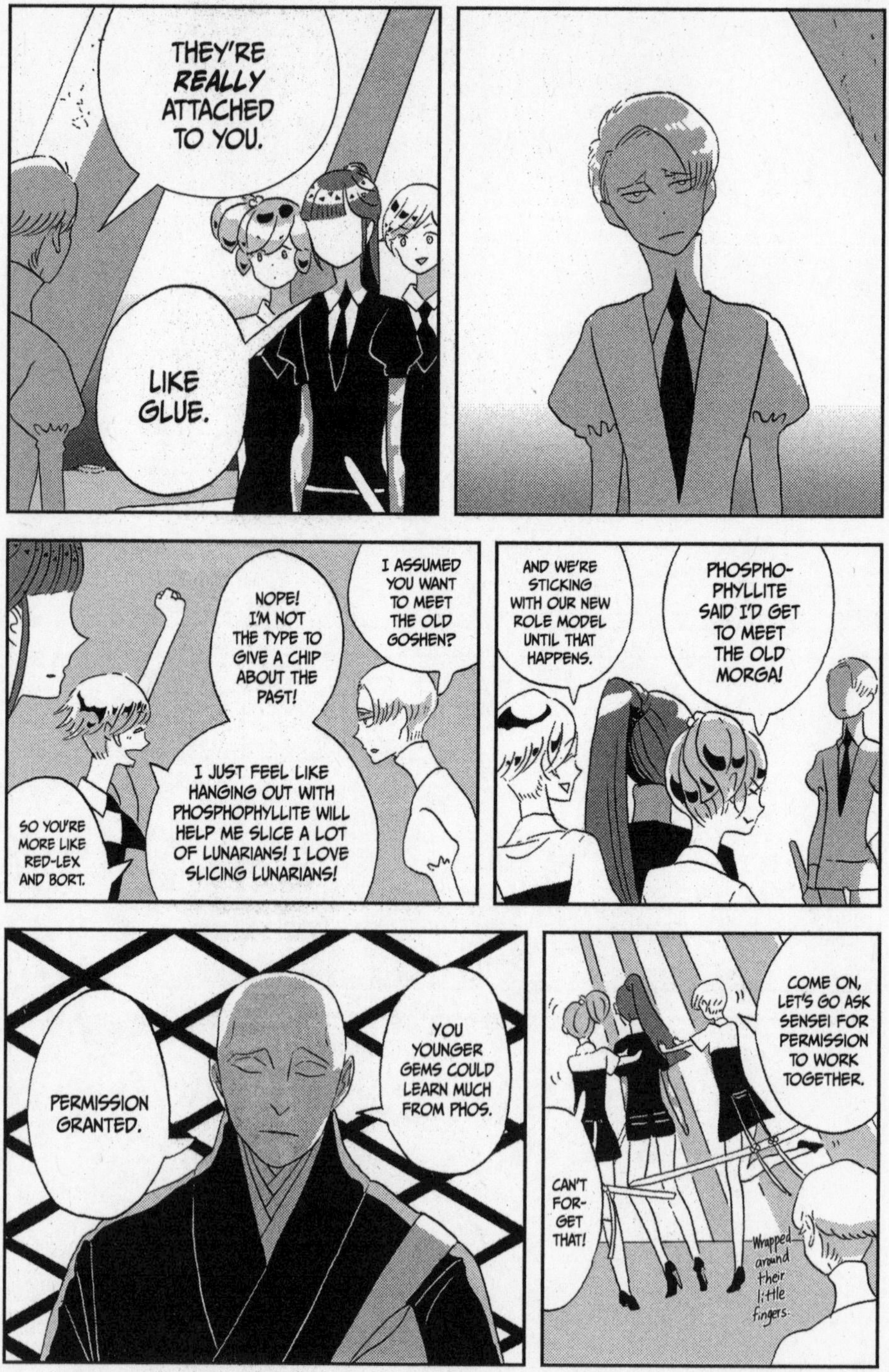
THEY'RE *REALLY* ATTACHED TO YOU.
LIKE GLUE.
PHOSPHO-PHYLLITE SAID I'D GET TO MEET THE OLD MORGA!
AND WE'RE STICKING WITH OUR NEW ROLE MODEL UNTIL THAT HAPPENS.
I ASSUMED YOU WANT TO MEET THE OLD GOSHEN?
NOPE! I'M NOT THE TYPE TO GIVE A CHIP ABOUT THE PAST!
I JUST FEEL LIKE HANGING OUT WITH PHOSPHOPHYLLITE WILL HELP ME SLICE A LOT OF LUNARIANS! I LOVE SLICING LUNARIANS!
SO YOU'RE MORE LIKE RED-LEX AND BORT.
COME ON, LET'S GO ASK SENSEI FOR PERMISSION TO WORK TOGETHER.
CAN'T FOR-GET THAT!
Wrapped around their little fingers.
YOU YOUNGER GEMS COULD LEARN MUCH FROM PHOS.
PERMISSION GRANTED.

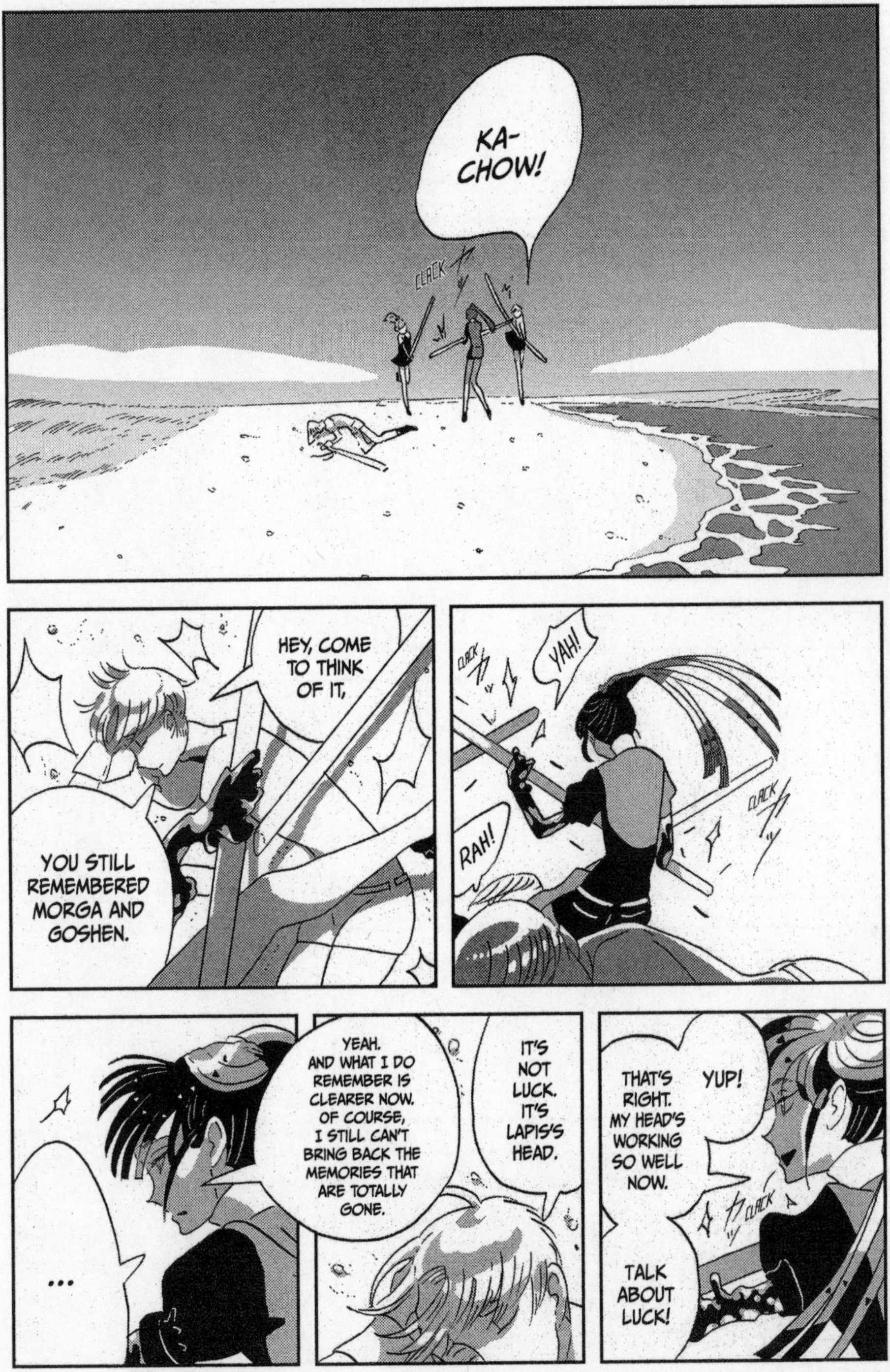
KA-
CHOW!
CLACK
YAH!
CLACK
CLACK
RAH!
HEY, COME TO THINK OF IT,
YOU STILL REMEMBERED MORGA AND GOSHEN.
THAT'S RIGHT. MY HEAD'S WORKING SO WELL NOW.
YUP!
CLACK
TALK ABOUT LUCK!
IT'S NOT LUCK. IT'S LAPIS'S HEAD.
YEAH. AND WHAT I DO REMEMBER IS CLEARER NOW. OF COURSE, I STILL CAN'T BRING BACK THE MEMORIES THAT ARE TOTALLY GONE.
...

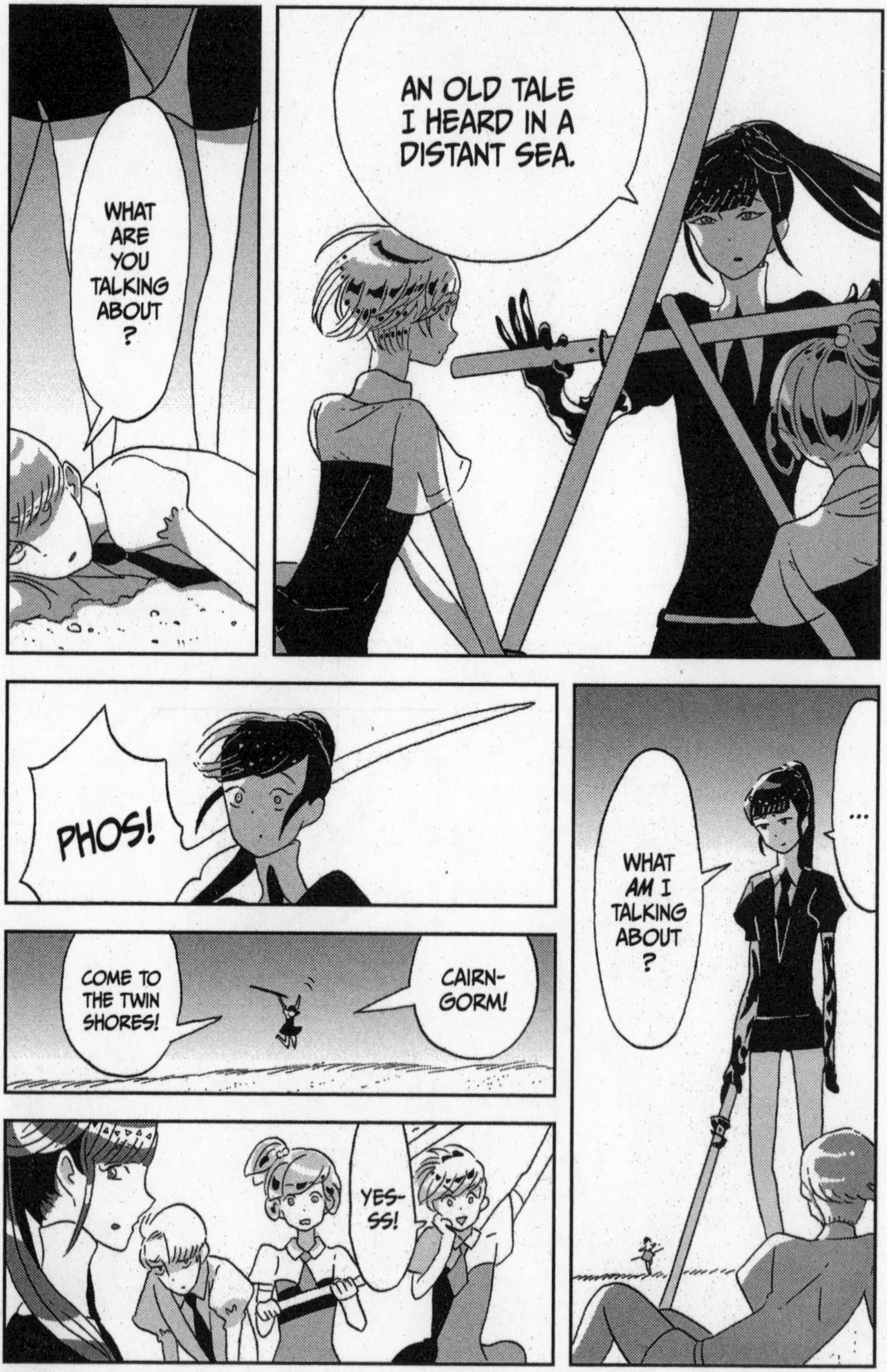
AN OLD TALE I HEARD IN A DISTANT SEA.
WHAT ARE YOU TALKING ABOUT?
...
WHAT *AM* I TALKING ABOUT?
PHOS!
CAIRN-GORM!
COME TO THE TWIN SHORES!
YESS-SS!

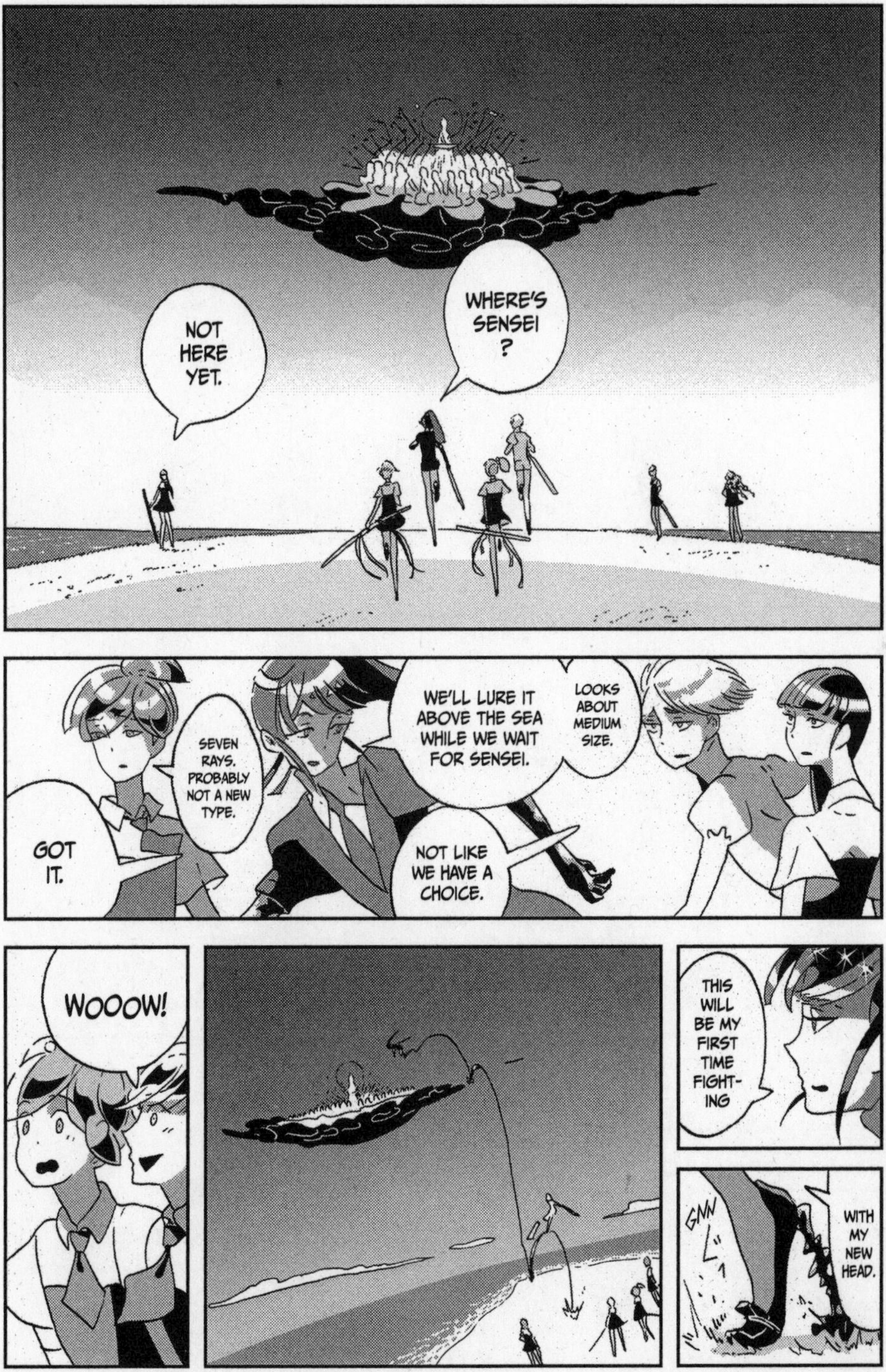
WHERE'S SENSEI ?
NOT HERE YET.
LOOKS ABOUT MEDIUM SIZE.
WE'LL LURE IT ABOVE THE SEA WHILE WE WAIT FOR SENSEI.
NOT LIKE WE HAVE A CHOICE.
SEVEN RAYS. PROBABLY NOT A NEW TYPE.
GOT IT.
THIS WILL BE MY FIRST TIME FIGHTING
WITH MY NEW HEAD.
GNN
WOOOW!

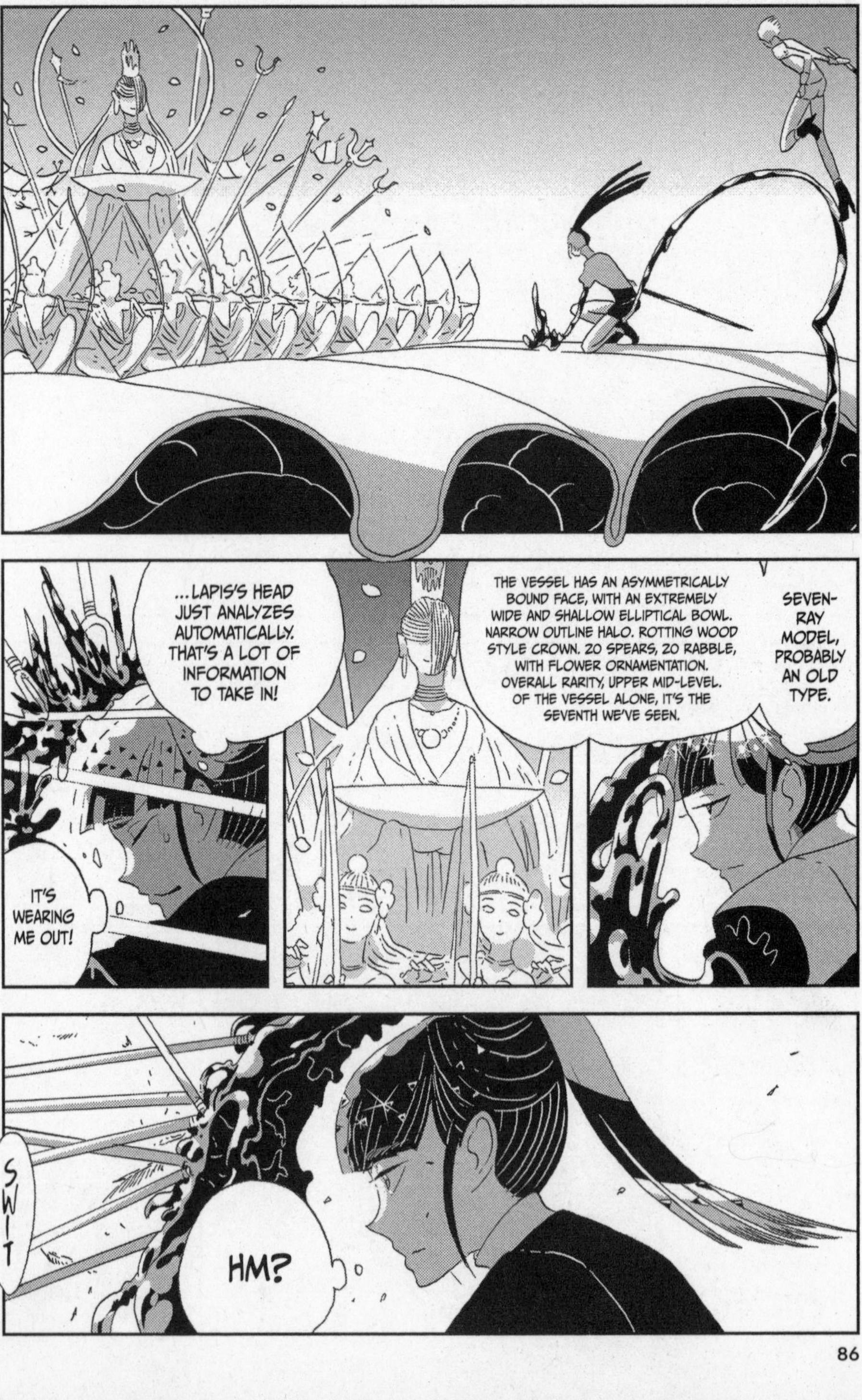
SEVEN-RAY MODEL, PROBABLY AN OLD TYPE.
THE VESSEL HAS AN ASYMMETRICALLY BOUND FACE, WITH AN EXTREMELY WIDE AND SHALLOW ELLIPTICAL BOWL. NARROW OUTLINE HALO. ROTTING WOOD STYLE CROWN. 20 SPEARS, 20 RABBLE, WITH FLOWER ORNAMENTATION. OVERALL RARITY, UPPER MID-LEVEL. OF THE VESSEL ALONE, IT'S THE SEVENTH WE'VE SEEN.
...LAPIS'S HEAD JUST ANALYZES AUTOMATICALLY. THAT'S A LOT OF INFORMATION TO TAKE IN!
IT'S WEARING ME OUT!
SWIT
HM?

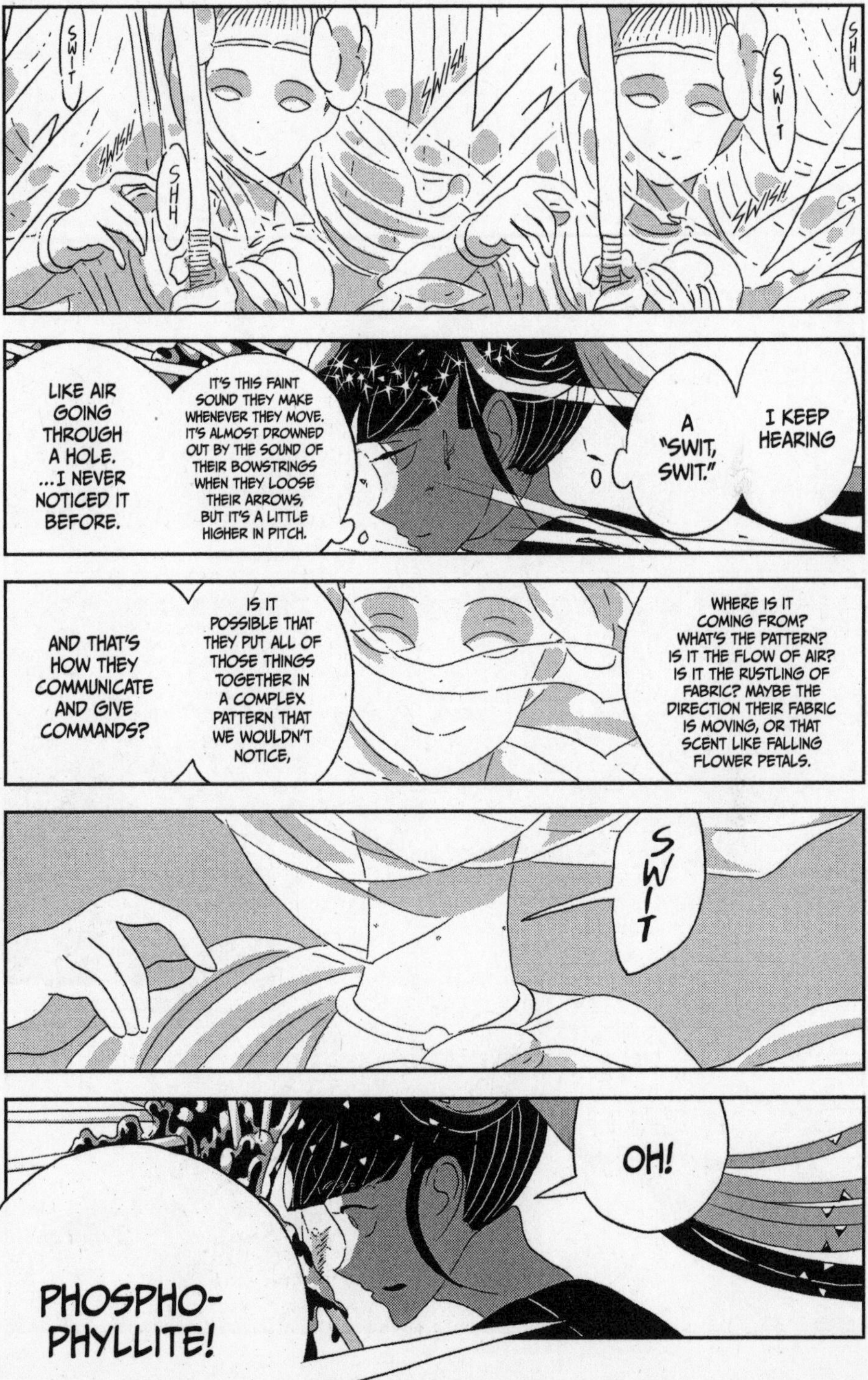
SHH
SWIT
SWISH
SWISH
SWIT
SWISH
SHH
I KEEP HEARING
A "SWIT, SWIT."
IT'S THIS FAINT SOUND THEY MAKE WHENEVER THEY MOVE. IT'S ALMOST DROWNED OUT BY THE SOUND OF THEIR BOWSTRINGS WHEN THEY LOOSE THEIR ARROWS, BUT IT'S A LITTLE HIGHER IN PITCH.
LIKE AIR GOING THROUGH A HOLE. ...I NEVER NOTICED IT BEFORE.
WHERE IS IT COMING FROM? WHAT'S THE PATTERN? IS IT THE FLOW OF AIR? IS IT THE RUSTLING OF FABRIC? MAYBE THE DIRECTION THEIR FABRIC IS MOVING, OR THAT SCENT LIKE FALLING FLOWER PETALS.
IS IT POSSIBLE THAT THEY PUT ALL OF THOSE THINGS TOGETHER IN A COMPLEX PATTERN THAT WE WOULDN'T NOTICE,
AND THAT'S HOW THEY COMMUNICATE AND GIVE COMMANDS?
SWIT
OH!
PHOSPHO-PHYLLITE!

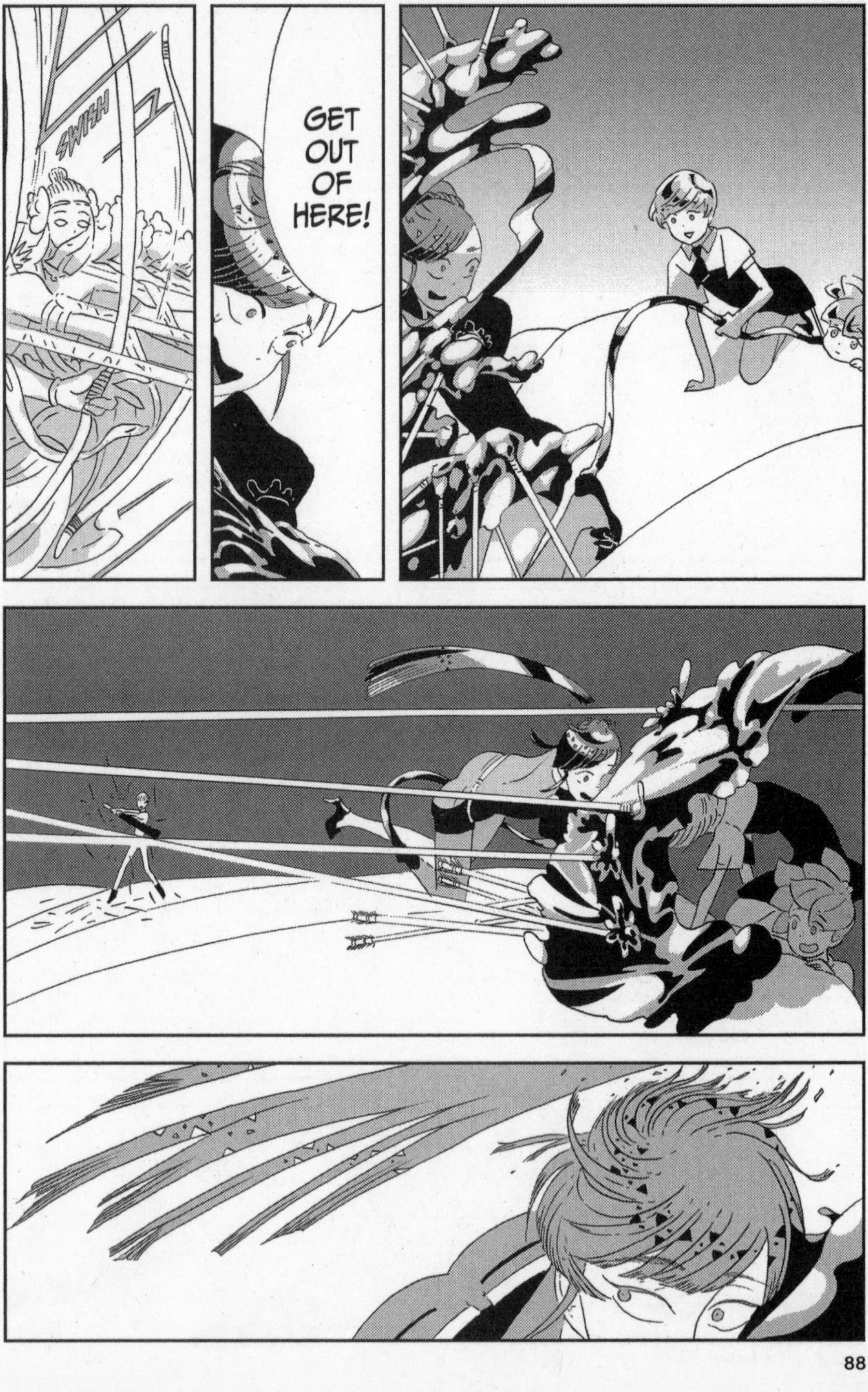
GET OUT OF HERE!
SWISH

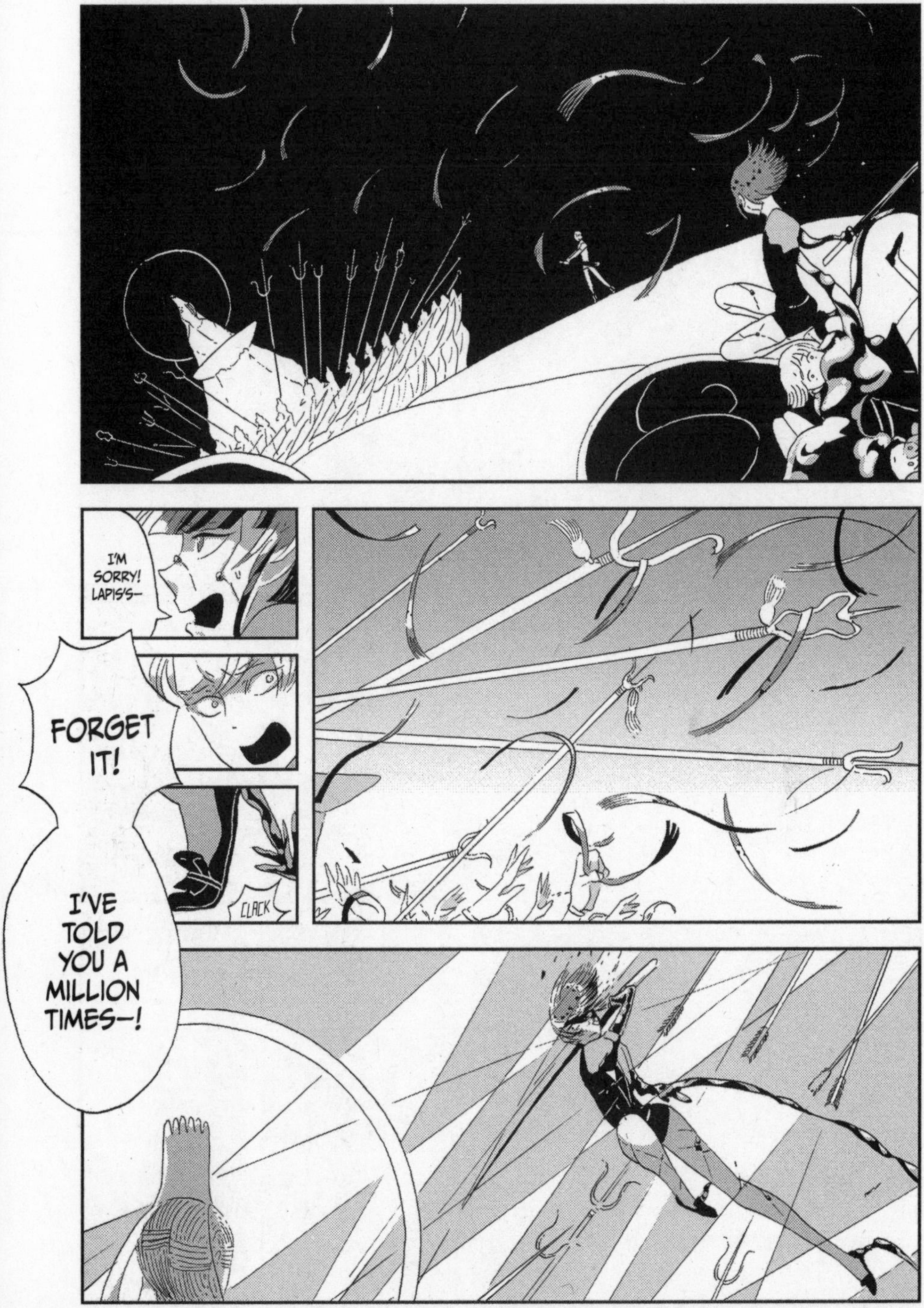

I'M SORRY! LAPIS'S—
FORGET IT!
I'VE TOLD YOU A MILLION TIMES—!
CLACK

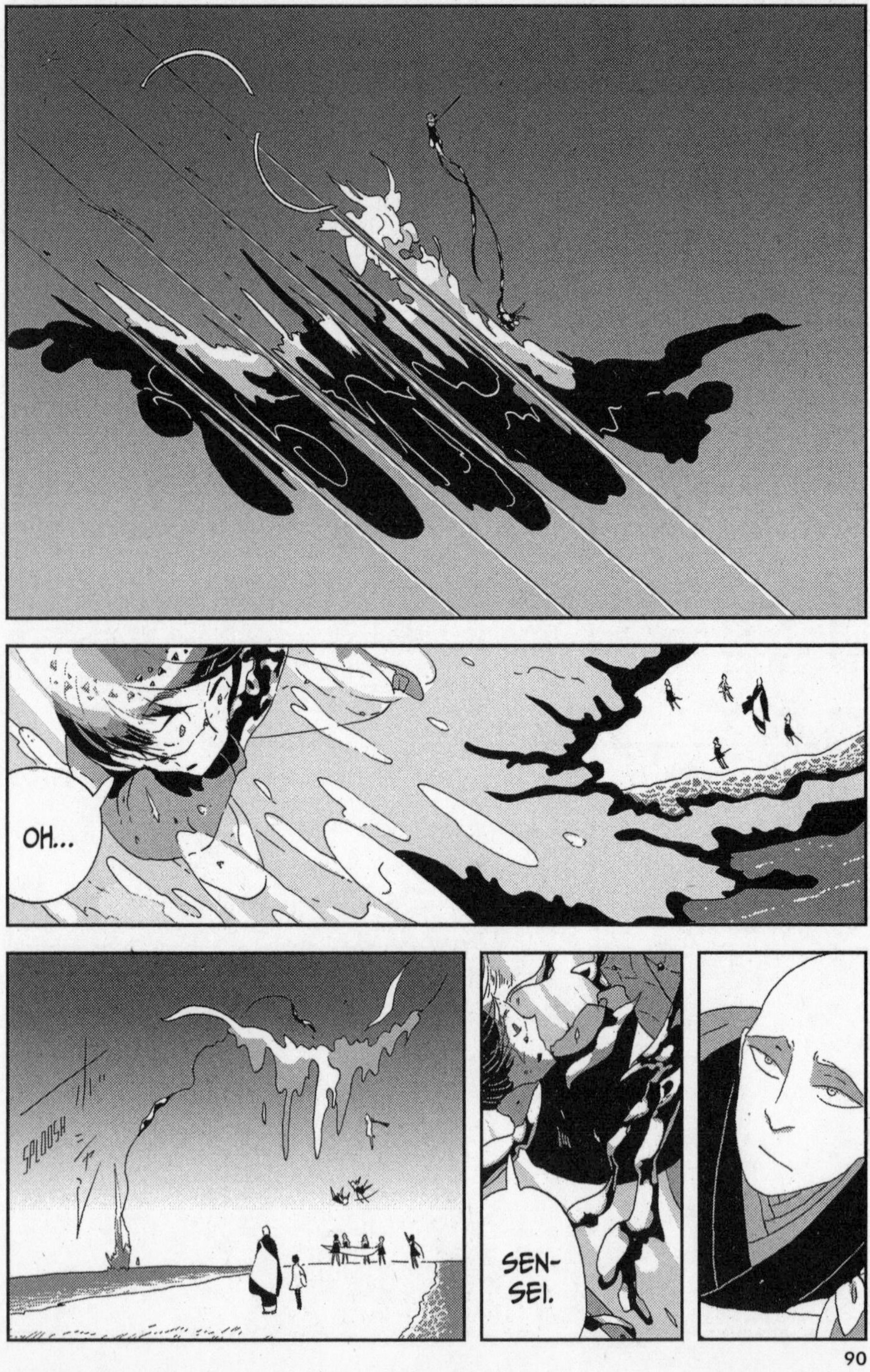
OH...
SEN-SEI.
SPLOOSH

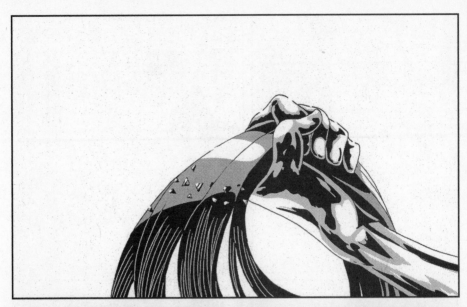

PHOSPHO-
PHYLLITE!

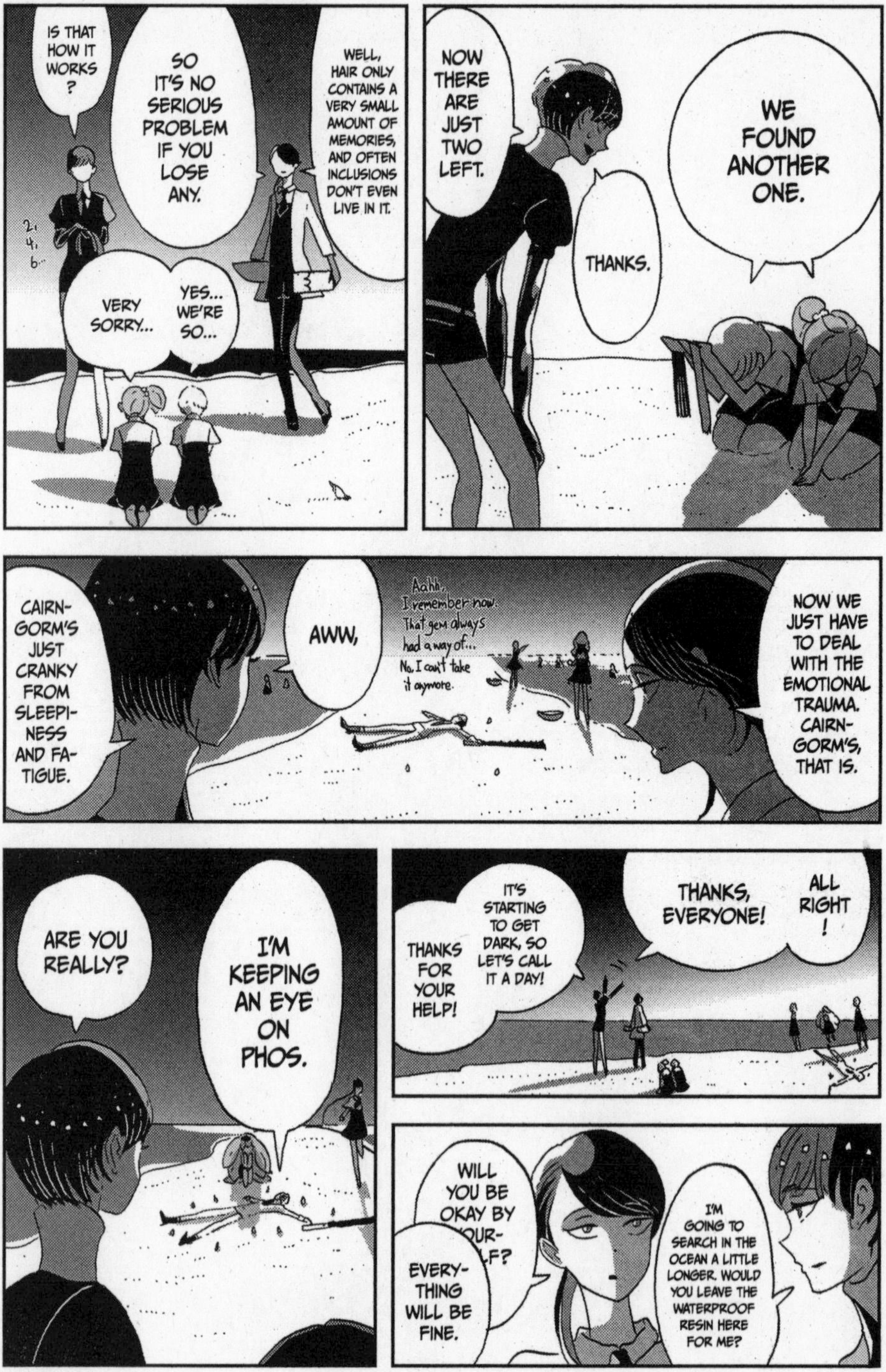

WE FOUND ANOTHER ONE.
THANKS.
NOW THERE ARE JUST TWO LEFT.
WELL, HAIR ONLY CONTAINS A VERY SMALL AMOUNT OF MEMORIES, AND OFTEN INCLUSIONS DON'T EVEN LIVE IN IT.
SO IT'S NO SERIOUS PROBLEM IF YOU LOSE ANY.
IS THAT HOW IT WORKS?
2, 4, 6...
YES... WE'RE SO...
VERY SORRY...
NOW WE JUST HAVE TO DEAL WITH THE EMOTIONAL TRAUMA. CAIRNGORM'S, THAT IS.
Aahh, I remember now. That gem always had a way of... No, I can't take it anymore.
AWW,
CAIRNGORM'S JUST CRANKY FROM SLEEPINESS AND FATIGUE.
ALL RIGHT!
THANKS, EVERYONE!
IT'S STARTING TO GET DARK, SO LET'S CALL IT A DAY!
THANKS FOR YOUR HELP!
I'M GOING TO SEARCH IN THE OCEAN A LITTLE LONGER. WOULD YOU LEAVE THE WATERPROOF RESIN HERE FOR ME?
WILL YOU BE OKAY BY OUR- LF?
EVERYTHING WILL BE FINE.
I'M KEEPING AN EYE ON PHOS.
ARE YOU REALLY?

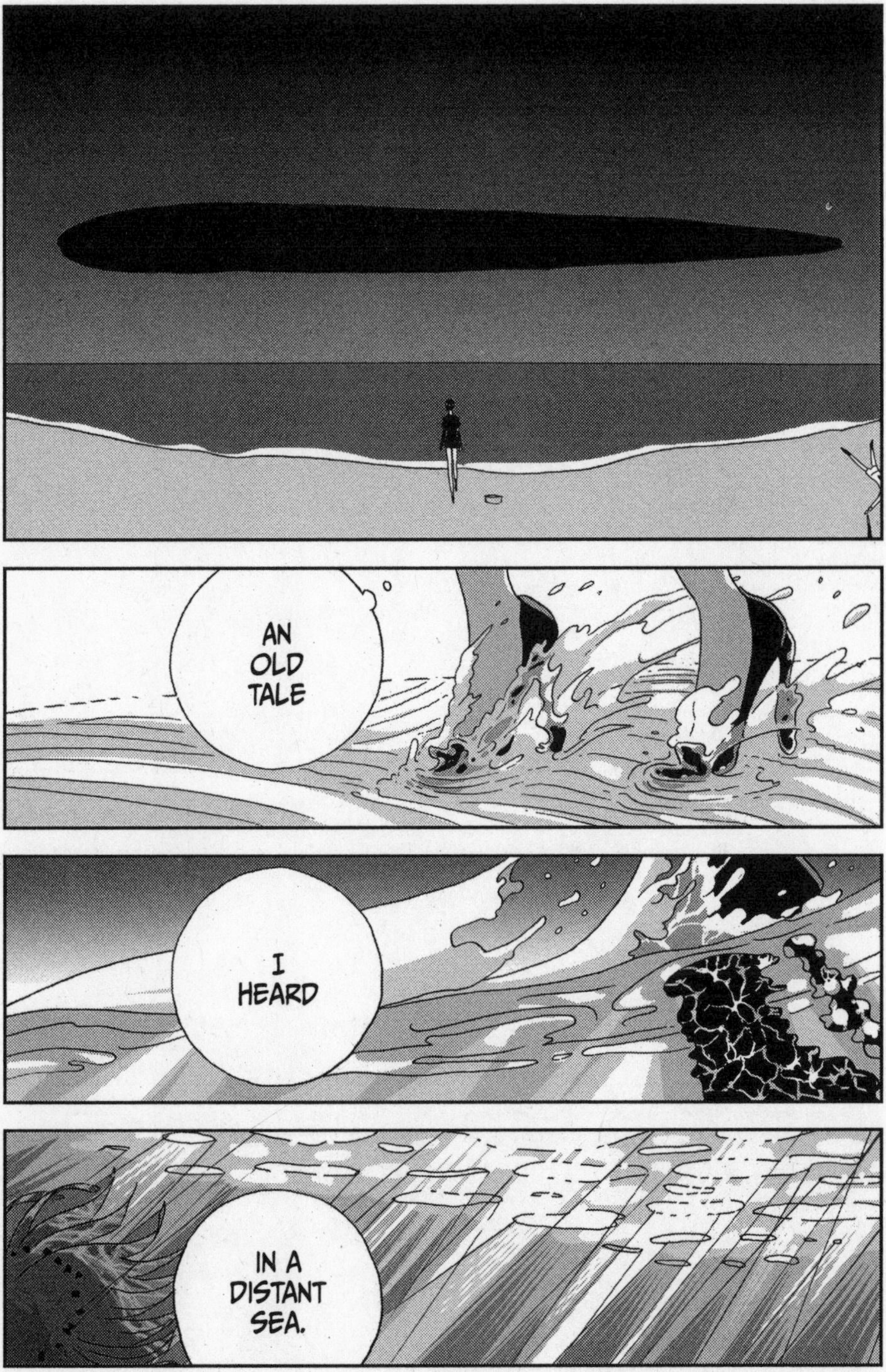
AN OLD TALE
I HEARD
IN A DISTANT SEA.

HMM, I WONDER WHAT IT WAS.

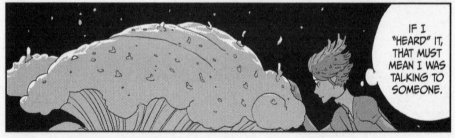

IF I "HEARD" IT, THAT MUST MEAN I WAS TALKING TO SOMEONE.

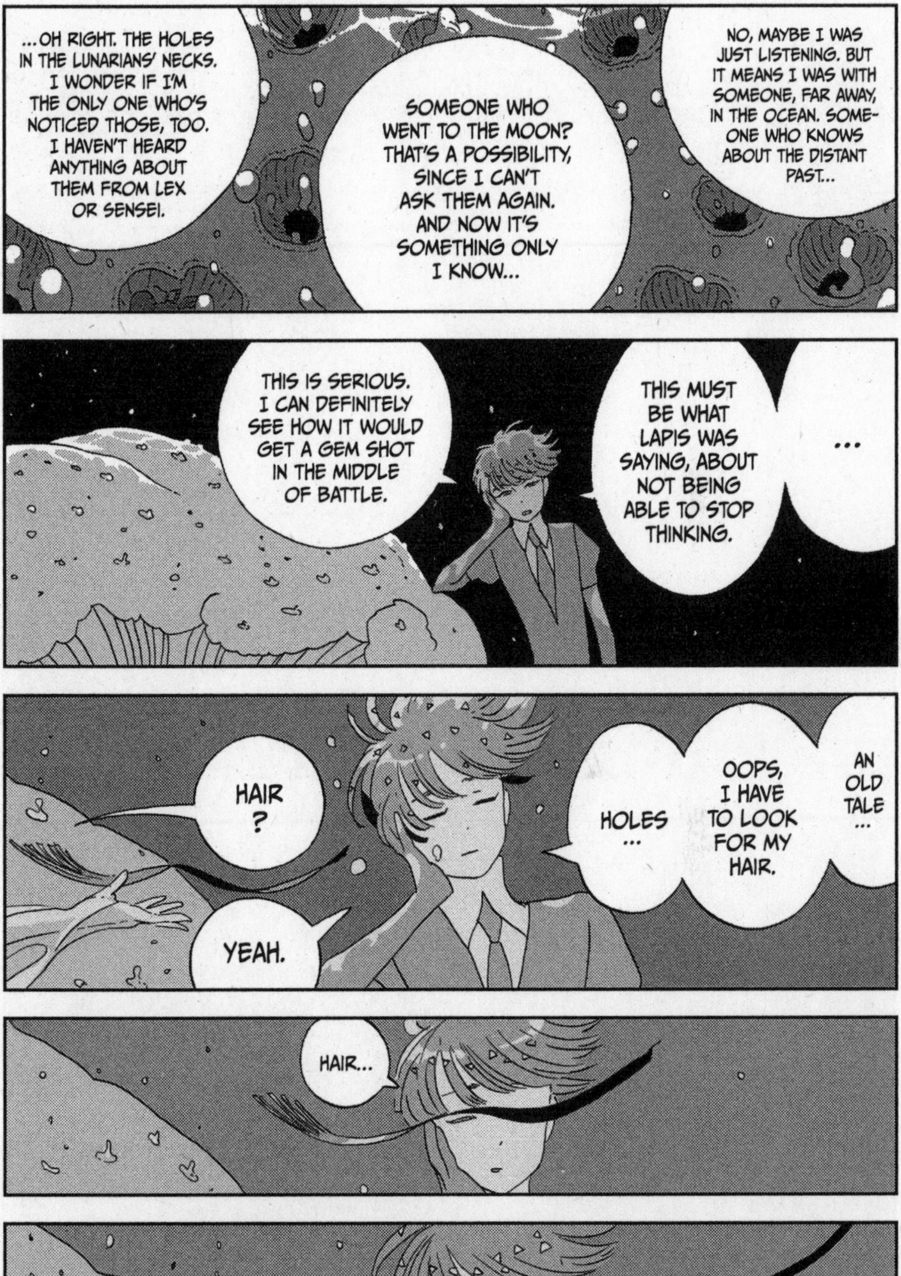
NO, MAYBE I WAS JUST LISTENING. BUT IT MEANS I WAS WITH SOMEONE, FAR AWAY, IN THE OCEAN. SOME-ONE WHO KNOWS ABOUT THE DISTANT PAST...
SOMEONE WHO WENT TO THE MOON? THAT'S A POSSIBILITY, SINCE I CAN'T ASK THEM AGAIN. AND NOW IT'S SOMETHING ONLY I KNOW...
...OH RIGHT. THE HOLES IN THE LUNARIANS' NECKS. I WONDER IF I'M THE ONLY ONE WHO'S NOTICED THOSE, TOO. I HAVEN'T HEARD ANYTHING ABOUT THEM FROM LEX OR SENSEI.
...
THIS MUST BE WHAT LAPIS WAS SAYING, ABOUT NOT BEING ABLE TO STOP THINKING.
THIS IS SERIOUS. I CAN DEFINITELY SEE HOW IT WOULD GET A GEM SHOT IN THE MIDDLE OF BATTLE.
AN OLD TALE ...
OOPS, I HAVE TO LOOK FOR MY HAIR.
HOLES ...
HAIR ?
YEAH.
HAIR...

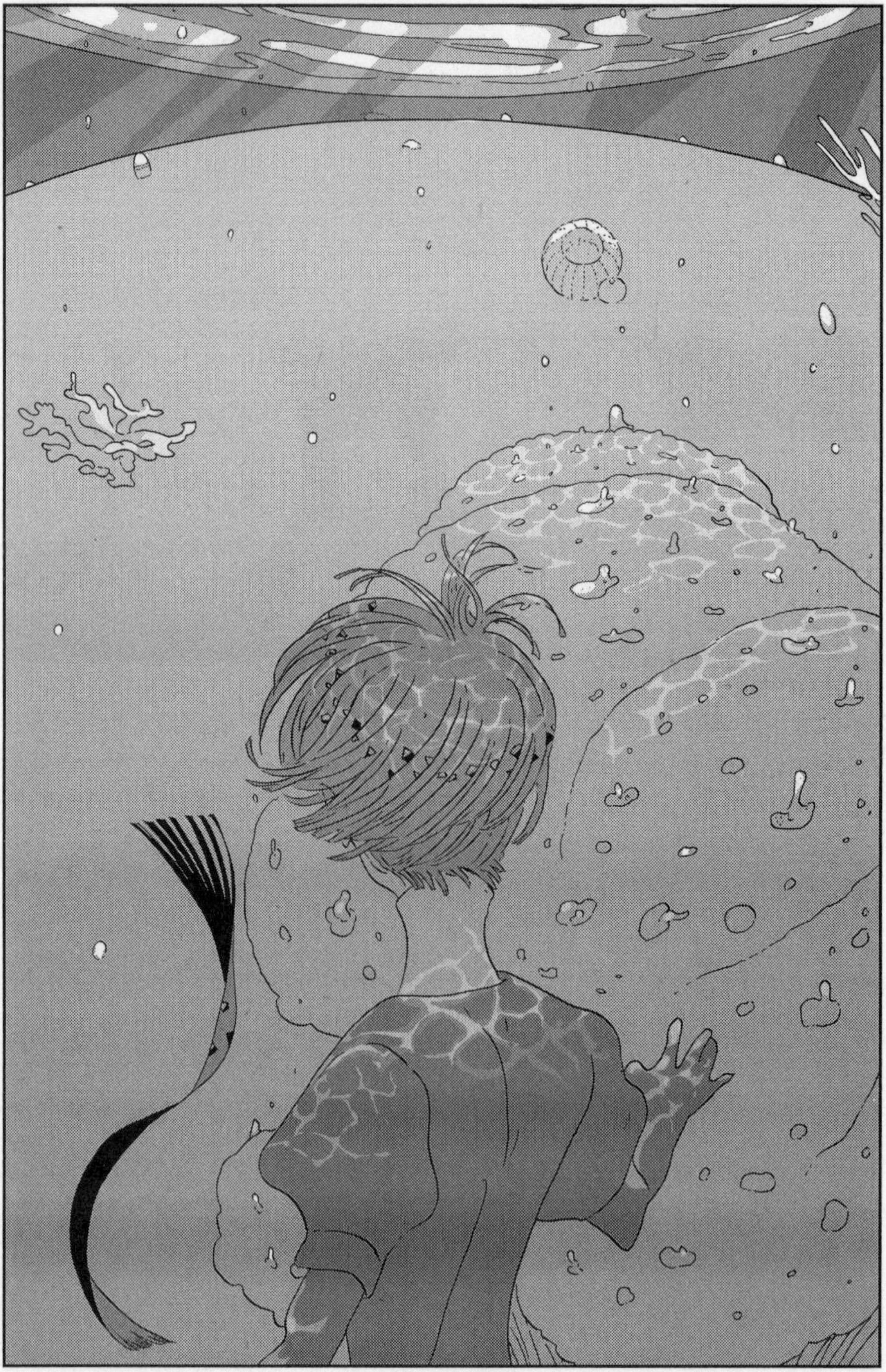

CHAPTER 48: An Old Tale Heard in the Sea END

CHAPTER 49:

On the Trail

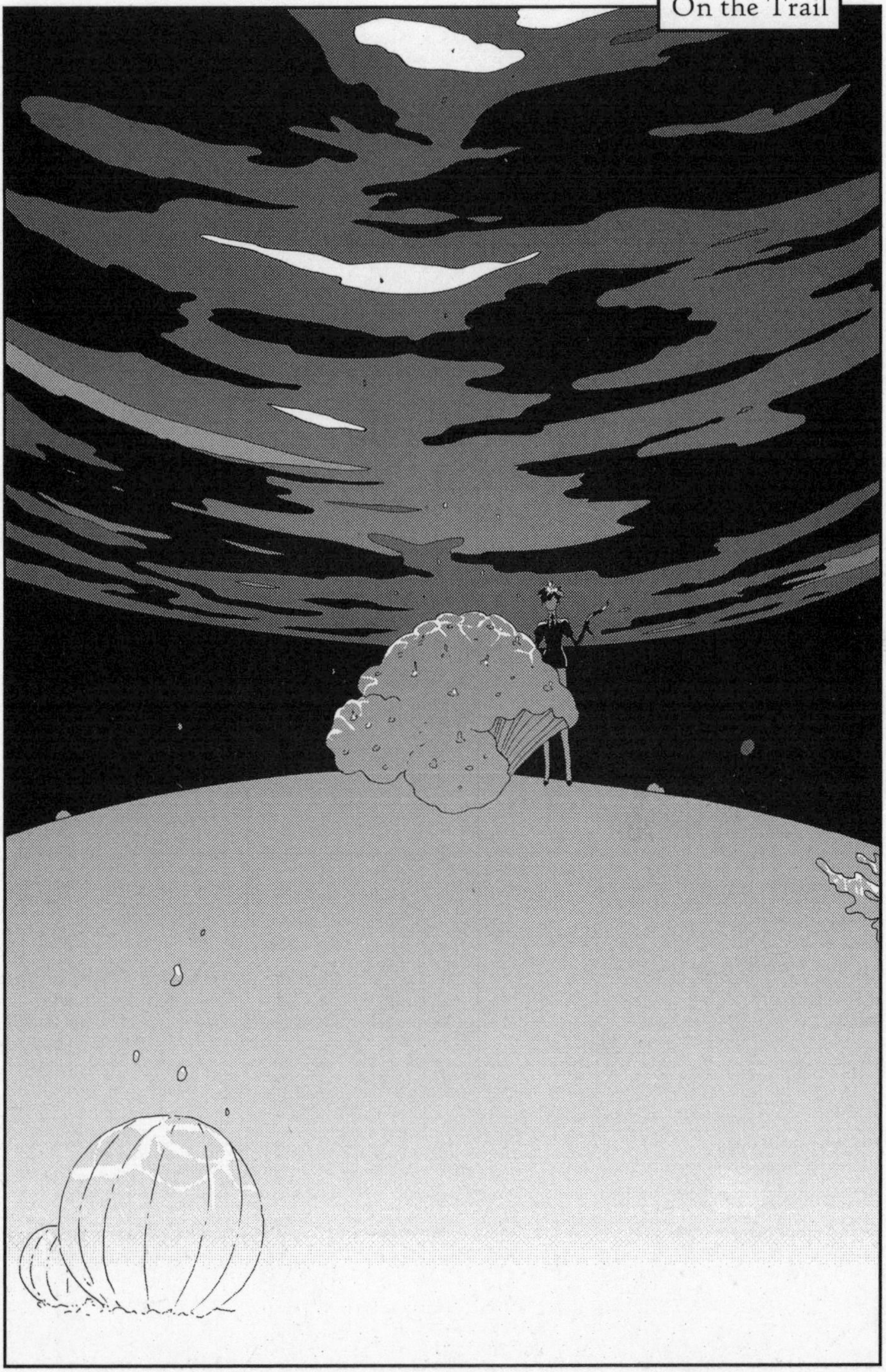

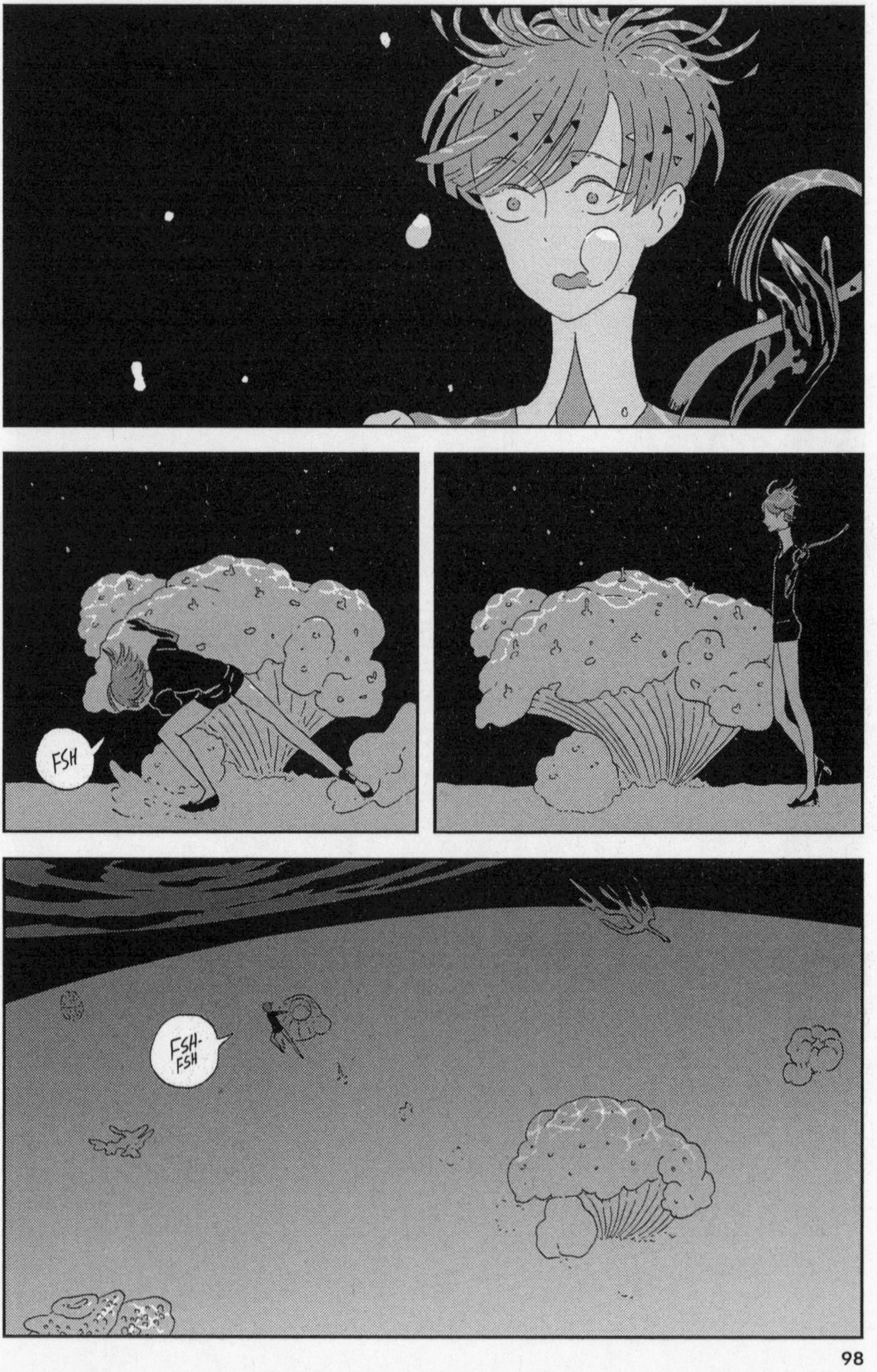
FSH
FSH-
FSH

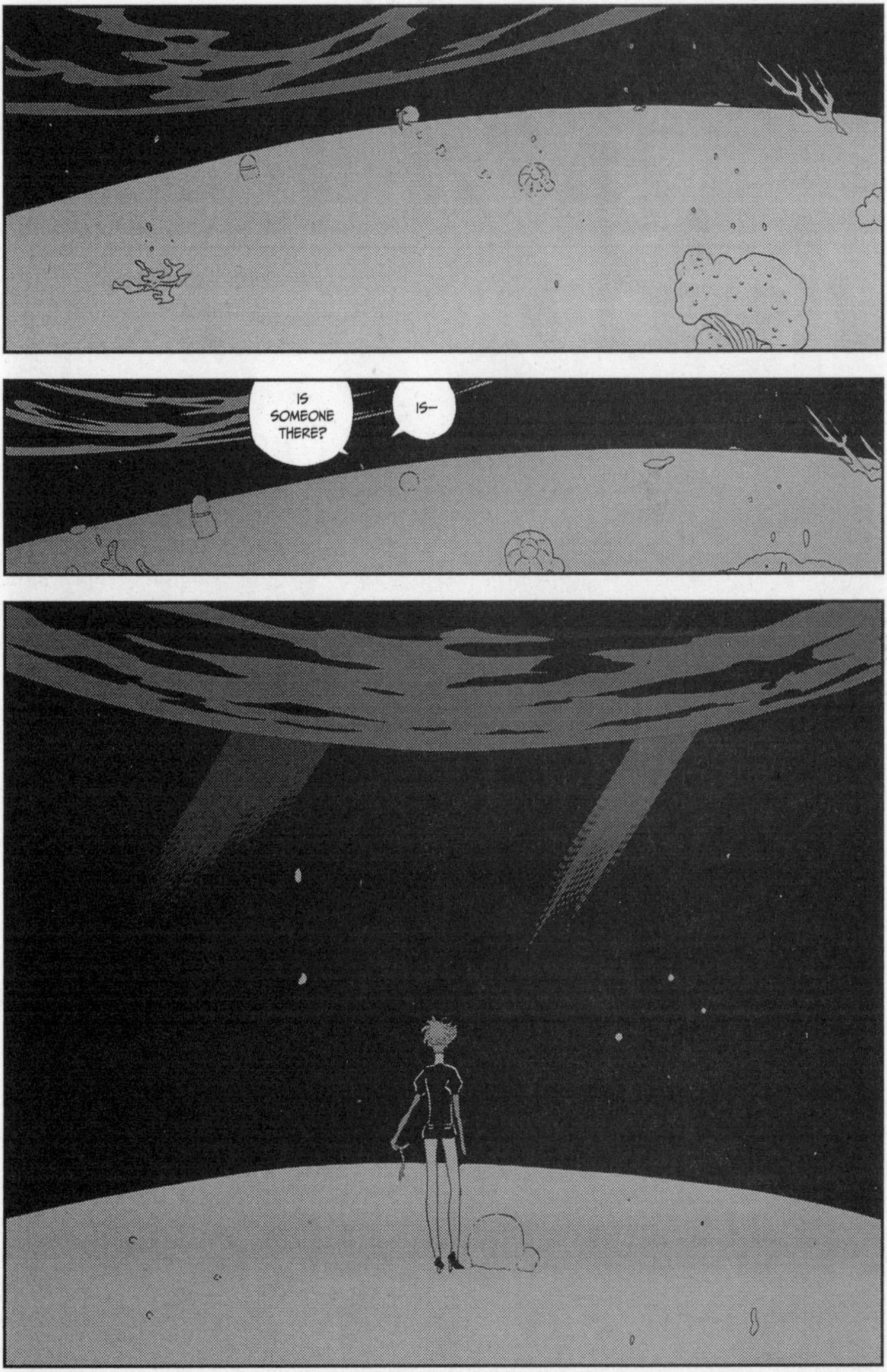
IS—
IS SOMEONE THERE?

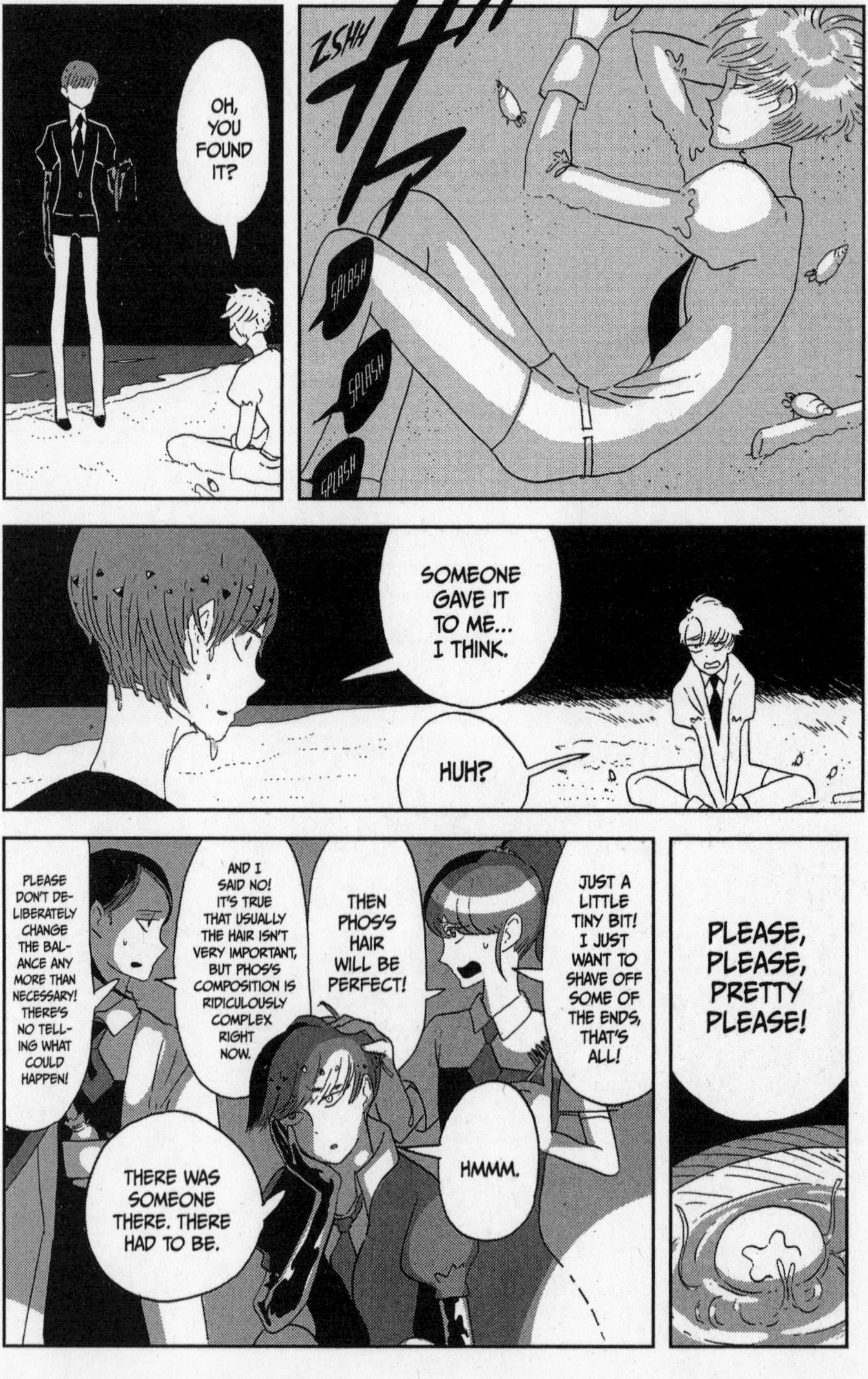
ZSHH
SPLASH
SPLASH
SPLASH
OH, YOU FOUND IT?
SOMEONE GAVE IT TO ME... I THINK.
HUH?
PLEASE, PLEASE, PRETTY PLEASE!
JUST A LITTLE TINY BIT! I JUST WANT TO SHAVE OFF SOME OF THE ENDS, THAT'S ALL!
THEN PHOS'S HAIR WILL BE PERFECT!
AND I SAID NO! IT'S TRUE THAT USUALLY THE HAIR ISN'T VERY IMPORTANT, BUT PHOS'S COMPOSITION IS RIDICULOUSLY COMPLEX RIGHT NOW.
PLEASE DON'T DE-LIBERATELY CHANGE THE BAL-ANCE ANY MORE THAN NECESSARY! THERE'S NO TELL-ING WHAT COULD HAPPEN!
HMMM.
THERE WAS SOMEONE THERE. THERE HAD TO BE.

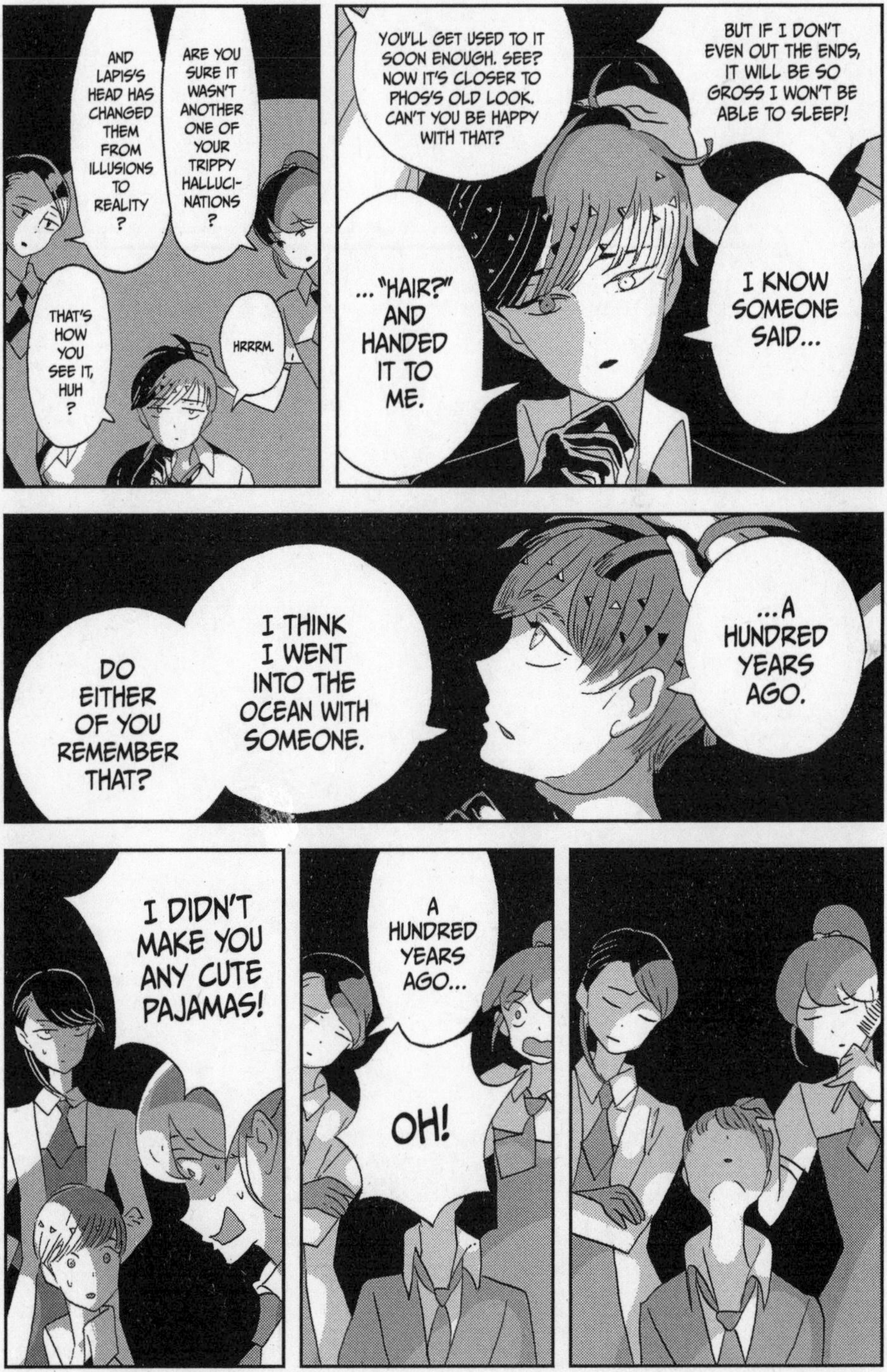
BUT IF I DON'T EVEN OUT THE ENDS, IT WILL BE SO GROSS I WON'T BE ABLE TO SLEEP!
YOU'LL GET USED TO IT SOON ENOUGH. SEE? NOW IT'S CLOSER TO PHOS'S OLD LOOK. CAN'T YOU BE HAPPY WITH THAT?
I KNOW SOMEONE SAID...
..."HAIR?" AND HANDED IT TO ME.
ARE YOU SURE IT WASN'T ANOTHER ONE OF YOUR TRIPPY HALLUCI-NATIONS?
AND LAPIS'S HEAD HAS CHANGED THEM FROM ILLUSIONS TO REALITY?
HRRRM.
THAT'S HOW YOU SEE IT, HUH?
...A HUNDRED YEARS AGO.
I THINK I WENT INTO THE OCEAN WITH SOMEONE.
DO EITHER OF YOU REMEMBER THAT?
A HUNDRED YEARS AGO...
OH!
I DIDN'T MAKE YOU ANY CUTE PAJAMAS!

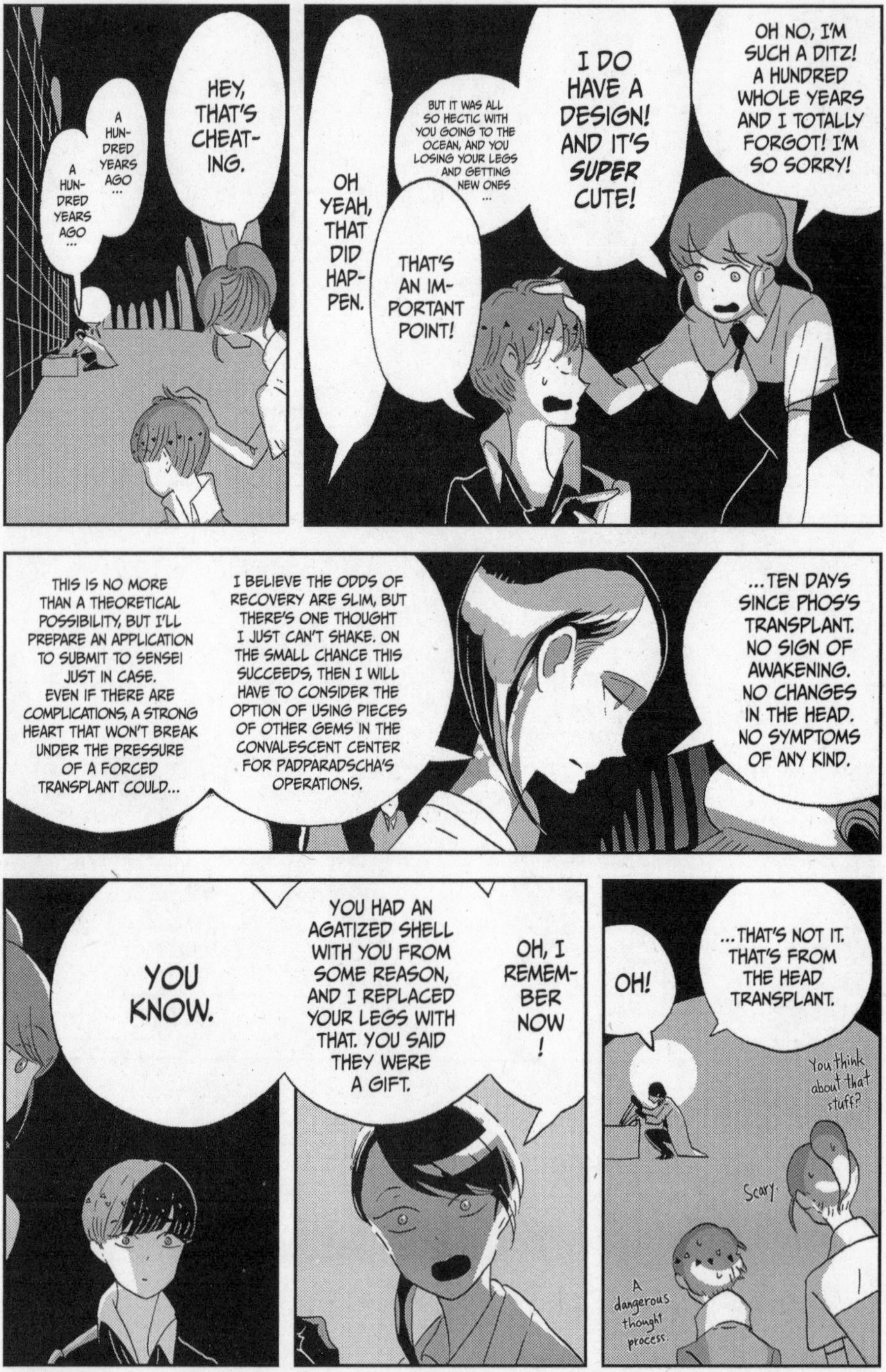
OH NO, I'M SUCH A DITZ! A HUNDRED WHOLE YEARS AND I TOTALLY FORGOT! I'M SO SORRY!
I DO HAVE A DESIGN! AND IT'S SUPER CUTE!
BUT IT WAS ALL SO HECTIC WITH YOU GOING TO THE OCEAN, AND YOU LOSING YOUR LEGS AND GETTING NEW ONES ...
THAT'S AN IMPORTANT POINT!
OH YEAH, THAT DID HAPPEN.
HEY, THAT'S CHEATING.
A HUNDRED YEARS AGO ...
A HUNDRED YEARS AGO ...
...TEN DAYS SINCE PHOS'S TRANSPLANT. NO SIGN OF AWAKENING. NO CHANGES IN THE HEAD. NO SYMPTOMS OF ANY KIND.
I BELIEVE THE ODDS OF RECOVERY ARE SLIM, BUT THERE'S ONE THOUGHT I JUST CAN'T SHAKE. ON THE SMALL CHANCE THIS SUCCEEDS, THEN I WILL HAVE TO CONSIDER THE OPTION OF USING PIECES OF OTHER GEMS IN THE CONVALESCENT CENTER FOR PADPARADSCHA'S OPERATIONS.
THIS IS NO MORE THAN A THEORETICAL POSSIBILITY, BUT I'LL PREPARE AN APPLICATION TO SUBMIT TO SENSEI JUST IN CASE. EVEN IF THERE ARE COMPLICATIONS, A STRONG HEART THAT WON'T BREAK UNDER THE PRESSURE OF A FORCED TRANSPLANT COULD...
...THAT'S NOT IT. THAT'S FROM THE HEAD TRANSPLANT.
OH!
You think about that stuff?
Scary.
A dangerous thought process.
OH, I REMEMBER NOW!
YOU HAD AN AGATIZED SHELL WITH YOU FROM SOME REASON, AND I REPLACED YOUR LEGS WITH THAT. YOU SAID THEY WERE A GIFT.
YOU KNOW.

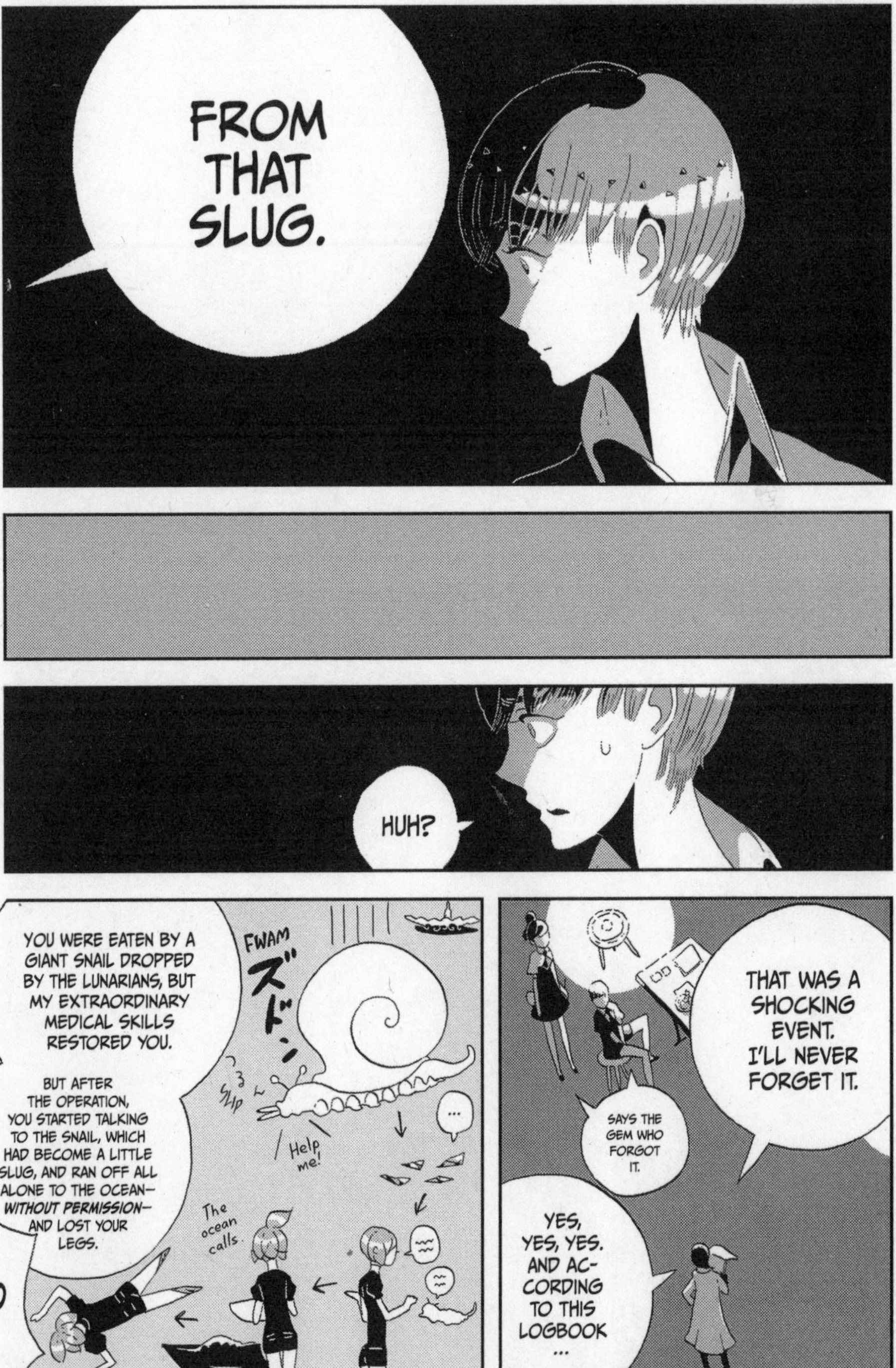
FROM THAT SLUG.
HUH?
THAT WAS A SHOCKING EVENT. I'LL NEVER FORGET IT.
SAYS THE GEM WHO FORGOT IT.
YES, YES, YES. AND AC-CORDING TO THIS LOGBOOK ...
YOU WERE EATEN BY A GIANT SNAIL DROPPED BY THE LUNARIANS, BUT MY EXTRAORDINARY MEDICAL SKILLS RESTORED YOU.
FWAM
SLIP
Help me!
BUT AFTER THE OPERATION, YOU STARTED TALKING TO THE SNAIL, WHICH HAD BECOME A LITTLE SLUG, AND RAN OFF ALL ALONE TO THE OCEAN—*WITHOUT PERMISSION*—AND LOST YOUR LEGS.
The ocean calls
NOOO!

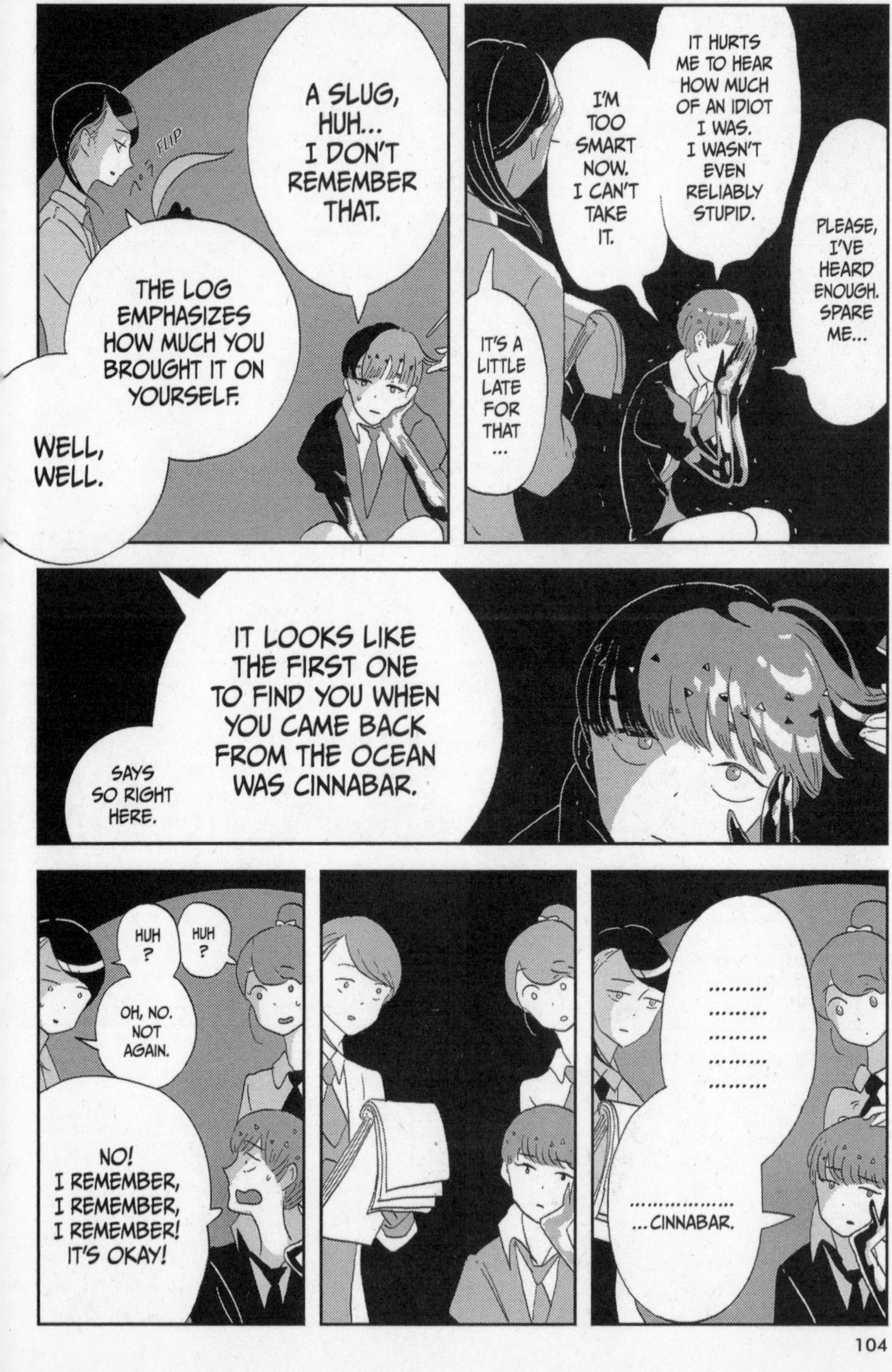
IT HURTS ME TO HEAR HOW MUCH OF AN IDIOT I WAS. I WASN'T EVEN RELIABLY STUPID.
I'M TOO SMART NOW. I CAN'T TAKE IT.
PLEASE, I'VE HEARD ENOUGH. SPARE ME...
IT'S A LITTLE LATE FOR THAT ...
FLIP
A SLUG, HUH... I DON'T REMEMBER THAT.
THE LOG EMPHASIZES HOW MUCH YOU BROUGHT IT ON YOURSELF.
WELL, WELL.
IT LOOKS LIKE THE FIRST ONE TO FIND YOU WHEN YOU CAME BACK FROM THE OCEAN WAS CINNABAR.
SAYS SO RIGHT HERE.
....
....
....
....
....
....
...CINNABAR.
HUH ?
HUH ?
OH, NO. NOT AGAIN.
NO! I REMEMBER, I REMEMBER, I REMEMBER! IT'S OKAY!

I HAVE
TO GO SEE
CINNABAR.

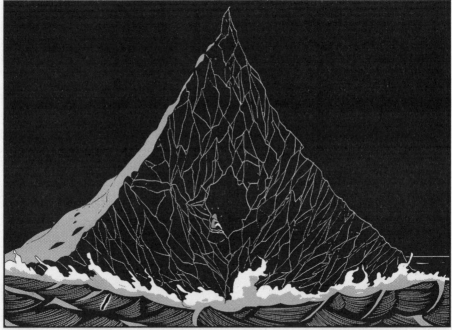

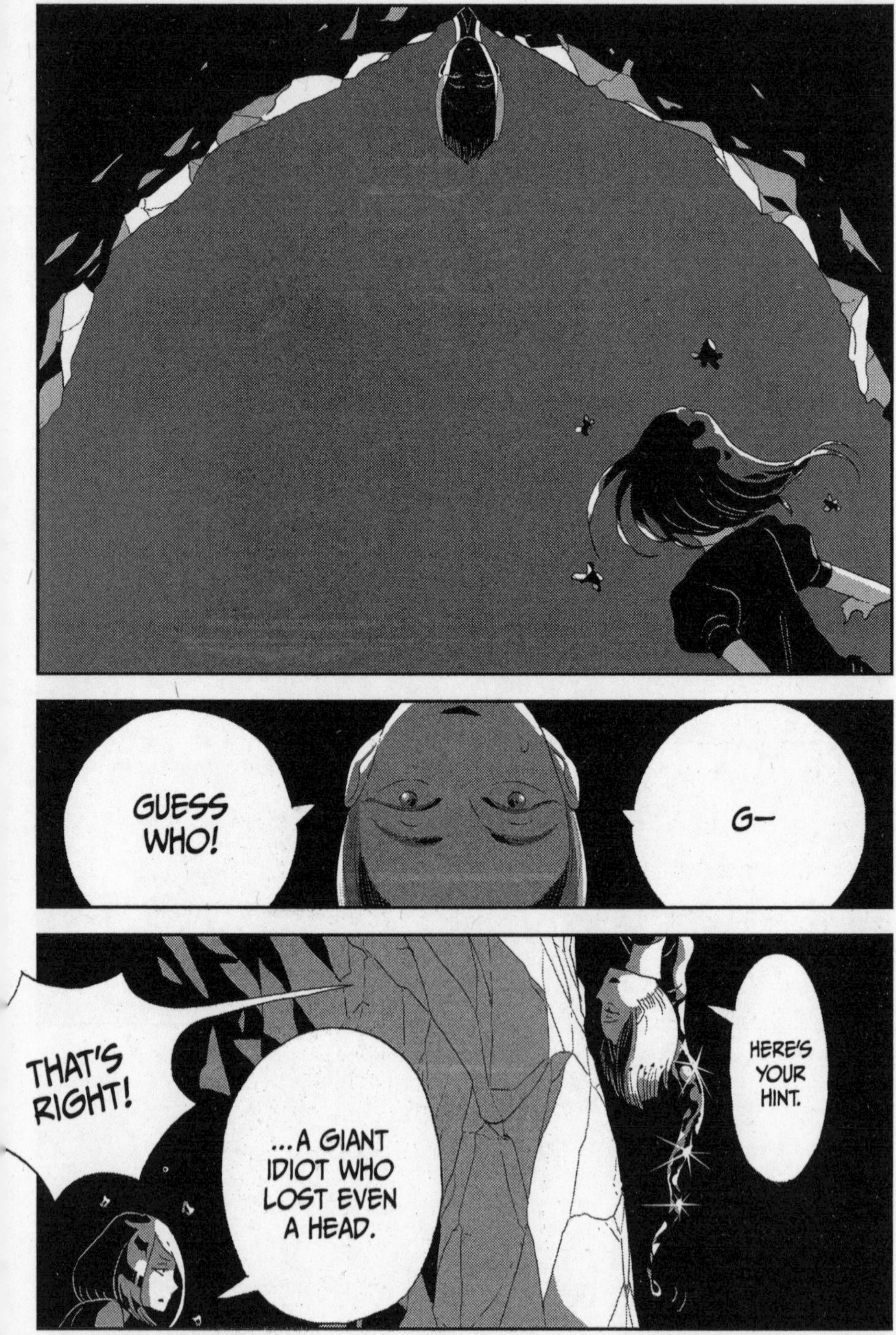
G—
GUESS WHO!
HERE'S YOUR HINT.
...A GIANT IDIOT WHO LOST EVEN A HEAD.
THAT'S RIGHT!

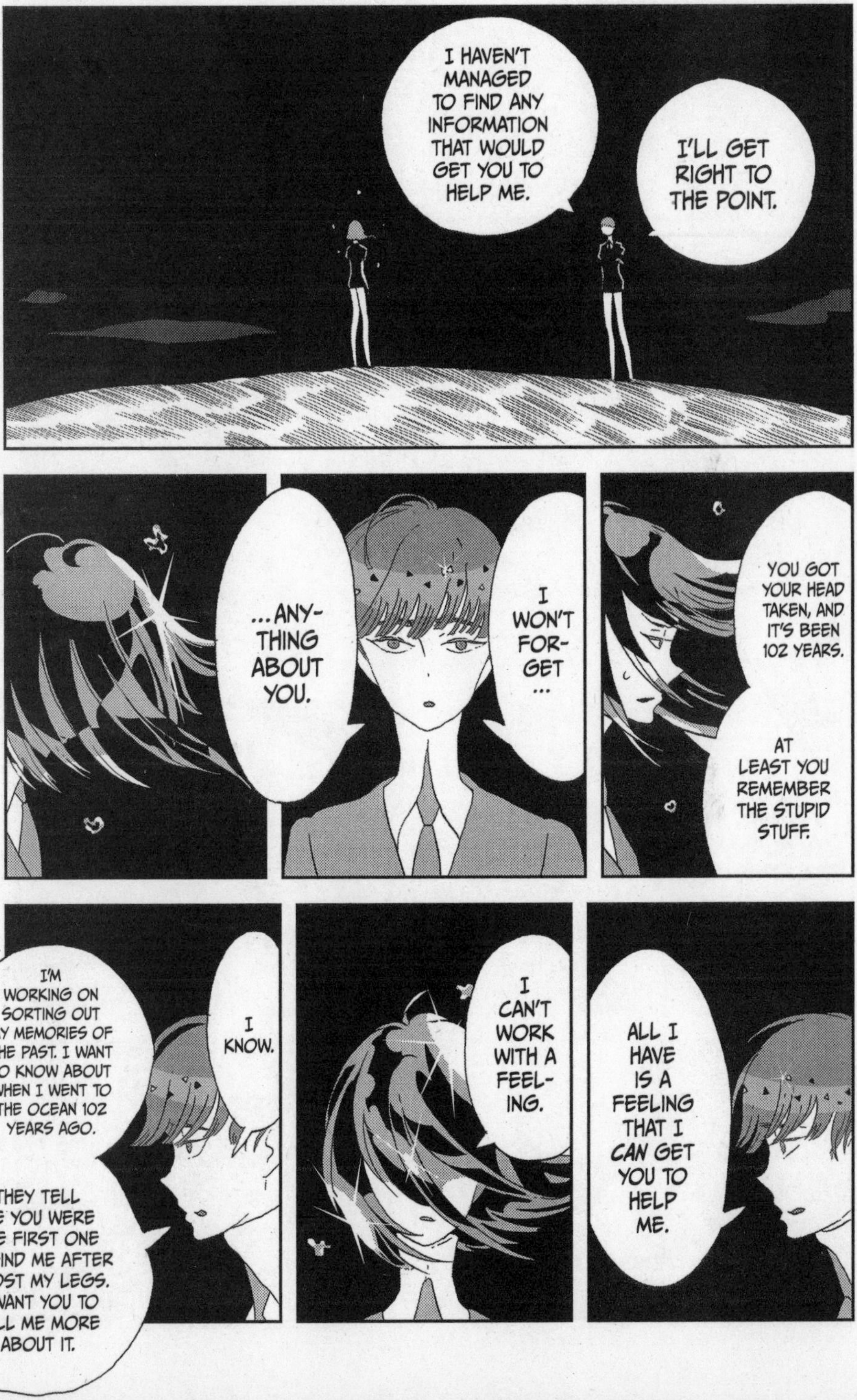
I'LL GET RIGHT TO THE POINT.
I HAVEN'T MANAGED TO FIND ANY INFORMATION THAT WOULD GET YOU TO HELP ME.
YOU GOT YOUR HEAD TAKEN, AND IT'S BEEN 102 YEARS.
AT LEAST YOU REMEMBER THE STUPID STUFF.
I WON'T FOR-GET...
...ANY-THING ABOUT YOU.
ALL I HAVE IS A FEELING THAT I *CAN* GET YOU TO HELP ME.
I CAN'T WORK WITH A FEEL-ING.
I KNOW.
I'M WORKING ON SORTING OUT MY MEMORIES OF THE PAST. I WANT TO KNOW ABOUT WHEN I WENT TO THE OCEAN 102 YEARS AGO.
THEY TELL ME YOU WERE THE FIRST ONE TO FIND ME AFTER I LOST MY LEGS. I WANT YOU TO TELL ME MORE ABOUT IT.

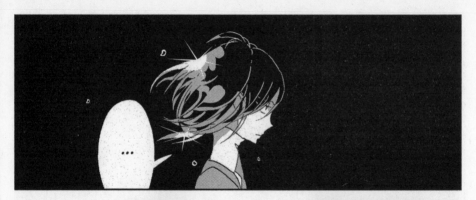

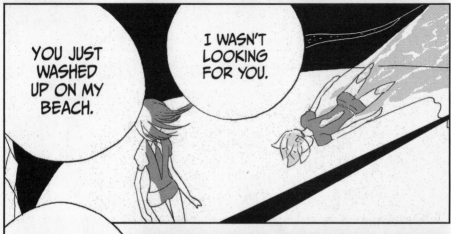

...
I WASN'T LOOKING FOR YOU.
YOU JUST WASHED UP ON MY BEACH.
THERE WAS A BOWL THAT HAD THE AGATE SHELLS AND A PIECE OF YOUR FACE.
THAT'S ALL. I DON'T KNOW ANYTHING THAT HAPPENED BEFORE OR AFTER THAT.
AND I DON'T CARE.
I SEE.
THANK YOU.
AND ONE MORE THING.

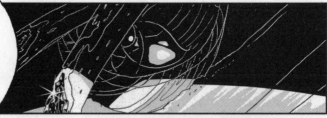

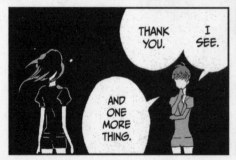

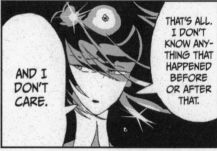

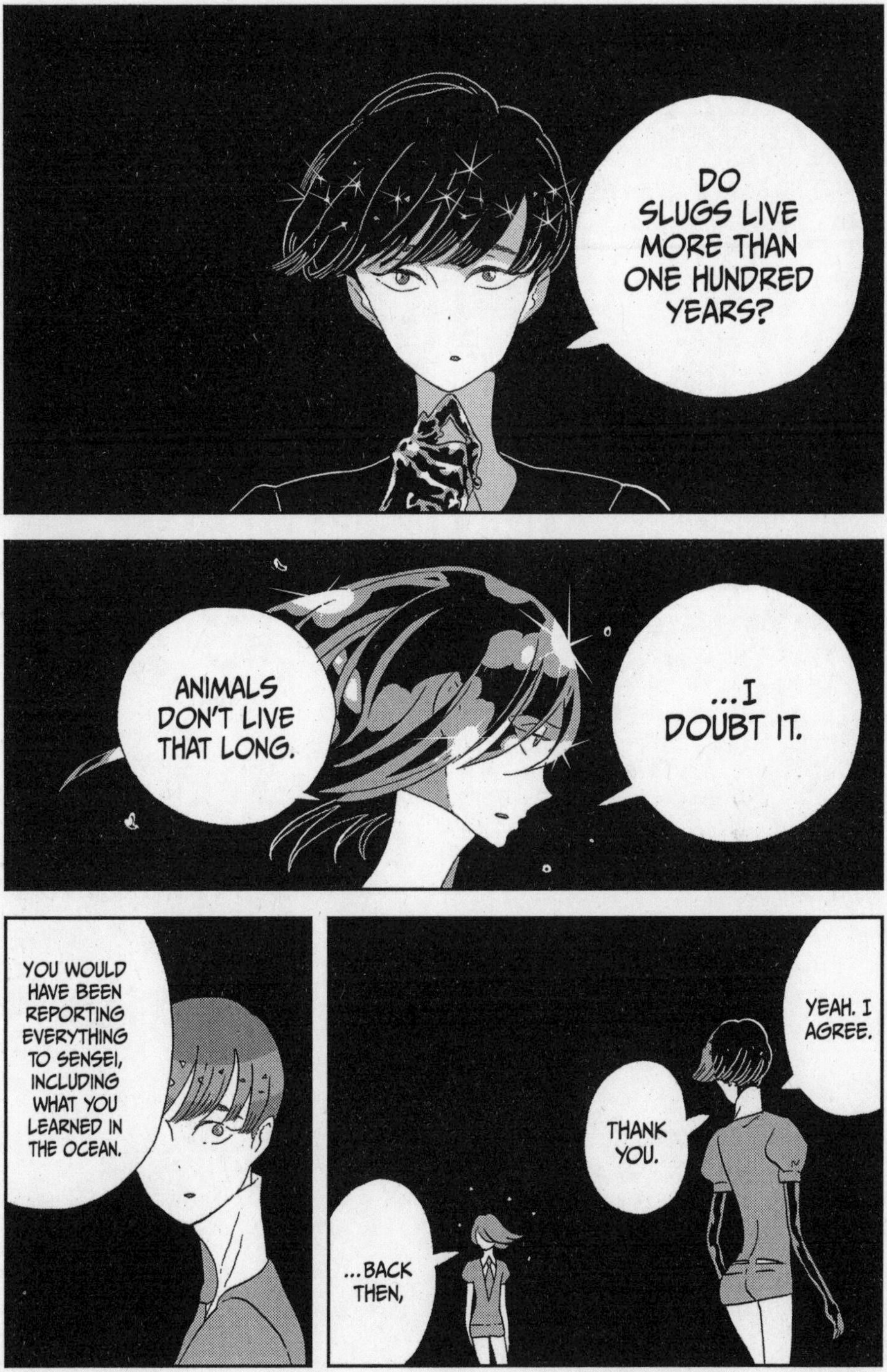
DO SLUGS LIVE MORE THAN ONE HUNDRED YEARS?
...I DOUBT IT.
ANIMALS DON'T LIVE THAT LONG.
YEAH. I AGREE.
THANK YOU.
...BACK THEN,
YOU WOULD HAVE BEEN REPORTING EVERYTHING TO SENSEI, INCLUDING WHAT YOU LEARNED IN THE OCEAN.

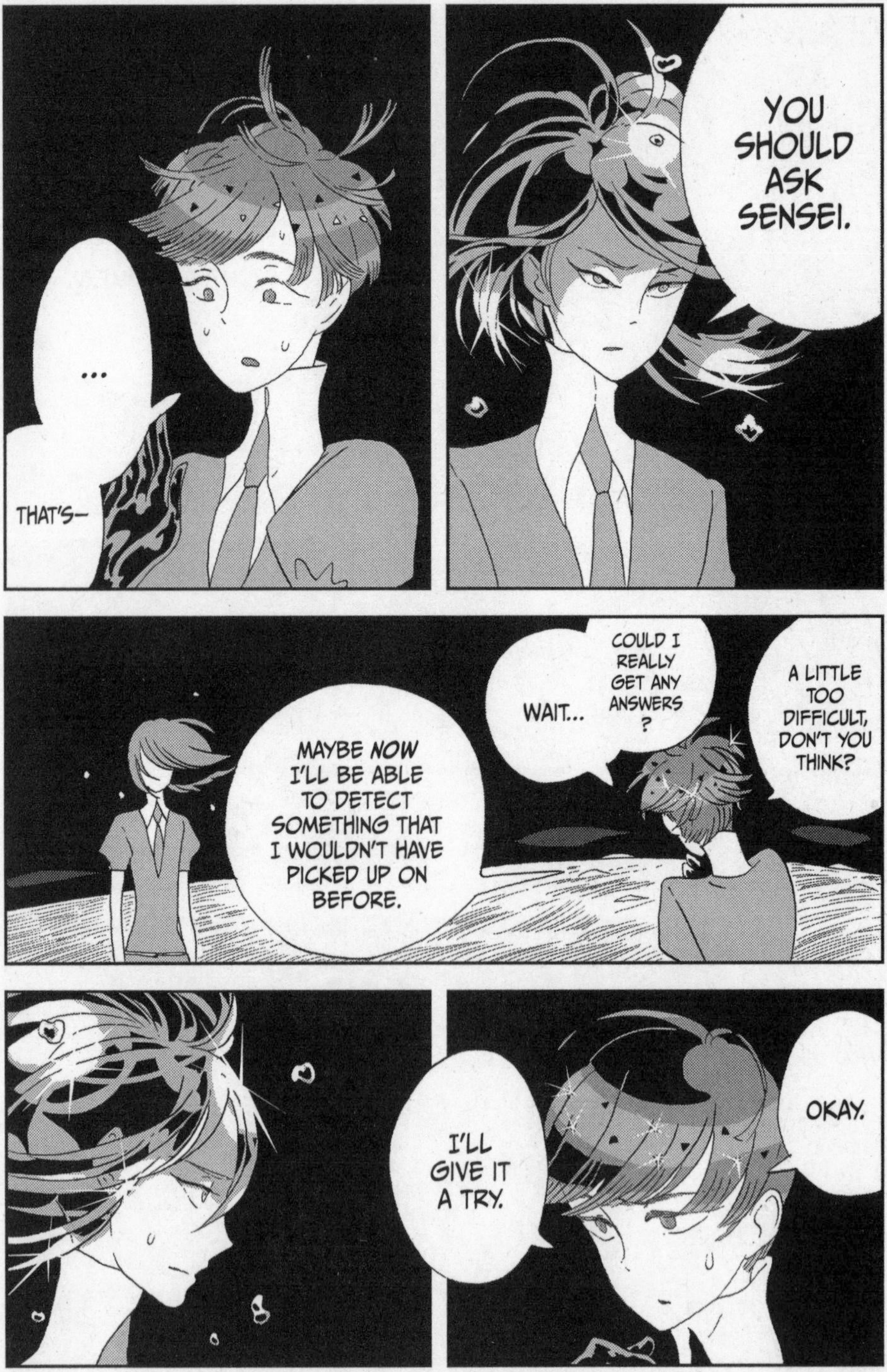
YOU SHOULD ASK SENSEI.
...
THAT'S—
A LITTLE TOO DIFFICULT, DON'T YOU THINK?
COULD I REALLY GET ANY ANSWERS ?
WAIT...
MAYBE *NOW* I'LL BE ABLE TO DETECT SOMETHING THAT I WOULDN'T HAVE PICKED UP ON BEFORE.
OKAY.
I'LL GIVE IT A TRY.

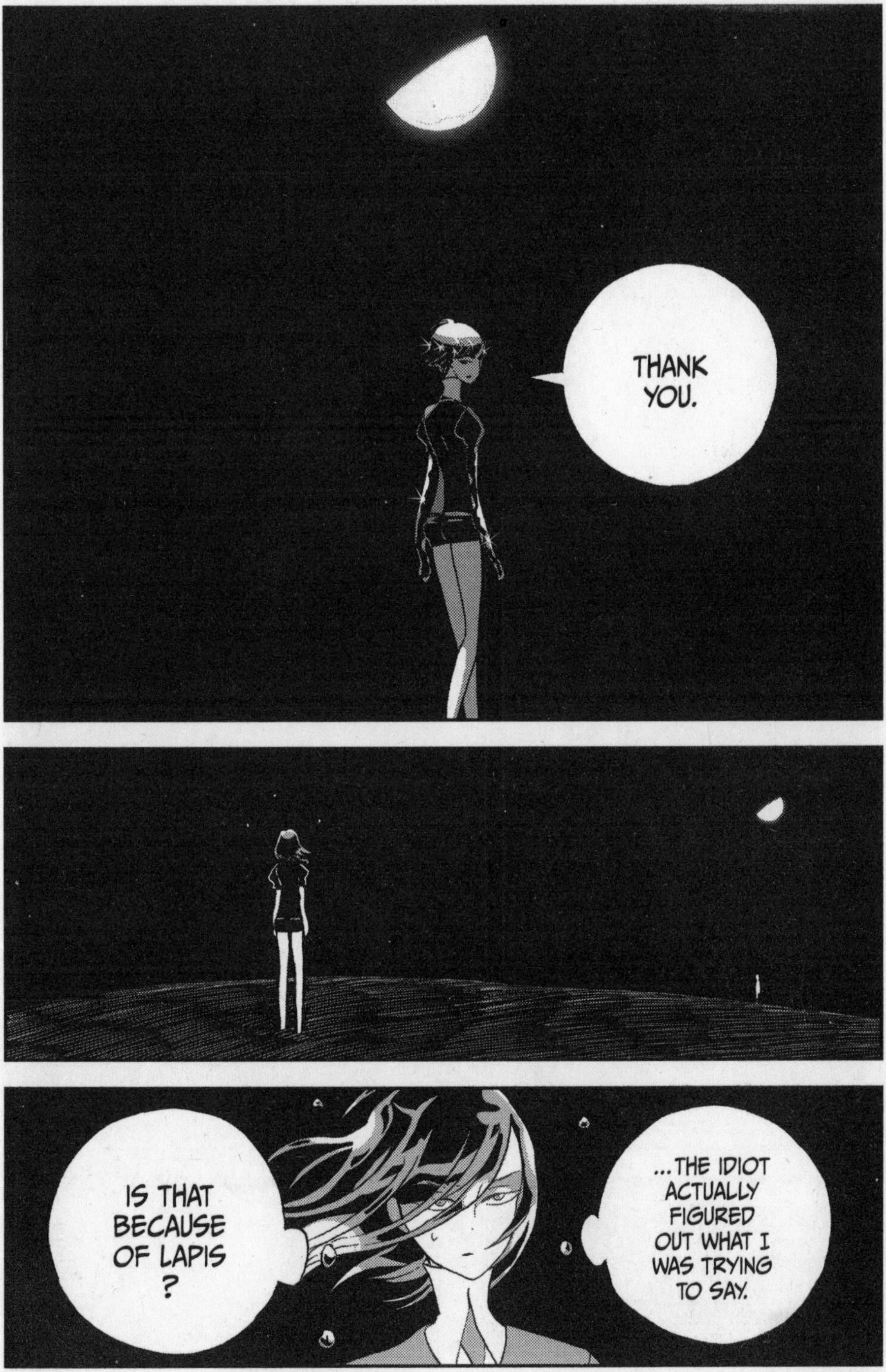
THANK YOU.
...THE IDIOT ACTUALLY FIGURED OUT WHAT I WAS TRYING TO SAY.
IS THAT BECAUSE OF LAPIS ?

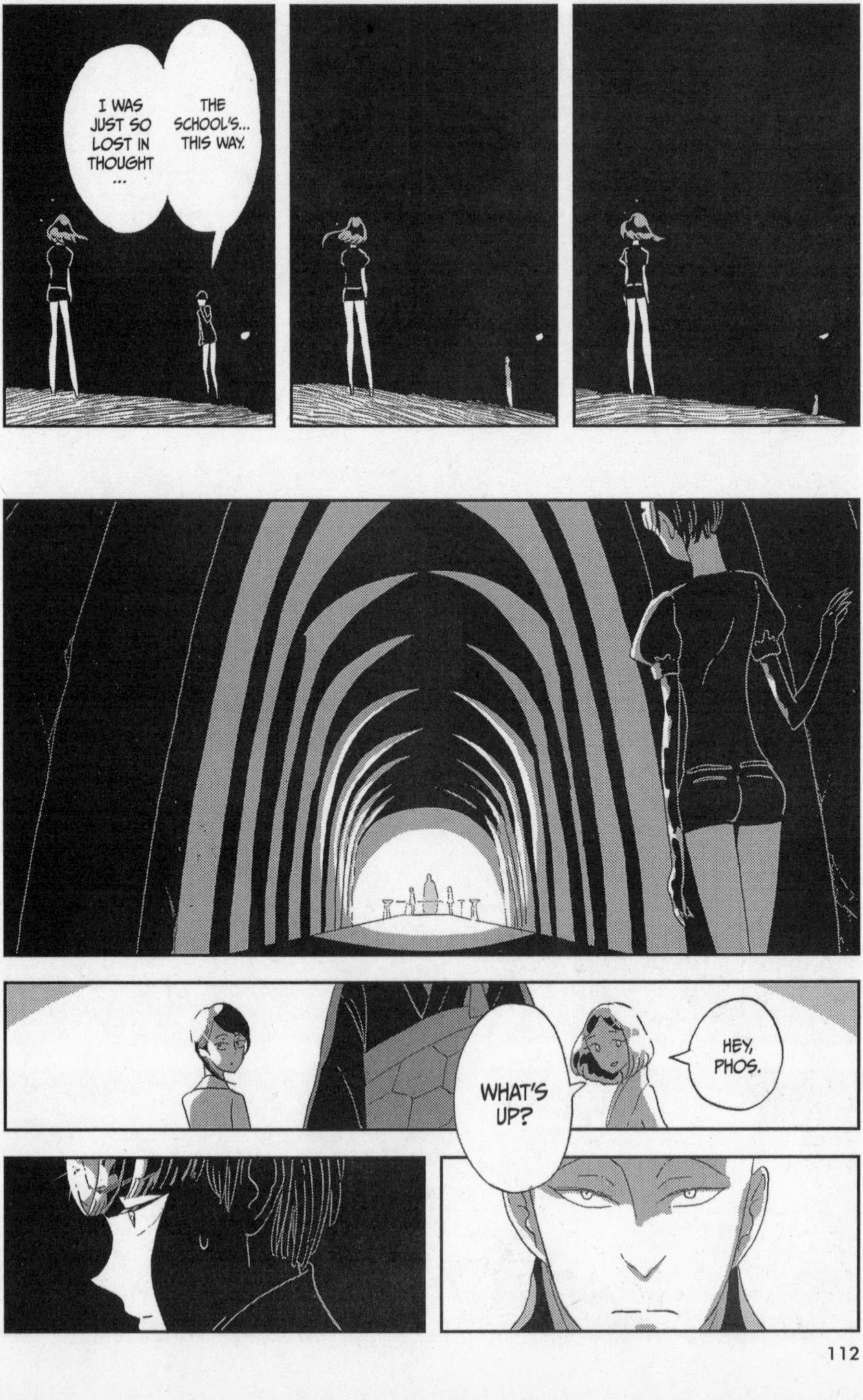
THE SCHOOL'S... THIS WAY.
I WAS JUST SO LOST IN THOUGHT ...
HEY, PHOS.
WHAT'S UP?

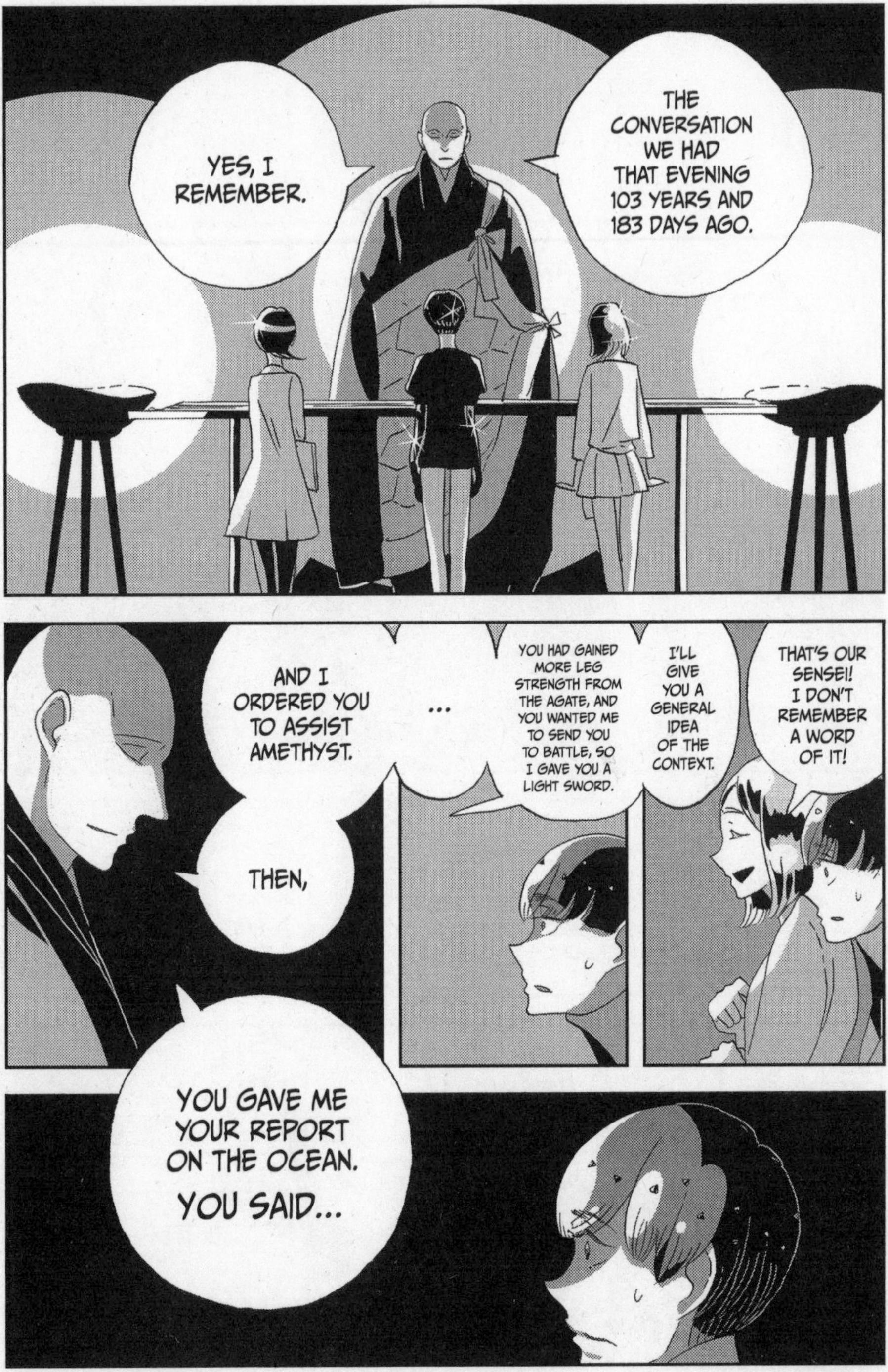
THE CONVERSATION WE HAD THAT EVENING 103 YEARS AND 183 DAYS AGO.
YES, I REMEMBER.
THAT'S OUR SENSEI! I DON'T REMEMBER A WORD OF IT!
I'LL GIVE YOU A GENERAL IDEA OF THE CONTEXT.
YOU HAD GAINED MORE LEG STRENGTH FROM THE AGATE, AND YOU WANTED ME TO SEND YOU TO BATTLE, SO I GAVE YOU A LIGHT SWORD.
...
AND I ORDERED YOU TO ASSIST AMETHYST.
THEN,
YOU GAVE ME YOUR REPORT ON THE OCEAN.
YOU SAID...

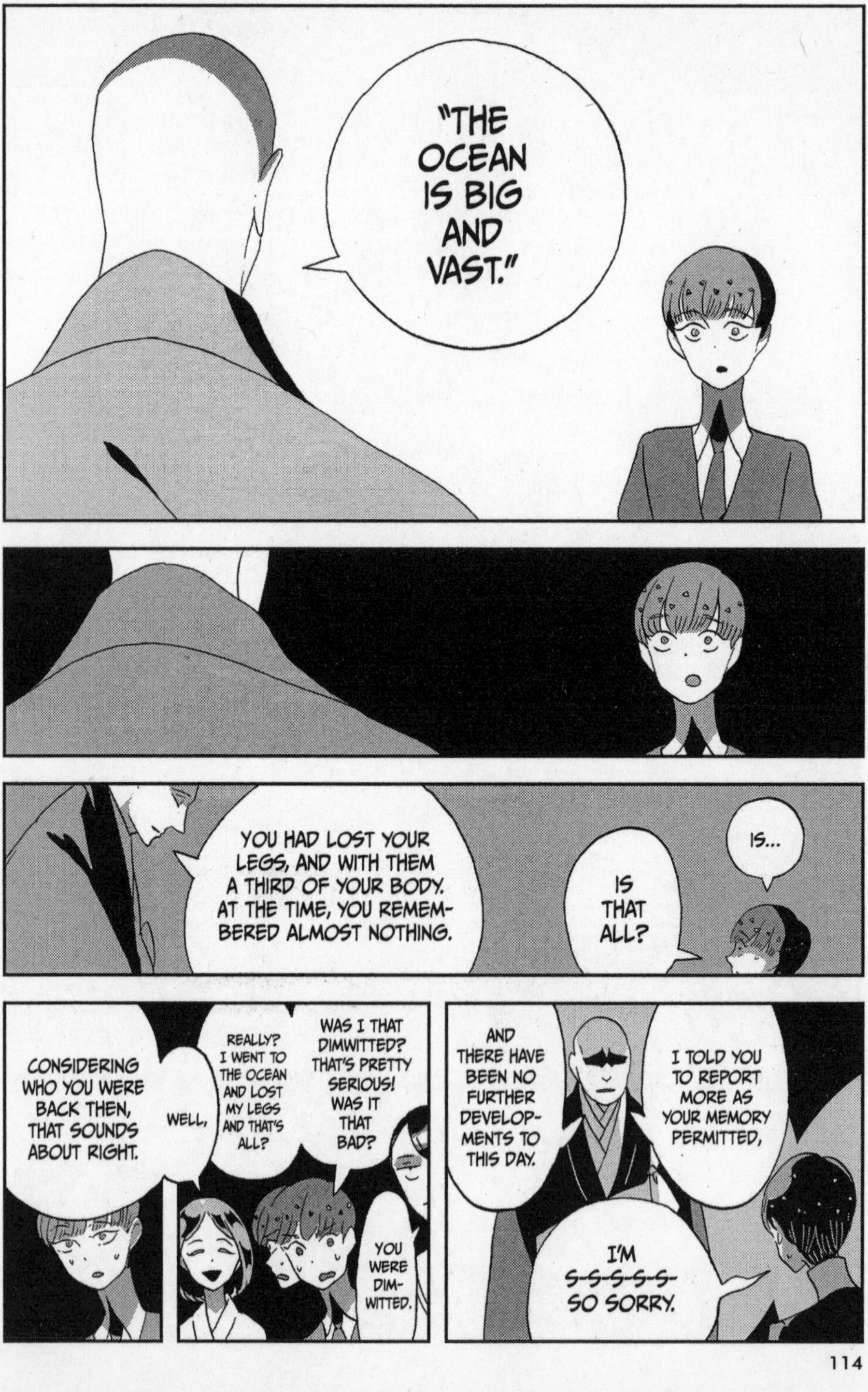
"THE OCEAN IS BIG AND VAST."
IS...
IS THAT ALL?
YOU HAD LOST YOUR LEGS, AND WITH THEM A THIRD OF YOUR BODY. AT THE TIME, YOU REMEMBERED ALMOST NOTHING.
I TOLD YOU TO REPORT MORE AS YOUR MEMORY PERMITTED,
AND THERE HAVE BEEN NO FURTHER DEVELOPMENTS TO THIS DAY.
I'M S-S-S-S-S-SO SORRY.
WAS I THAT DIMWITTED? THAT'S PRETTY SERIOUS! WAS IT THAT BAD?
REALLY? I WENT TO THE OCEAN AND LOST MY LEGS AND THAT'S ALL?
WELL,
CONSIDERING WHO YOU WERE BACK THEN, THAT SOUNDS ABOUT RIGHT.
YOU WERE DIMWITTED.

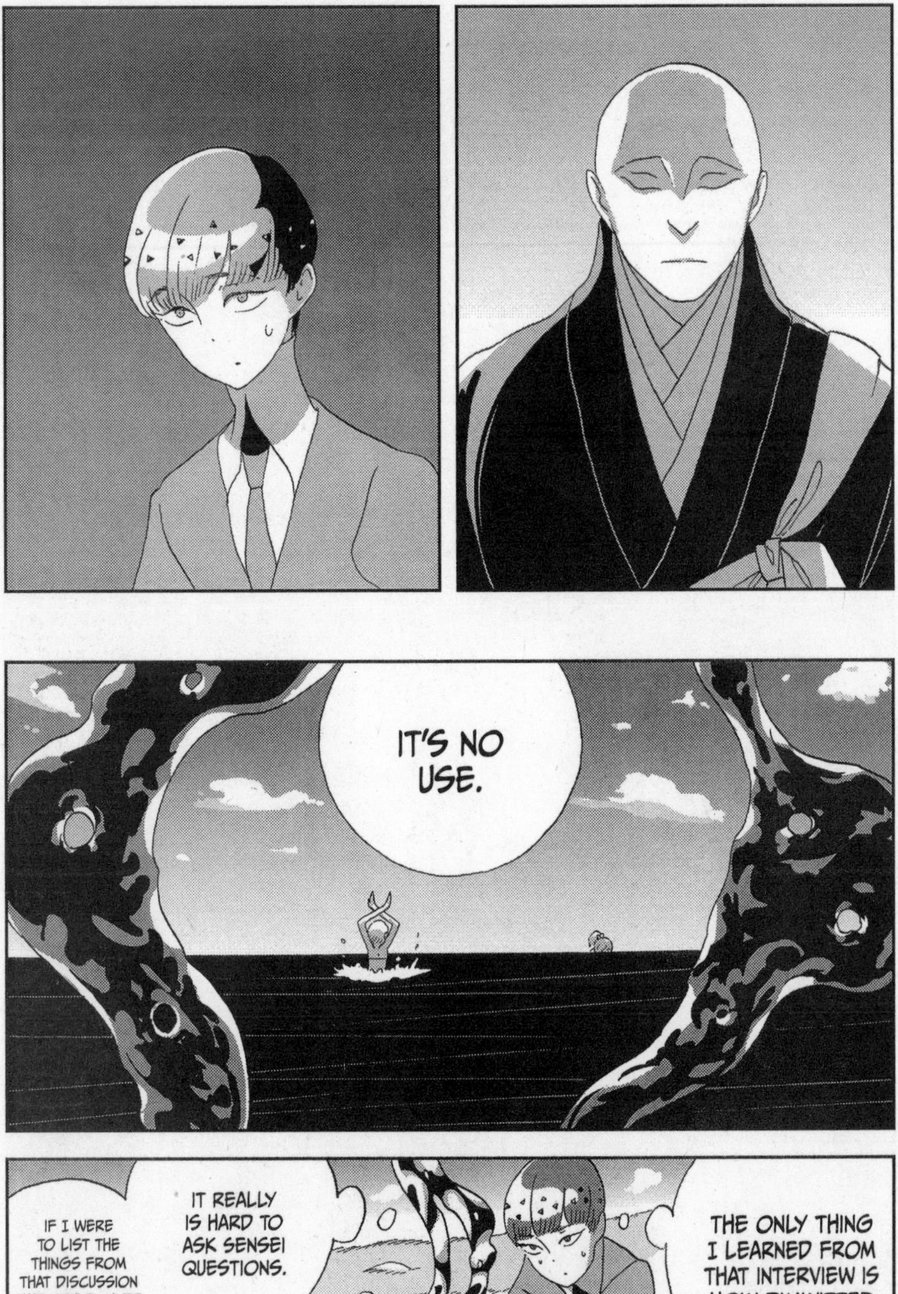
IT'S NO USE.
THE ONLY THING I LEARNED FROM THAT INTERVIEW IS HOW DIMWITTED I WAS.
IT REALLY IS HARD TO ASK SENSEI QUESTIONS.
IF I WERE TO LIST THE THINGS FROM THAT DISCUSSION THAT COULD MAYBE EVEN POSSIBLY BE CONSIDERED SUSPICIOUS...

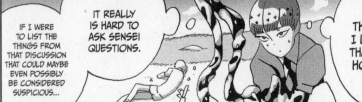

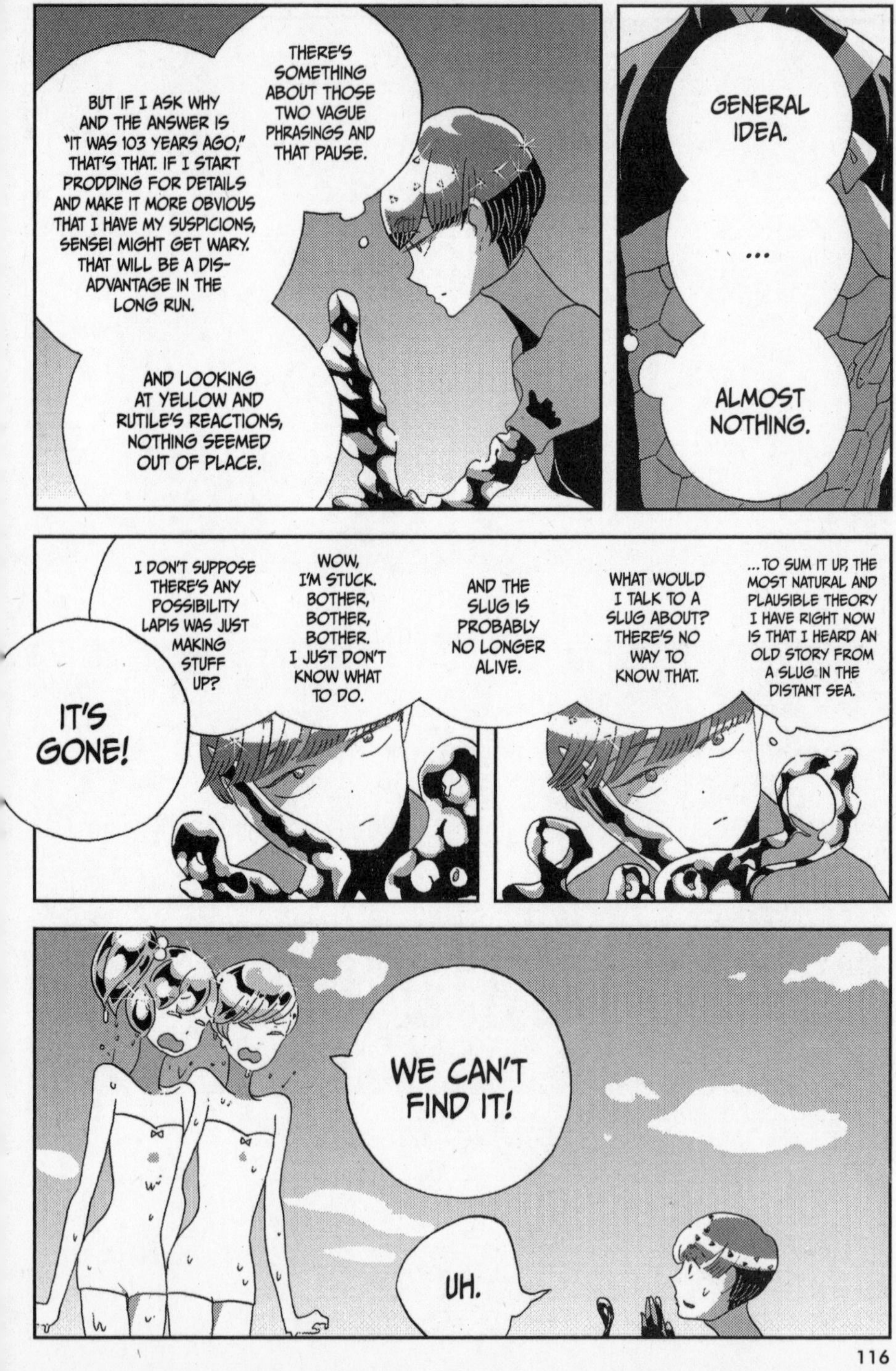
GENERAL IDEA.
...
ALMOST NOTHING.
THERE'S SOMETHING ABOUT THOSE TWO VAGUE PHRASINGS AND THAT PAUSE.
BUT IF I ASK WHY AND THE ANSWER IS "IT WAS 103 YEARS AGO," THAT'S THAT. IF I START PRODDING FOR DETAILS AND MAKE IT MORE OBVIOUS THAT I HAVE MY SUSPICIONS, SENSEI MIGHT GET WARY. THAT WILL BE A DIS-ADVANTAGE IN THE LONG RUN.
AND LOOKING AT YELLOW AND RUTILE'S REACTIONS, NOTHING SEEMED OUT OF PLACE.
...TO SUM IT UP, THE MOST NATURAL AND PLAUSIBLE THEORY I HAVE RIGHT NOW IS THAT I HEARD AN OLD STORY FROM A SLUG IN THE DISTANT SEA.
WHAT WOULD I TALK TO A SLUG ABOUT? THERE'S NO WAY TO KNOW THAT.
AND THE SLUG IS PROBABLY NO LONGER ALIVE.
WOW, I'M STUCK. BOTHER, BOTHER, BOTHER. I JUST DON'T KNOW WHAT TO DO.
I DON'T SUPPOSE THERE'S ANY POSSIBILITY LAPIS WAS JUST MAKING STUFF UP?
IT'S GONE!
WE CAN'T FIND IT!
UH.

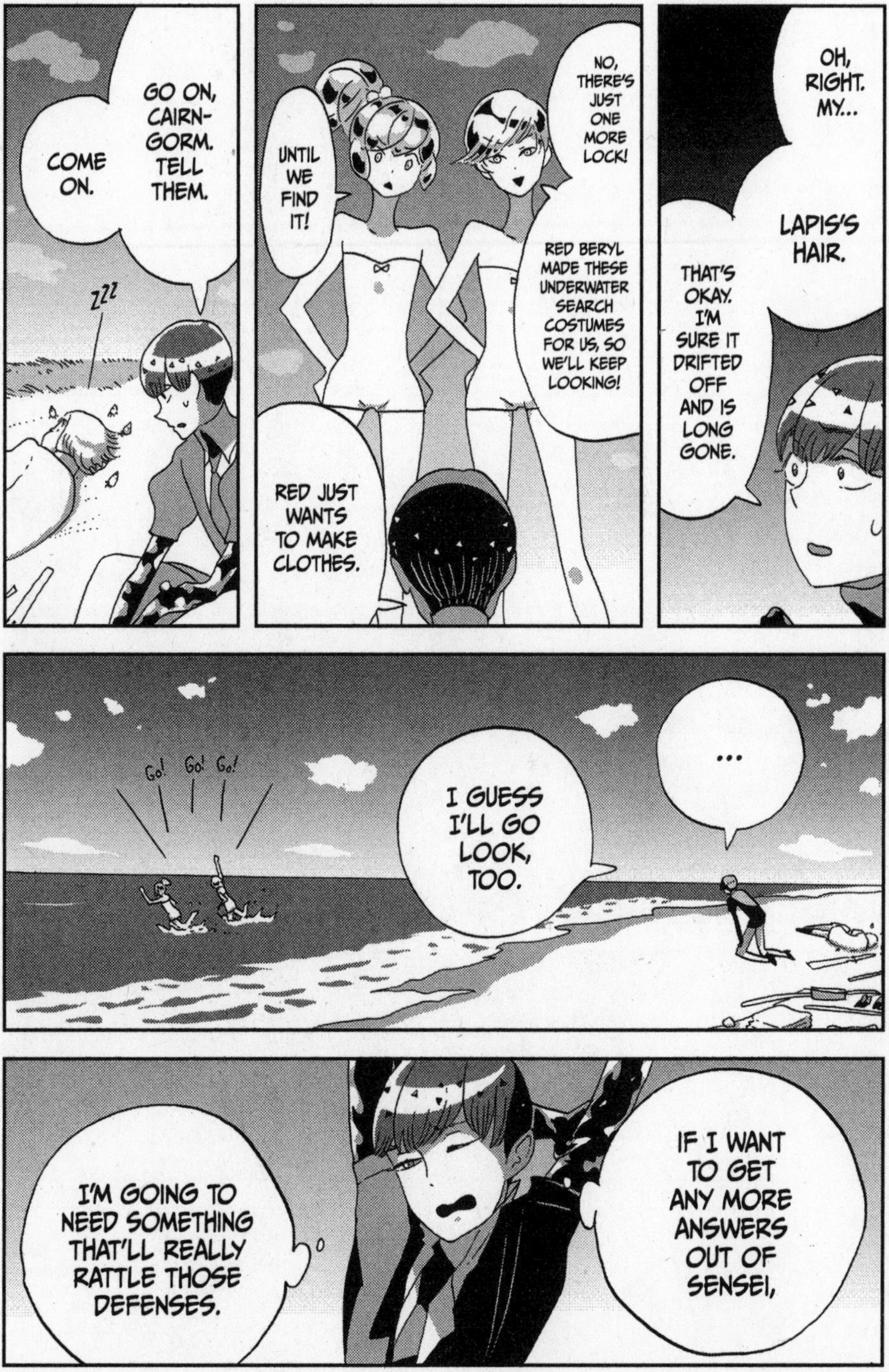
OH, RIGHT. MY...
LAPIS'S HAIR.
THAT'S OKAY. I'M SURE IT DRIFTED OFF AND IS LONG GONE.
NO, THERE'S JUST ONE MORE LOCK!
UNTIL WE FIND IT!
RED BERYL MADE THESE UNDERWATER SEARCH COSTUMES FOR US, SO WE'LL KEEP LOOKING!
RED JUST WANTS TO MAKE CLOTHES.
GO ON, CAIRN-GORM. TELL THEM.
COME ON.
ZZZ
...
I GUESS I'LL GO LOOK, TOO.
Go! Go! Go!
IF I WANT TO GET ANY MORE ANSWERS OUT OF SENSEI,
I'M GOING TO NEED SOMETHING THAT'LL REALLY RATTLE THOSE DEFENSES.

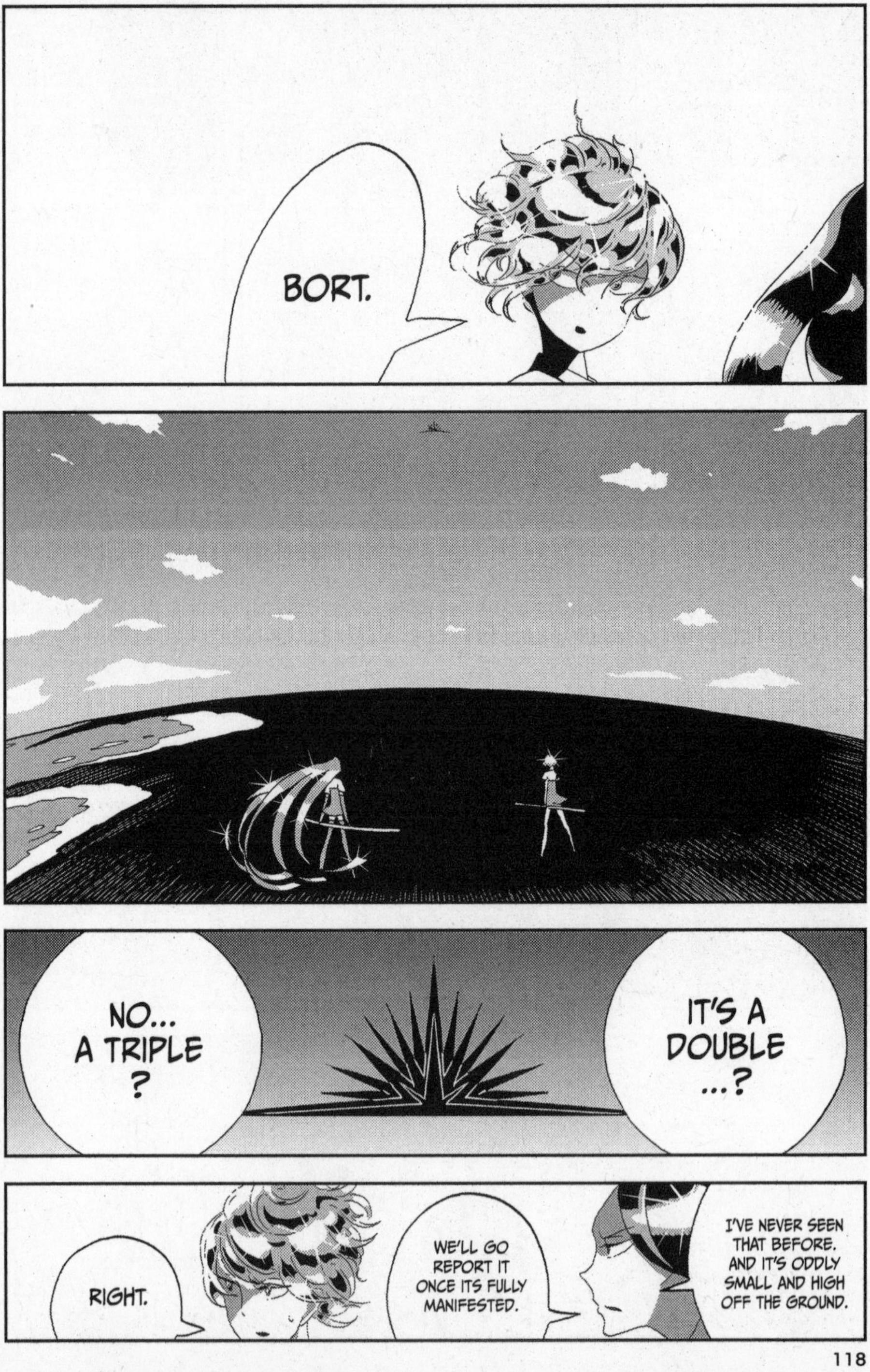
BORT.
IT'S A DOUBLE ...?
NO... A TRIPLE ?
I'VE NEVER SEEN THAT BEFORE. AND IT'S ODDLY SMALL AND HIGH OFF THE GROUND.
WE'LL GO REPORT IT ONCE ITS FULLY MANIFESTED.
RIGHT.

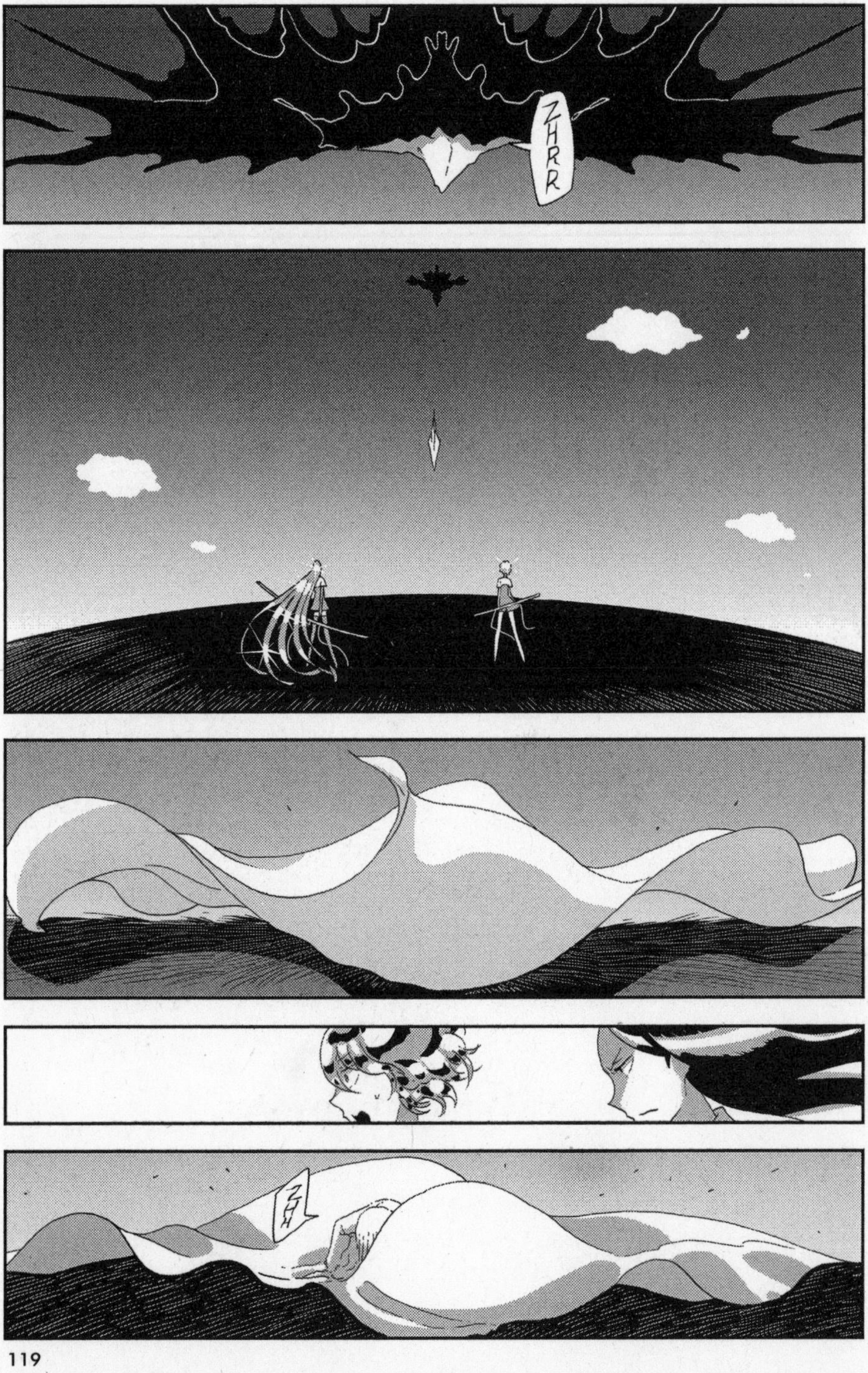
ZHRR
ZHH

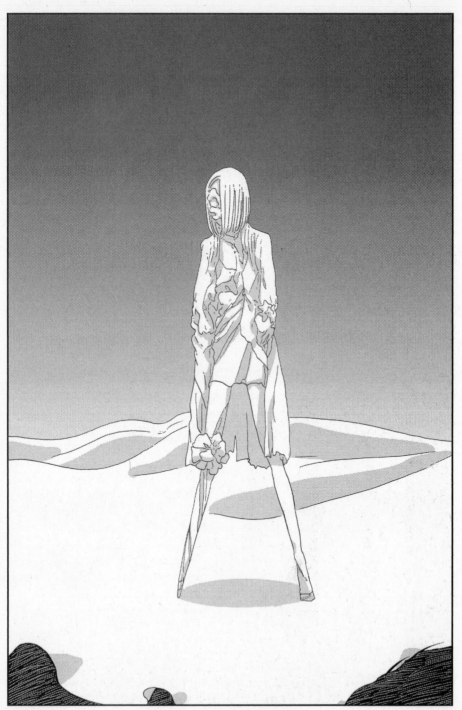

CHAPTER 49: On the Trail END

CHAPTER 50:

The Doctor

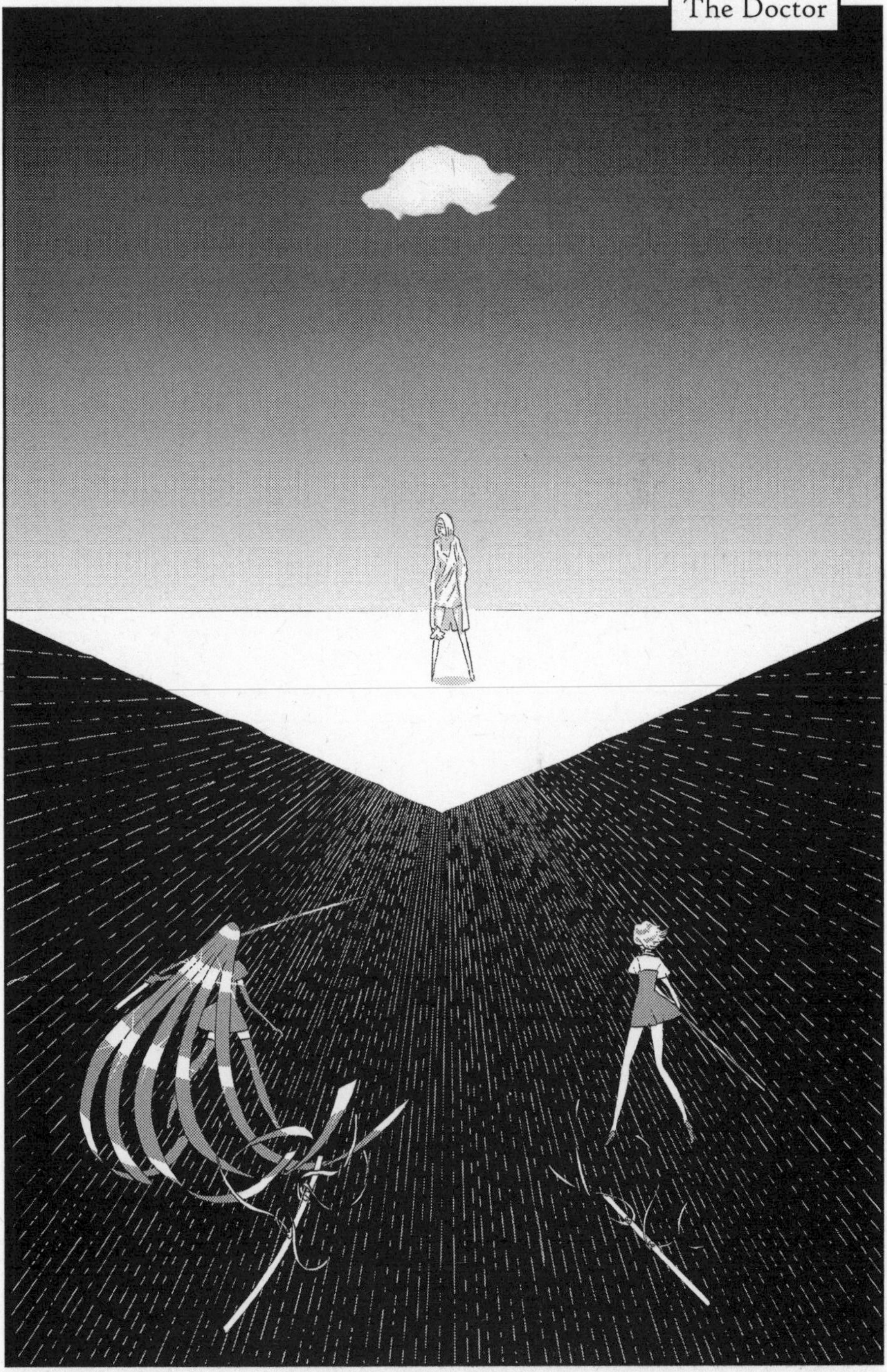

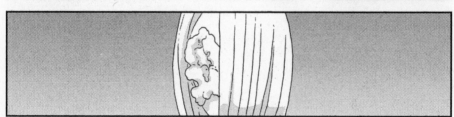

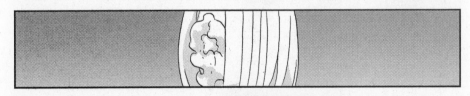

GO GET
SENSEI.

ZIRCON.

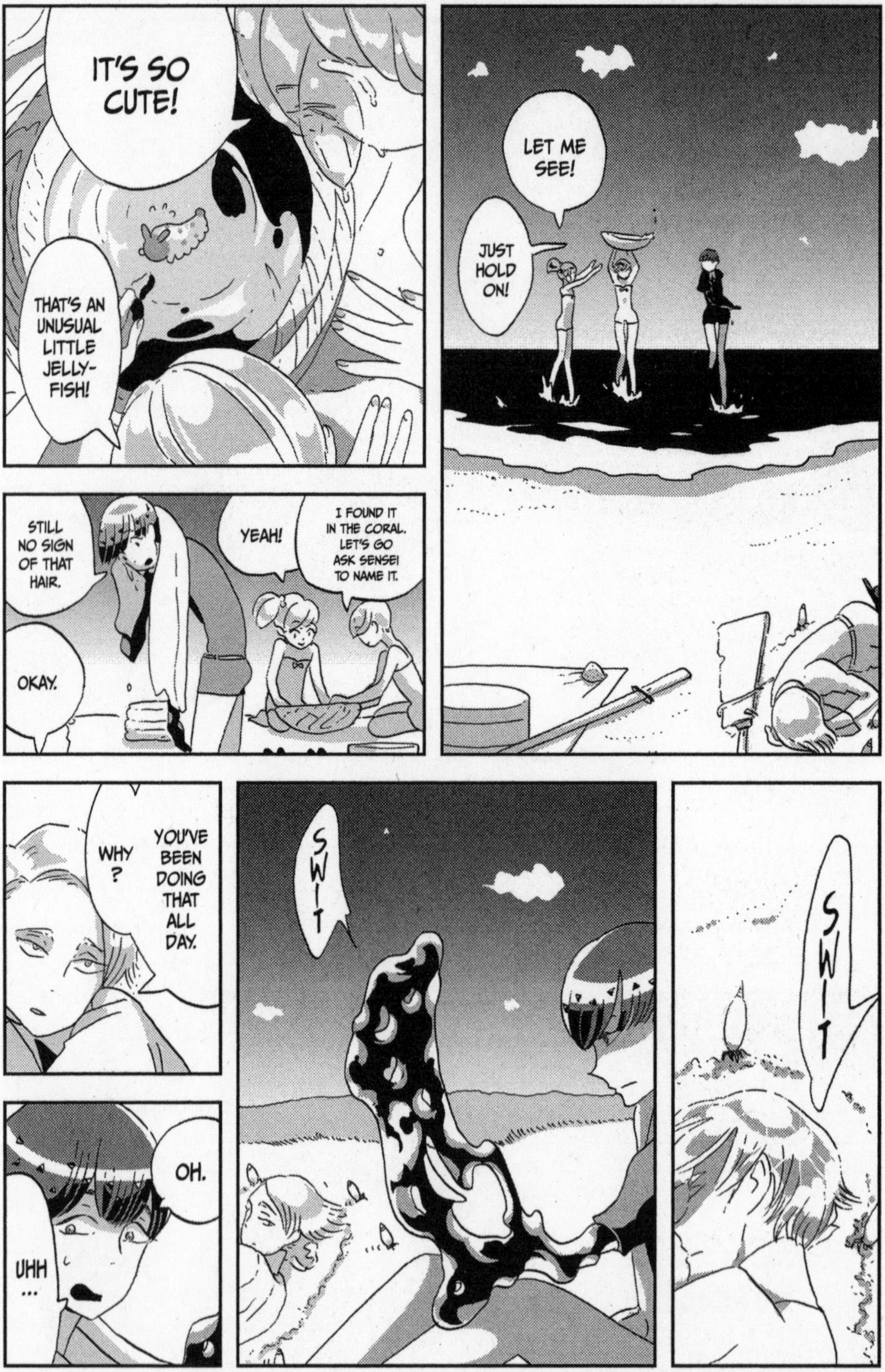
LET ME SEE!
JUST HOLD ON!
IT'S SO CUTE!
THAT'S AN UNUSUAL LITTLE JELLY-FISH!
I FOUND IT IN THE CORAL. LET'S GO ASK SENSEI TO NAME IT.
YEAH!
STILL NO SIGN OF THAT HAIR.
OKAY.
SWIT
SWIT
YOU'VE BEEN DOING THAT ALL DAY.
WHY?
OH.
UHH...

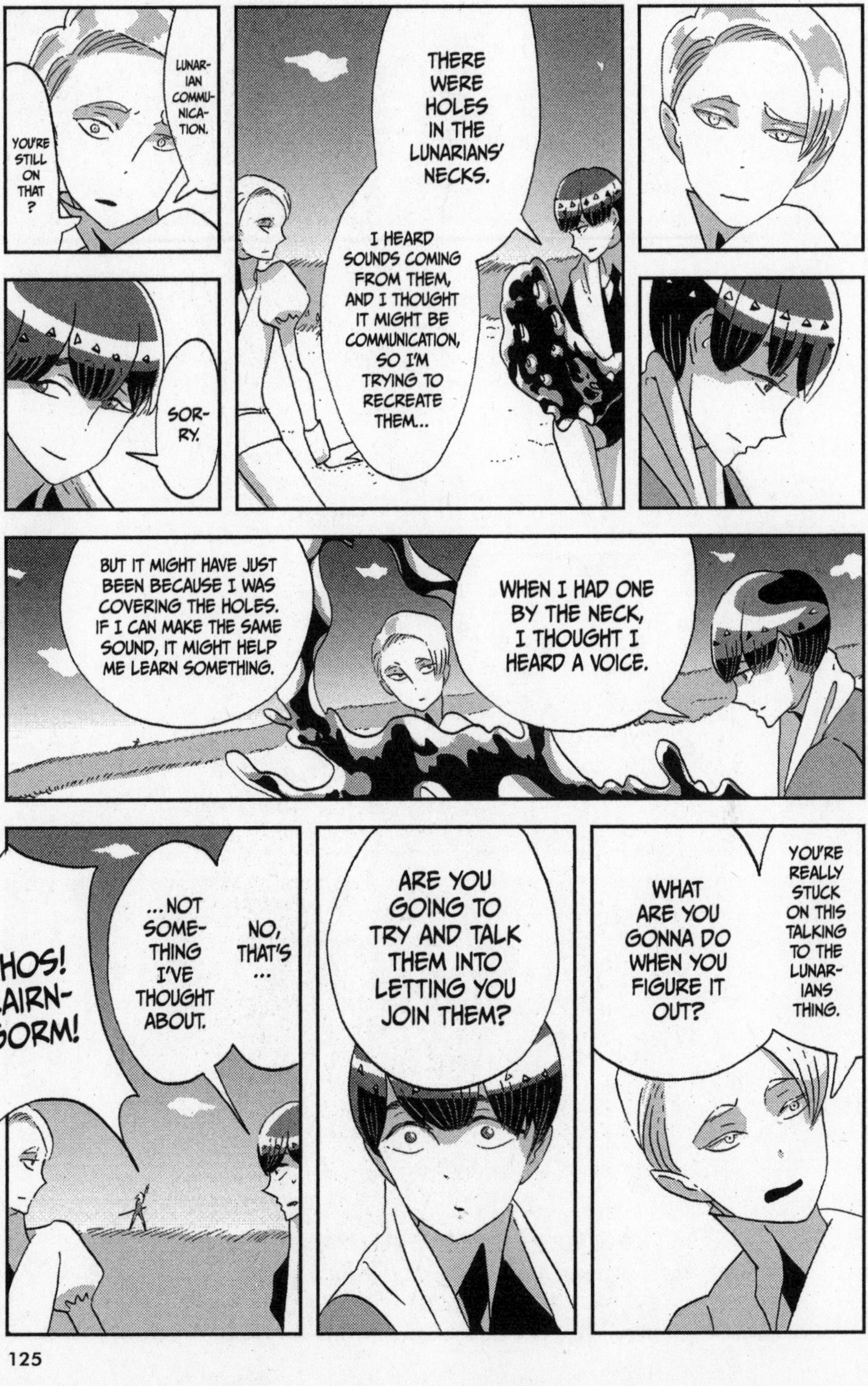
THERE WERE HOLES IN THE LUNARIANS' NECKS.
I HEARD SOUNDS COMING FROM THEM, AND I THOUGHT IT MIGHT BE COMMUNICATION, SO I'M TRYING TO RECREATE THEM...
LUNARIAN COMMUNICATION.
YOU'RE STILL ON THAT?
SORRY.
WHEN I HAD ONE BY THE NECK, I THOUGHT I HEARD A VOICE.
BUT IT MIGHT HAVE JUST BEEN BECAUSE I WAS COVERING THE HOLES. IF I CAN MAKE THE SAME SOUND, IT MIGHT HELP ME LEARN SOMETHING.
YOU'RE REALLY STUCK ON THIS TALKING TO THE LUNARIANS THING.
WHAT ARE YOU GONNA DO WHEN YOU FIGURE IT OUT?
ARE YOU GOING TO TRY AND TALK THEM INTO LETTING YOU JOIN THEM?
NO, THAT'S...
...NOT SOMETHING I'VE THOUGHT ABOUT.
PHOS! CAIRNGORM!

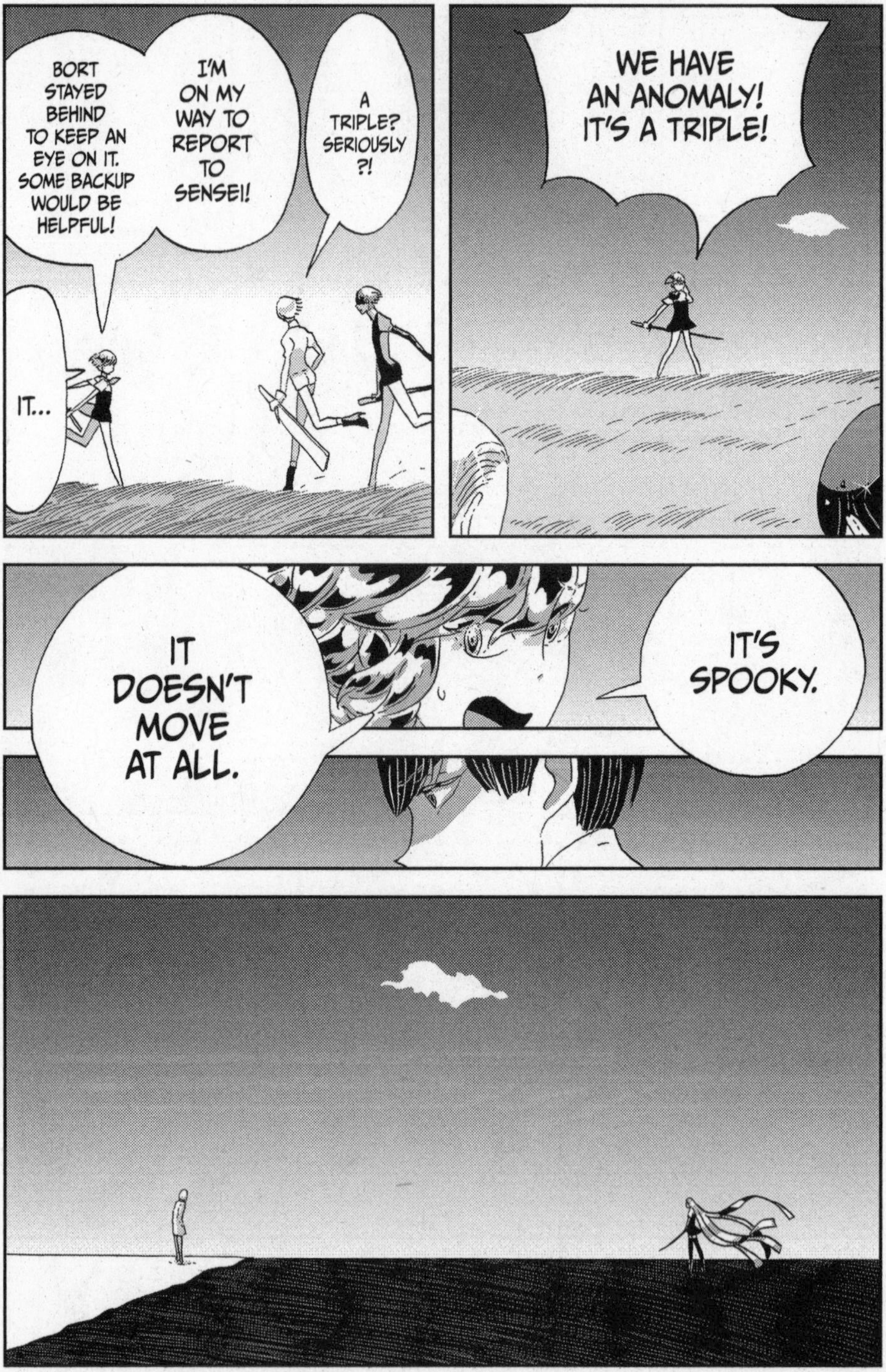
WE HAVE AN ANOMALY! IT'S A TRIPLE!
A TRIPLE? SERIOUSLY?!
I'M ON MY WAY TO REPORT TO SENSEI!
BORT STAYED BEHIND TO KEEP AN EYE ON IT. SOME BACKUP WOULD BE HELPFUL!
IT...
IT'S SPOOKY.
IT DOESN'T MOVE AT ALL.

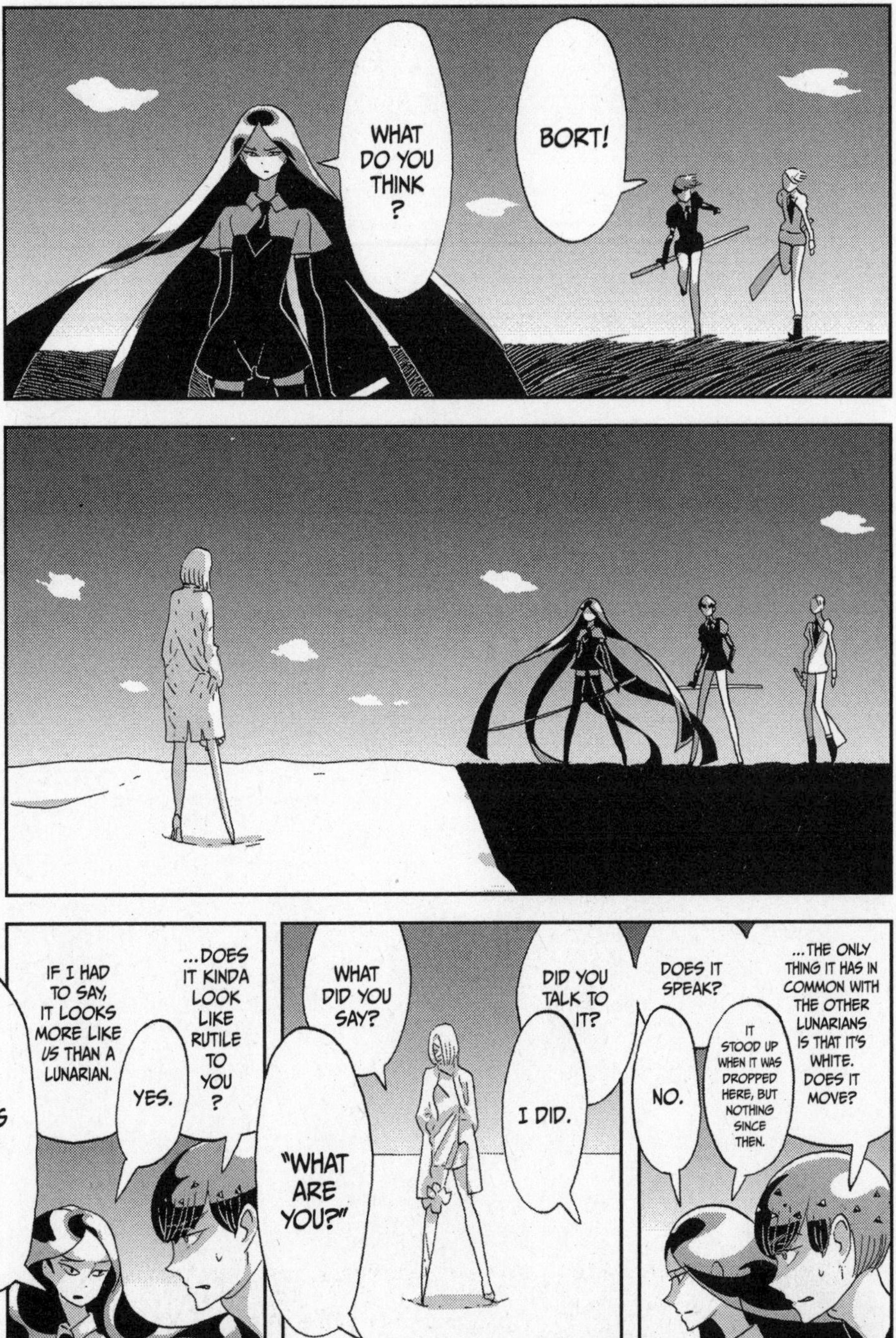
BORT!
WHAT DO YOU THINK?
...THE ONLY THING IT HAS IN COMMON WITH THE OTHER LUNARIANS IS THAT IT'S WHITE. DOES IT MOVE?
DOES IT SPEAK?
IT STOOD UP WHEN IT WAS DROPPED HERE, BUT NOTHING SINCE THEN.
NO.
DID YOU TALK TO IT?
I DID.
WHAT DID YOU SAY?
"WHAT ARE YOU?"
...DOES IT KINDA LOOK LIKE RUTILE TO YOU?
YES.
IF I HAD TO SAY, IT LOOKS MORE LIKE *US* THAN A LUNARIAN.
THERE'S SEN-SEI.

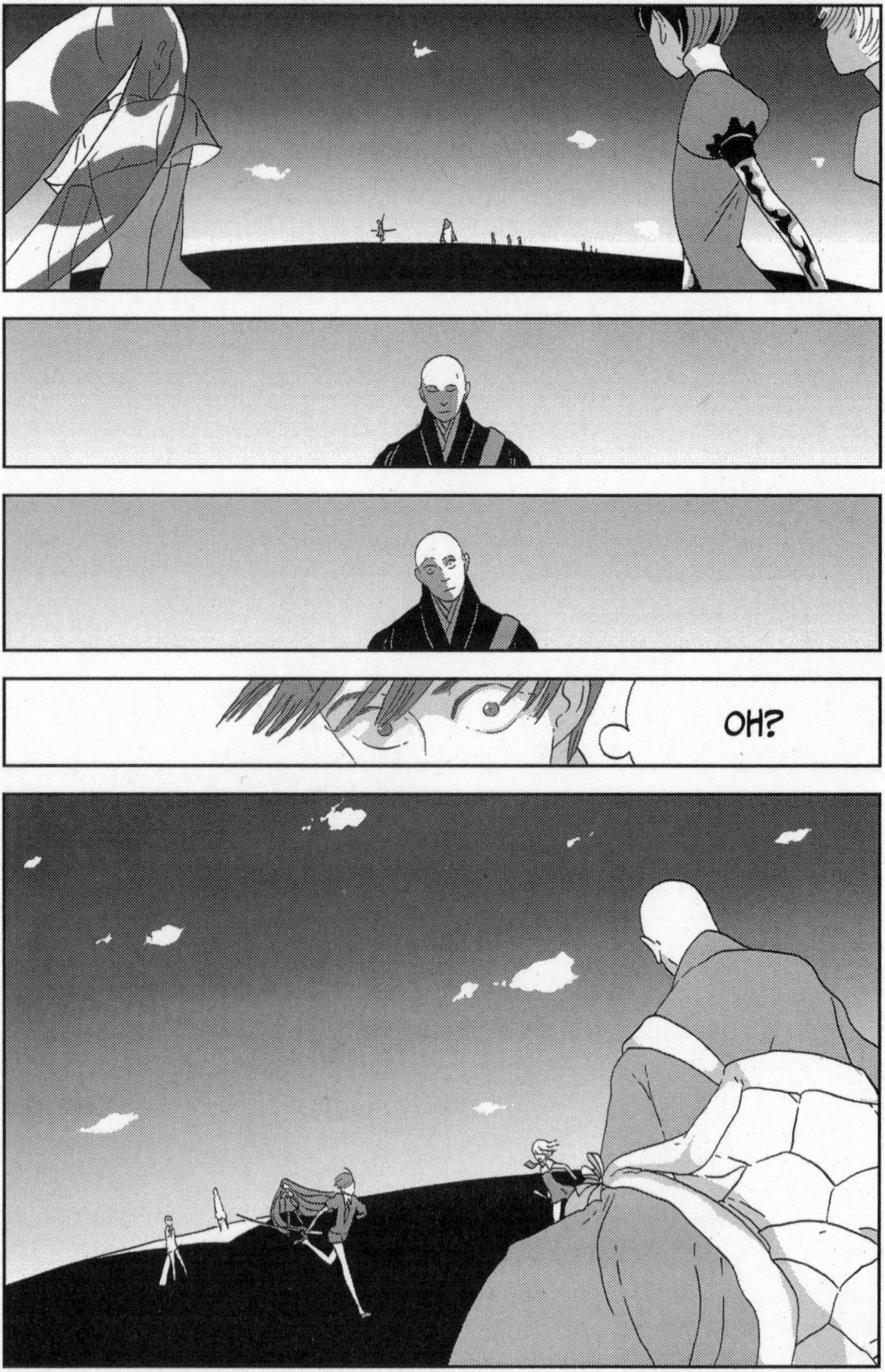
OH?

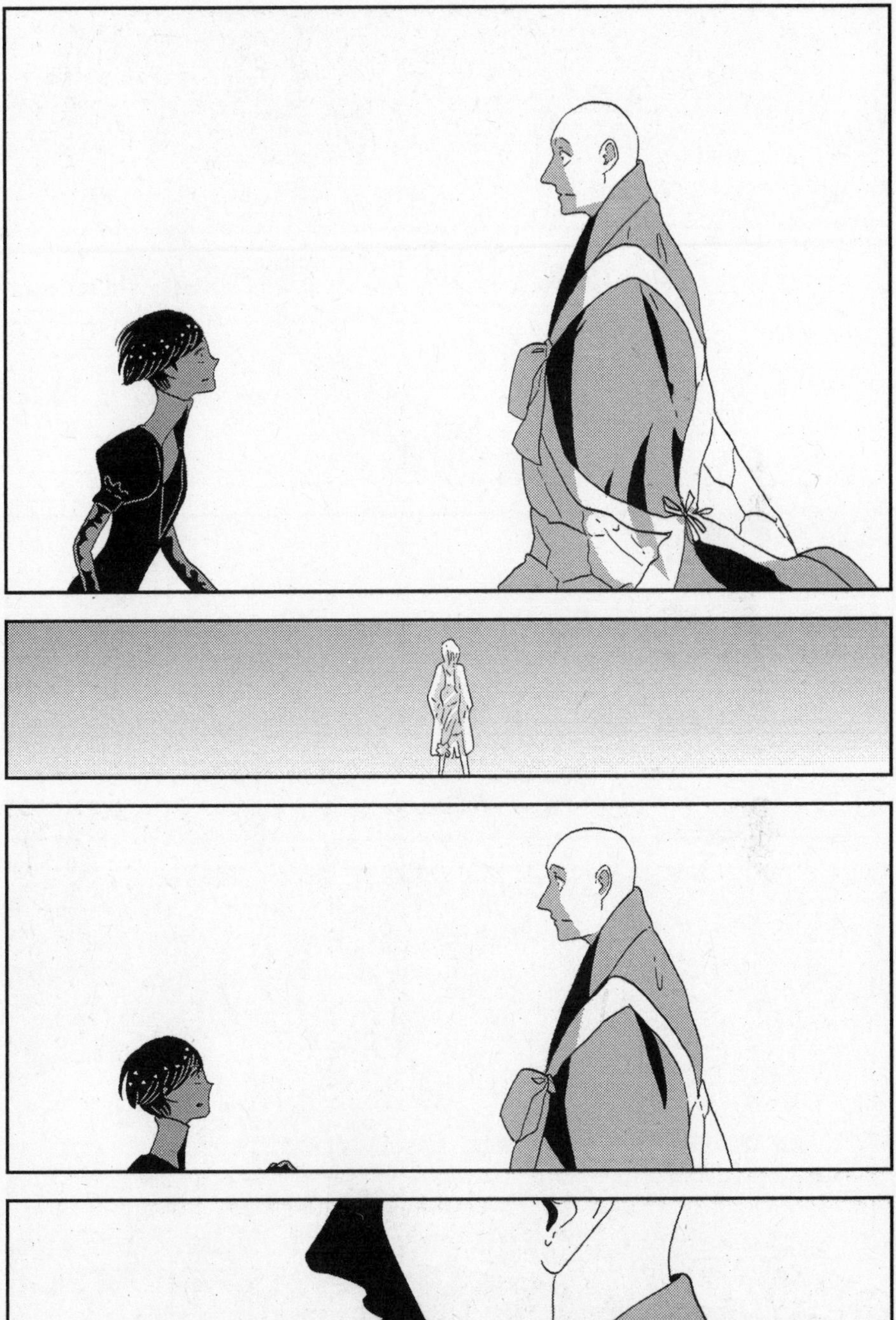

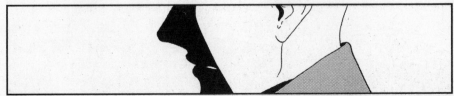

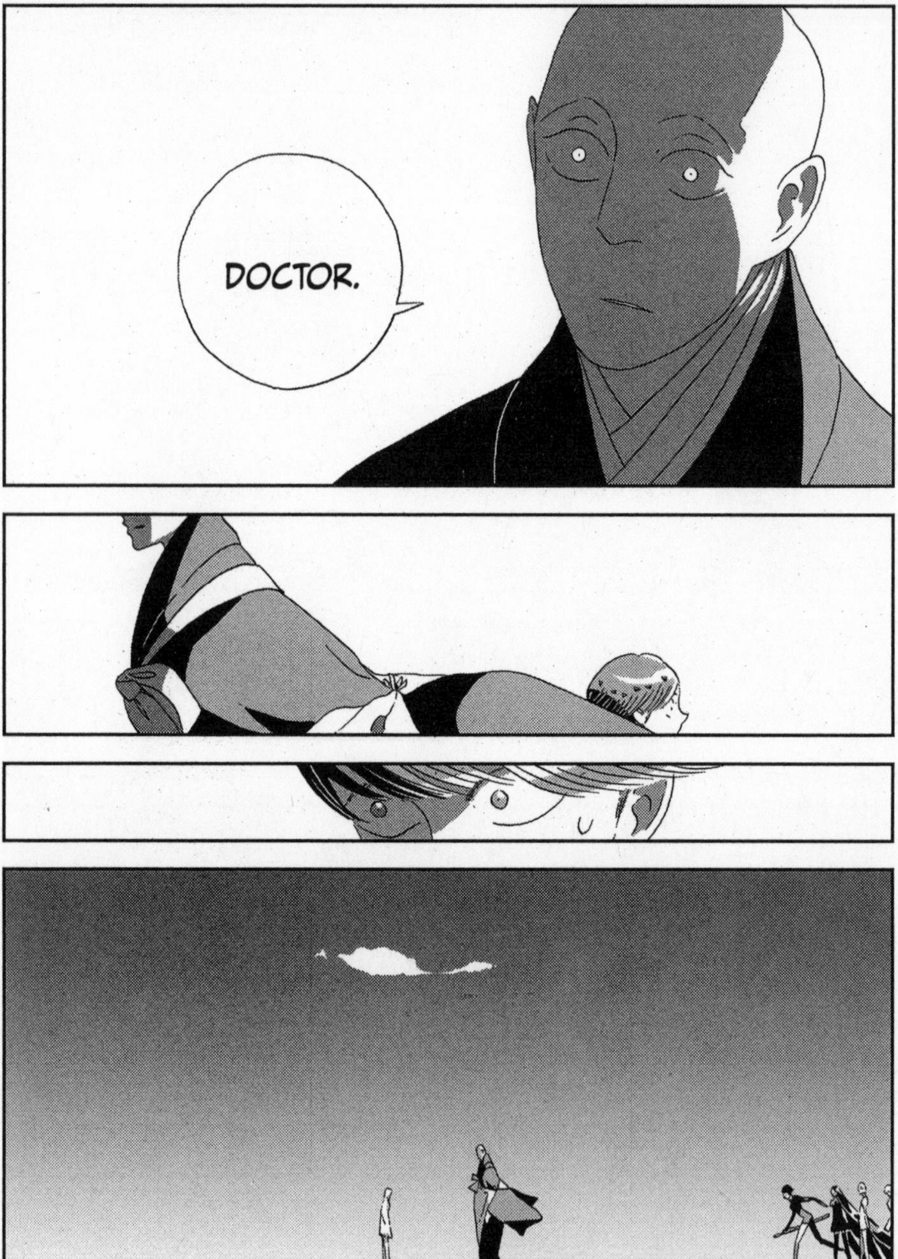
DOCTOR.

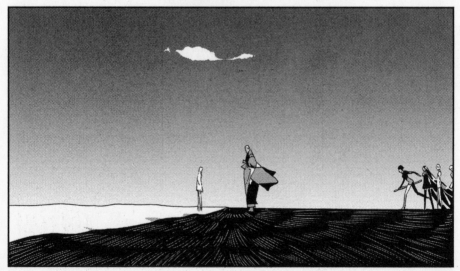

A
FAKE
...

...

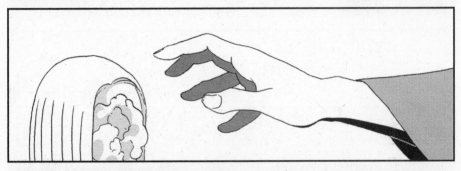

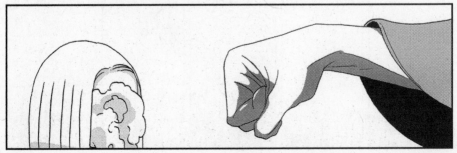

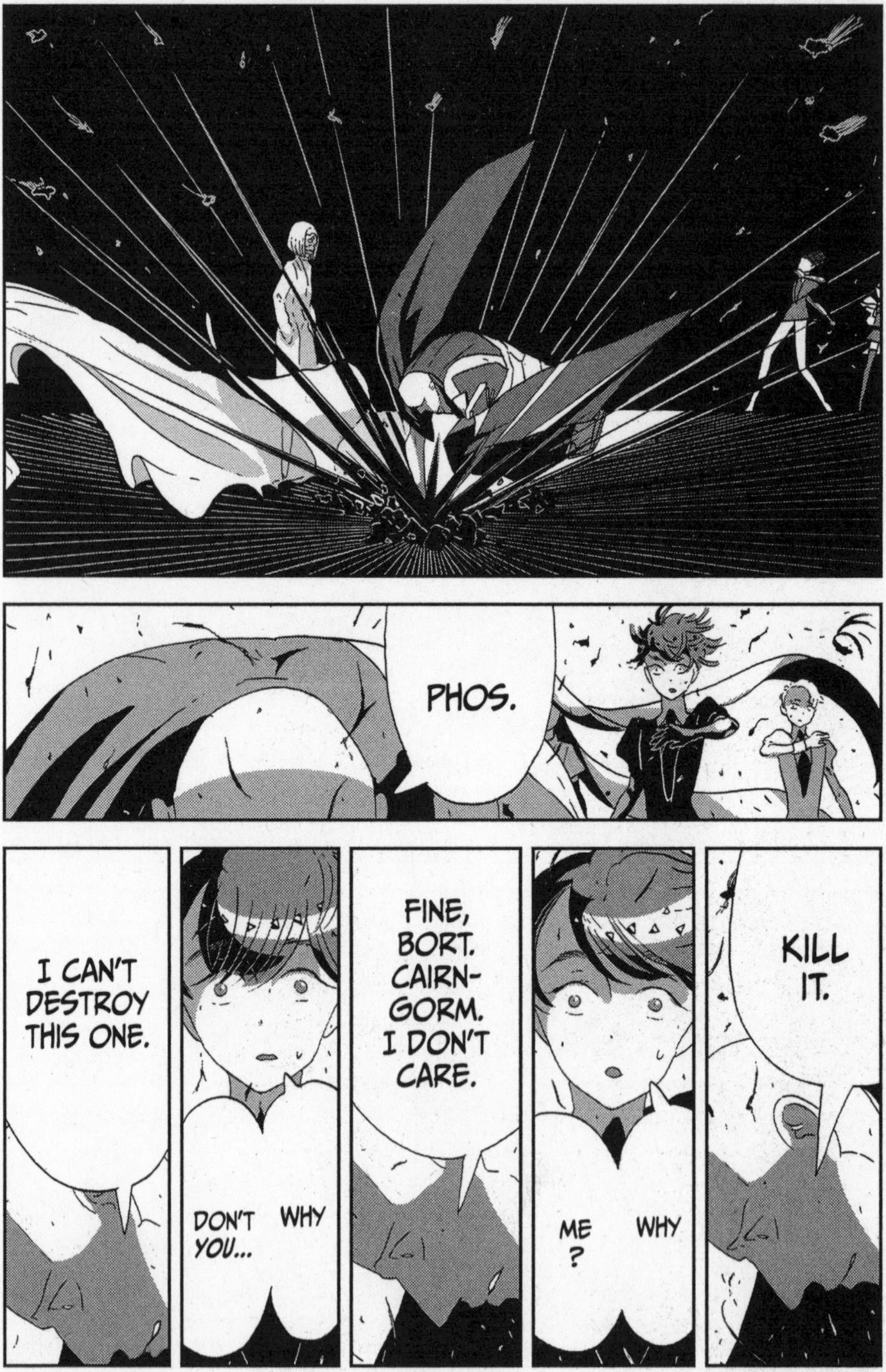
PHOS.
KILL IT.
WHY
ME ?
FINE, BORT. CAIRN-GORM. I DON'T CARE.
WHY
DON'T YOU...
I CAN'T DESTROY THIS ONE.

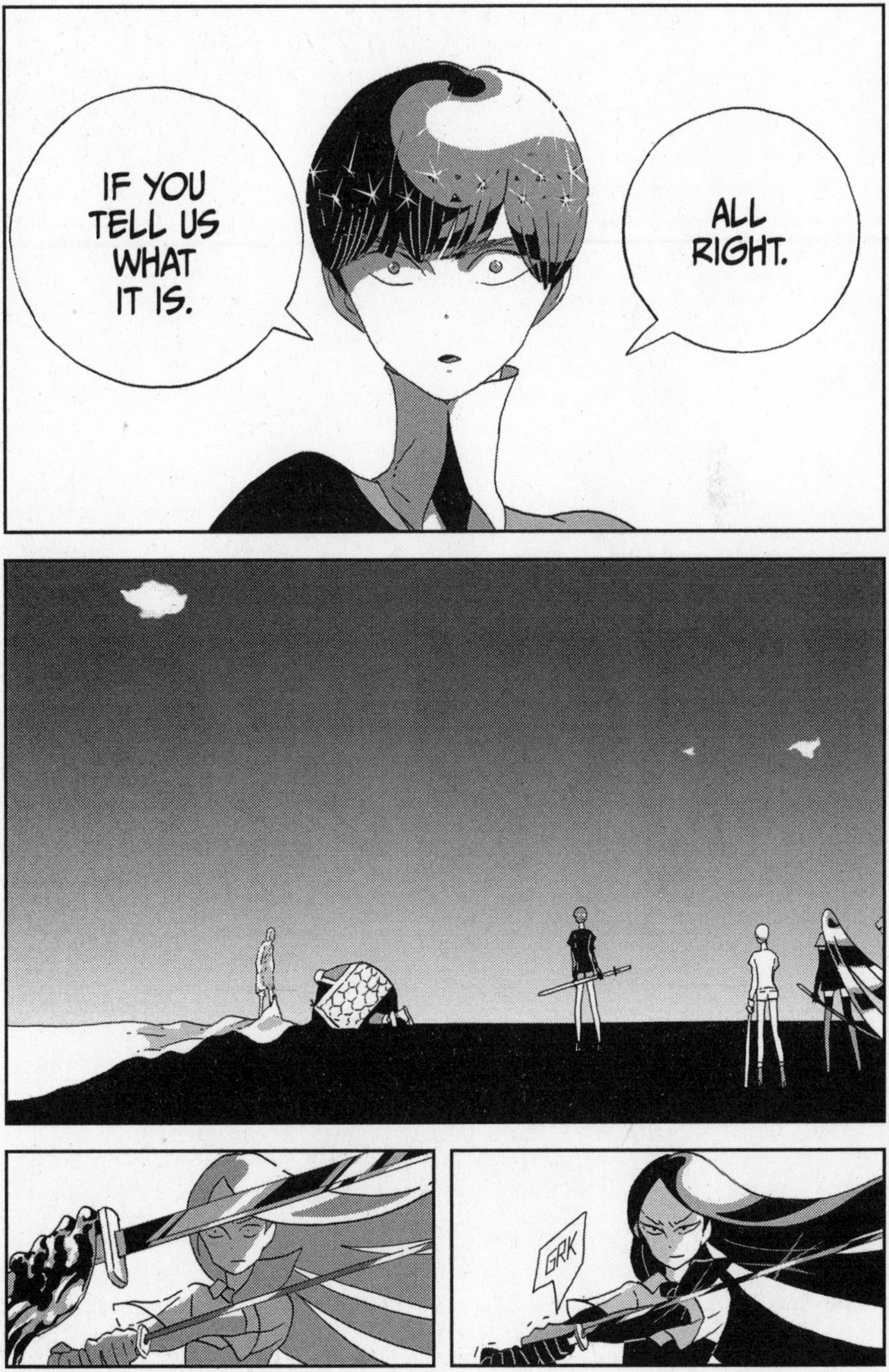
ALL RIGHT.
IF YOU TELL US WHAT IT IS.
GRK

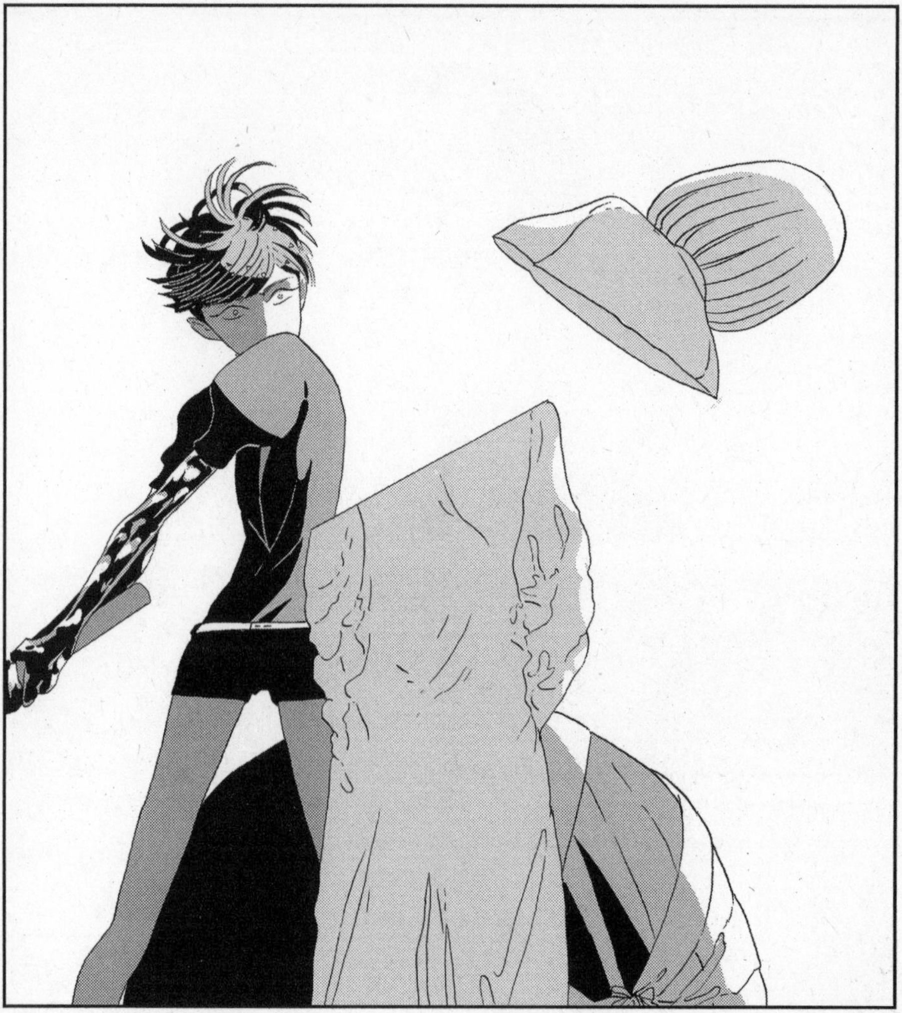
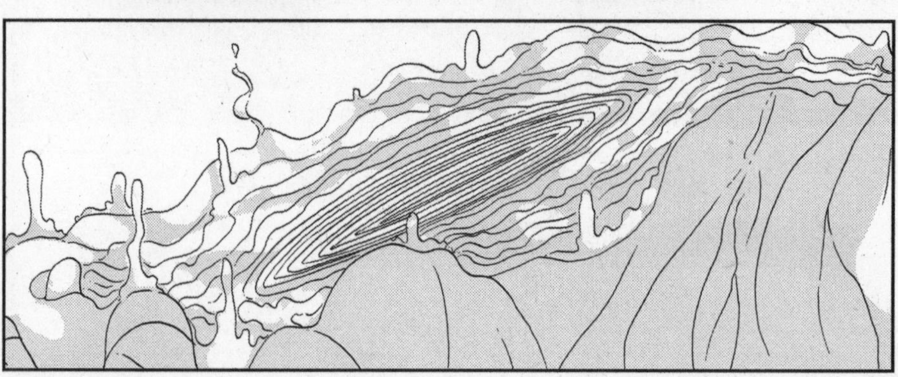

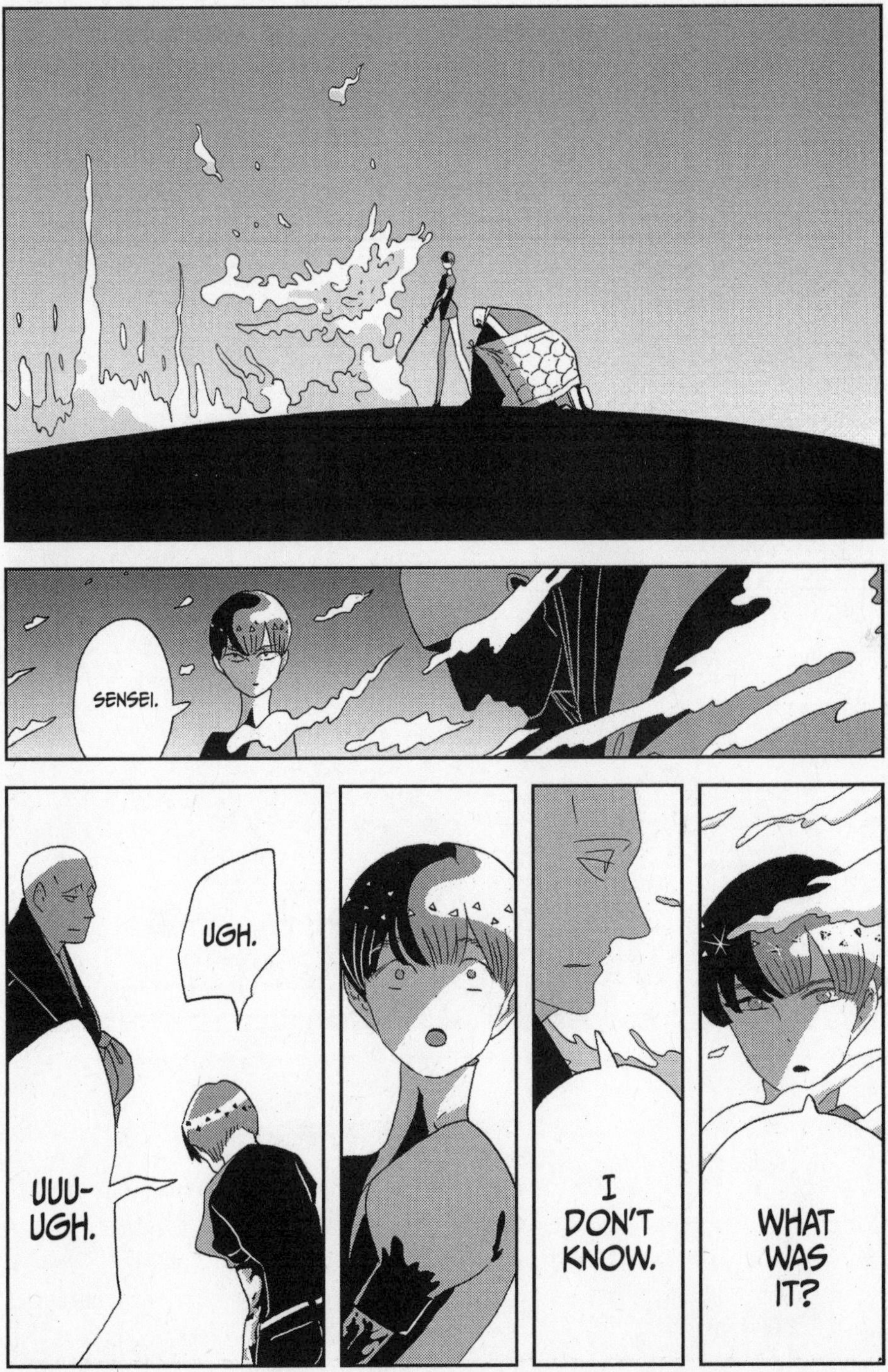
SENSEI.
WHAT WAS IT?
I DON'T KNOW.
UGH.
UUU-UGH.

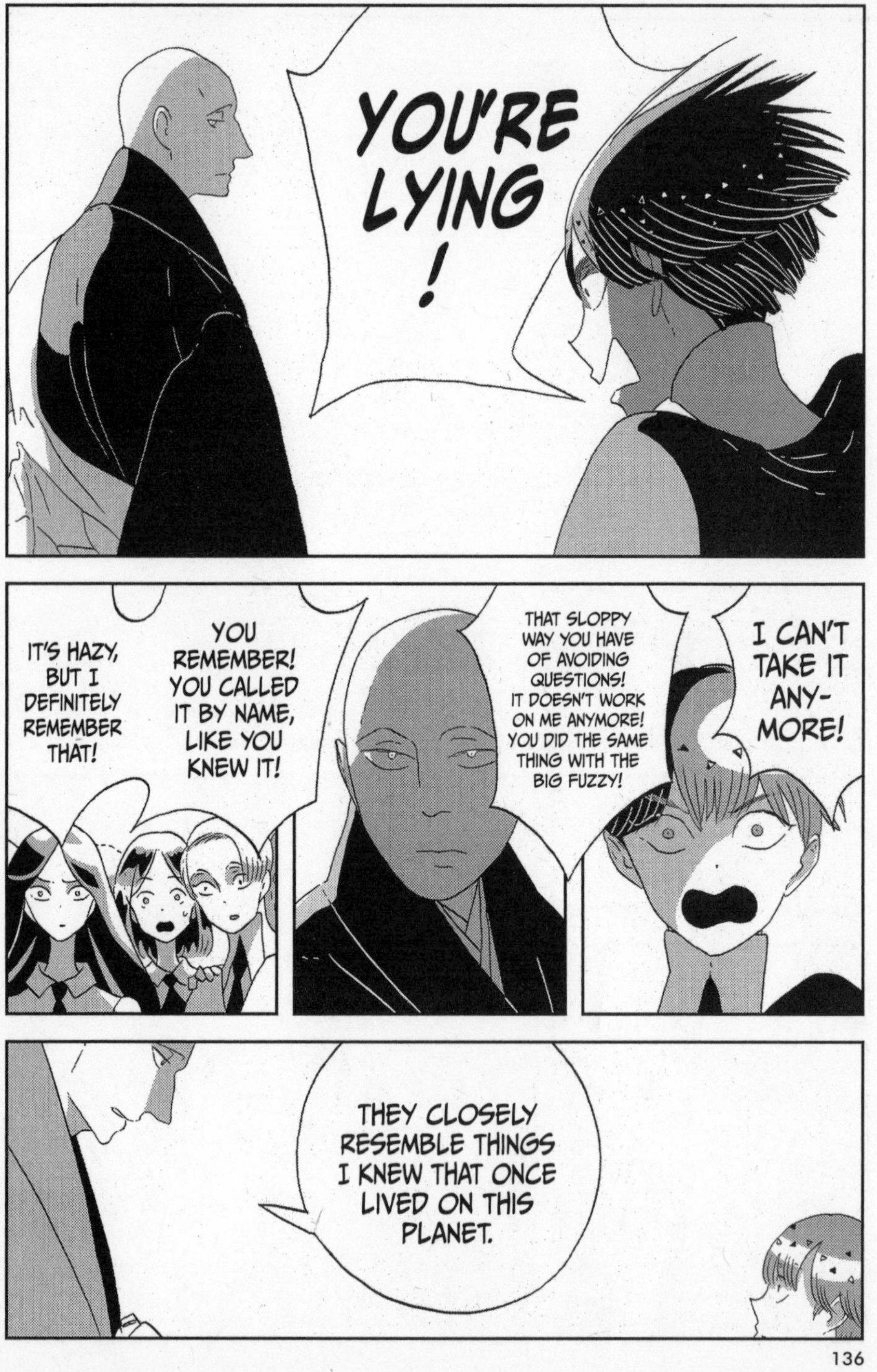
YOU'RE LYING!
I CAN'T TAKE IT ANY-MORE!
THAT SLOPPY WAY YOU HAVE OF AVOIDING QUESTIONS! IT DOESN'T WORK ON ME ANYMORE! YOU DID THE SAME THING WITH THE BIG FUZZY!
YOU REMEMBER! YOU CALLED IT BY NAME, LIKE YOU KNEW IT!
IT'S HAZY, BUT I DEFINITELY REMEMBER THAT!
THEY CLOSELY RESEMBLE THINGS I KNEW THAT ONCE LIVED ON THIS PLANET.

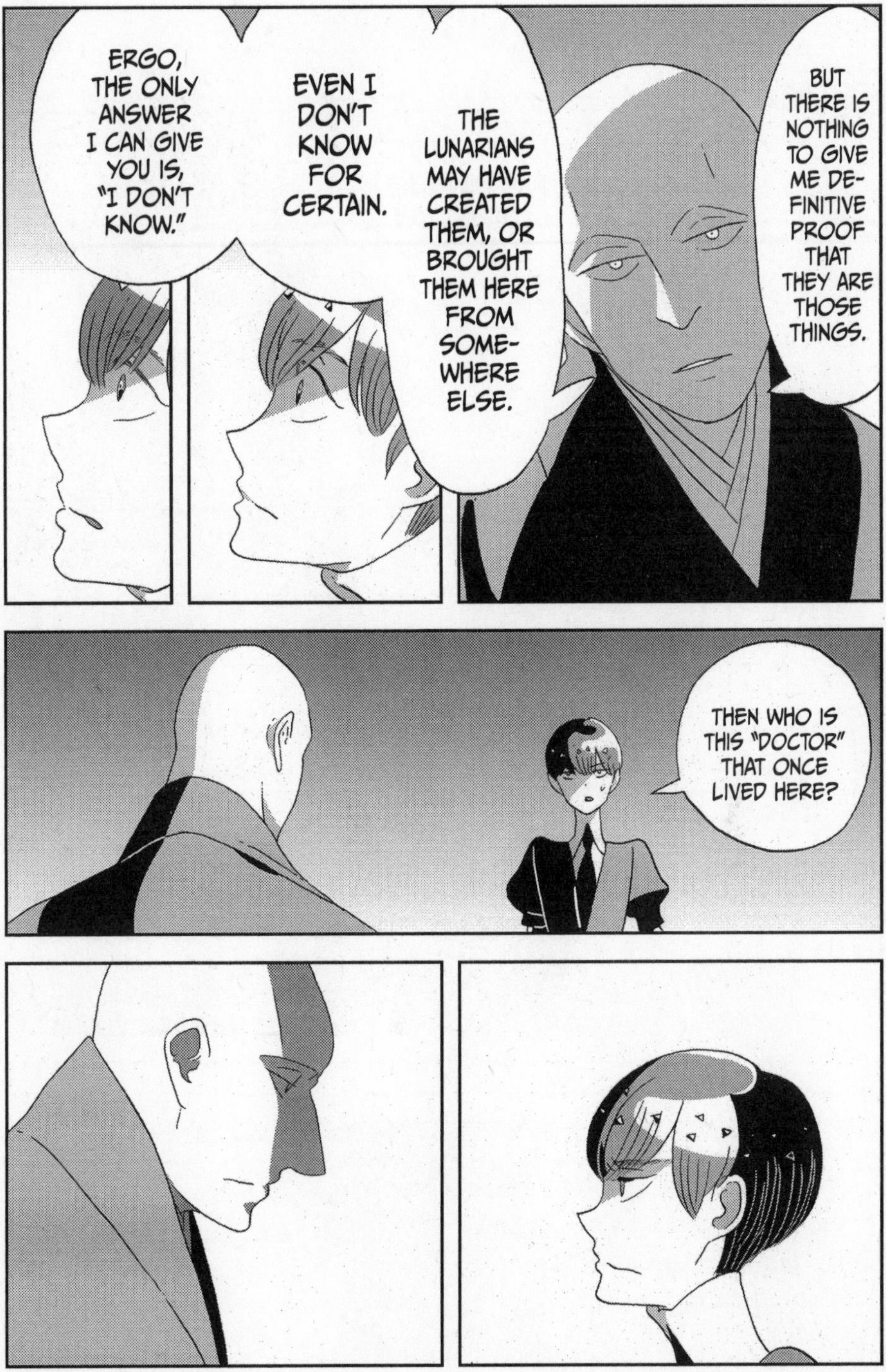
BUT THERE IS NOTHING TO GIVE ME DEFINITIVE PROOF THAT THEY ARE THOSE THINGS.
THE LUNARIANS MAY HAVE CREATED THEM, OR BROUGHT THEM HERE FROM SOMEWHERE ELSE.
EVEN I DON'T KNOW FOR CERTAIN.
ERGO, THE ONLY ANSWER I CAN GIVE YOU IS, "I DON'T KNOW."
THEN WHO IS THIS "DOCTOR" THAT ONCE LIVED HERE?

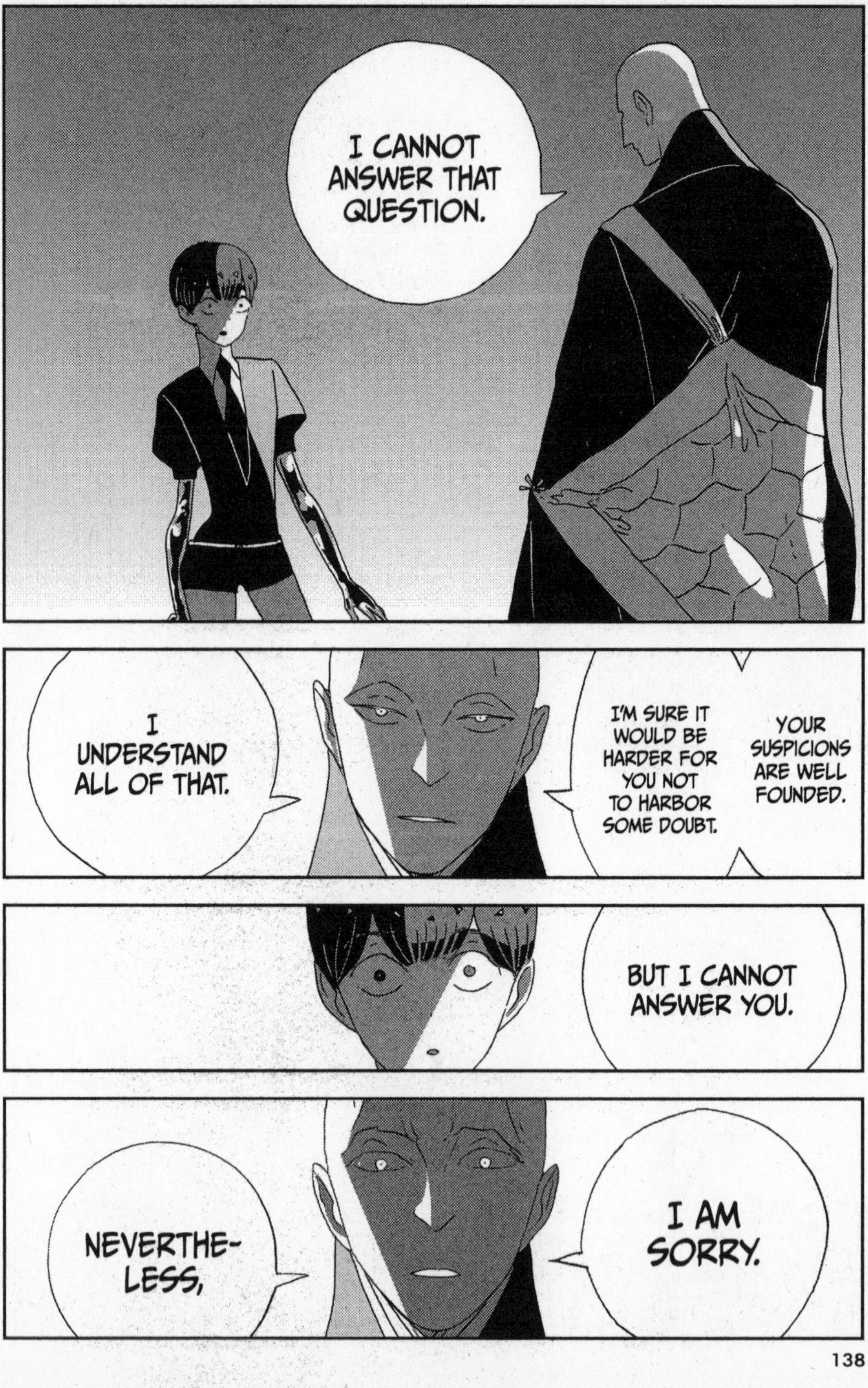
I CANNOT ANSWER THAT QUESTION.
YOUR SUSPICIONS ARE WELL FOUNDED.
I'M SURE IT WOULD BE HARDER FOR YOU NOT TO HARBOR SOME DOUBT.
I UNDERSTAND ALL OF THAT.
BUT I CANNOT ANSWER YOU.
I AM SORRY.
NEVERTHE-LESS,

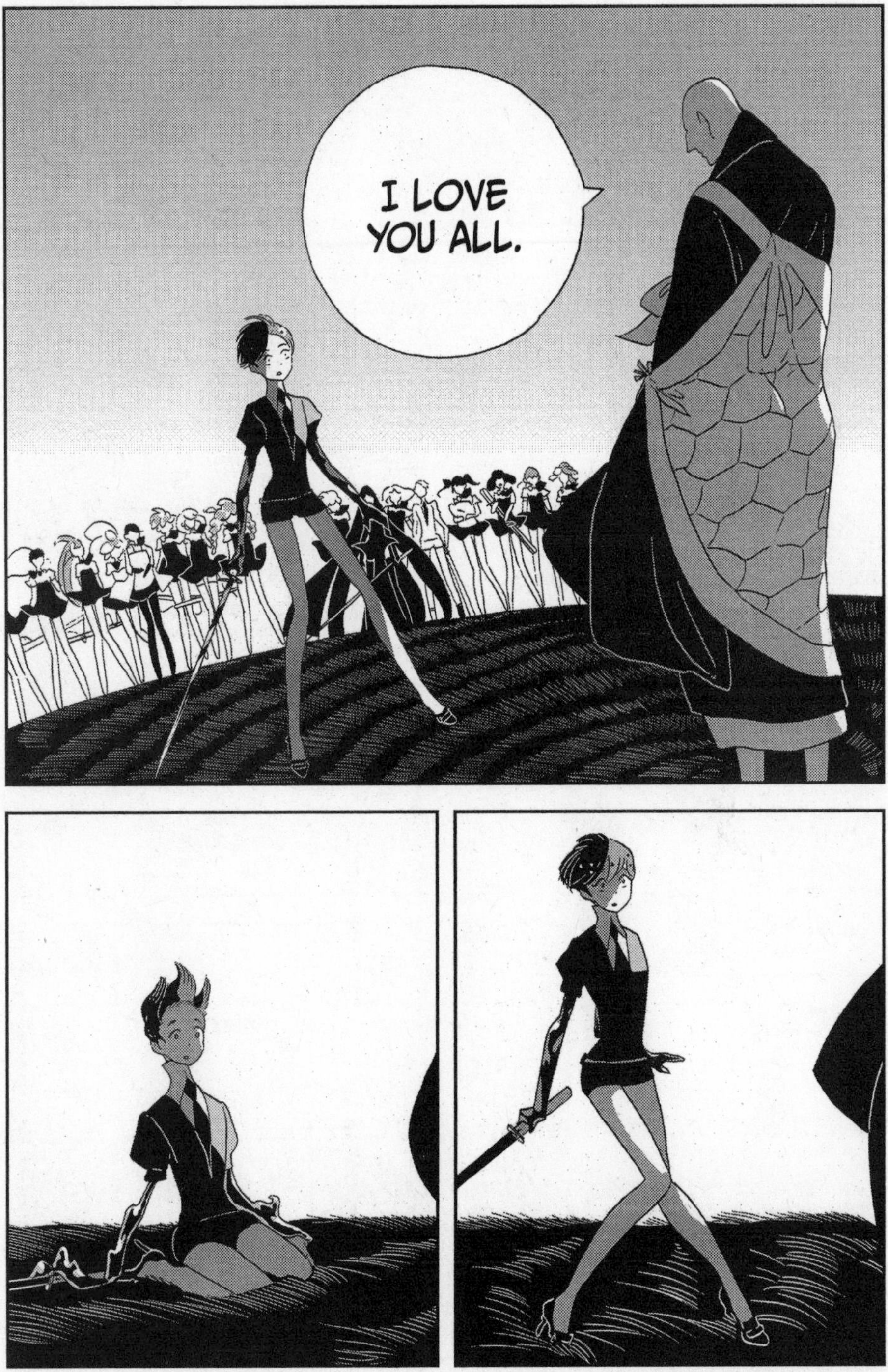
I LOVE YOU ALL.

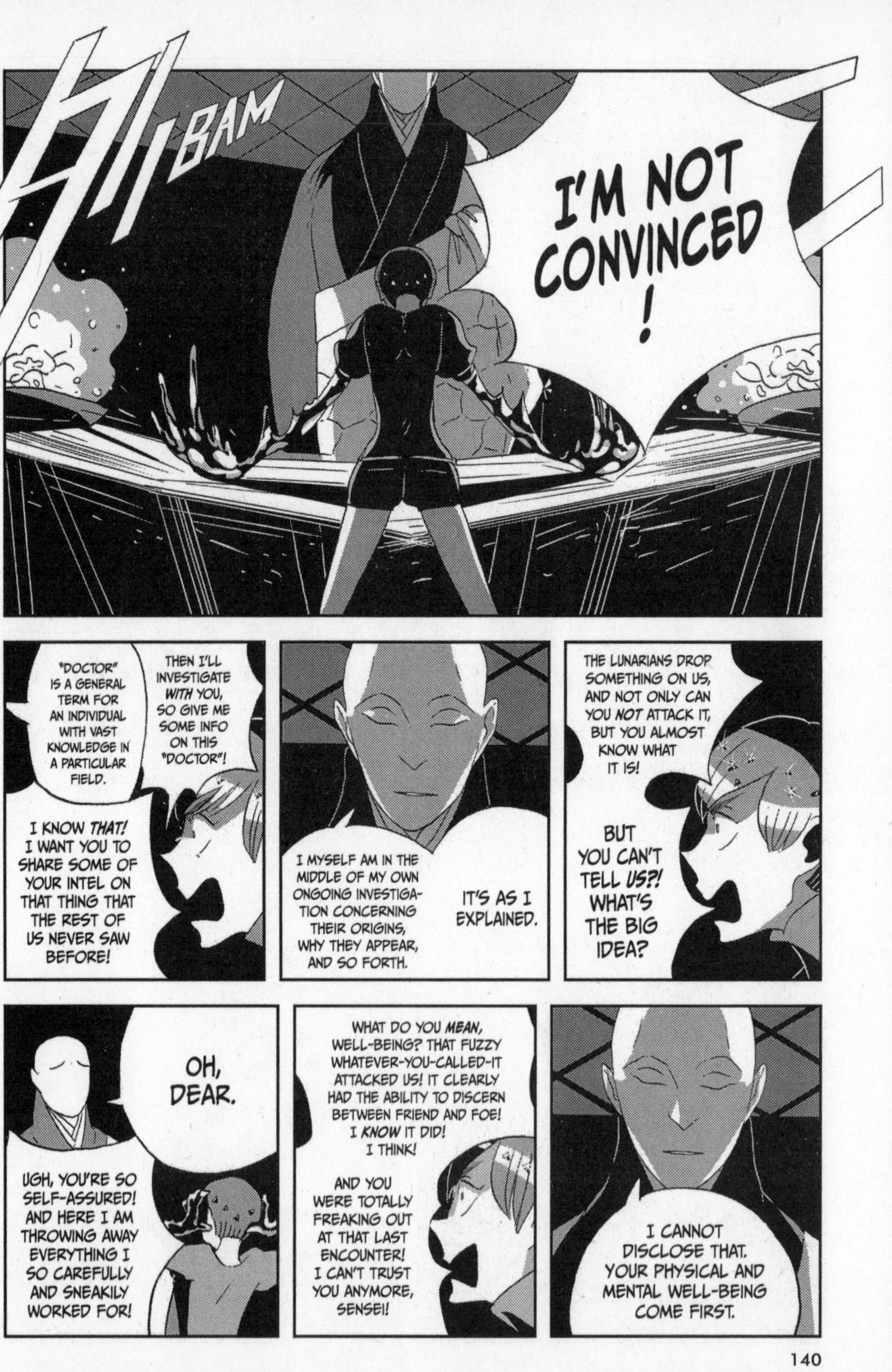
I'M NOT CONVINCED!
BAM
THE LUNARIANS DROP SOMETHING ON US, AND NOT ONLY CAN YOU *NOT* ATTACK IT, BUT YOU ALMOST KNOW WHAT IT IS!
BUT YOU CAN'T TELL *US?!* WHAT'S THE BIG IDEA?
IT'S AS I EXPLAINED.
I MYSELF AM IN THE MIDDLE OF MY OWN ONGOING INVESTIGATION CONCERNING THEIR ORIGINS, WHY THEY APPEAR, AND SO FORTH.
THEN I'LL INVESTIGATE *WITH* YOU, SO GIVE ME SOME INFO ON THIS "DOCTOR"!
"DOCTOR" IS A GENERAL TERM FOR AN INDIVIDUAL WITH VAST KNOWLEDGE IN A PARTICULAR FIELD.
I KNOW *THAT!* I WANT YOU TO SHARE SOME OF YOUR INTEL ON THAT THING THAT THE REST OF US NEVER SAW BEFORE!
I CANNOT DISCLOSE THAT. YOUR PHYSICAL AND MENTAL WELL-BEING COME FIRST.
WHAT DO YOU *MEAN*, WELL-BEING? THAT FUZZY WHATEVER-YOU-CALLED-IT ATTACKED US! IT CLEARLY HAD THE ABILITY TO DISCERN BETWEEN FRIEND AND FOE! I *KNOW* IT DID! I THINK!
AND YOU WERE TOTALLY FREAKING OUT AT THAT LAST ENCOUNTER! I CAN'T TRUST YOU ANYMORE, SENSEI!
OH, DEAR.
UGH, YOU'RE SO SELF-ASSURED! AND HERE I AM THROWING AWAY EVERYTHING I SO CAREFULLY AND SNEAKILY WORKED FOR!

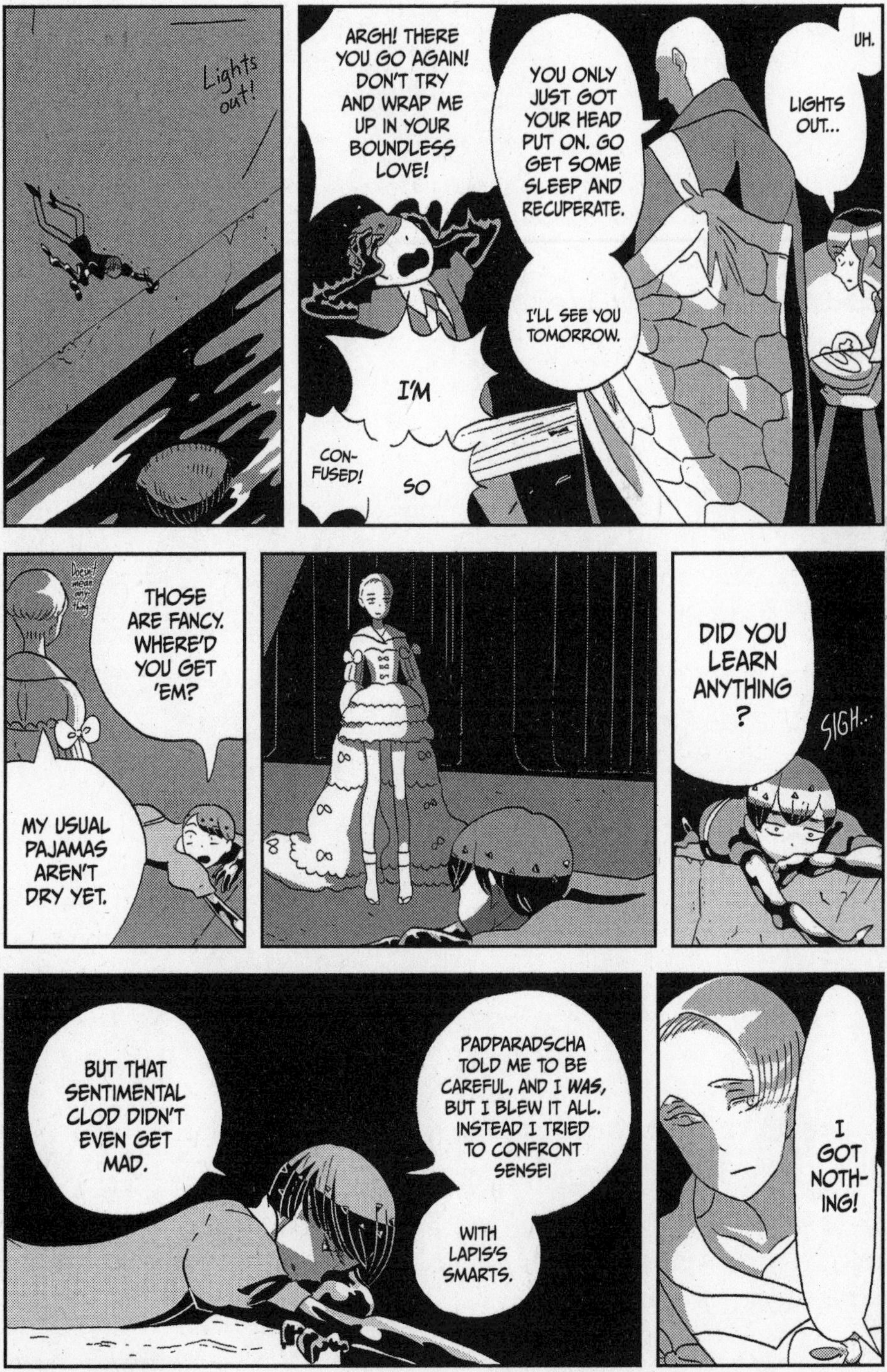
UH.
LIGHTS OUT...
YOU ONLY JUST GOT YOUR HEAD PUT ON. GO GET SOME SLEEP AND RECUPERATE.
I'LL SEE YOU TOMORROW.
ARGH! THERE YOU GO AGAIN! DON'T TRY AND WRAP ME UP IN YOUR BOUNDLESS LOVE!
I'M SO CON-FUSED!
Lights out!
DID YOU LEARN ANYTHING?
SIGH...
Doesn't mean any-thing
THOSE ARE FANCY. WHERE'D YOU GET 'EM?
MY USUAL PAJAMAS AREN'T DRY YET.
I GOT NOTH-ING!
PADPARADSCHA TOLD ME TO BE CAREFUL, AND I *WAS*, BUT I BLEW IT ALL. INSTEAD I TRIED TO CONFRONT SENSEI
WITH LAPIS'S SMARTS.
BUT THAT SENTIMENTAL CLOD DIDN'T EVEN GET MAD.

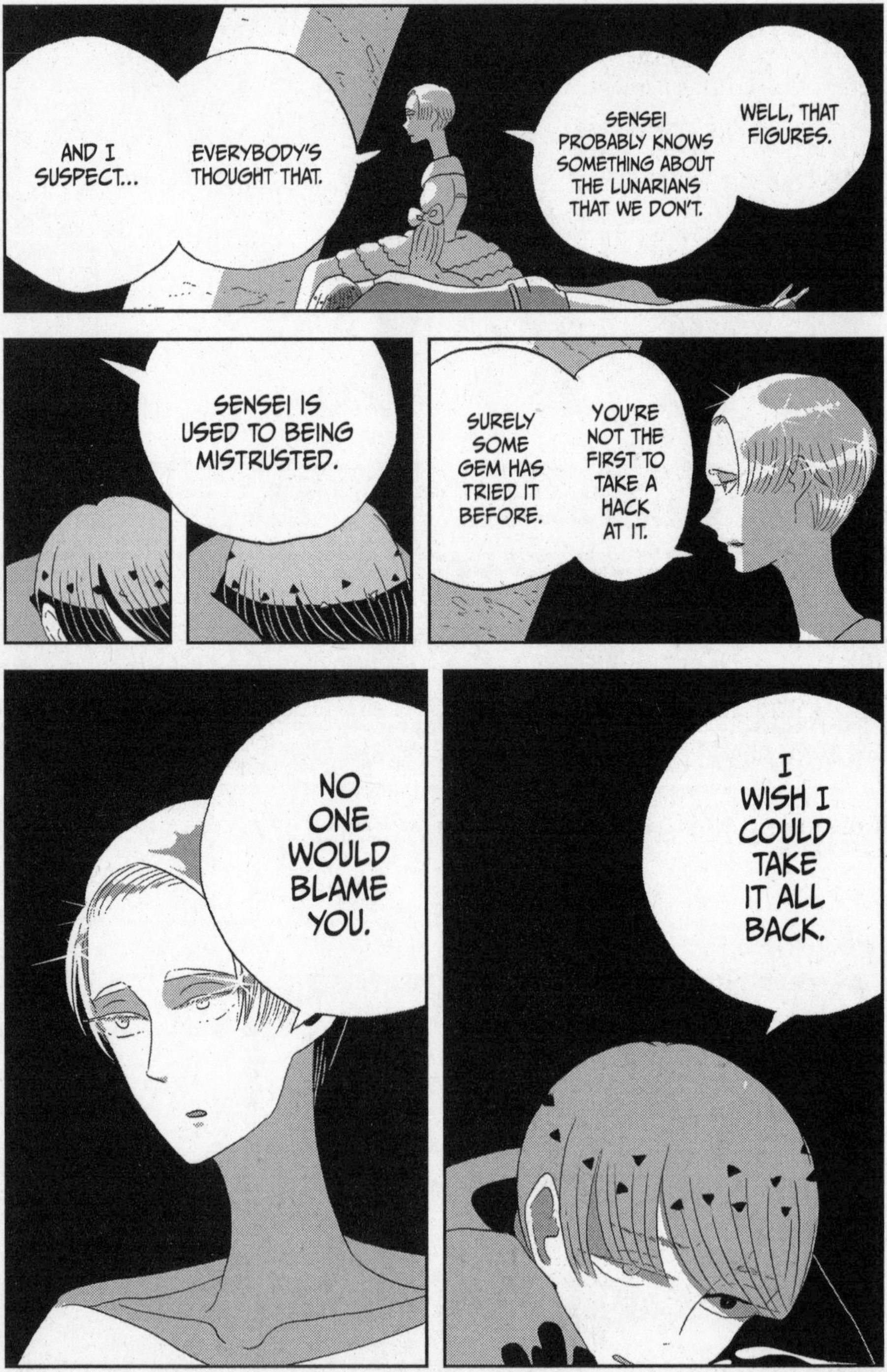
WELL, THAT FIGURES.
SENSEI PROBABLY KNOWS SOMETHING ABOUT THE LUNARIANS THAT WE DON'T.
EVERYBODY'S THOUGHT THAT.
AND I SUSPECT...
YOU'RE NOT THE FIRST TO TAKE A HACK AT IT.
SURELY SOME GEM HAS TRIED IT BEFORE.
SENSEI IS USED TO BEING MISTRUSTED.
I WISH I COULD TAKE IT ALL BACK.
NO ONE WOULD BLAME YOU.

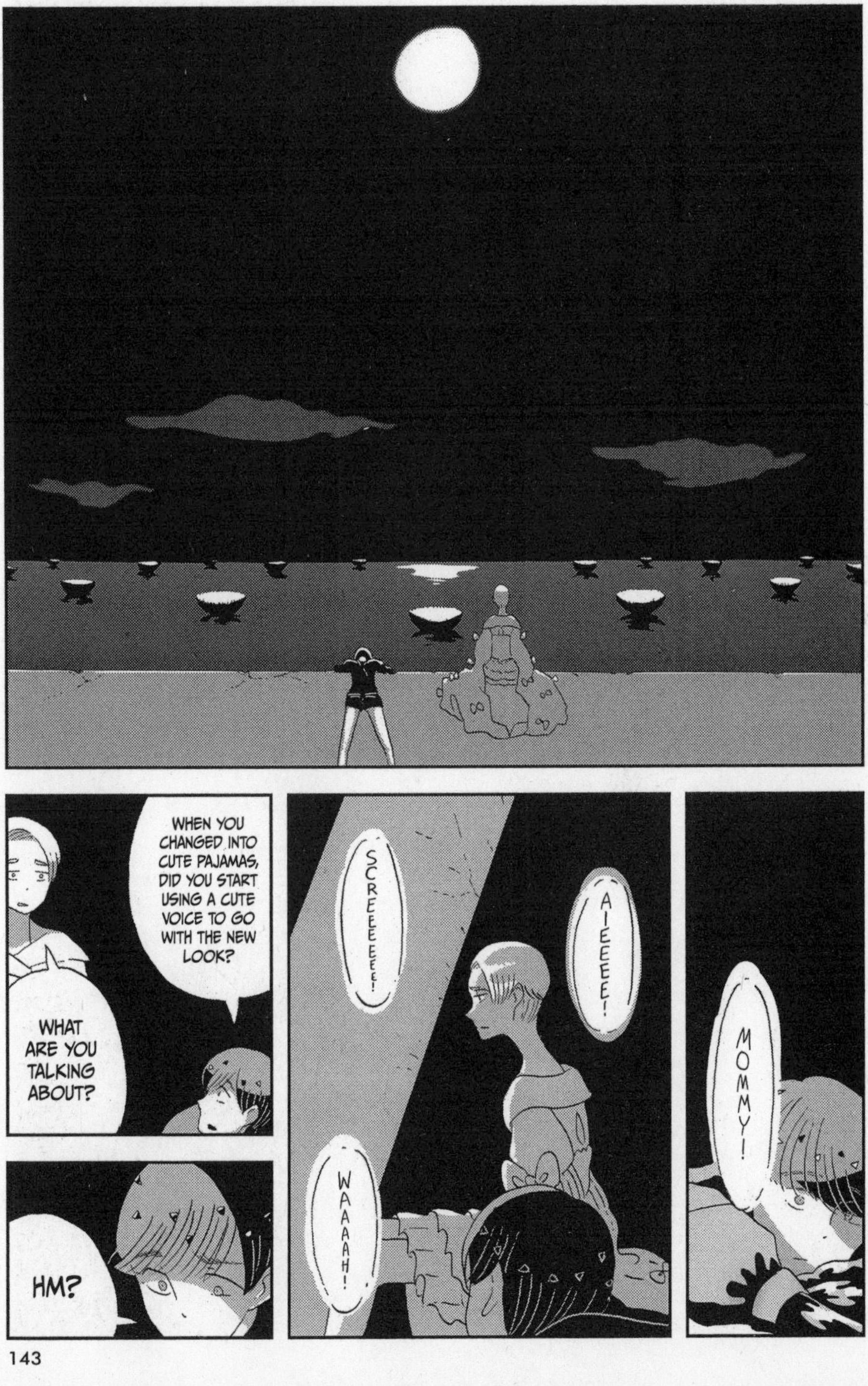

MOMMY!
AIEEEEE!
SCREEEEEEE!
WAAAAH!
WHEN YOU CHANGED INTO CUTE PAJAMAS, DID YOU START USING A CUTE VOICE TO GO WITH THE NEW LOOK?
WHAT ARE YOU TALKING ABOUT?
HM?

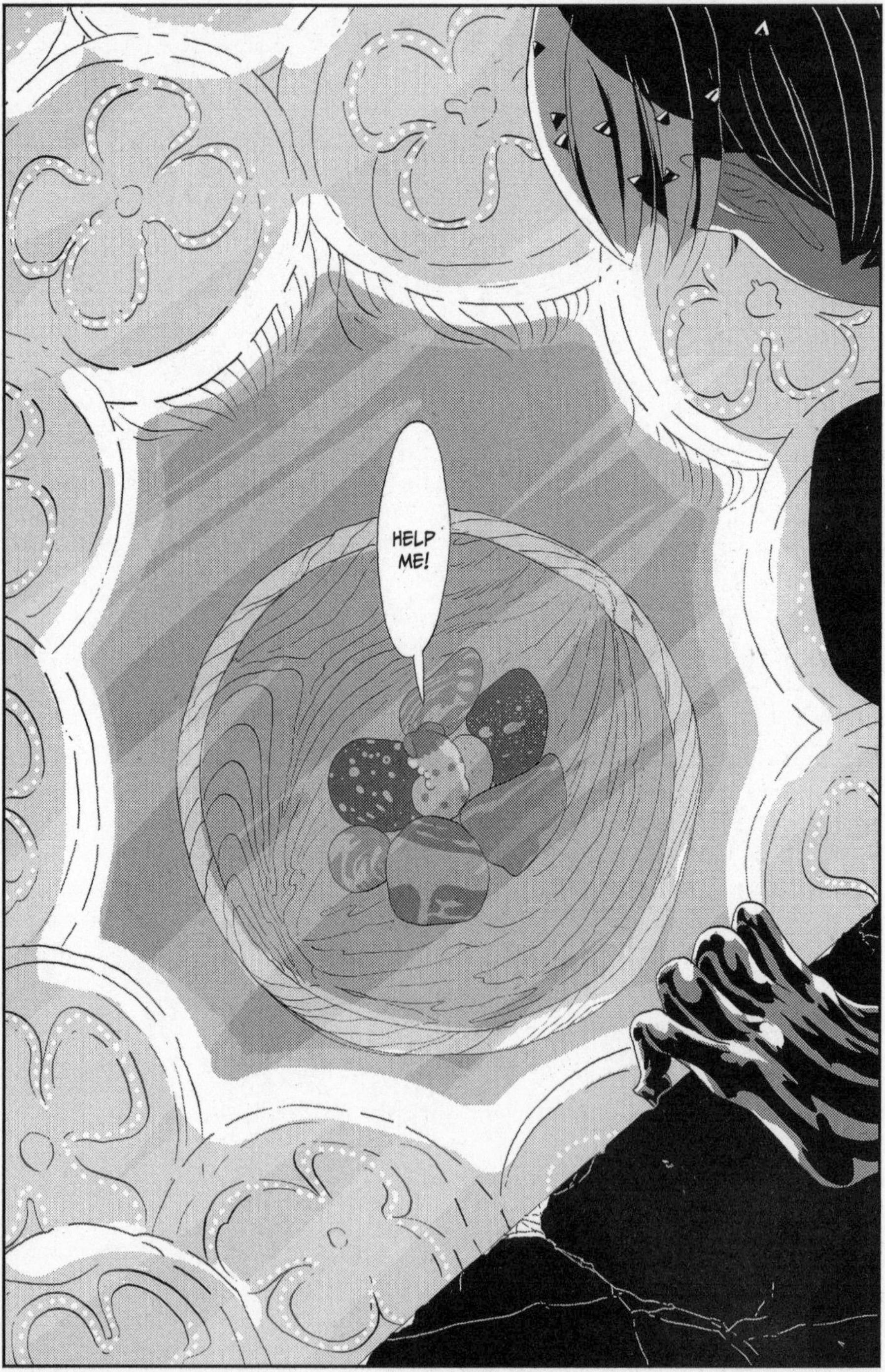
HELP ME!

CHAPTER 50: The Doctor END

CHAPTER 51:

Legend

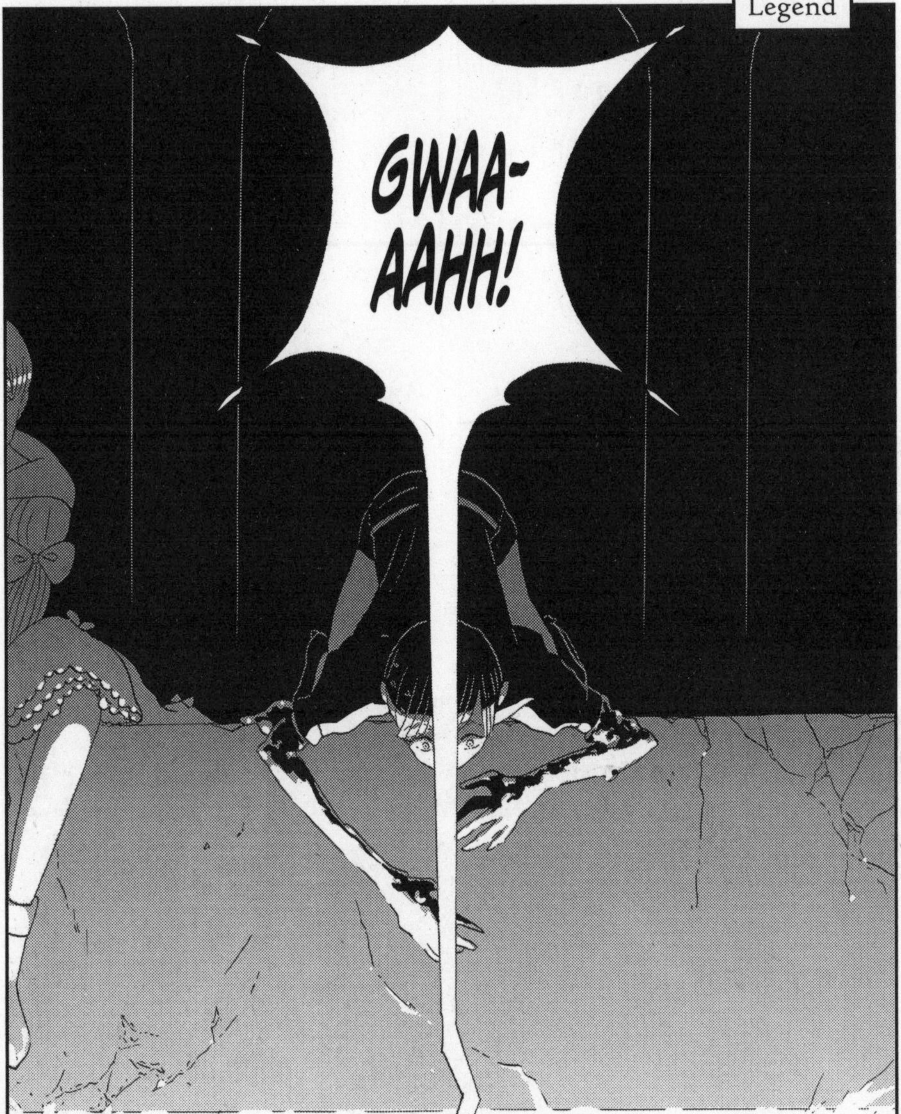

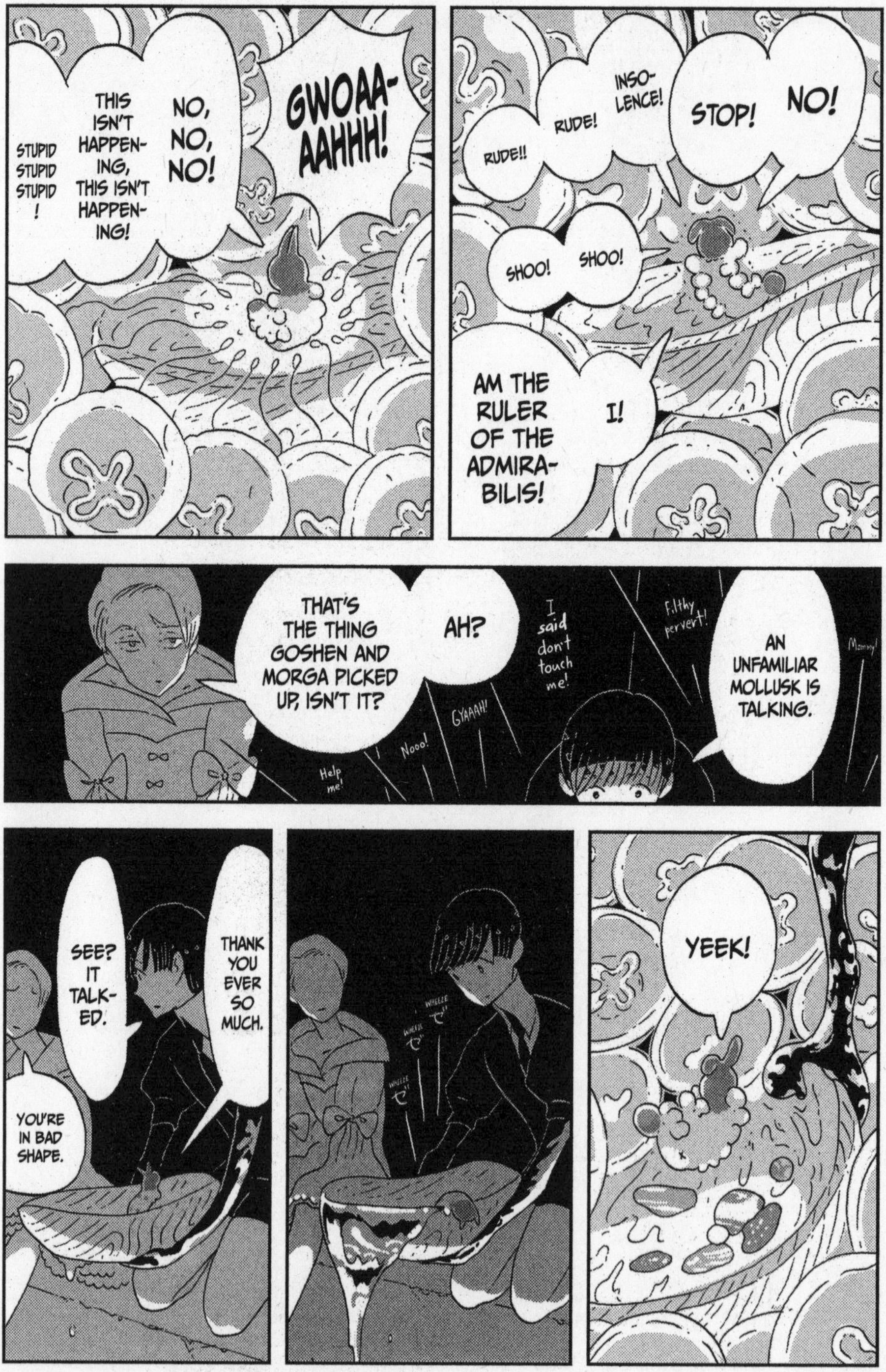
NO!
STOP!
INSO-LENCE!
RUDE!
RUDE!!
SHOO!
SHOO!
I!
AM THE RULER OF THE ADMIRA-BILIS!
GWOAA-AAHHH!
NO, NO, NO!
THIS ISN'T HAPPEN-ING, THIS ISN'T HAPPEN-ING!
STUPID STUPID STUPID!
Mommy!
AN UNFAMILIAR MOLLUSK IS TALKING.
Filthy pervert!
I said don't touch me!
AH?
THAT'S THE THING GOSHEN AND MORGA PICKED UP, ISN'T IT?
GYAAAH!
Nooo!
Help me!
YEEK!
THANK YOU EVER SO MUCH.
SEE? IT TALK-ED.
YOU'RE IN BAD SHAPE.

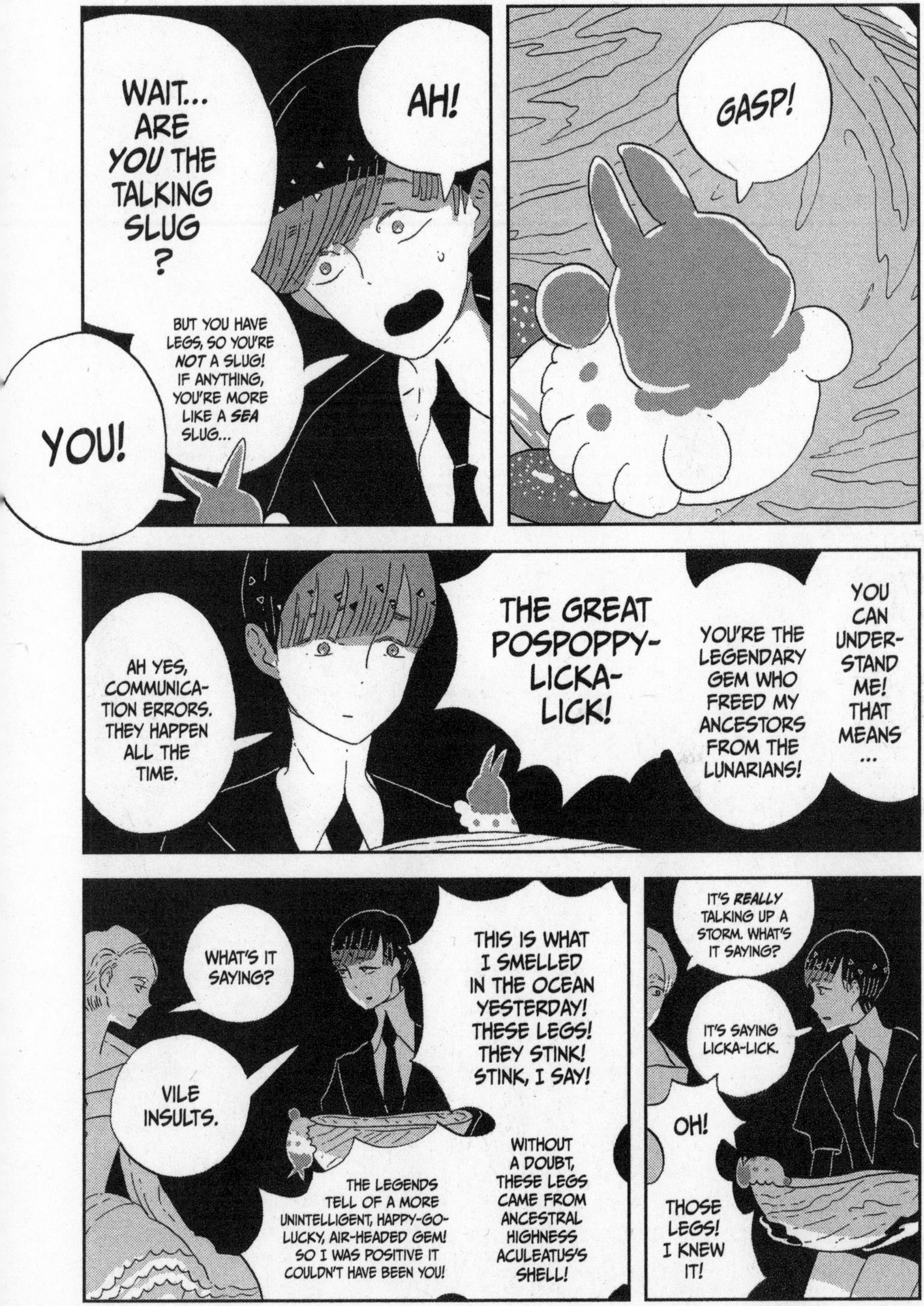

GASP!
AH!
WAIT... ARE *YOU* THE TALKING SLUG?
BUT YOU HAVE LEGS, SO YOU'RE *NOT* A SLUG! IF ANYTHING, YOU'RE MORE LIKE A *SEA* SLUG...
YOU!
YOU CAN UNDER-STAND ME! THAT MEANS ...
YOU'RE THE LEGENDARY GEM WHO FREED MY ANCESTORS FROM THE LUNARIANS!
THE GREAT POSPOPPY-LICKA-LICK!
AH YES, COMMUNICA-TION ERRORS. THEY HAPPEN ALL THE TIME.
IT'S *REALLY* TALKING UP A STORM. WHAT'S IT SAYING?
IT'S SAYING LICKA-LICK.
OH!
THOSE LEGS! I KNEW IT!
THIS IS WHAT I SMELLED IN THE OCEAN YESTERDAY! THESE LEGS! THEY STINK! STINK, I SAY!
WHAT'S IT SAYING?
VILE INSULTS.
WITHOUT A DOUBT, THESE LEGS CAME FROM ANCESTRAL HIGHNESS ACULEATUS'S SHELL!
THE LEGENDS TELL OF A MORE UNINTELLIGENT, HAPPY-GO-LUCKY, AIR-HEADED GEM! SO I WAS POSITIVE IT COULDN'T HAVE BEEN YOU!

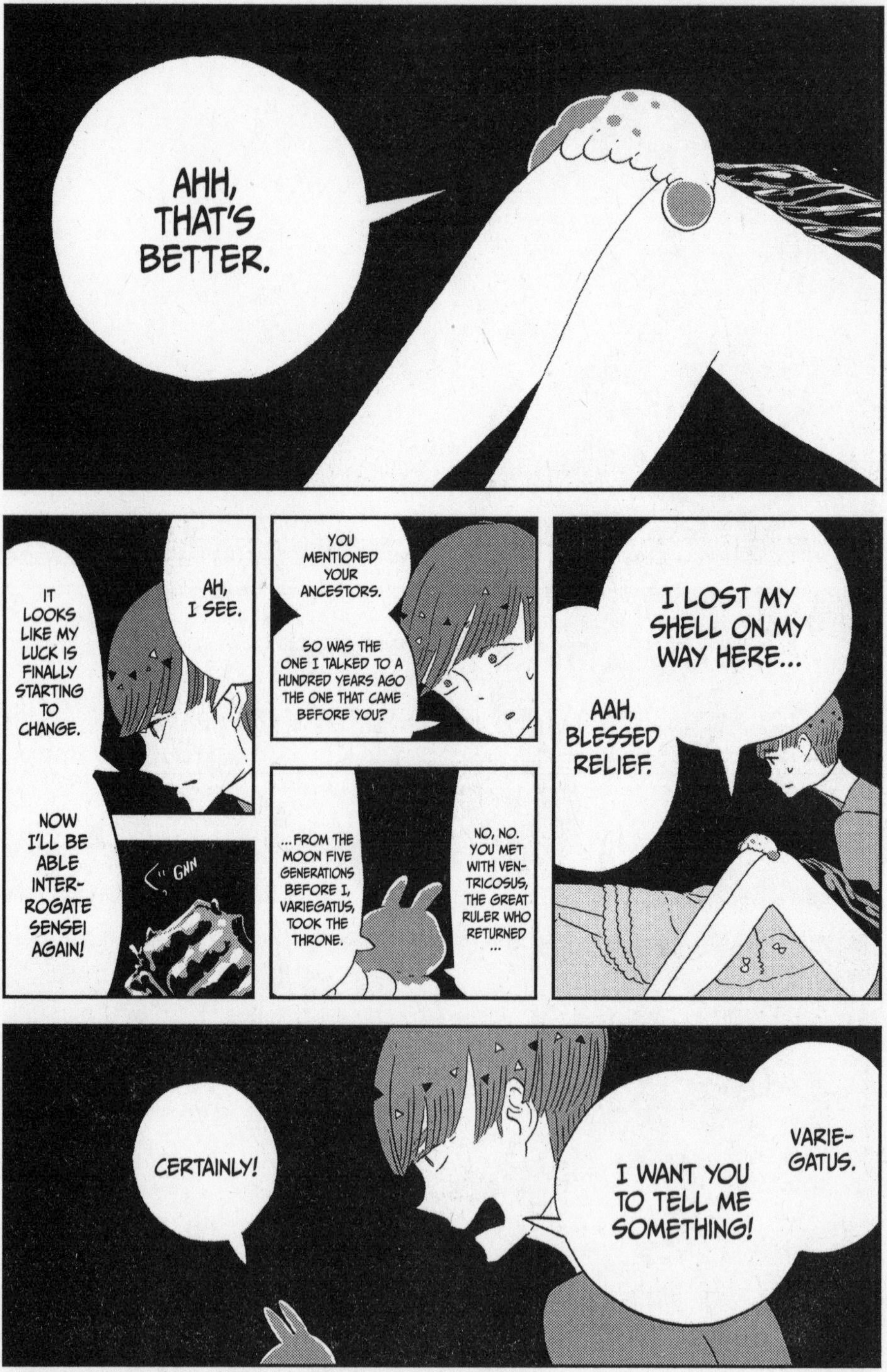
AHH, THAT'S BETTER.
I LOST MY SHELL ON MY WAY HERE...
AAH, BLESSED RELIEF.
YOU MENTIONED YOUR ANCESTORS.
SO WAS THE ONE I TALKED TO A HUNDRED YEARS AGO THE ONE THAT CAME BEFORE YOU?
NO, NO. YOU MET WITH VEN-TRICOSUS, THE GREAT RULER WHO RETURNED ...
...FROM THE MOON FIVE GENERATIONS BEFORE I, VARIEGATUS, TOOK THE THRONE.
AH, I SEE.
IT LOOKS LIKE MY LUCK IS FINALLY STARTING TO CHANGE.
GNN
NOW I'LL BE ABLE INTER-ROGATE SENSEI AGAIN!
VARIE-GATUS.
I WANT YOU TO TELL ME SOMETHING!
CERTAINLY!

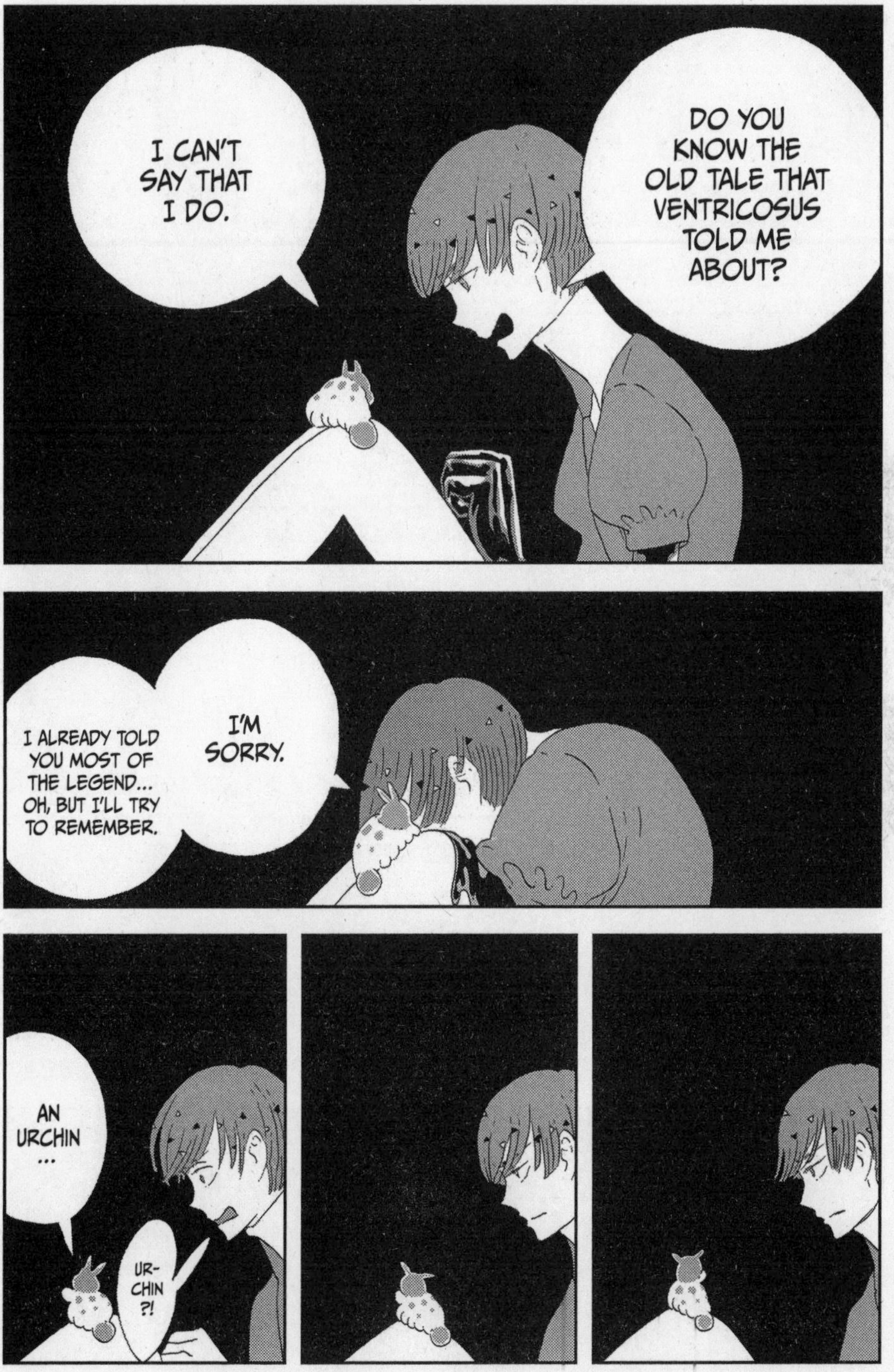
DO YOU KNOW THE OLD TALE THAT VENTRICOSUS TOLD ME ABOUT?
I CAN'T SAY THAT I DO.
I'M SORRY.
I ALREADY TOLD YOU MOST OF THE LEGEND... OH, BUT I'LL TRY TO REMEMBER.
AN URCHIN ...
UR-CHIN ?!

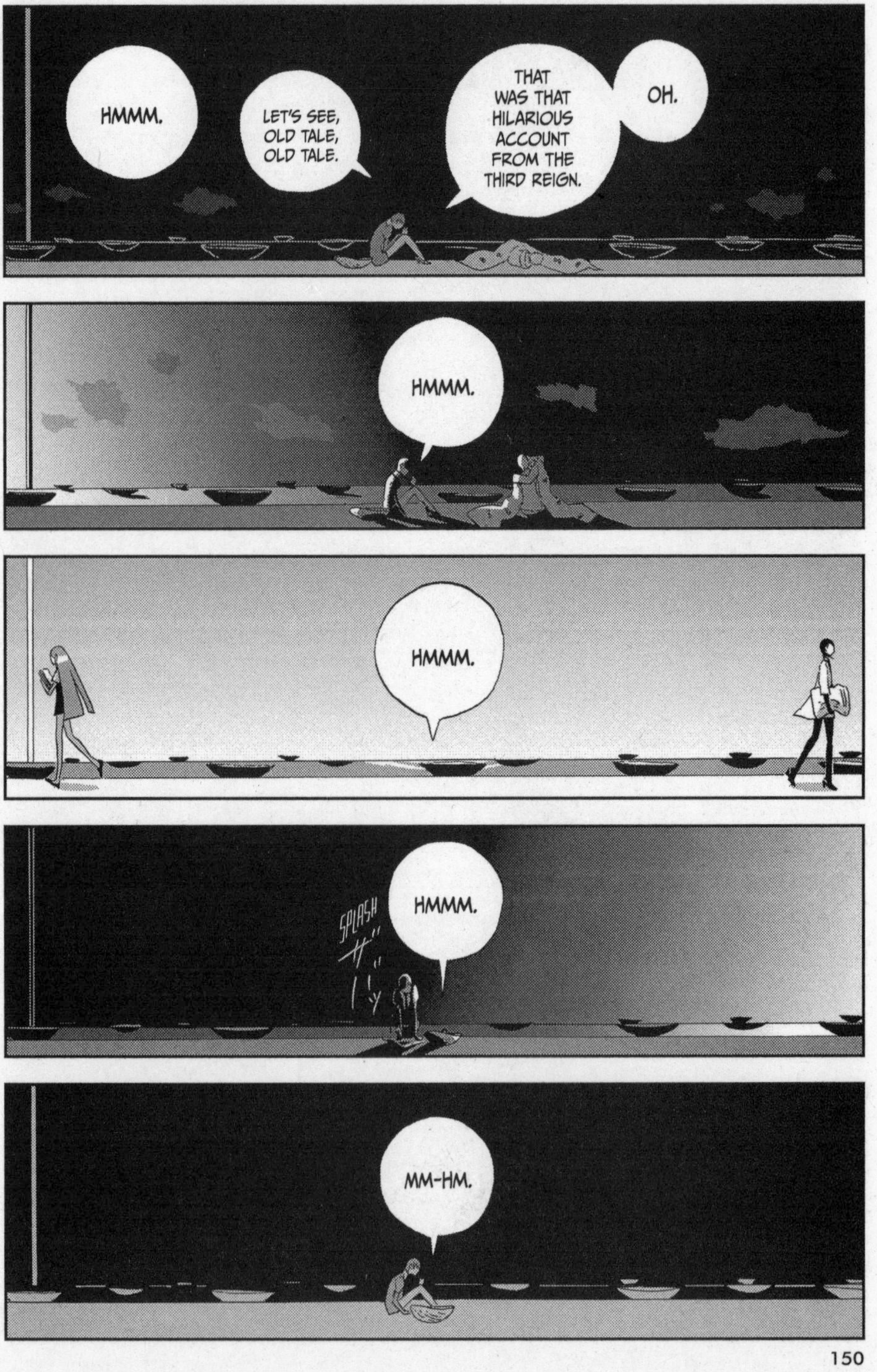
OH.
THAT WAS THAT HILARIOUS ACCOUNT FROM THE THIRD REIGN.
LET'S SEE, OLD TALE, OLD TALE.
HMMM.
HMMM.
HMMM.
HMMM.
SPLASH
MM-HM.

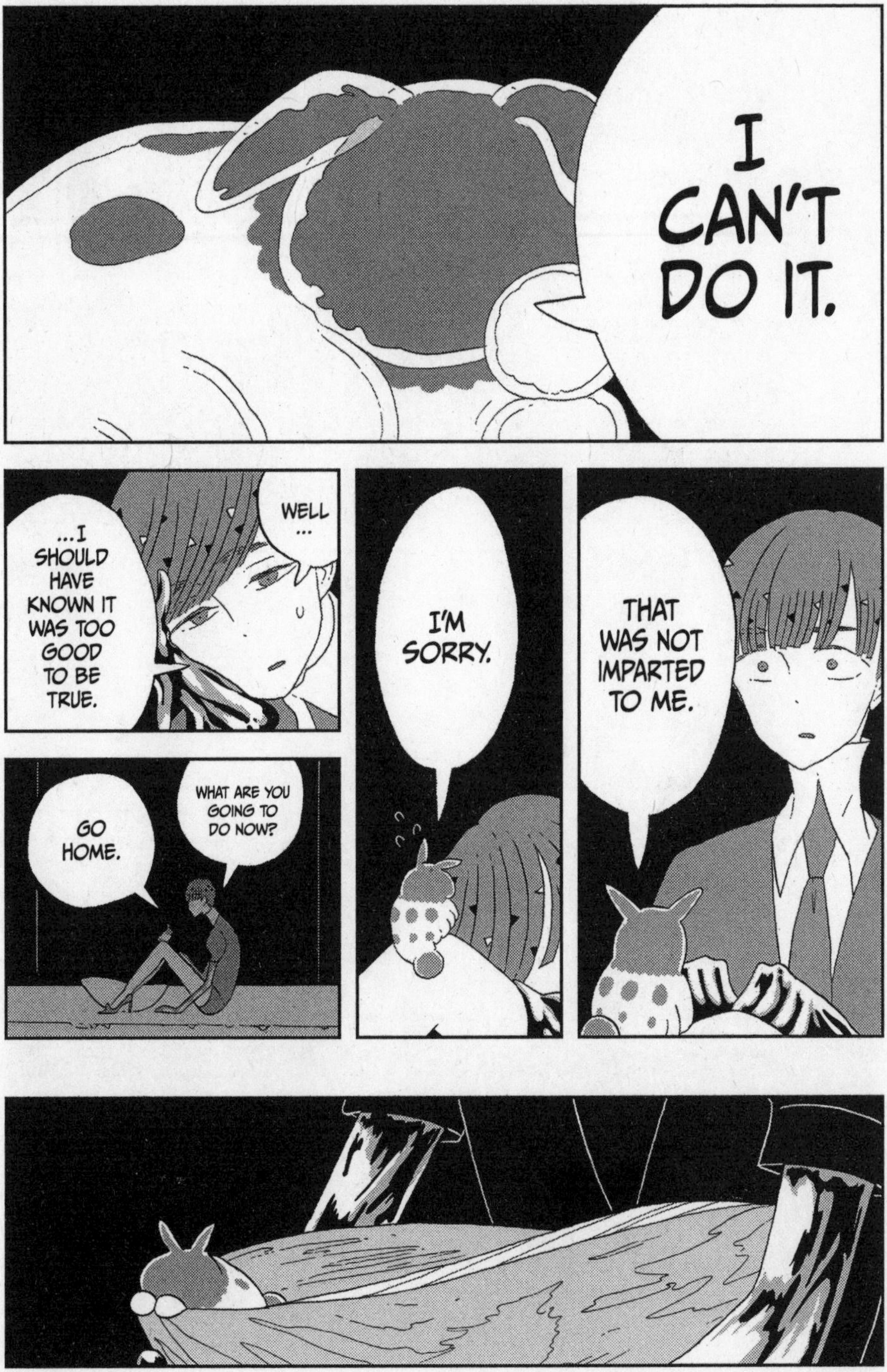
I CAN'T DO IT.
THAT WAS NOT IMPARTED TO ME.
I'M SORRY.
WELL ...
...I SHOULD HAVE KNOWN IT WAS TOO GOOD TO BE TRUE.
WHAT ARE YOU GOING TO DO NOW?
GO HOME.

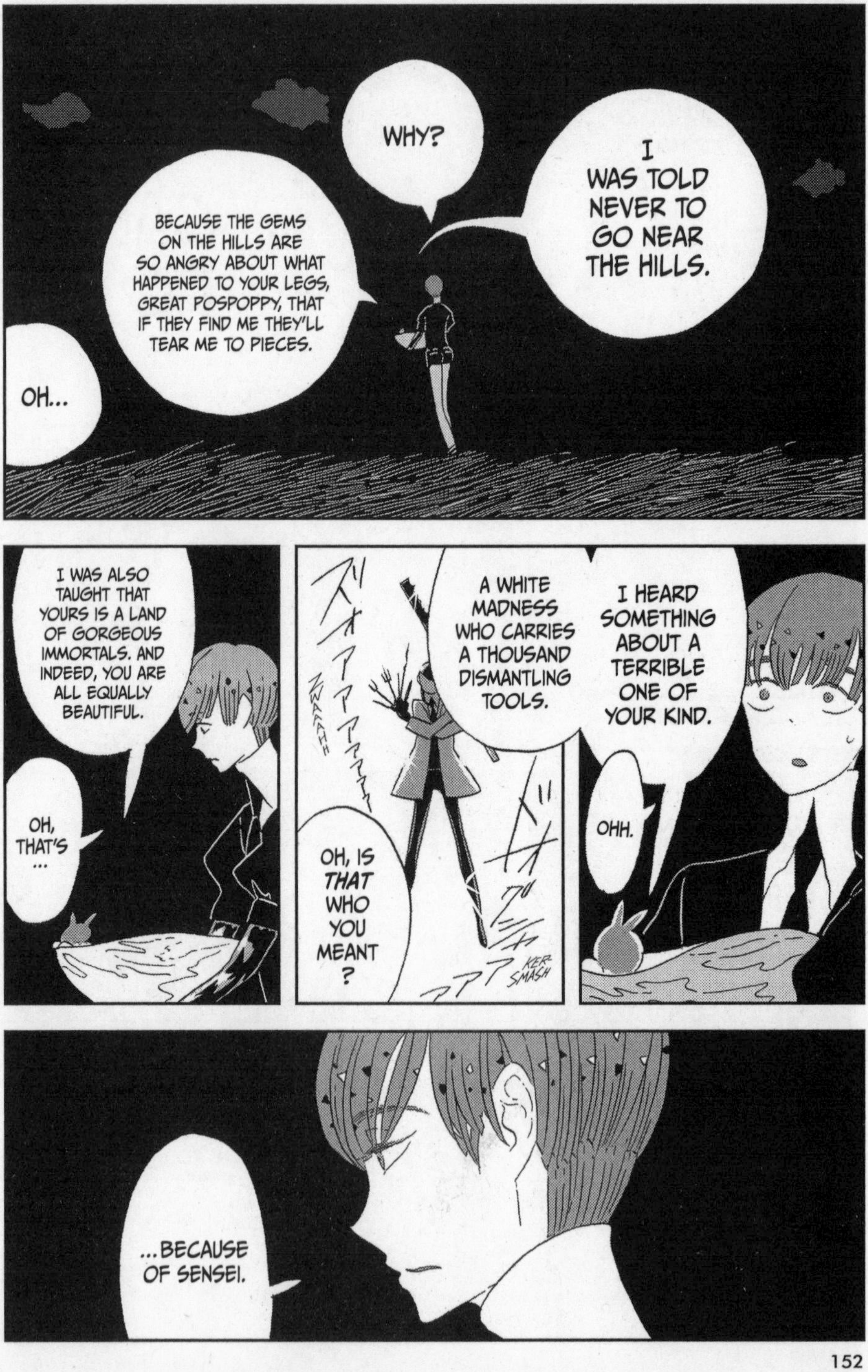
I WAS TOLD NEVER TO GO NEAR THE HILLS.
WHY?
BECAUSE THE GEMS ON THE HILLS ARE SO ANGRY ABOUT WHAT HAPPENED TO YOUR LEGS, GREAT POSPOPPY, THAT IF THEY FIND ME THEY'LL TEAR ME TO PIECES.
OH...
I HEARD SOMETHING ABOUT A TERRIBLE ONE OF YOUR KIND.
OHH.
A WHITE MADNESS WHO CARRIES A THOUSAND DISMANTLING TOOLS.
ZWAAAHH
KER-SMASH
OH, IS *THAT* WHO YOU MEANT?
I WAS ALSO TAUGHT THAT YOURS IS A LAND OF GORGEOUS IMMORTALS. AND INDEED, YOU ARE ALL EQUALLY BEAUTIFUL.
OH, THAT'S ...
...BECAUSE OF SENSEI.

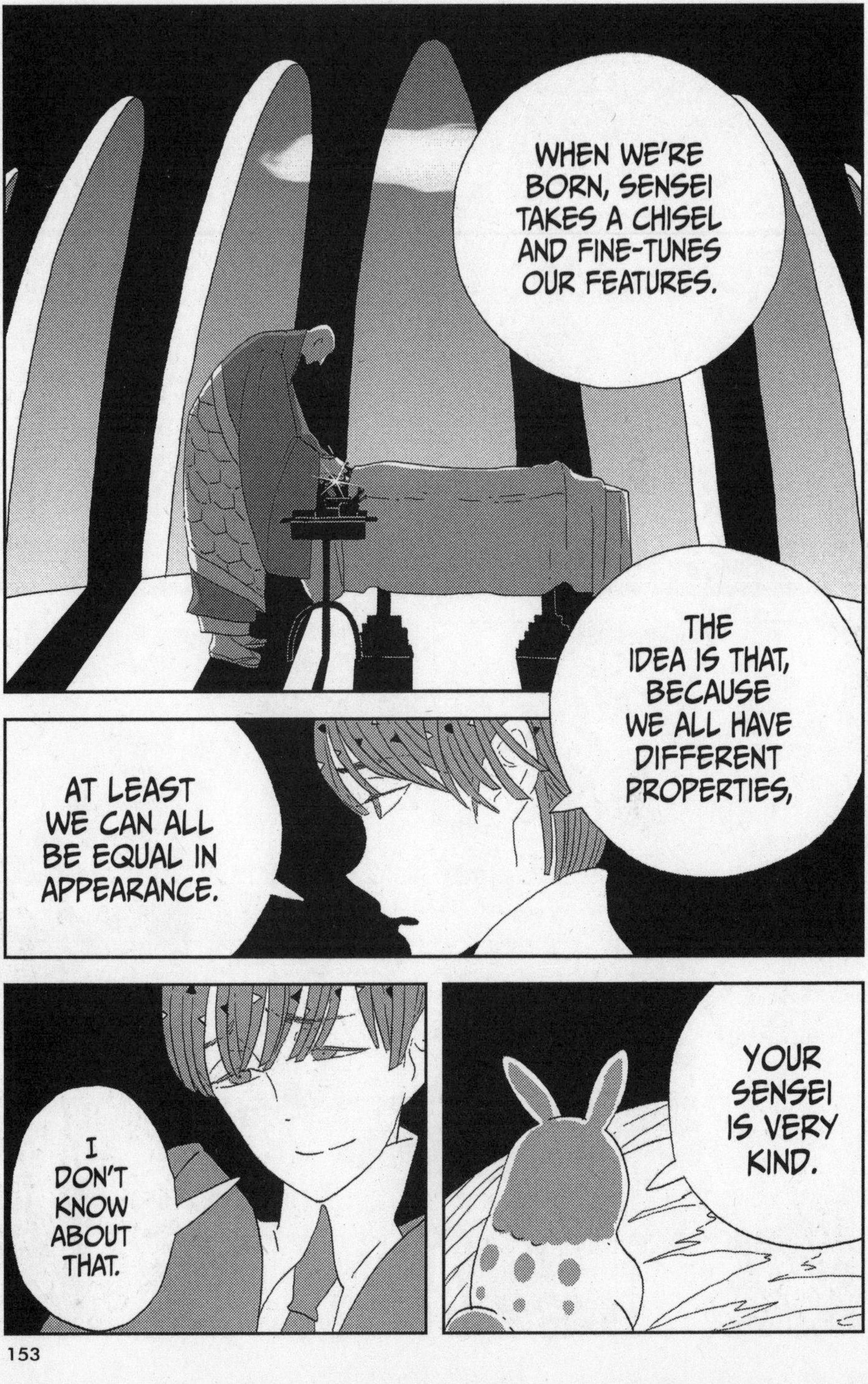
WHEN WE'RE BORN, SENSEI TAKES A CHISEL AND FINE-TUNES OUR FEATURES.
THE IDEA IS THAT, BECAUSE WE ALL HAVE DIFFERENT PROPERTIES,
AT LEAST WE CAN ALL BE EQUAL IN APPEARANCE.
YOUR SENSEI IS VERY KIND.
I DON'T KNOW ABOUT THAT.

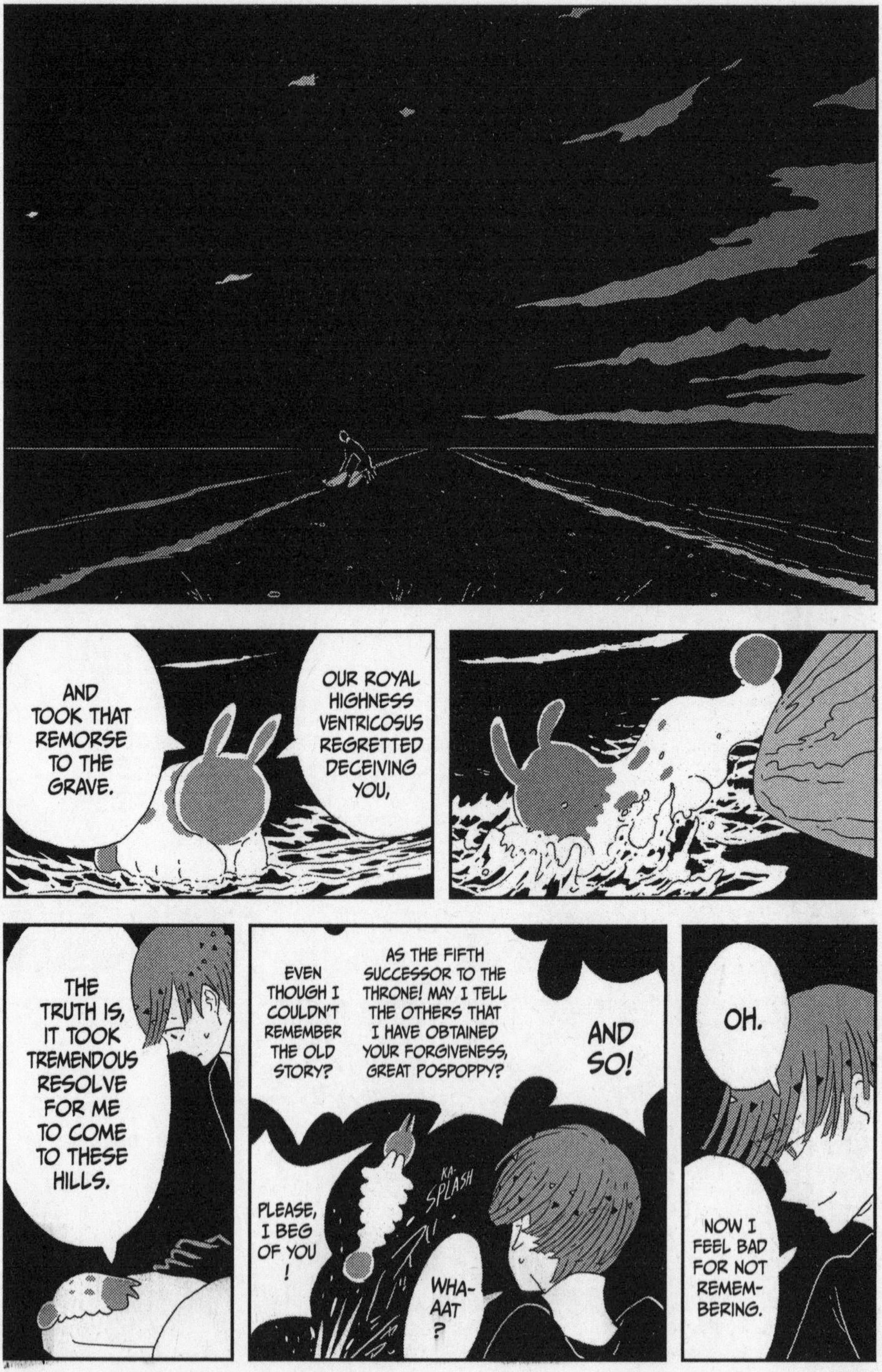
OUR ROYAL HIGHNESS VENTRICOSUS REGRETTED DECEIVING YOU,
AND TOOK THAT REMORSE TO THE GRAVE.
OH.
NOW I FEEL BAD FOR NOT REMEMBERING.
AND SO!
AS THE FIFTH SUCCESSOR TO THE THRONE! MAY I TELL THE OTHERS THAT I HAVE OBTAINED YOUR FORGIVENESS, GREAT POSPOPPY?
EVEN THOUGH I COULDN'T REMEMBER THE OLD STORY?
KA-SPLASH
WHA-AAT?
PLEASE, I BEG OF YOU!
THE TRUTH IS, IT TOOK TREMENDOUS RESOLVE FOR ME TO COME TO THESE HILLS.

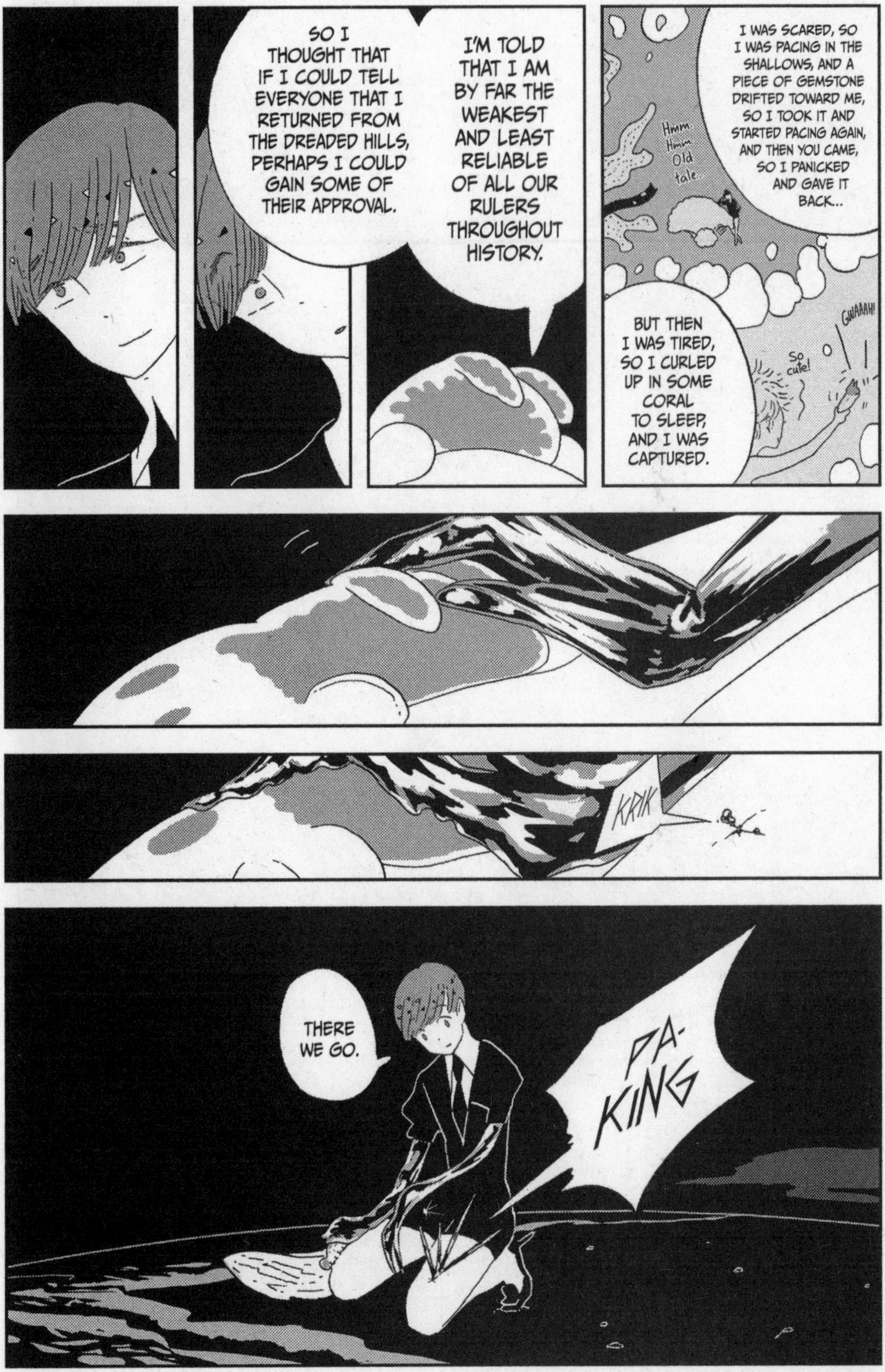
I WAS SCARED, SO I WAS PACING IN THE SHALLOWS, AND A PIECE OF GEMSTONE DRIFTED TOWARD ME, SO I TOOK IT AND STARTED PACING AGAIN, AND THEN YOU CAME, SO I PANICKED AND GAVE IT BACK...
Hmm Hmm Old tale...
GWAAAH!
So cute!
BUT THEN I WAS TIRED, SO I CURLED UP IN SOME CORAL TO SLEEP, AND I WAS CAPTURED.
I'M TOLD THAT I AM BY FAR THE WEAKEST AND LEAST RELIABLE OF ALL OUR RULERS THROUGHOUT HISTORY.
SO I THOUGHT THAT IF I COULD TELL EVERYONE THAT I RETURNED FROM THE DREADED HILLS, PERHAPS I COULD GAIN SOME OF THEIR APPROVAL.
KRIK
PA-KING
THERE WE GO.

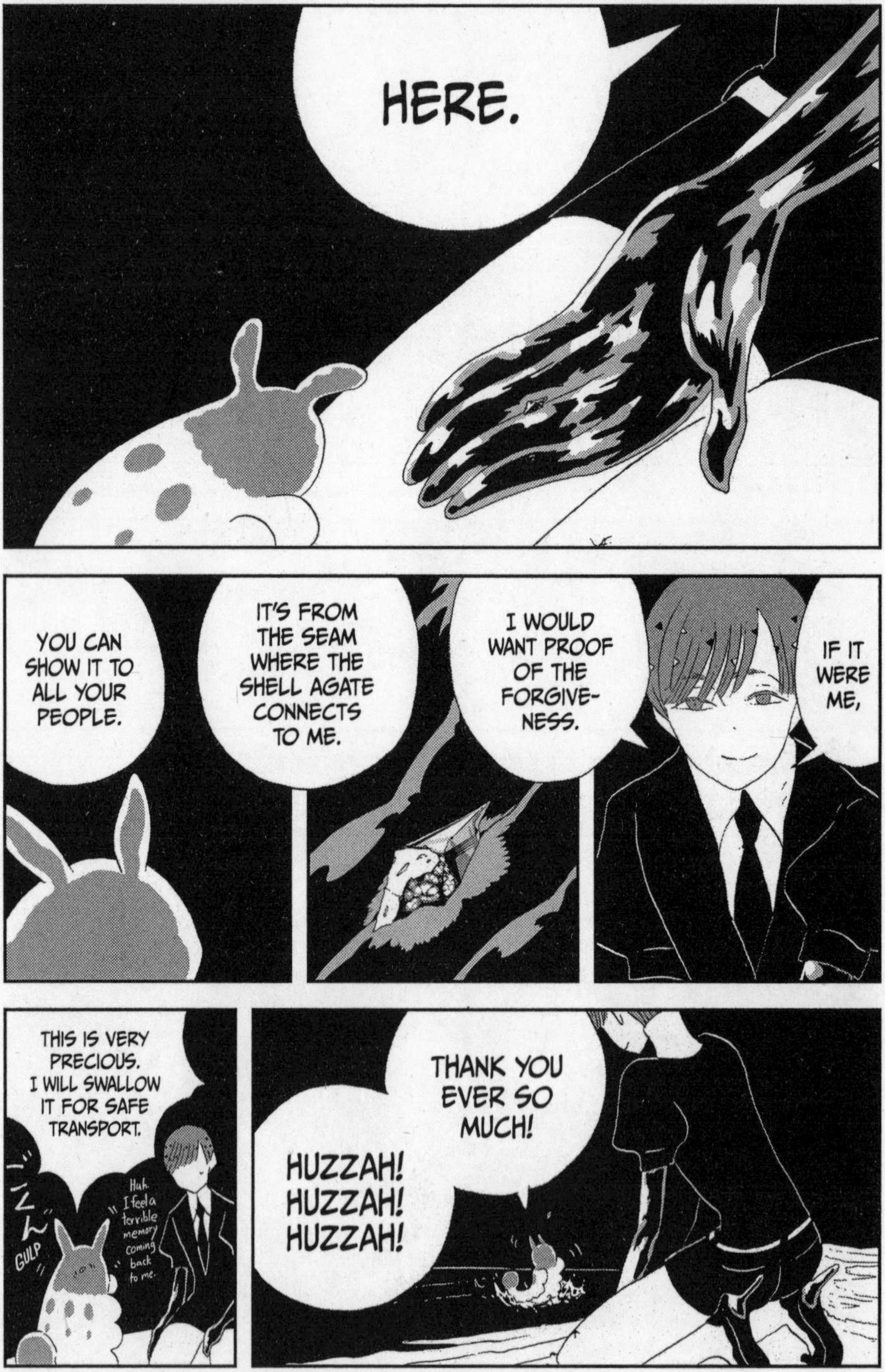
HERE.
IF IT WERE ME,
I WOULD WANT PROOF OF THE FORGIVE-NESS.
IT'S FROM THE SEAM WHERE THE SHELL AGATE CONNECTS TO ME.
YOU CAN SHOW IT TO ALL YOUR PEOPLE.
THANK YOU EVER SO MUCH!
HUZZAH! HUZZAH! HUZZAH!
THIS IS VERY PRECIOUS. I WILL SWALLOW IT FOR SAFE TRANSPORT.
Huh. I feel a terrible memory coming back to me.
GULP

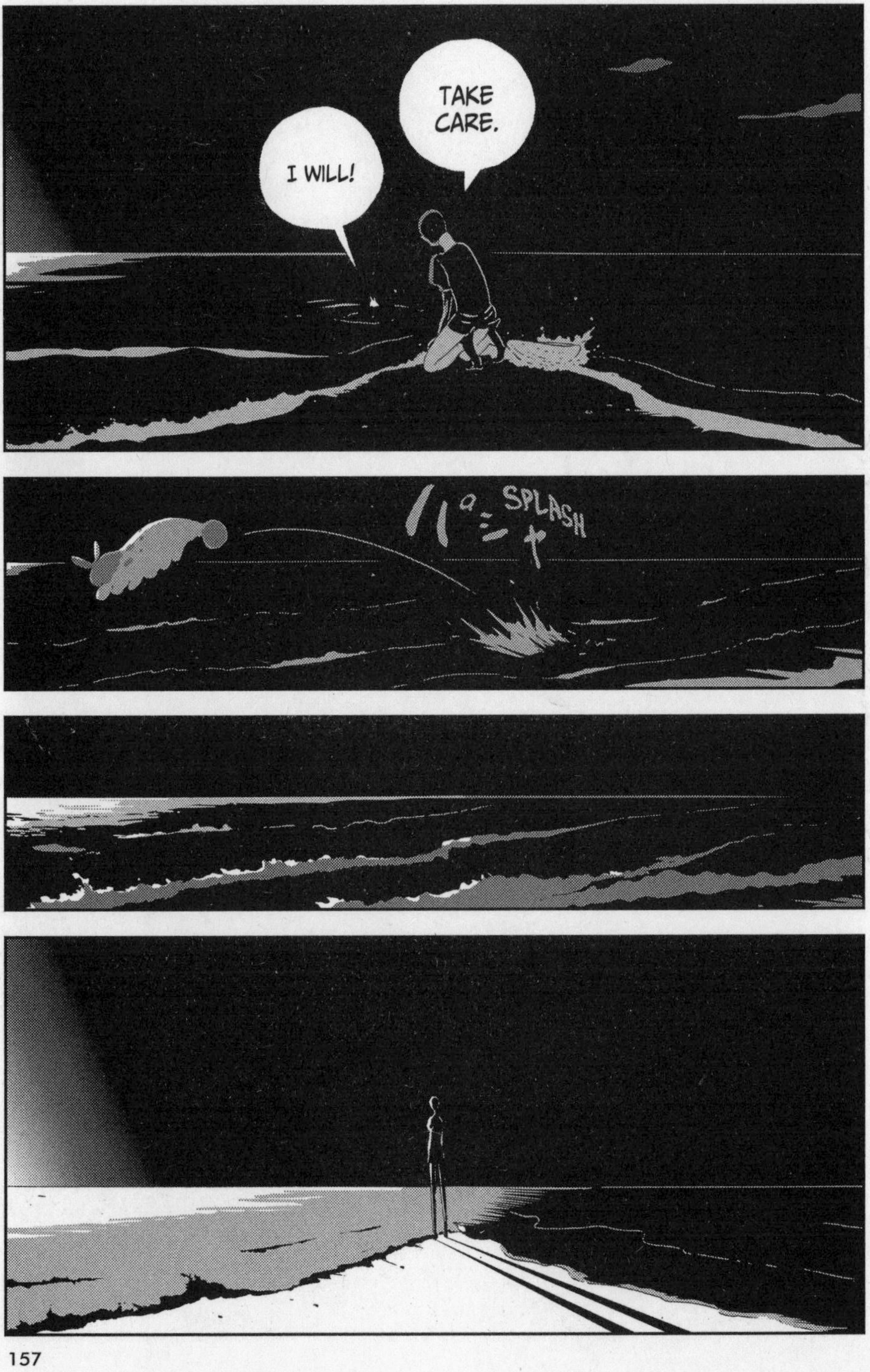
TAKE CARE.
I WILL!
パシャ
SPLASH

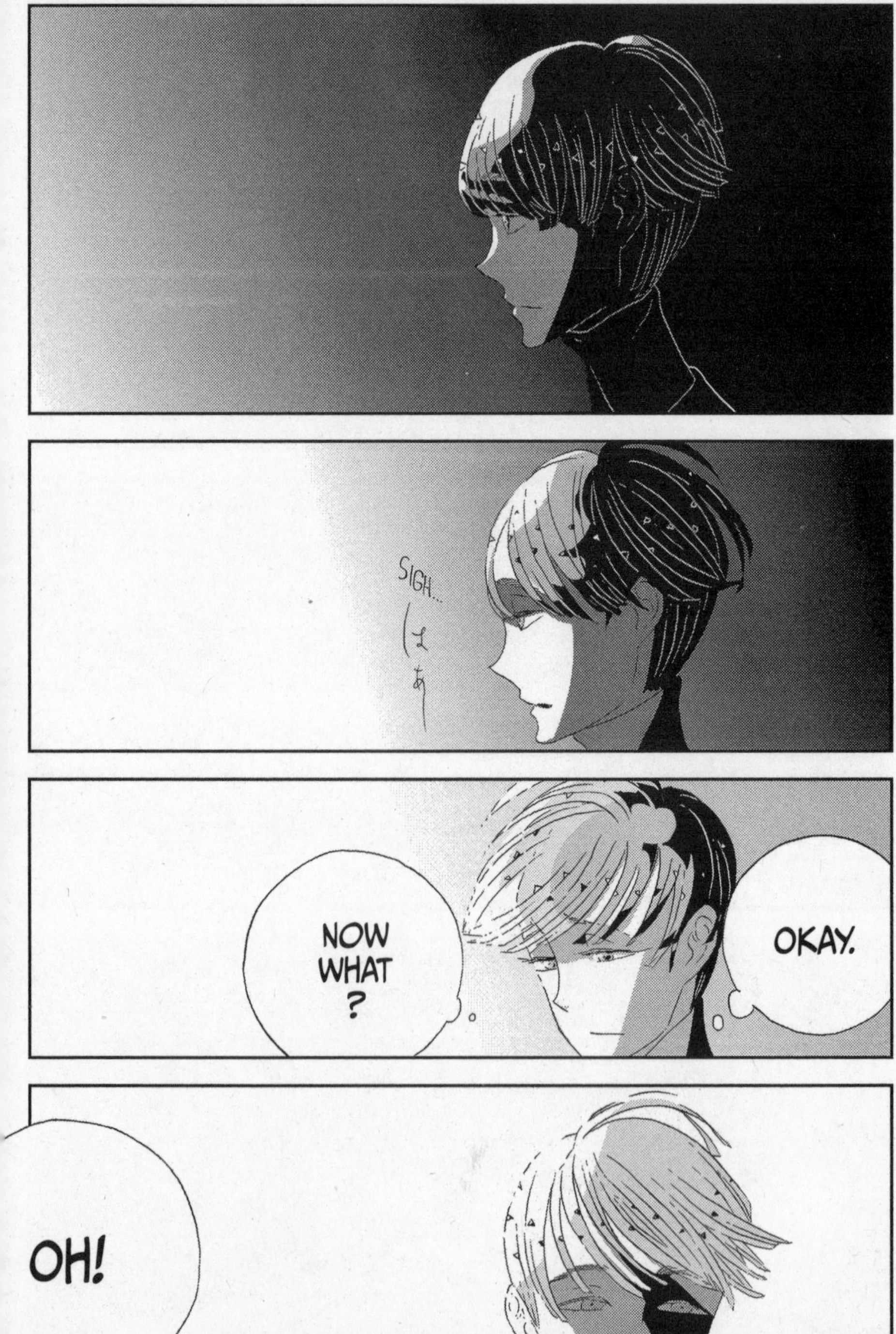
SIGH...
はあ
OKAY.
NOW WHAT?
OH!

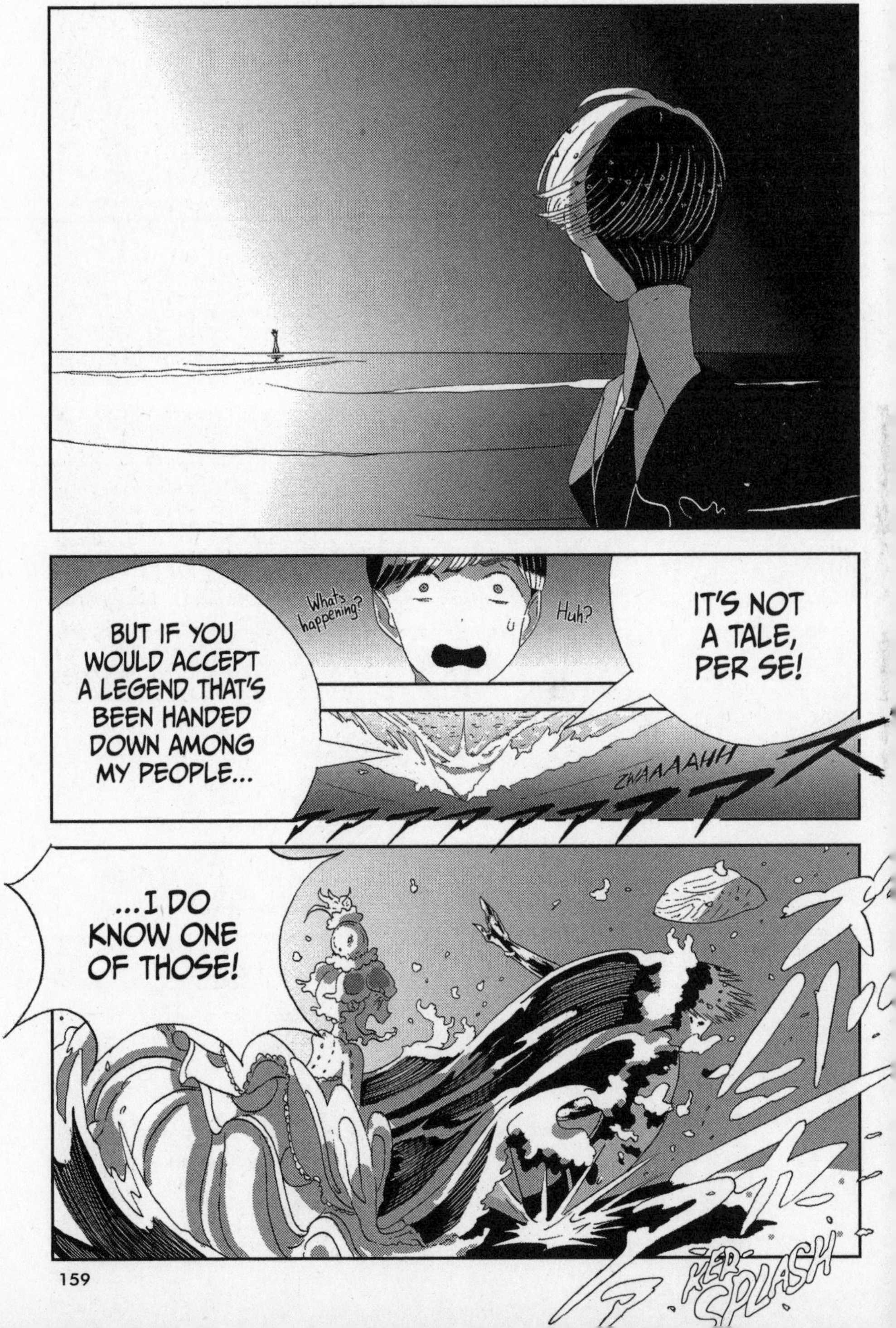
IT'S NOT A TALE, PER SE!
Huh?
What's happening?
BUT IF YOU WOULD ACCEPT A LEGEND THAT'S BEEN HANDED DOWN AMONG MY PEOPLE...
ZWAAAAHH
...I DO KNOW ONE OF THOSE!
KER-SPLASH

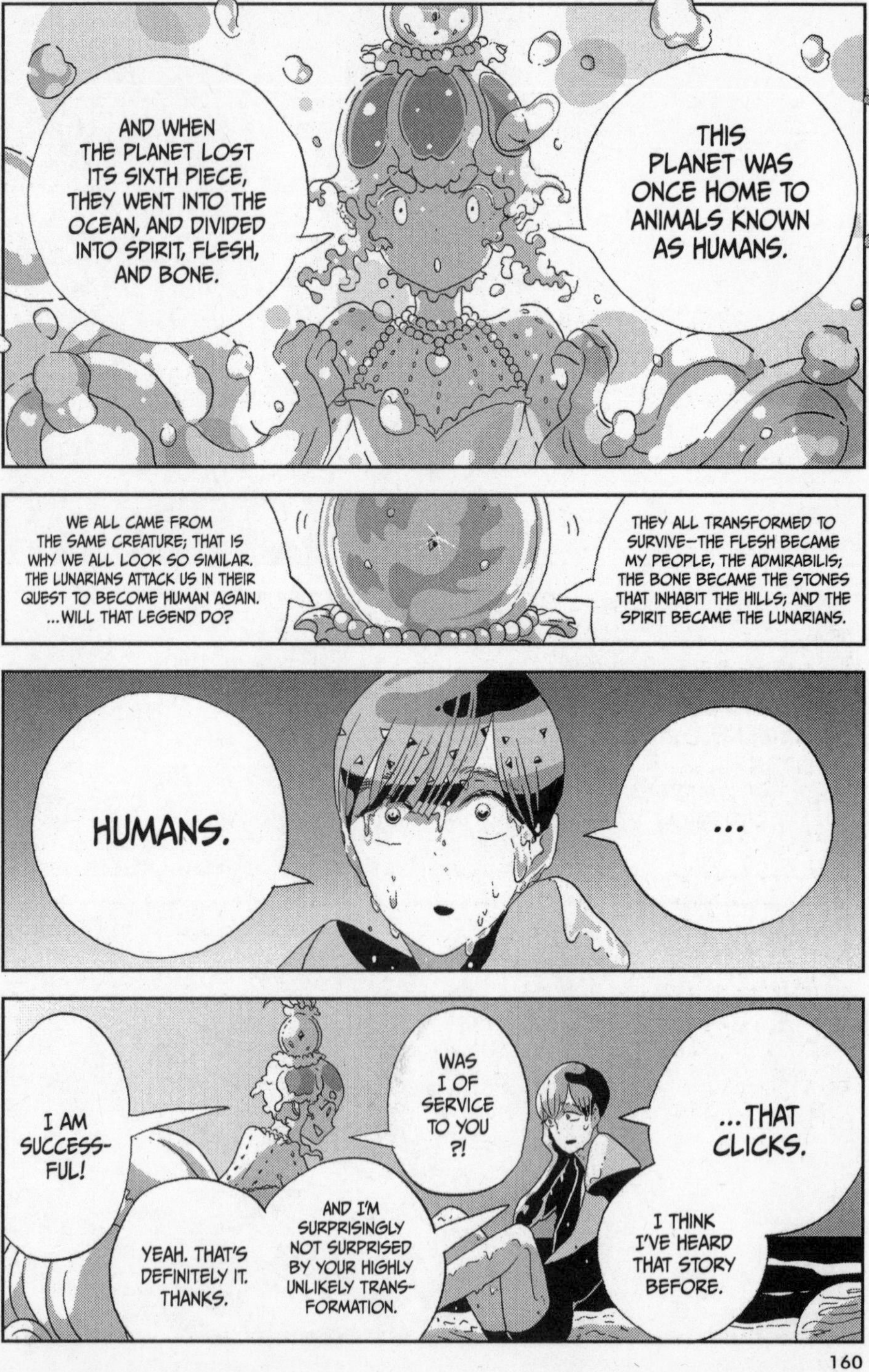
THIS PLANET WAS ONCE HOME TO ANIMALS KNOWN AS HUMANS.
AND WHEN THE PLANET LOST ITS SIXTH PIECE, THEY WENT INTO THE OCEAN, AND DIVIDED INTO SPIRIT, FLESH, AND BONE.
THEY ALL TRANSFORMED TO SURVIVE—THE FLESH BECAME MY PEOPLE, THE ADMIRABILIS; THE BONE BECAME THE STONES THAT INHABIT THE HILLS; AND THE SPIRIT BECAME THE LUNARIANS.
WE ALL CAME FROM THE SAME CREATURE; THAT IS WHY WE ALL LOOK SO SIMILAR. THE LUNARIANS ATTACK US IN THEIR QUEST TO BECOME HUMAN AGAIN. ...WILL THAT LEGEND DO?
...
HUMANS.
...THAT CLICKS.
I THINK I'VE HEARD THAT STORY BEFORE.
WAS I OF SERVICE TO YOU ?!
AND I'M SURPRISINGLY NOT SURPRISED BY YOUR HIGHLY UNLIKELY TRANS-FORMATION.
I AM SUCCESS-FUL!
YEAH. THAT'S DEFINITELY IT. THANKS.

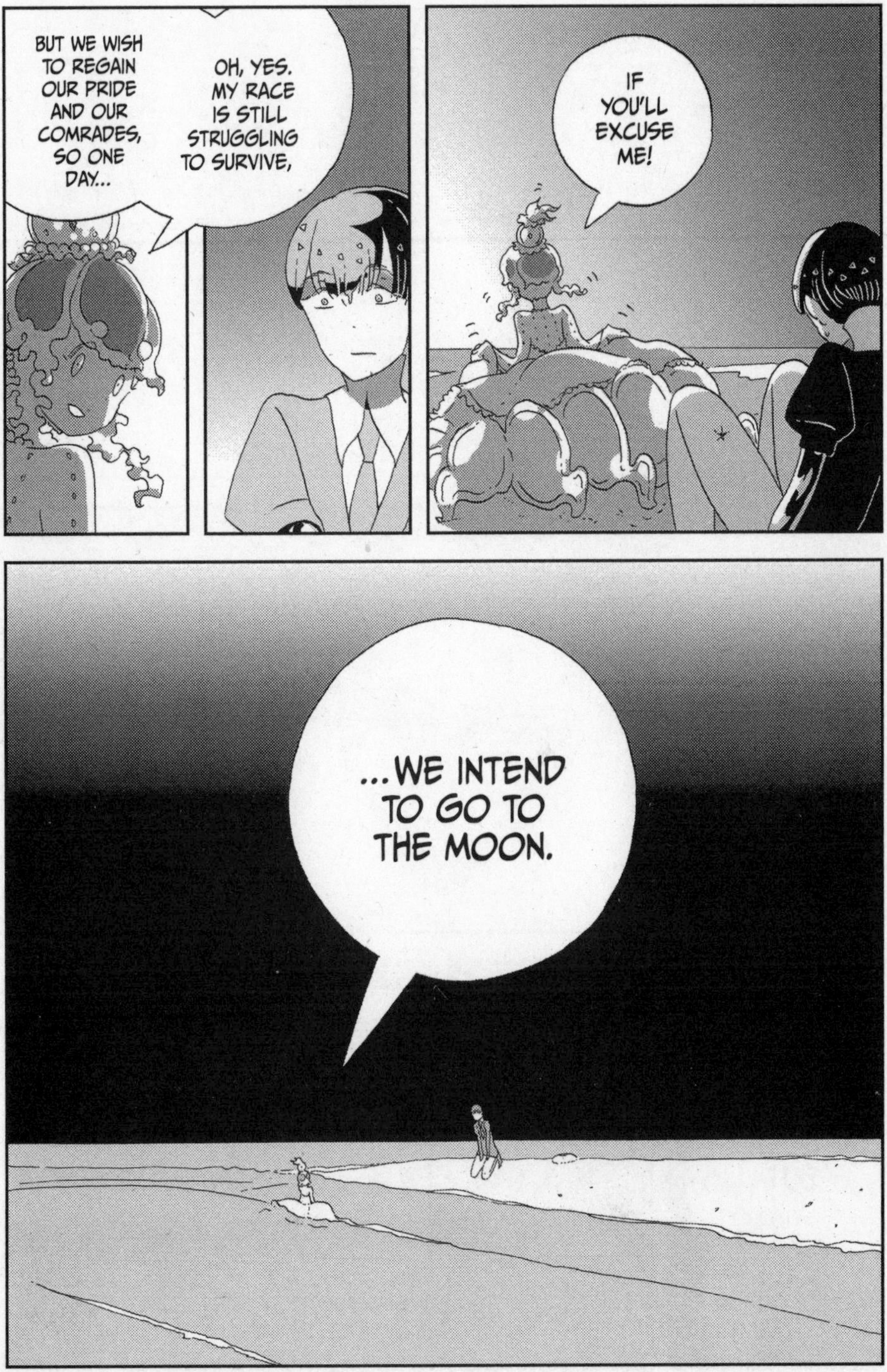
IF YOU'LL EXCUSE ME!
OH, YES. MY RACE IS STILL STRUGGLING TO SURVIVE,
BUT WE WISH TO REGAIN OUR PRIDE AND OUR COMRADES, SO ONE DAY...
...WE INTEND TO GO TO THE MOON.

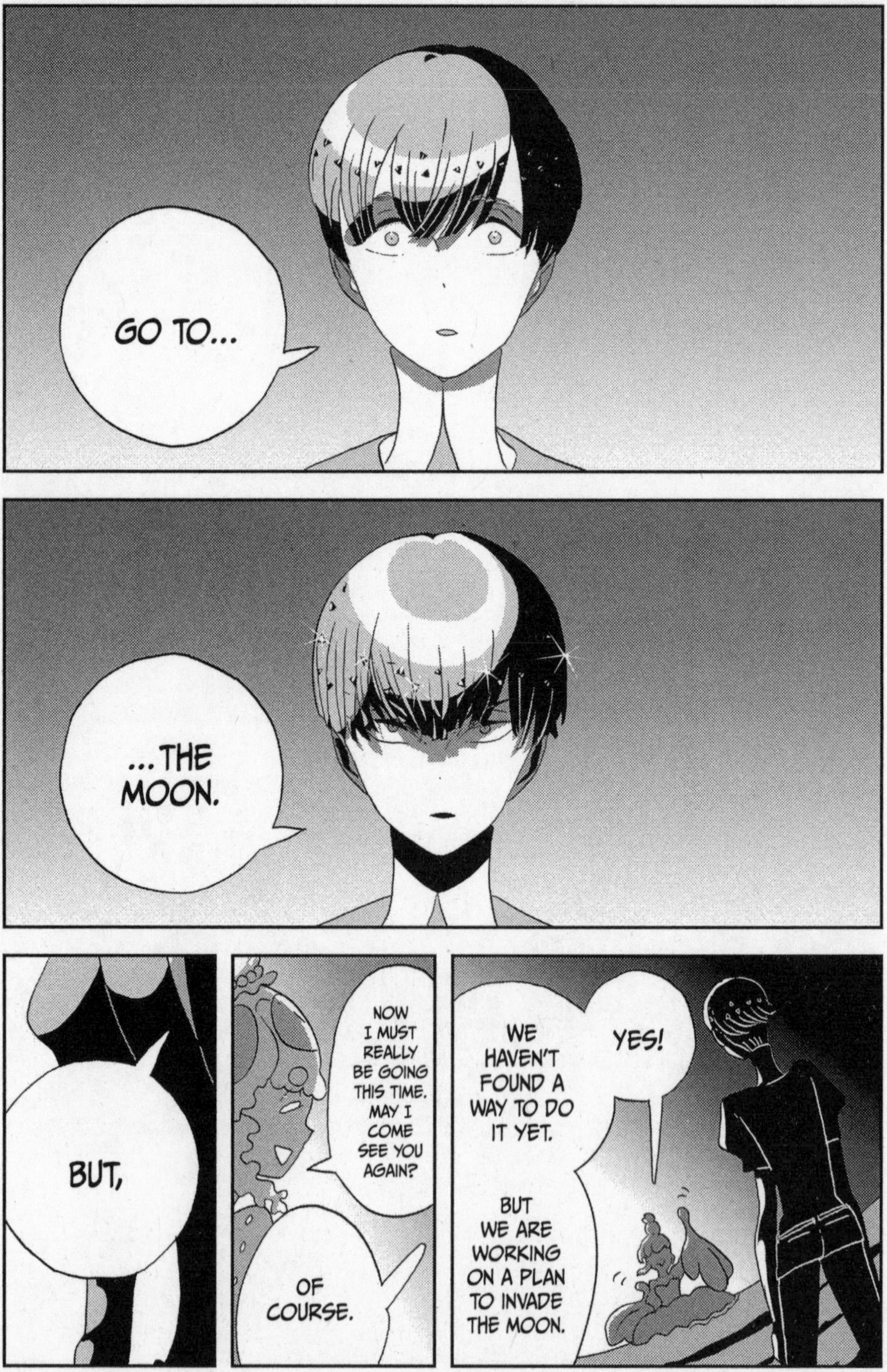
GO TO...
...THE MOON.
YES!
WE HAVEN'T FOUND A WAY TO DO IT YET.
BUT WE ARE WORKING ON A PLAN TO INVADE THE MOON.
NOW I MUST REALLY BE GOING THIS TIME. MAY I COME SEE YOU AGAIN?
OF COURSE.
BUT,

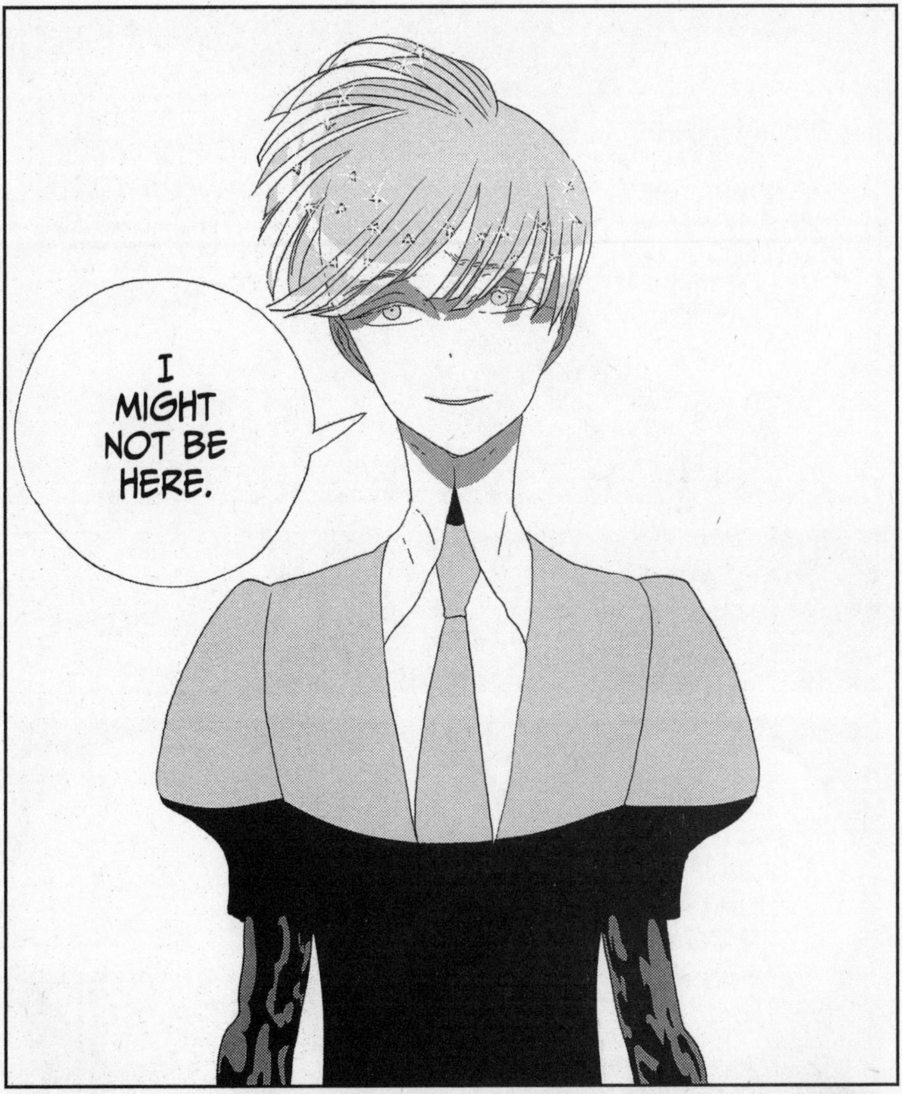
I MIGHT NOT BE HERE.
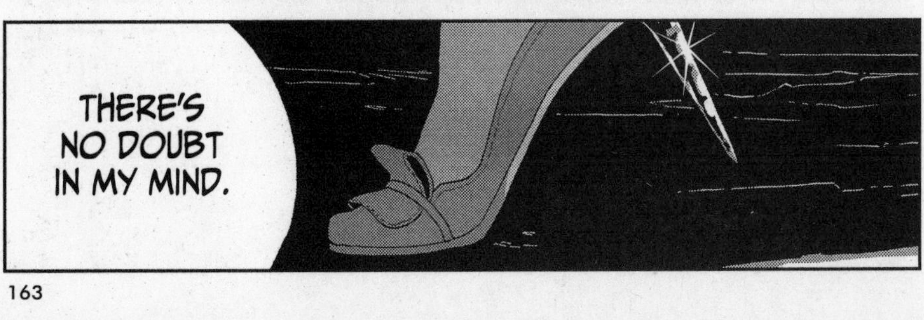
THERE'S NO DOUBT IN MY MIND.

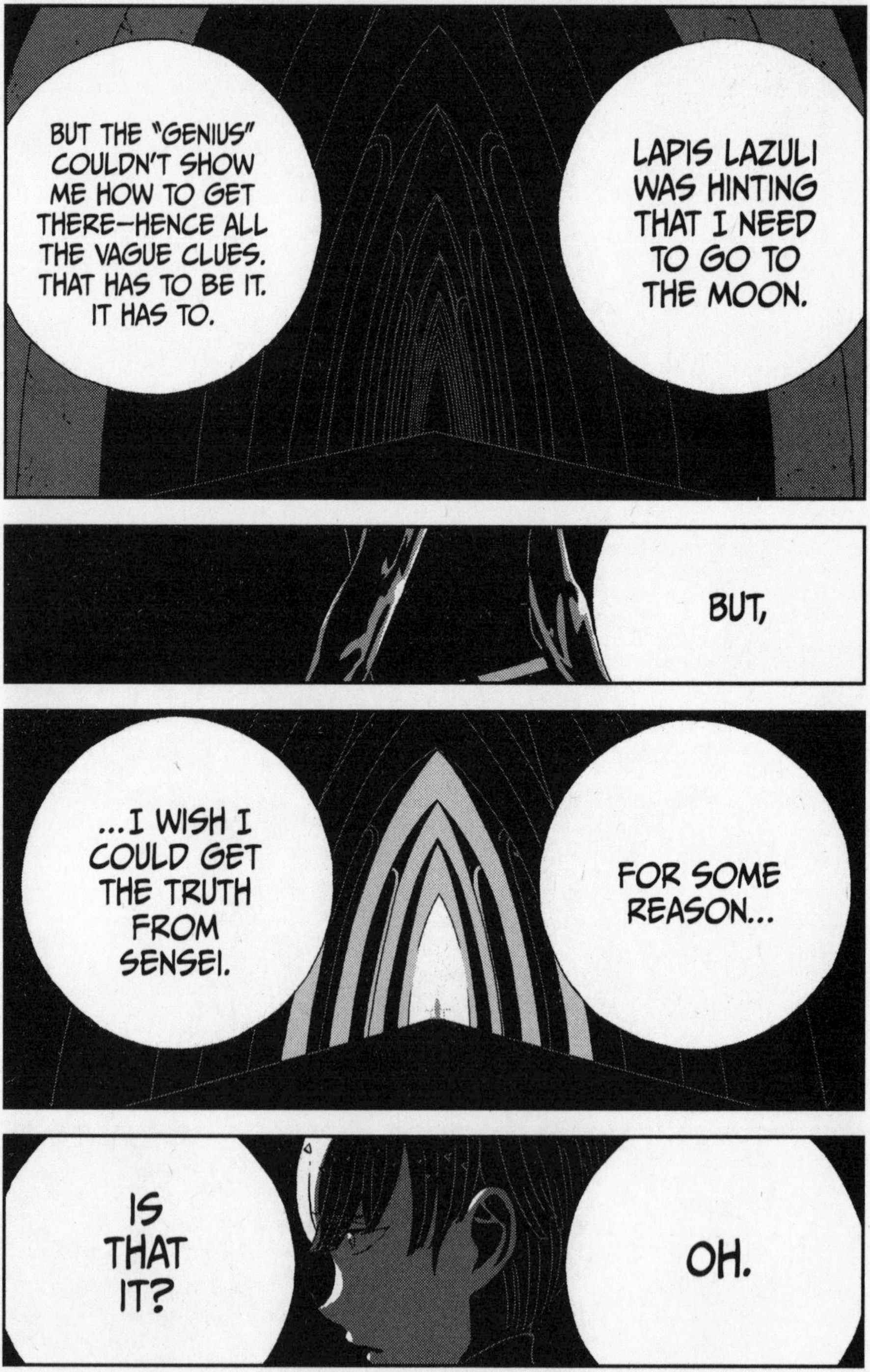
LAPIS LAZULI WAS HINTING THAT I NEED TO GO TO THE MOON.
BUT THE "GENIUS" COULDN'T SHOW ME HOW TO GET THERE—HENCE ALL THE VAGUE CLUES. THAT HAS TO BE IT. IT HAS TO.
BUT,
FOR SOME REASON...
...I WISH I COULD GET THE TRUTH FROM SENSEI.
OH.
IS THAT IT?

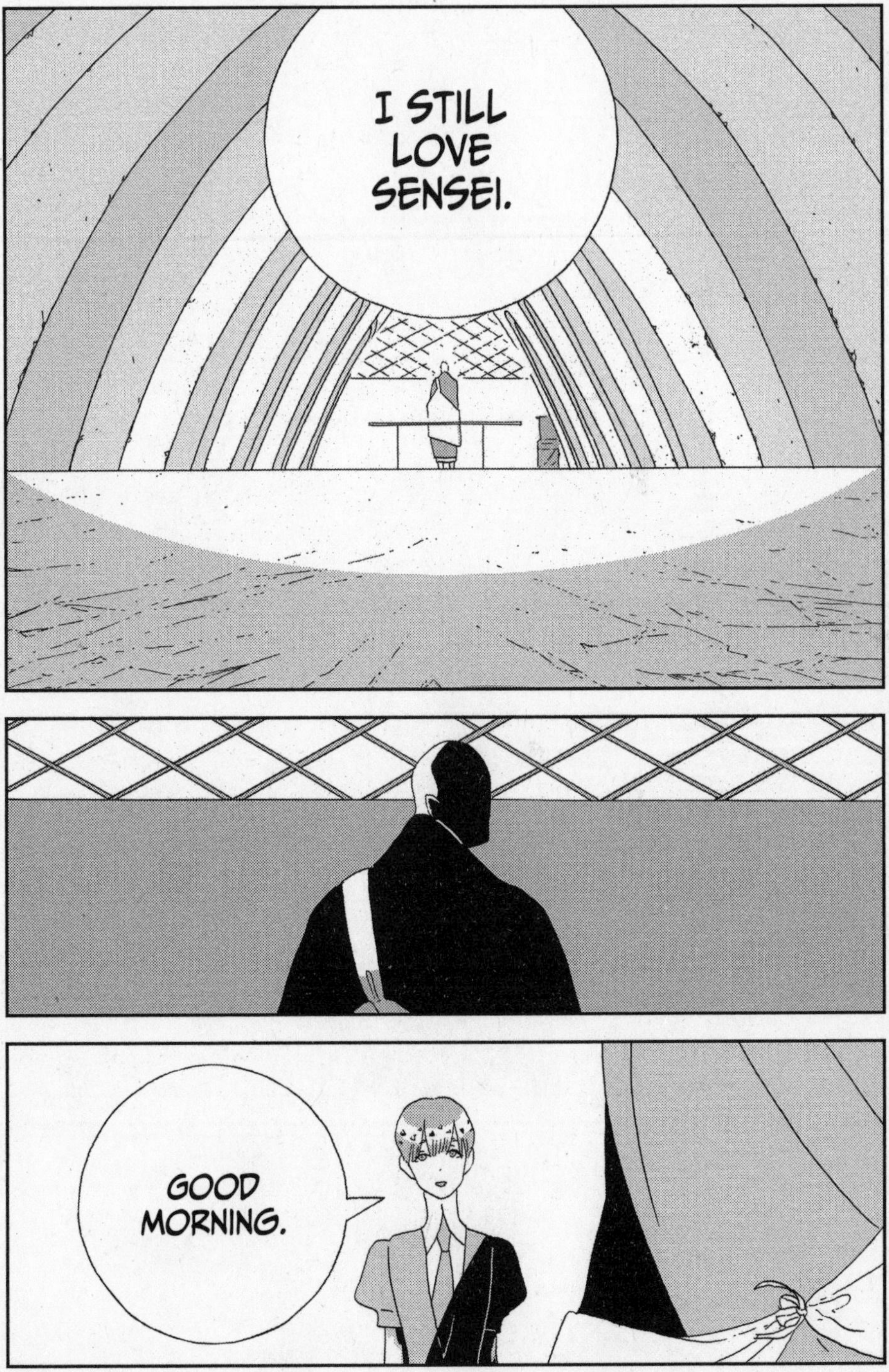
I STILL LOVE SENSEI.
GOOD MORNING.

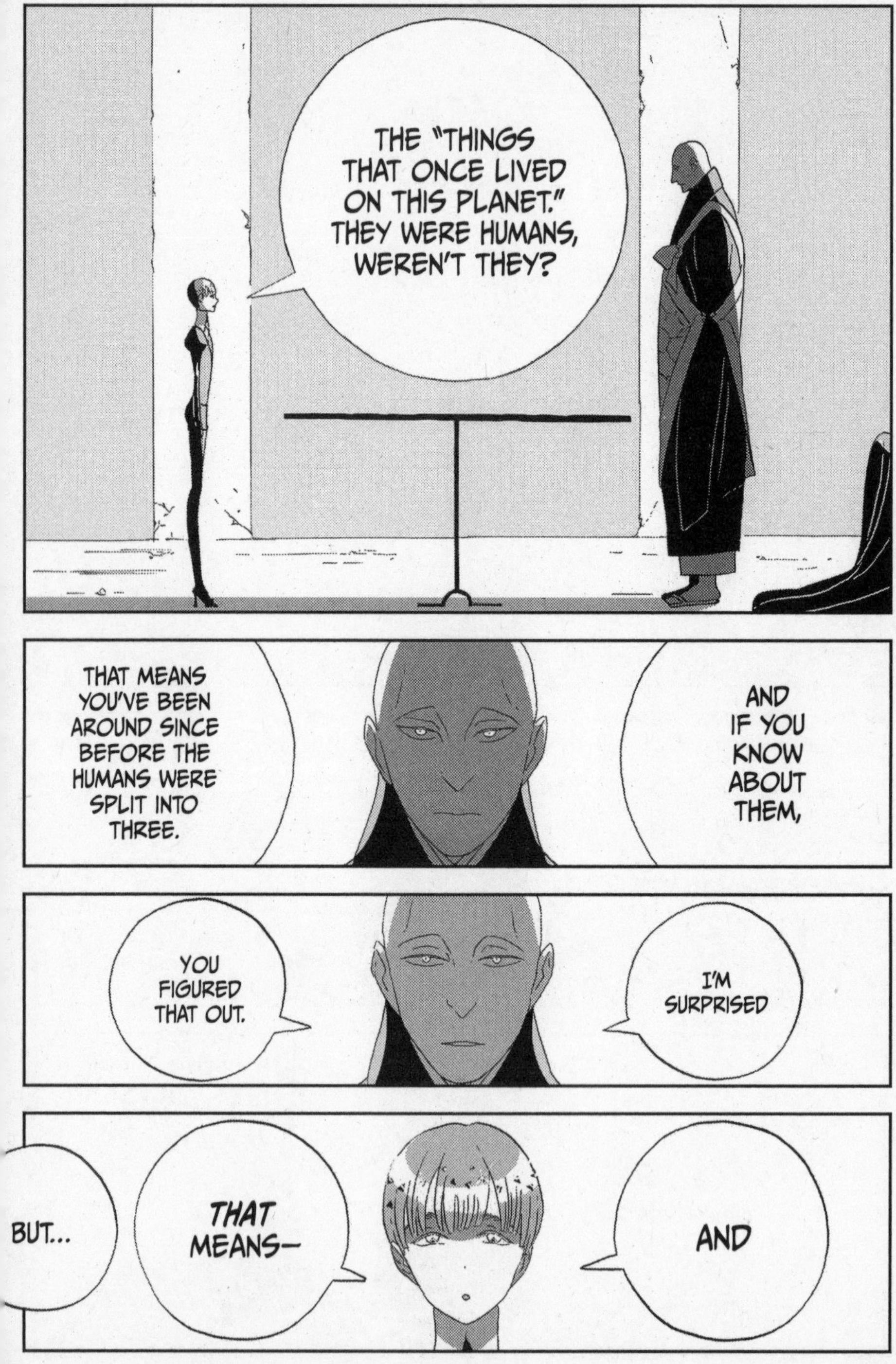
THE "THINGS THAT ONCE LIVED ON THIS PLANET." THEY WERE HUMANS, WEREN'T THEY?
AND IF YOU KNOW ABOUT THEM,
THAT MEANS YOU'VE BEEN AROUND SINCE BEFORE THE HUMANS WERE SPLIT INTO THREE.
I'M SURPRISED
YOU FIGURED THAT OUT.
AND
THAT MEANS—
BUT...

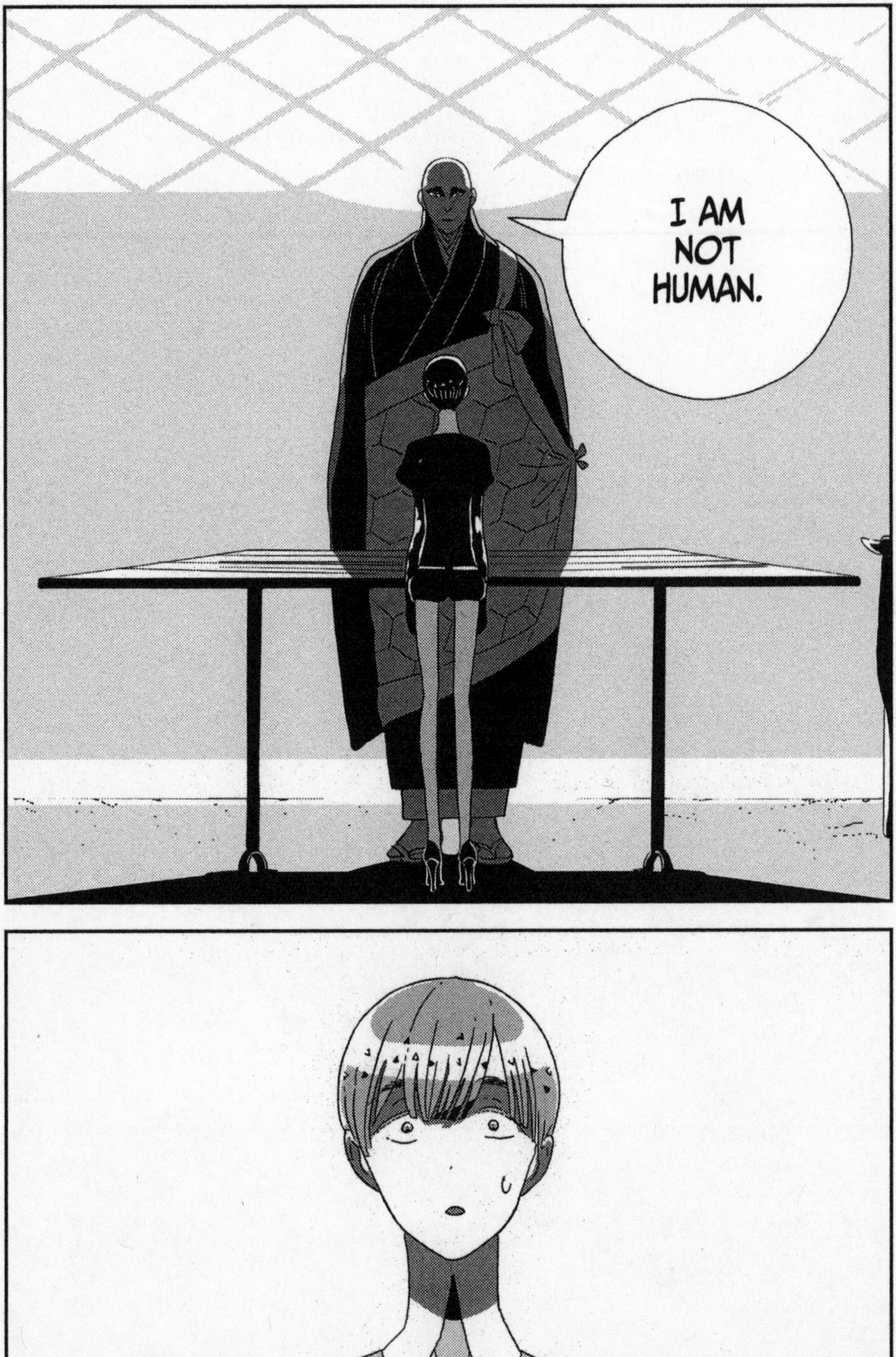
I AM NOT HUMAN.

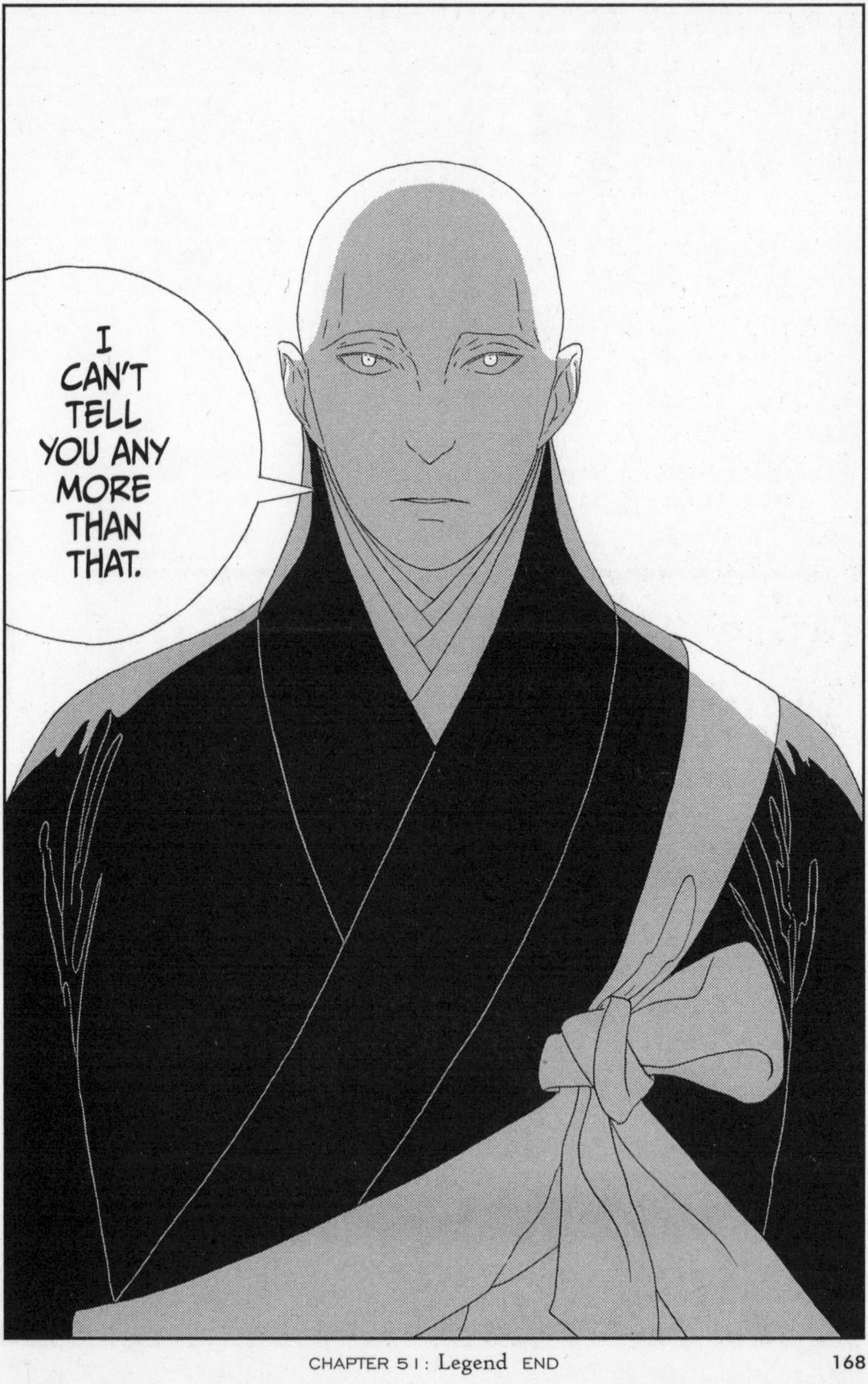
I CAN'T TELL YOU ANY MORE THAN THAT.

CHAPTER 51: Legend END

CHAPTER 52:

Journey

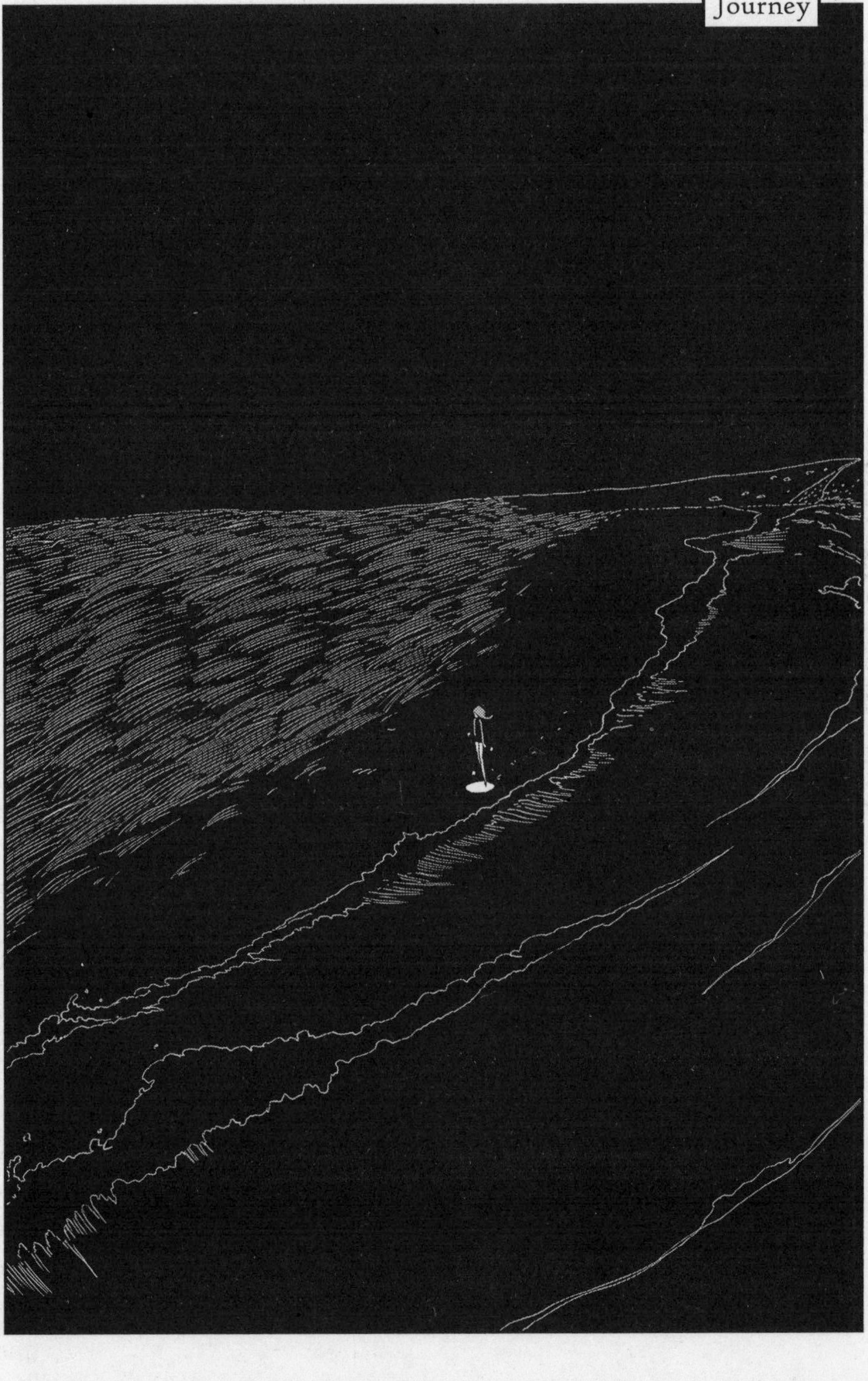

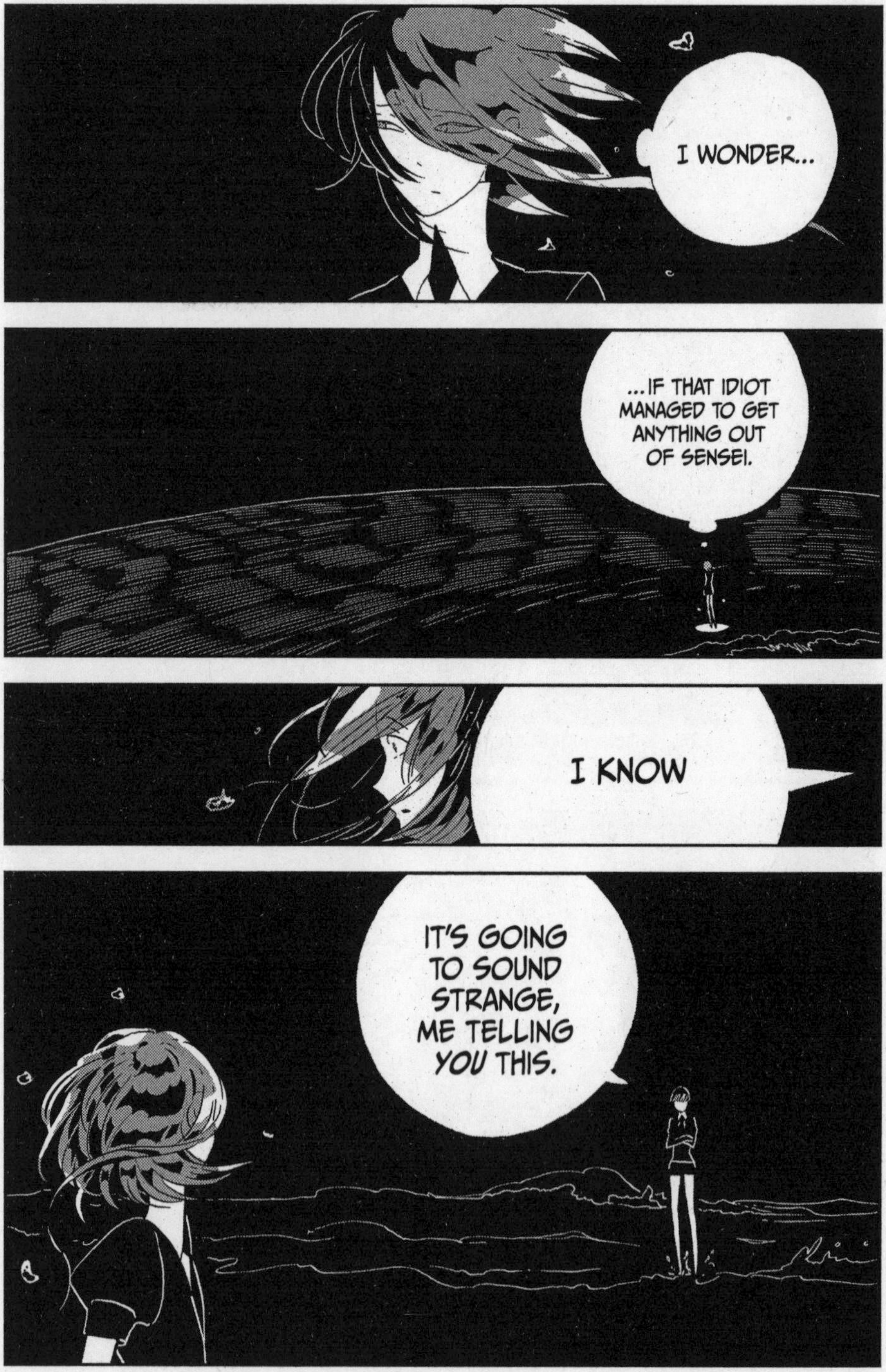
I WONDER...
...IF THAT IDIOT MANAGED TO GET ANYTHING OUT OF SENSEI.
I KNOW
IT'S GOING TO SOUND STRANGE, ME TELLING *YOU* THIS.

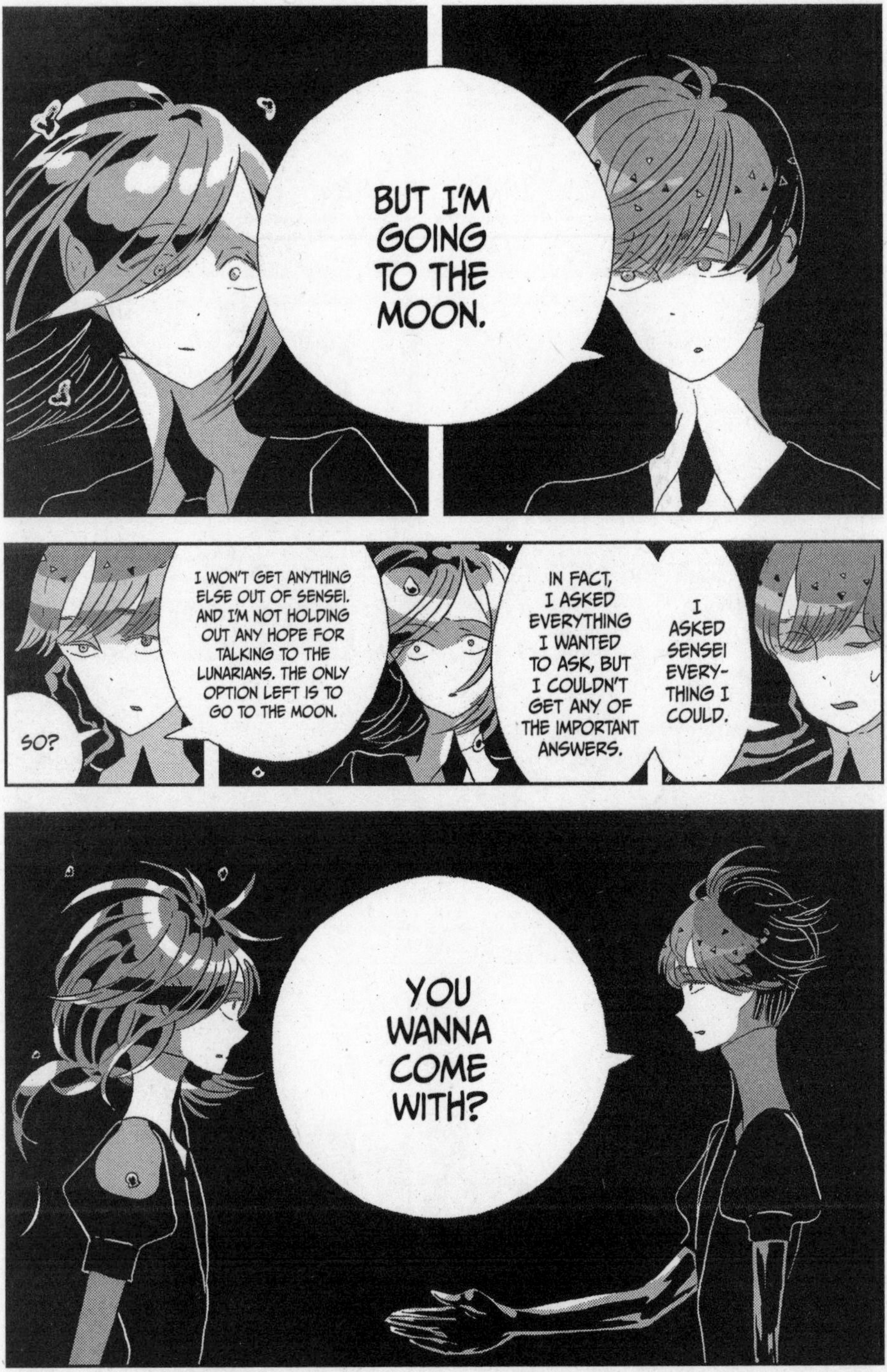
BUT I'M GOING TO THE MOON.
I ASKED SENSEI EVERY-THING I COULD.
IN FACT, I ASKED EVERYTHING I WANTED TO ASK, BUT I COULDN'T GET ANY OF THE IMPORTANT ANSWERS.
SO?
I WON'T GET ANYTHING ELSE OUT OF SENSEI. AND I'M NOT HOLDING OUT ANY HOPE FOR TALKING TO THE LUNARIANS. THE ONLY OPTION LEFT IS TO GO TO THE MOON.
YOU WANNA COME WITH?

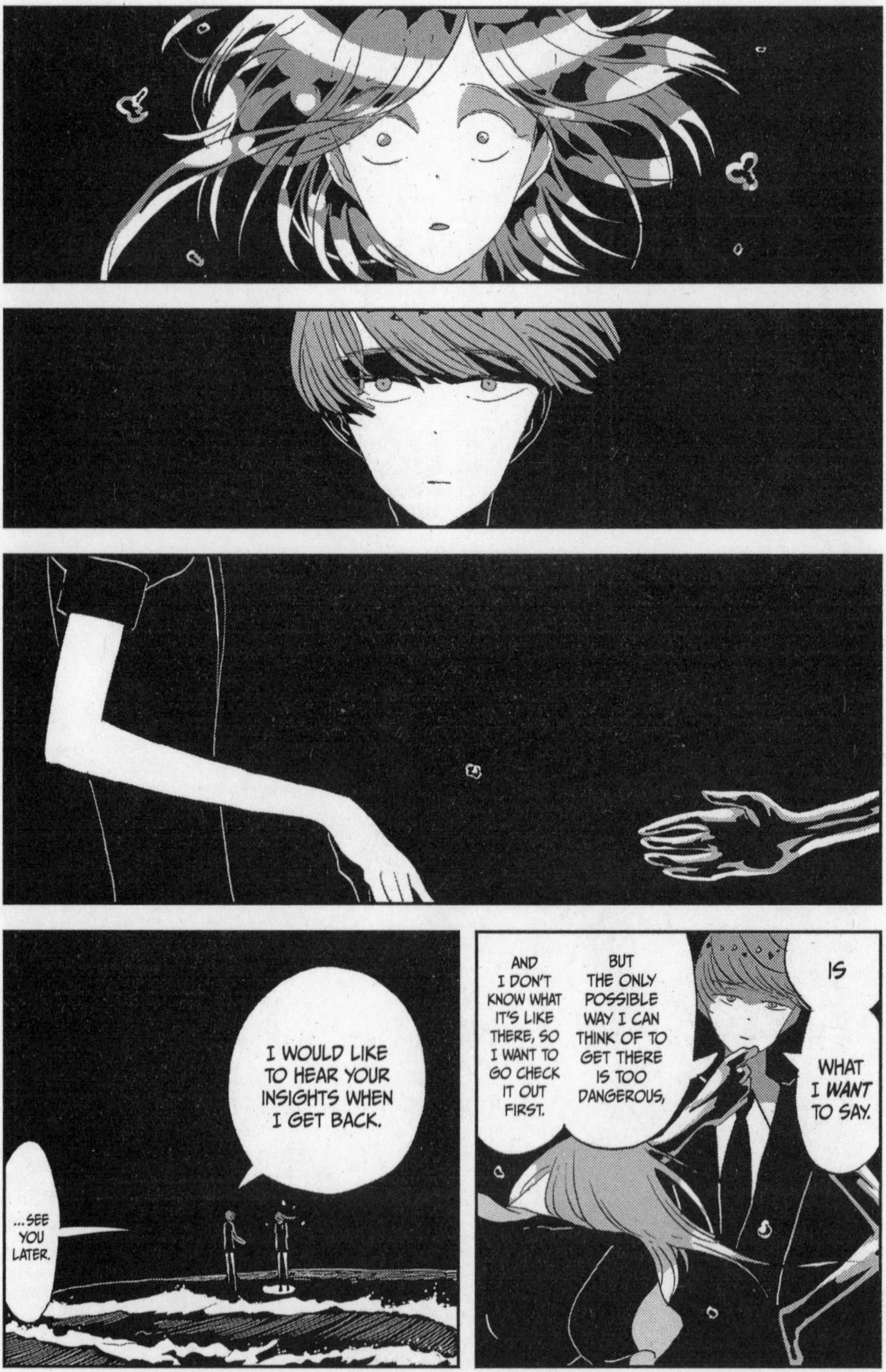
IS WHAT I *WANT* TO SAY.
BUT THE ONLY POSSIBLE WAY I CAN THINK OF TO GET THERE IS TOO DANGEROUS,
AND I DON'T KNOW WHAT IT'S LIKE THERE, SO I WANT TO GO CHECK IT OUT FIRST.
I WOULD LIKE TO HEAR YOUR INSIGHTS WHEN I GET BACK.
...SEE YOU LATER.

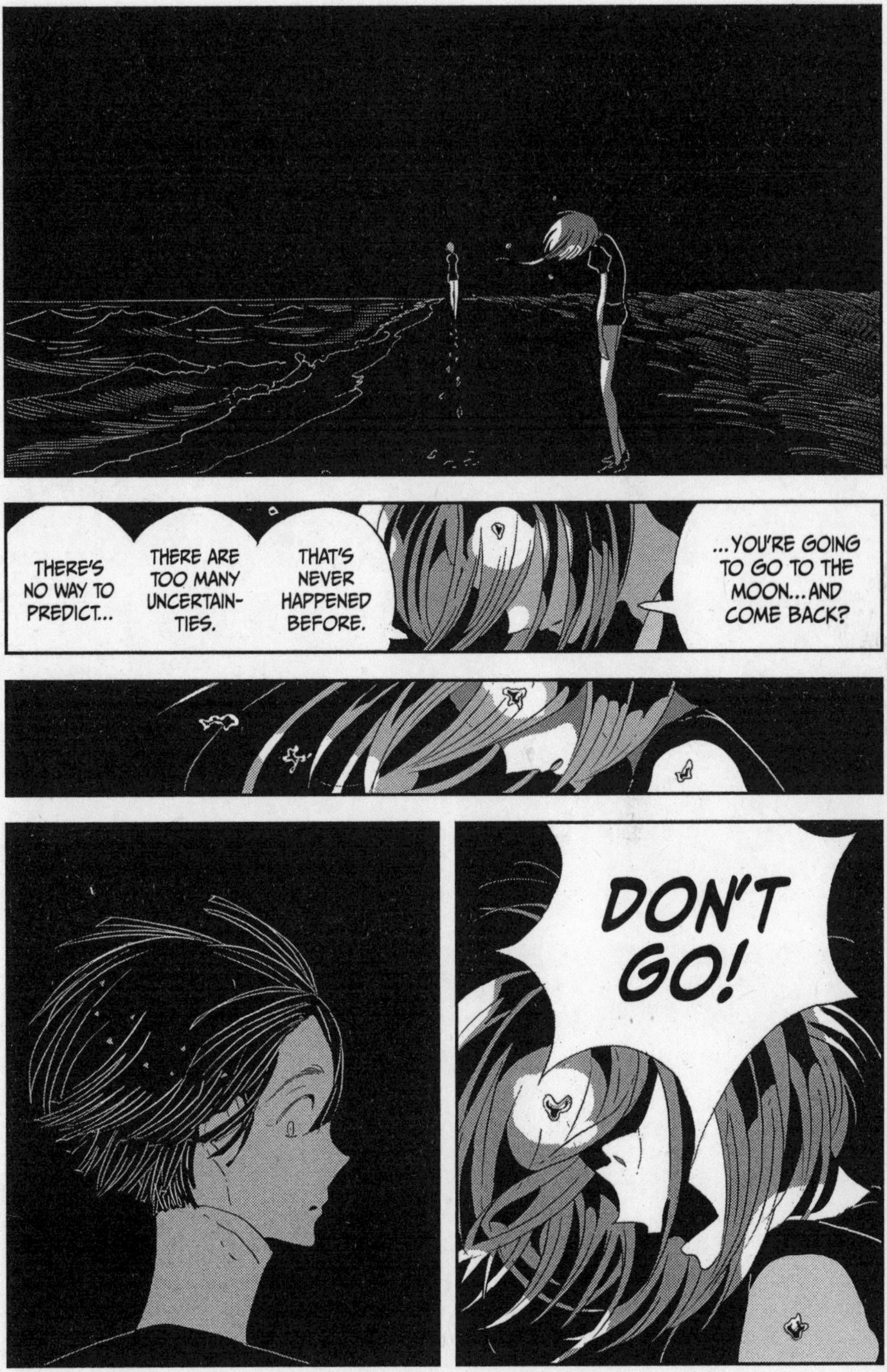
...YOU'RE GOING TO GO TO THE MOON...AND COME BACK?
THAT'S NEVER HAPPENED BEFORE.
THERE ARE TOO MANY UNCERTAIN-TIES.
THERE'S NO WAY TO PREDICT...
DON'T GO!

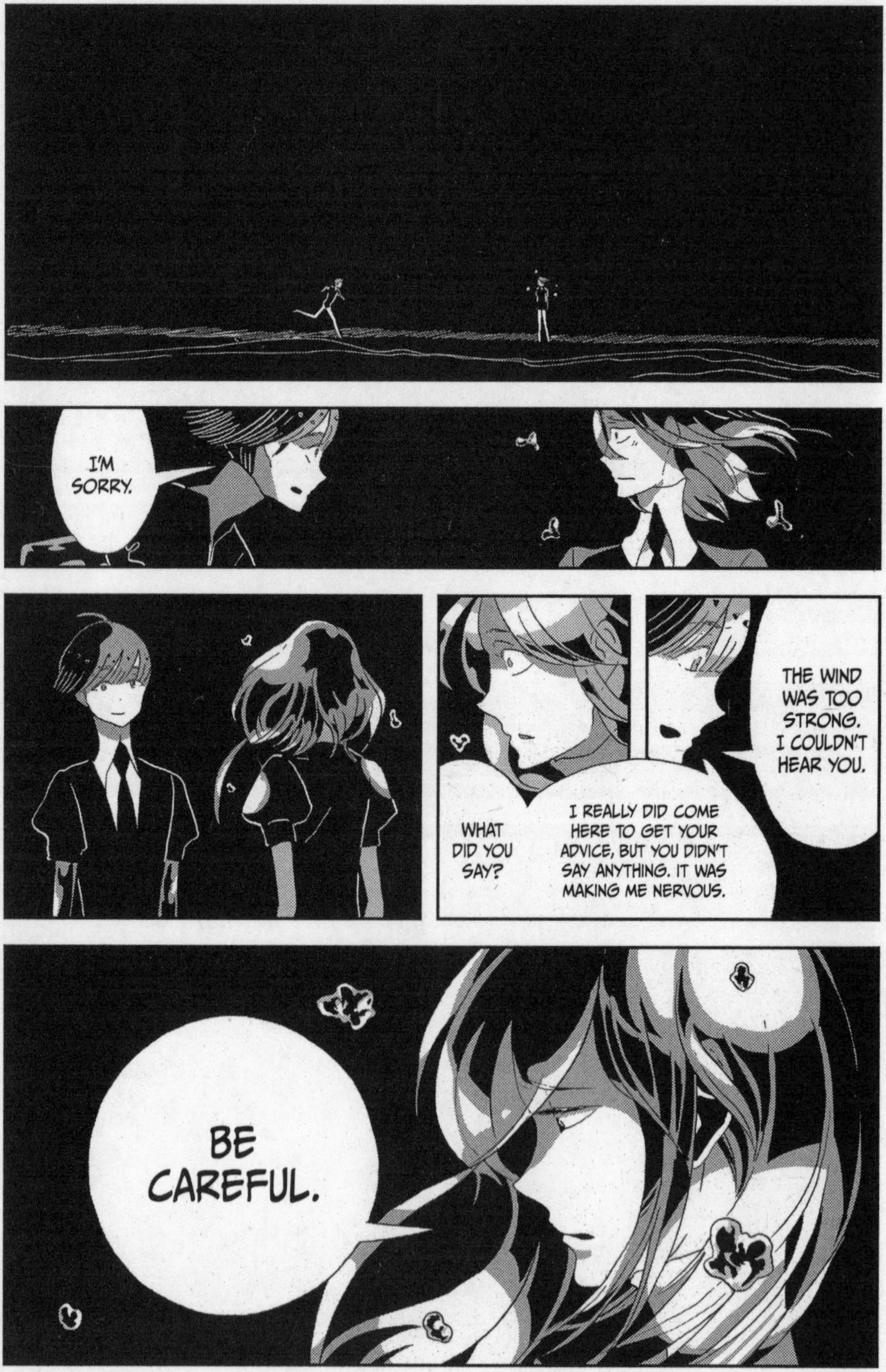

I'M SORRY.
THE WIND WAS TOO STRONG. I COULDN'T HEAR YOU.
I REALLY DID COME HERE TO GET YOUR ADVICE, BUT YOU DIDN'T SAY ANYTHING. IT WAS MAKING ME NERVOUS.
WHAT DID YOU SAY?
BE CAREFUL.

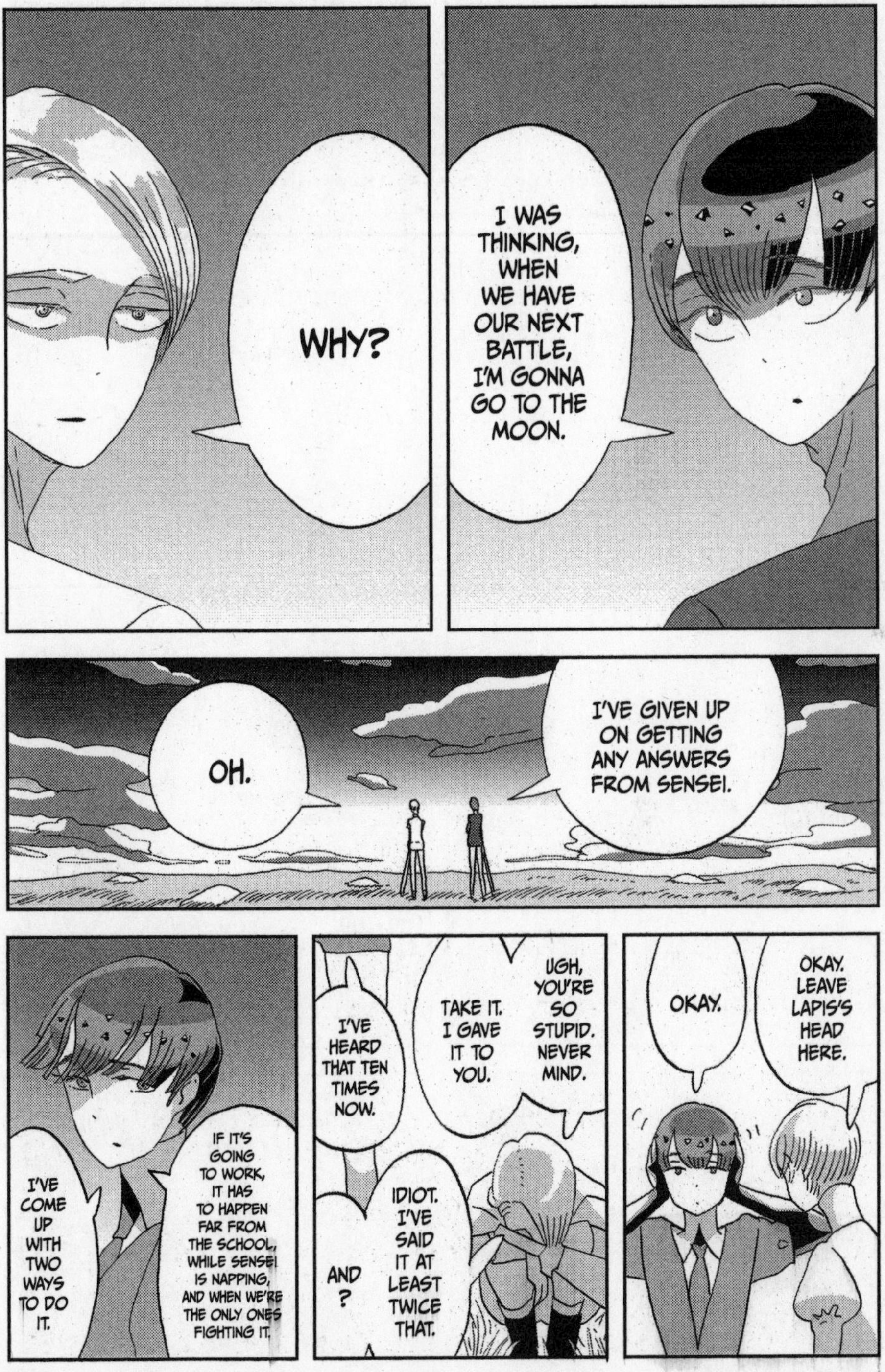
I WAS THINKING, WHEN WE HAVE OUR NEXT BATTLE, I'M GONNA GO TO THE MOON.
WHY?
I'VE GIVEN UP ON GETTING ANY ANSWERS FROM SENSEI.
OH.
OKAY. LEAVE LAPIS'S HEAD HERE.
OKAY.
UGH, YOU'RE SO STUPID. NEVER MIND.
TAKE IT. I GAVE IT TO YOU.
I'VE HEARD THAT TEN TIMES NOW.
IDIOT. I'VE SAID IT AT LEAST TWICE THAT.
AND ?
IF IT'S GOING TO WORK, IT HAS TO HAPPEN FAR FROM THE SCHOOL, WHILE SENSEI IS NAPPING, AND WHEN WE'RE THE ONLY ONES FIGHTING IT.
I'VE COME UP WITH TWO WAYS TO DO IT.

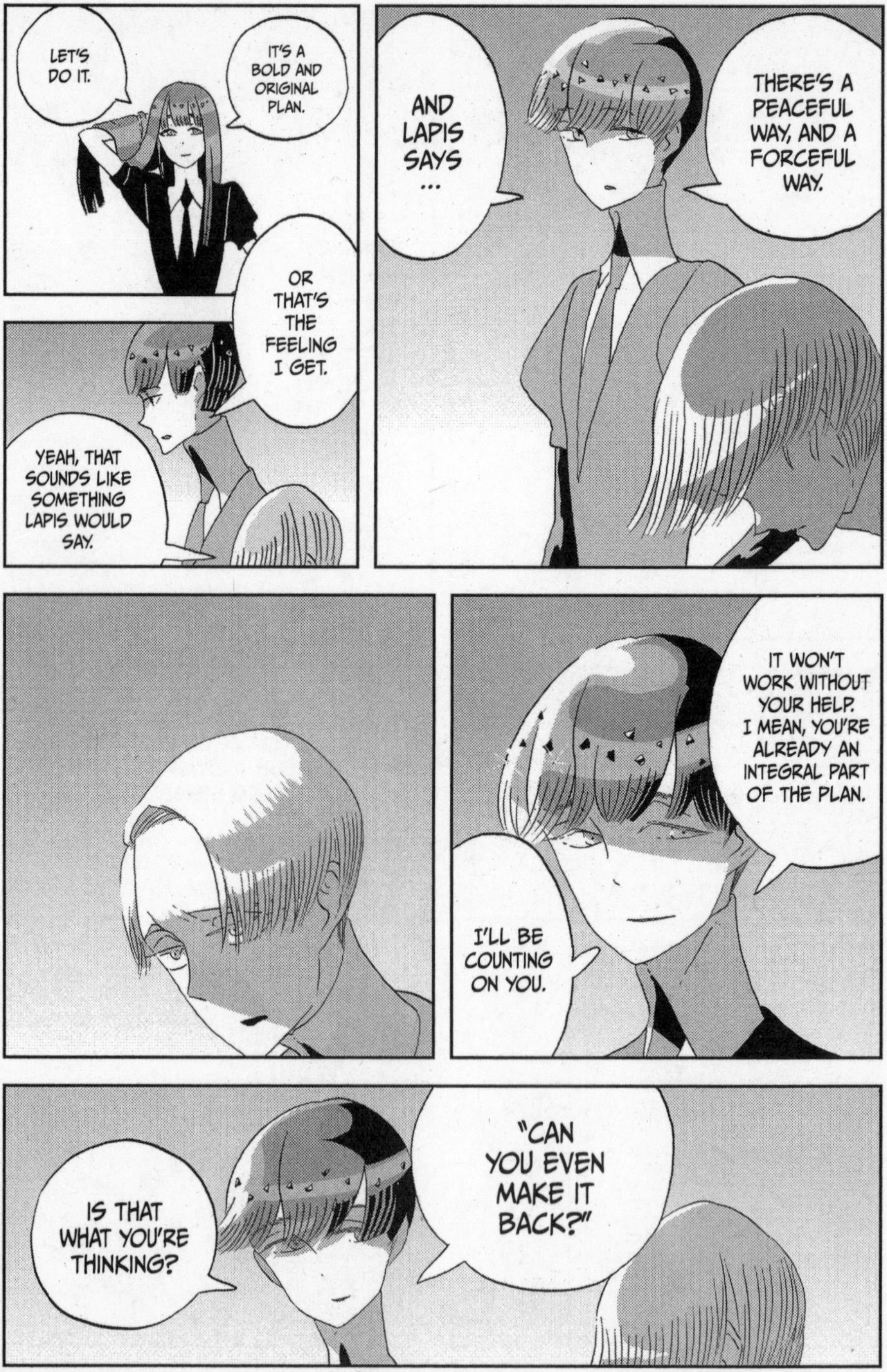
THERE'S A PEACEFUL WAY, AND A FORCEFUL WAY.
AND LAPIS SAYS ...
IT'S A BOLD AND ORIGINAL PLAN.
LET'S DO IT.
OR THAT'S THE FEELING I GET.
YEAH, THAT SOUNDS LIKE SOMETHING LAPIS WOULD SAY.
IT WON'T WORK WITHOUT YOUR HELP. I MEAN, YOU'RE ALREADY AN INTEGRAL PART OF THE PLAN.
I'LL BE COUNTING ON YOU.
"CAN YOU EVEN MAKE IT BACK?"
IS THAT WHAT YOU'RE THINKING?

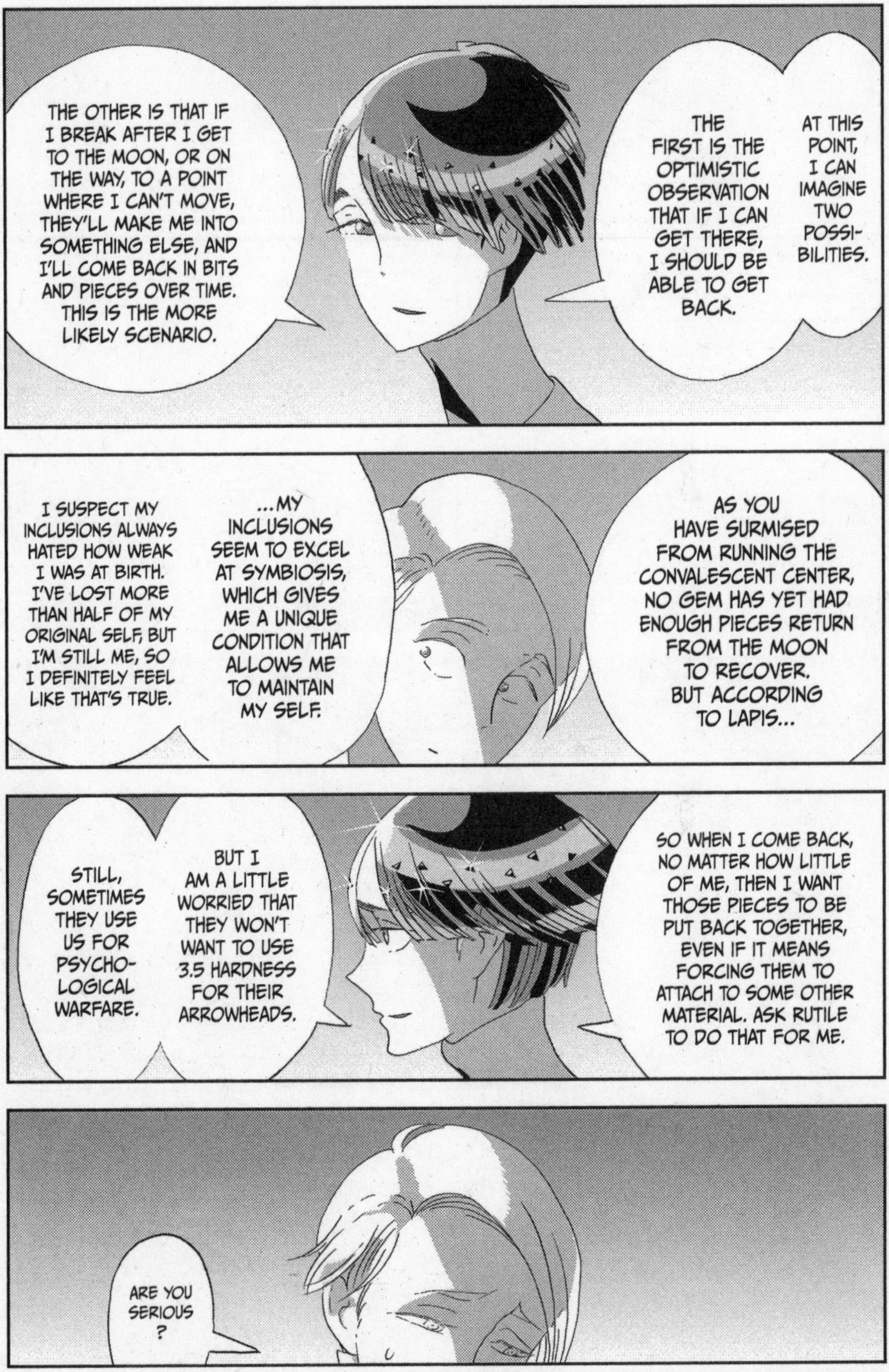
AT THIS POINT, I CAN IMAGINE TWO POSSIBILITIES.
THE FIRST IS THE OPTIMISTIC OBSERVATION THAT IF I CAN GET THERE, I SHOULD BE ABLE TO GET BACK.
THE OTHER IS THAT IF I BREAK AFTER I GET TO THE MOON, OR ON THE WAY, TO A POINT WHERE I CAN'T MOVE, THEY'LL MAKE ME INTO SOMETHING ELSE, AND I'LL COME BACK IN BITS AND PIECES OVER TIME. THIS IS THE MORE LIKELY SCENARIO.
AS YOU HAVE SURMISED FROM RUNNING THE CONVALESCENT CENTER, NO GEM HAS YET HAD ENOUGH PIECES RETURN FROM THE MOON TO RECOVER. BUT ACCORDING TO LAPIS...
...MY INCLUSIONS SEEM TO EXCEL AT SYMBIOSIS, WHICH GIVES ME A UNIQUE CONDITION THAT ALLOWS ME TO MAINTAIN MY SELF.
I SUSPECT MY INCLUSIONS ALWAYS HATED HOW WEAK I WAS AT BIRTH. I'VE LOST MORE THAN HALF OF MY ORIGINAL SELF, BUT I'M STILL ME, SO I DEFINITELY FEEL LIKE THAT'S TRUE.
SO WHEN I COME BACK, NO MATTER HOW LITTLE OF ME, THEN I WANT THOSE PIECES TO BE PUT BACK TOGETHER, EVEN IF IT MEANS FORCING THEM TO ATTACH TO SOME OTHER MATERIAL. ASK RUTILE TO DO THAT FOR ME.
BUT I AM A LITTLE WORRIED THAT THEY WON'T WANT TO USE 3.5 HARDNESS FOR THEIR ARROWHEADS.
STILL, SOMETIMES THEY USE US FOR PSYCHO-LOGICAL WARFARE.
ARE YOU SERIOUS ?

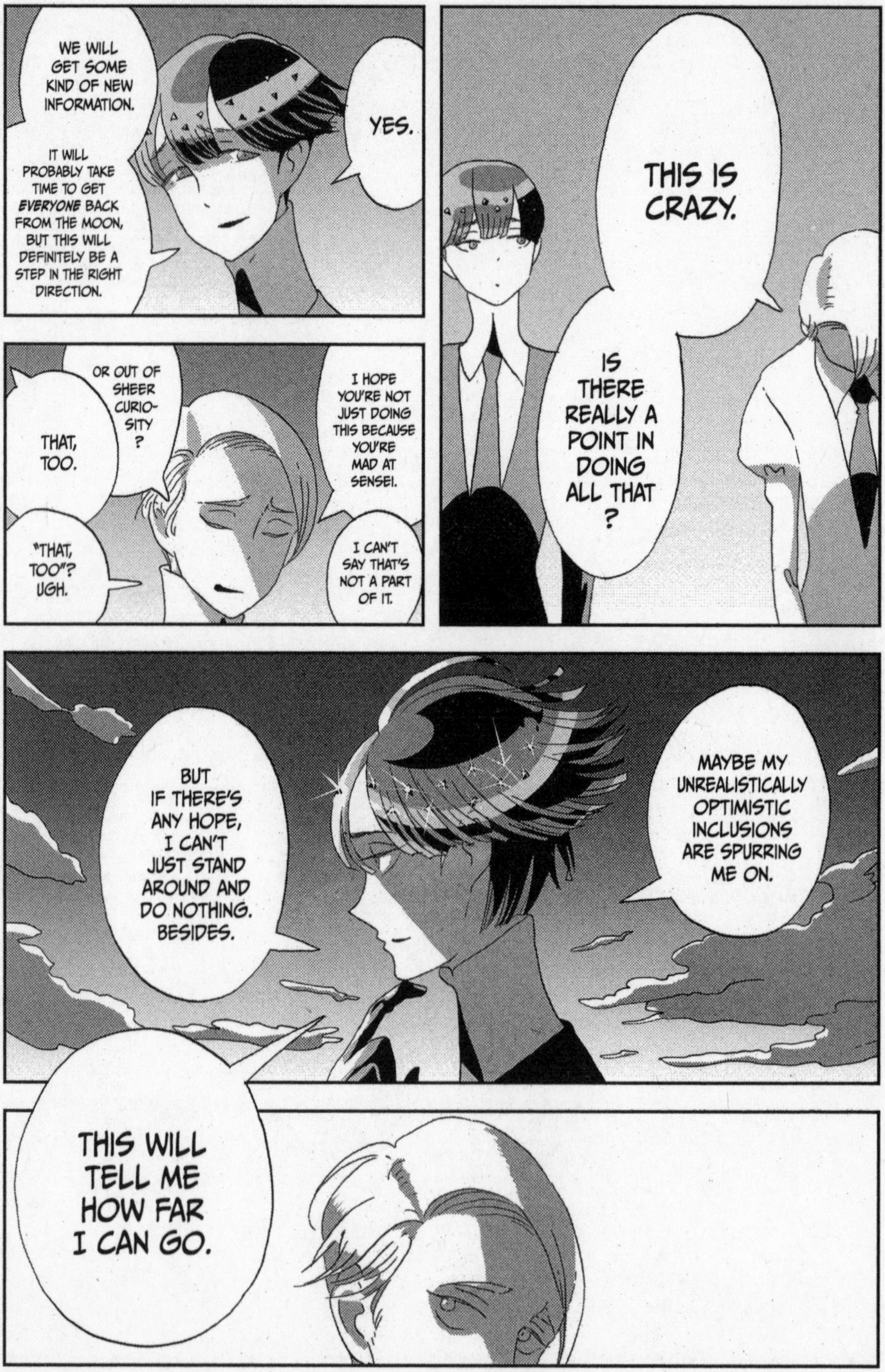
THIS IS CRAZY.
IS THERE REALLY A POINT IN DOING ALL THAT?
WE WILL GET SOME KIND OF NEW INFORMATION.
IT WILL PROBABLY TAKE TIME TO GET *EVERYONE* BACK FROM THE MOON, BUT THIS WILL DEFINITELY BE A STEP IN THE RIGHT DIRECTION.
YES.
I HOPE YOU'RE NOT JUST DOING THIS BECAUSE YOU'RE MAD AT SENSEI.
I CAN'T SAY THAT'S NOT A PART OF IT.
OR OUT OF SHEER CURIO-SITY?
THAT, TOO.
"THAT, TOO"? UGH.
MAYBE MY UNREALISTICALLY OPTIMISTIC INCLUSIONS ARE SPURRING ME ON.
BUT IF THERE'S ANY HOPE, I CAN'T JUST STAND AROUND AND DO NOTHING. BESIDES.
THIS WILL TELL ME HOW FAR I CAN GO.

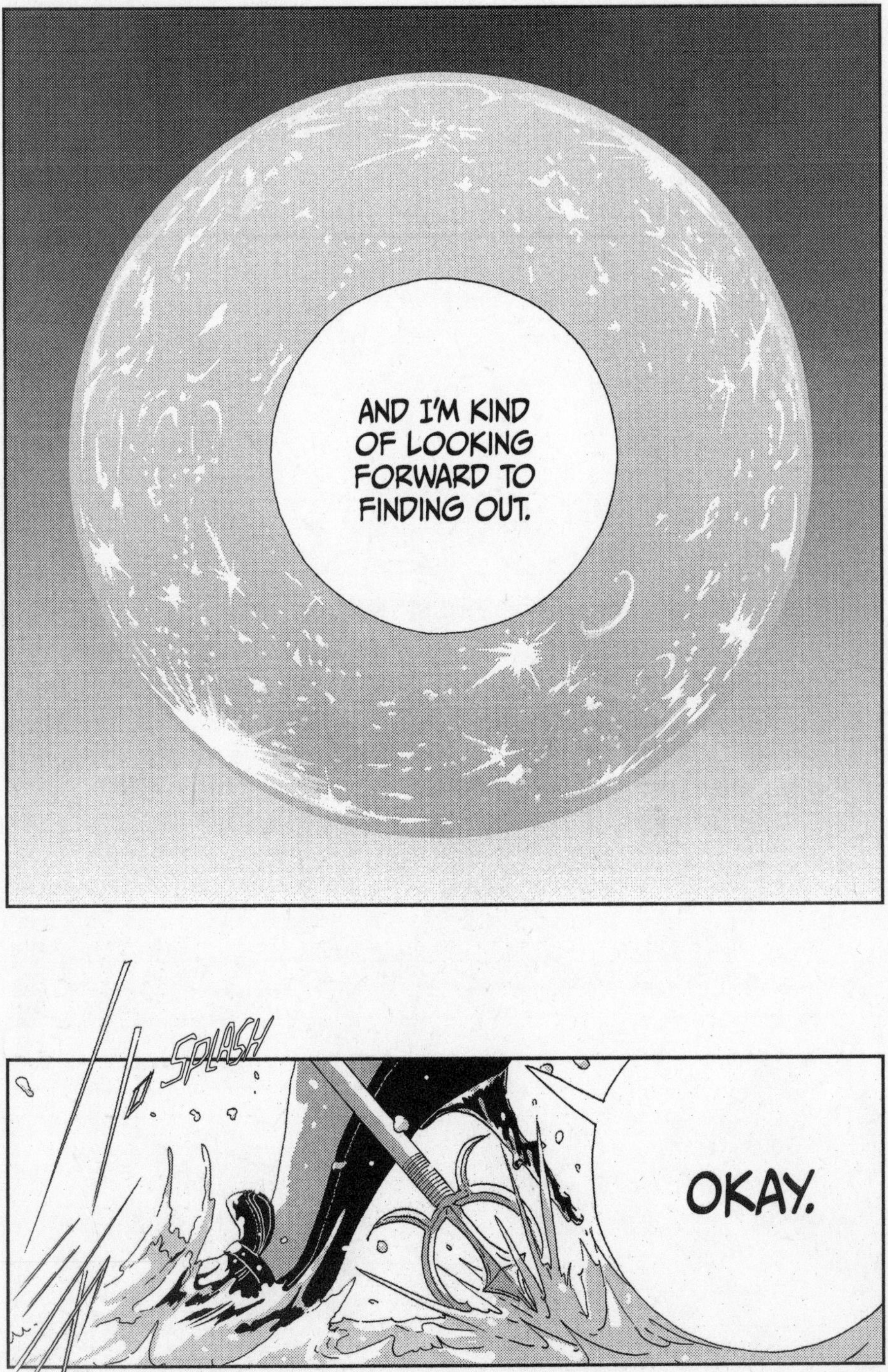
AND I'M KIND OF LOOKING FORWARD TO FINDING OUT.
OKAY.
SPLASH

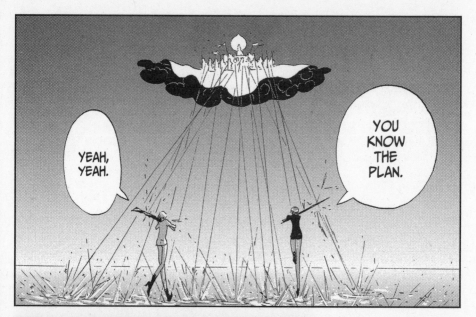

YEAH, YEAH.

YOU KNOW THE PLAN.

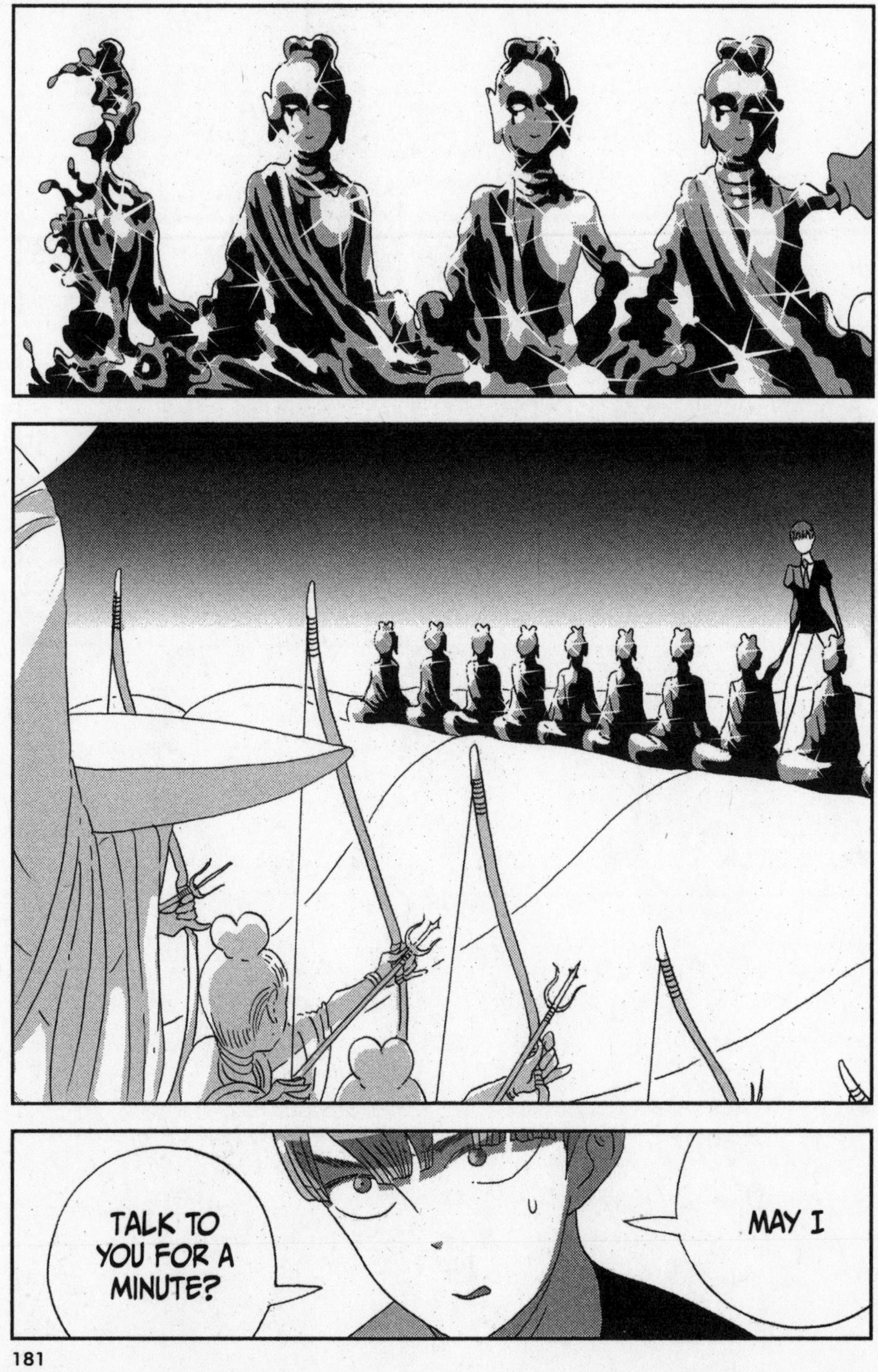
MAY I
TALK TO YOU FOR A MINUTE?

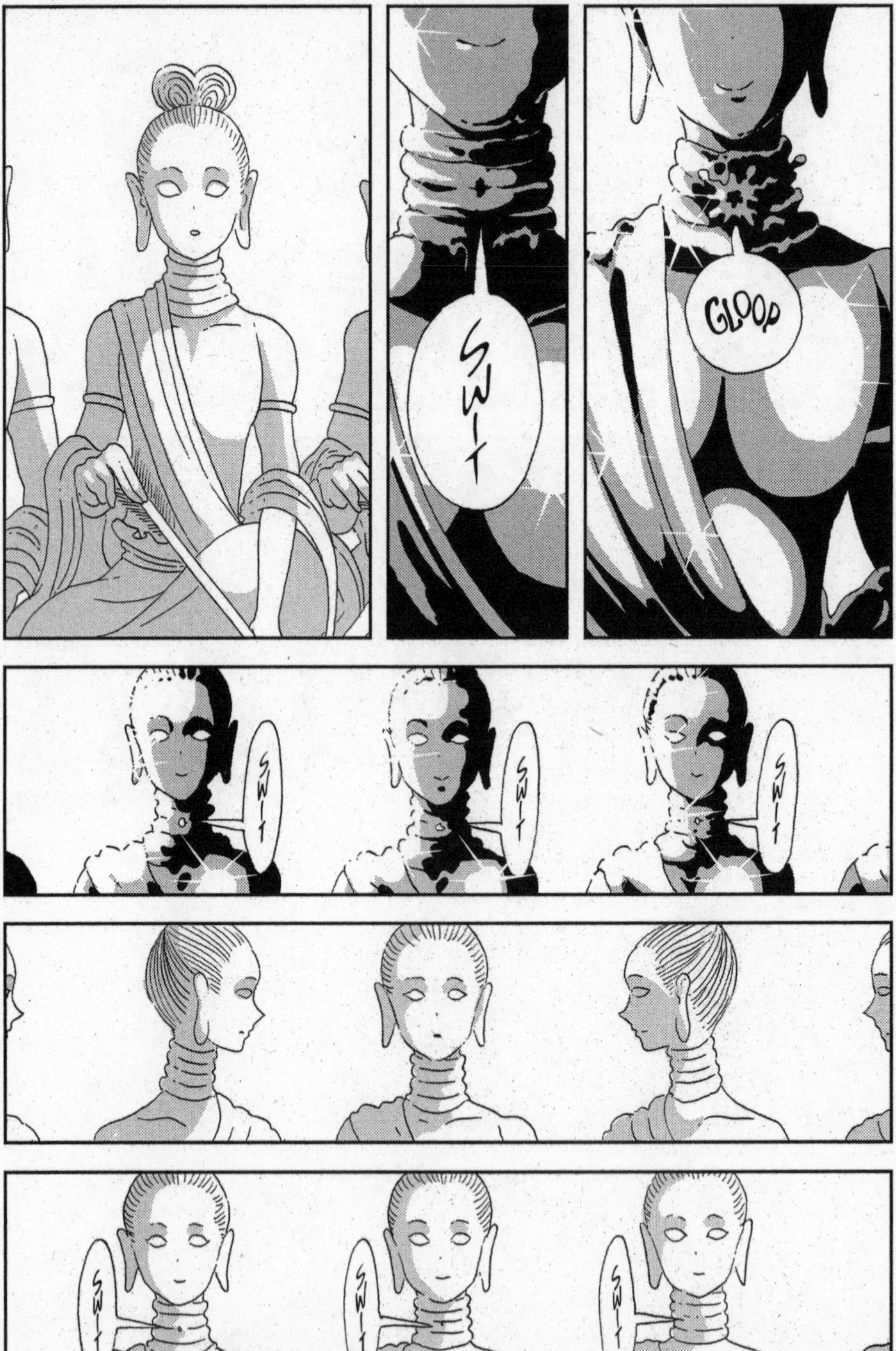
GLOOP
SWIT
SWIT
SWIT
SWIT
SWIT
SWIT
SWIT

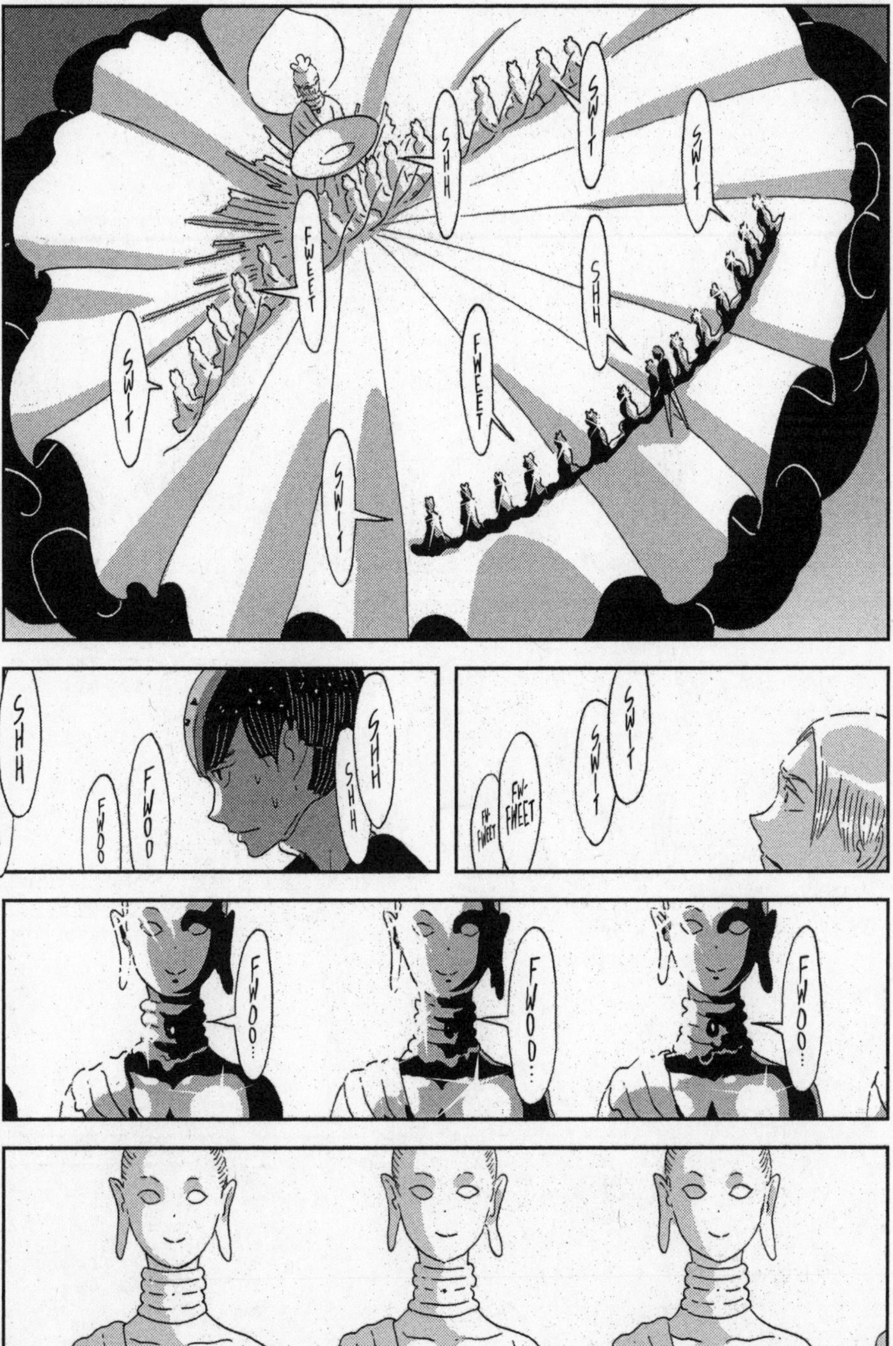
SWIT
SWIT
SHH
SHH
FWEET
FWEET
SWIT
SWIT
SWIT
SWIT
FW-FWEET
FW-FWEET
SHH
SHH
SHH
SHH
FWOO
FWOO
FWOO...
FWOO...
FWOO...

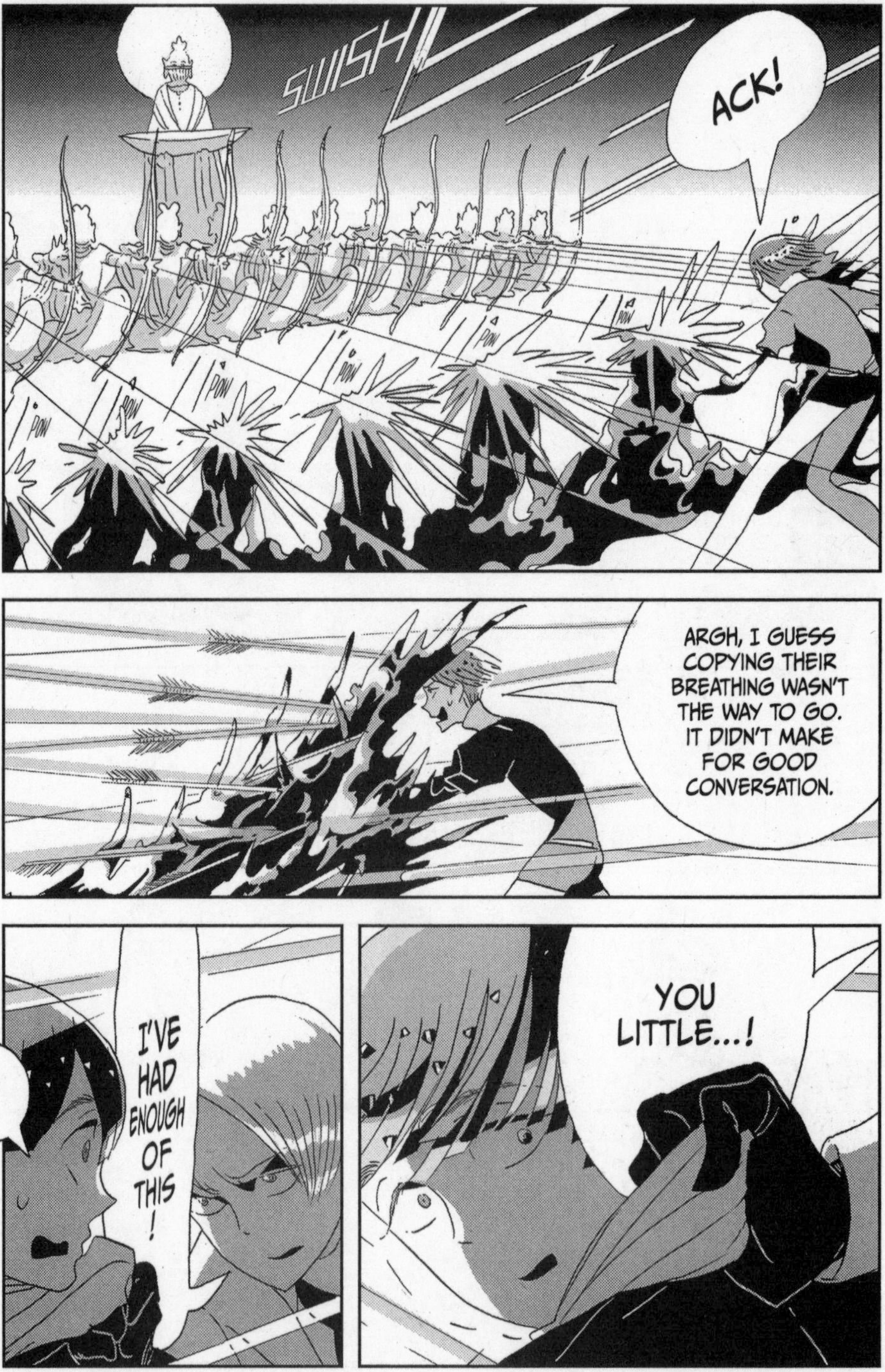
ACK!
SWISH
POW
POW
POW
POW
POW
POW
ARGH, I GUESS COPYING THEIR BREATHING WASN'T THE WAY TO GO. IT DIDN'T MAKE FOR GOOD CONVERSATION.
YOU LITTLE...!
I'VE HAD ENOUGH OF THIS!
HUH?

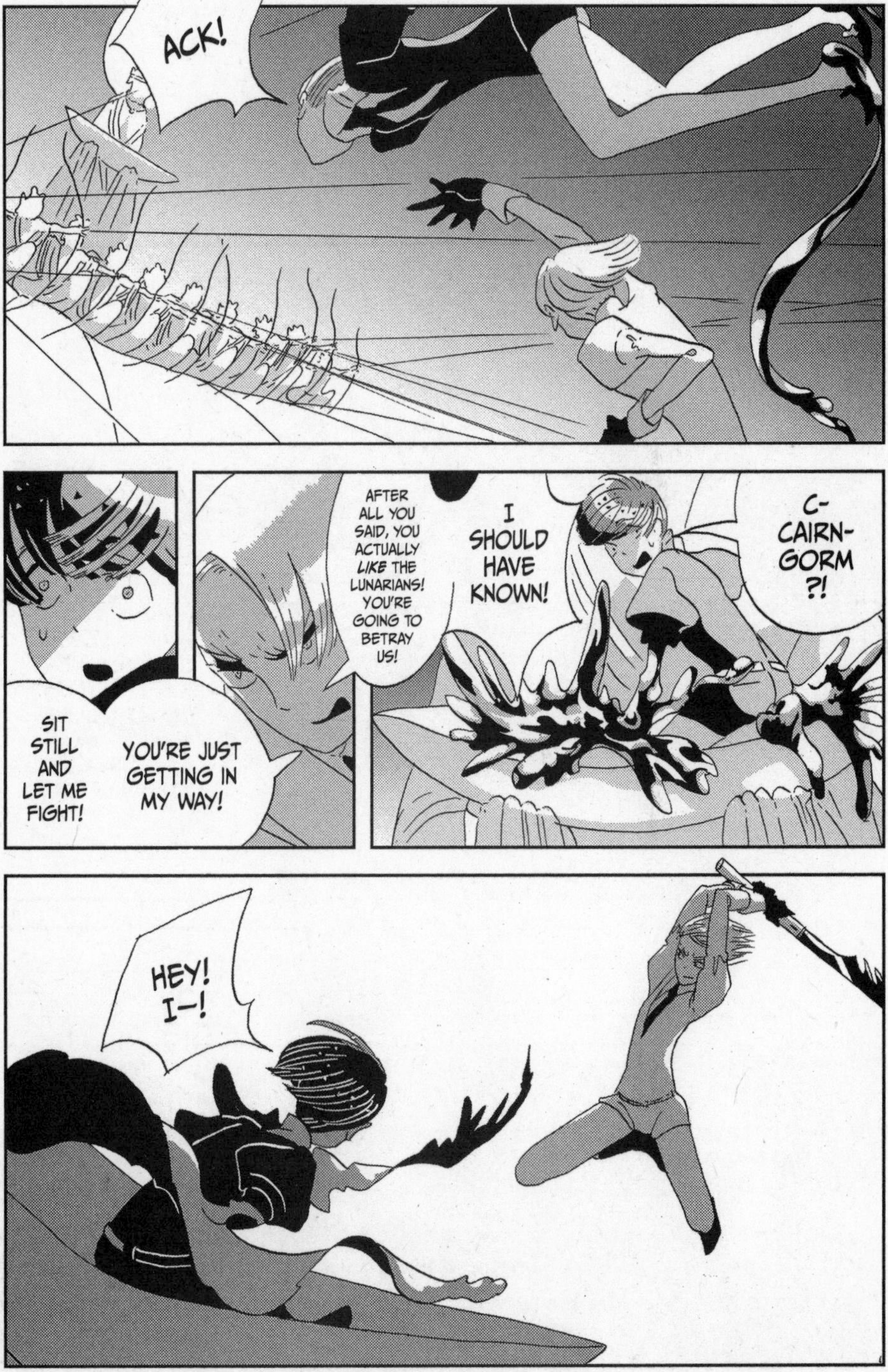
ACK!
C-CAIRNGORM?!
I SHOULD HAVE KNOWN!
AFTER ALL YOU SAID, YOU ACTUALLY *LIKE* THE LUNARIANS! YOU'RE GOING TO BETRAY US!
YOU'RE JUST GETTING IN MY WAY!
SIT STILL AND LET ME FIGHT!
HEY! I–!

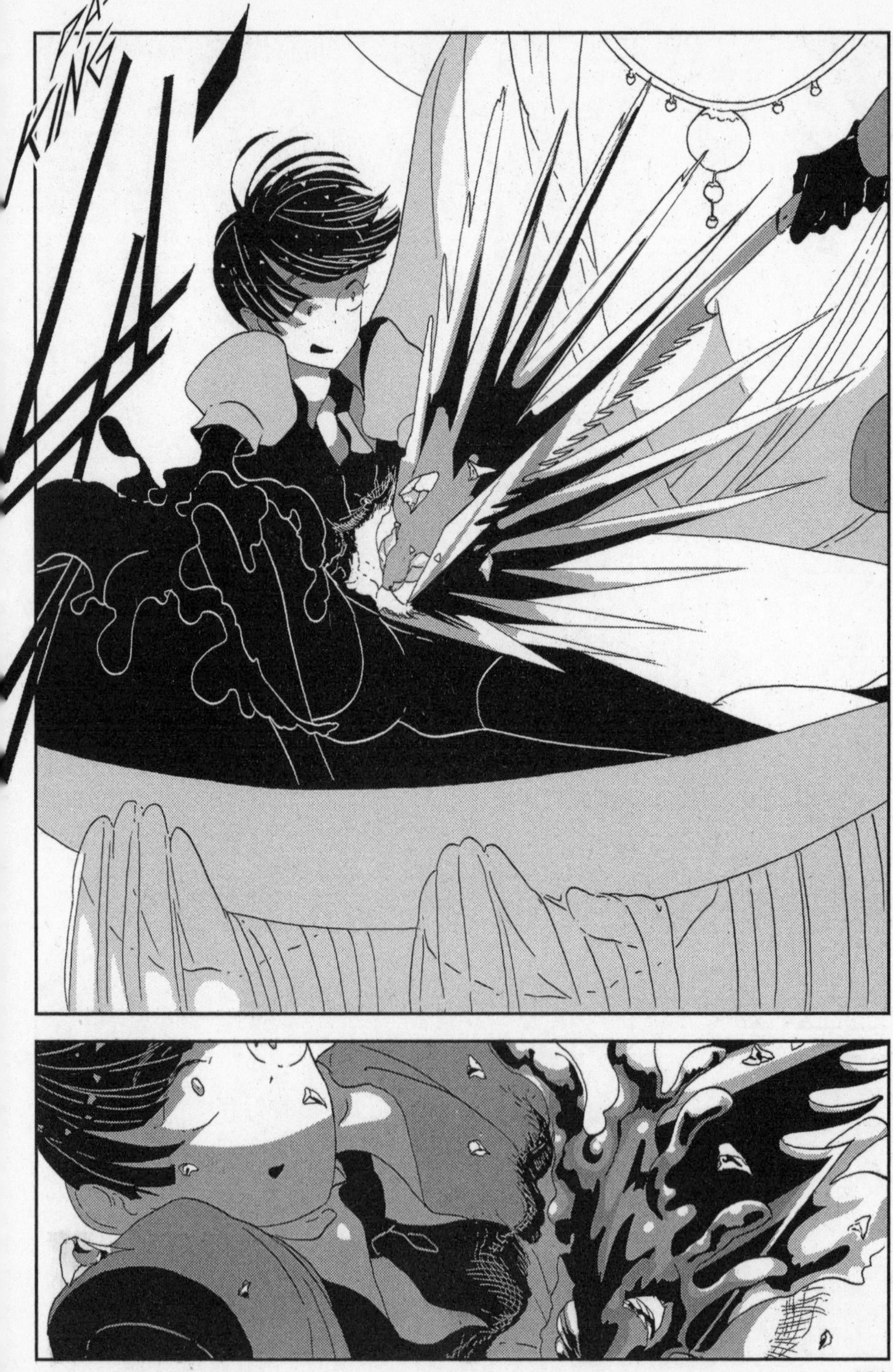
DA-KING

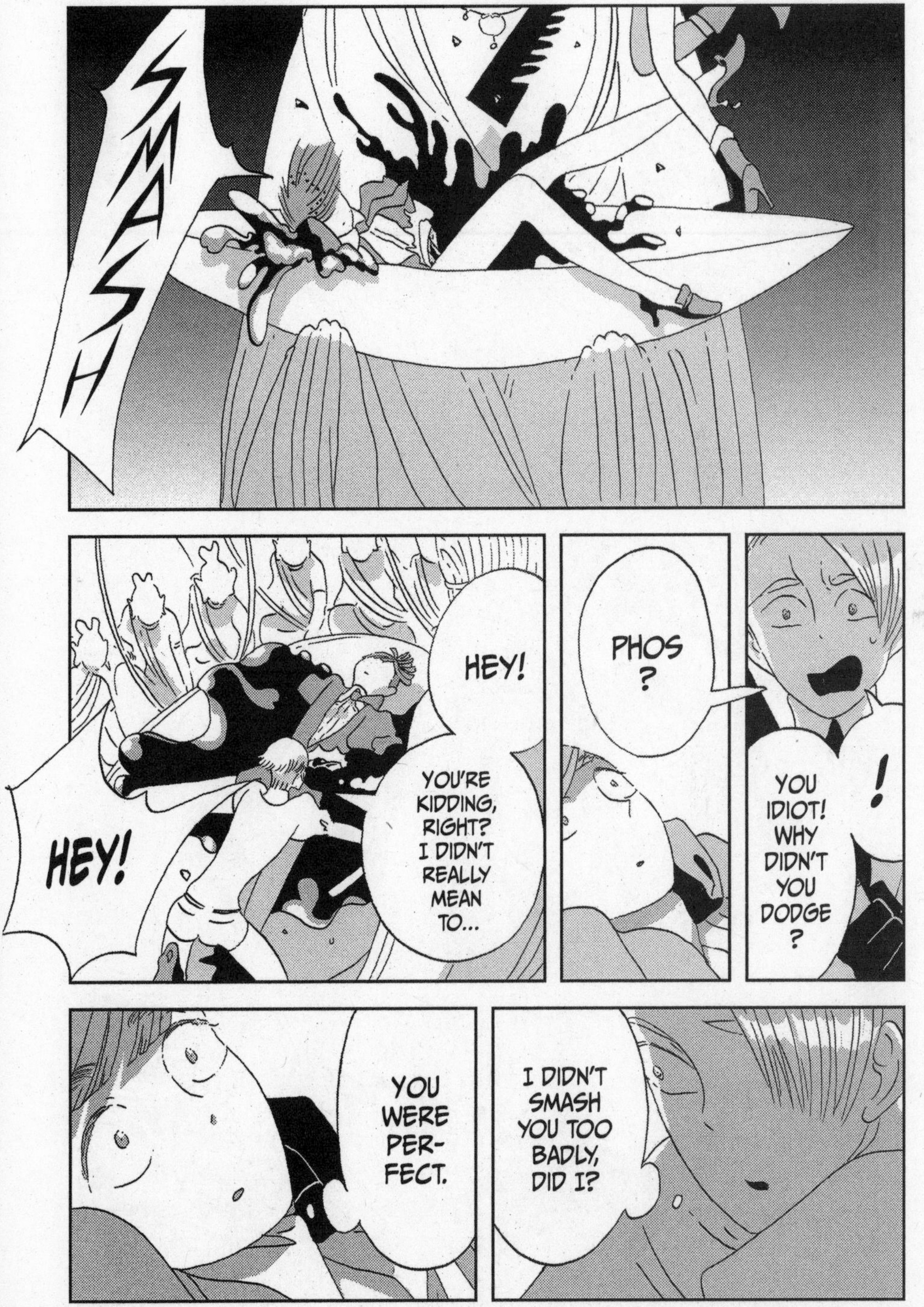
SMASH
!
YOU IDIOT! WHY DIDN'T YOU DODGE?
PHOS?
HEY!
YOU'RE KIDDING, RIGHT? I DIDN'T REALLY MEAN TO...
HEY!
I DIDN'T SMASH YOU TOO BADLY, DID I?
YOU WERE PERFECT.

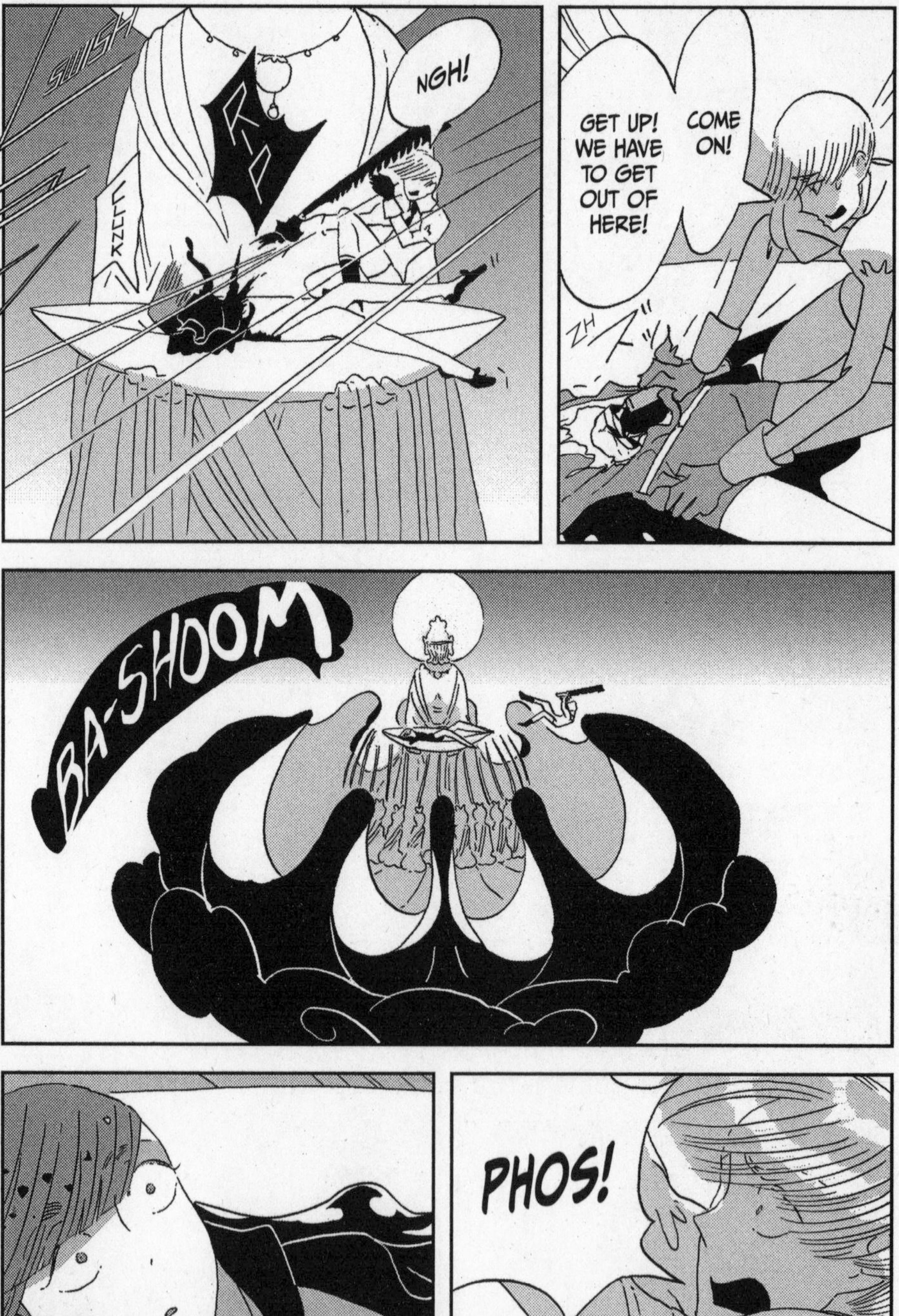
COME ON!
GET UP! WE HAVE TO GET OUT OF HERE!
ZH
NGH!
RIP
SWISH
CLUNK
BA-SHOOM
PHOS!

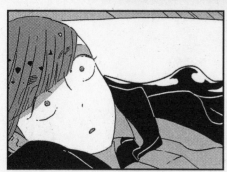

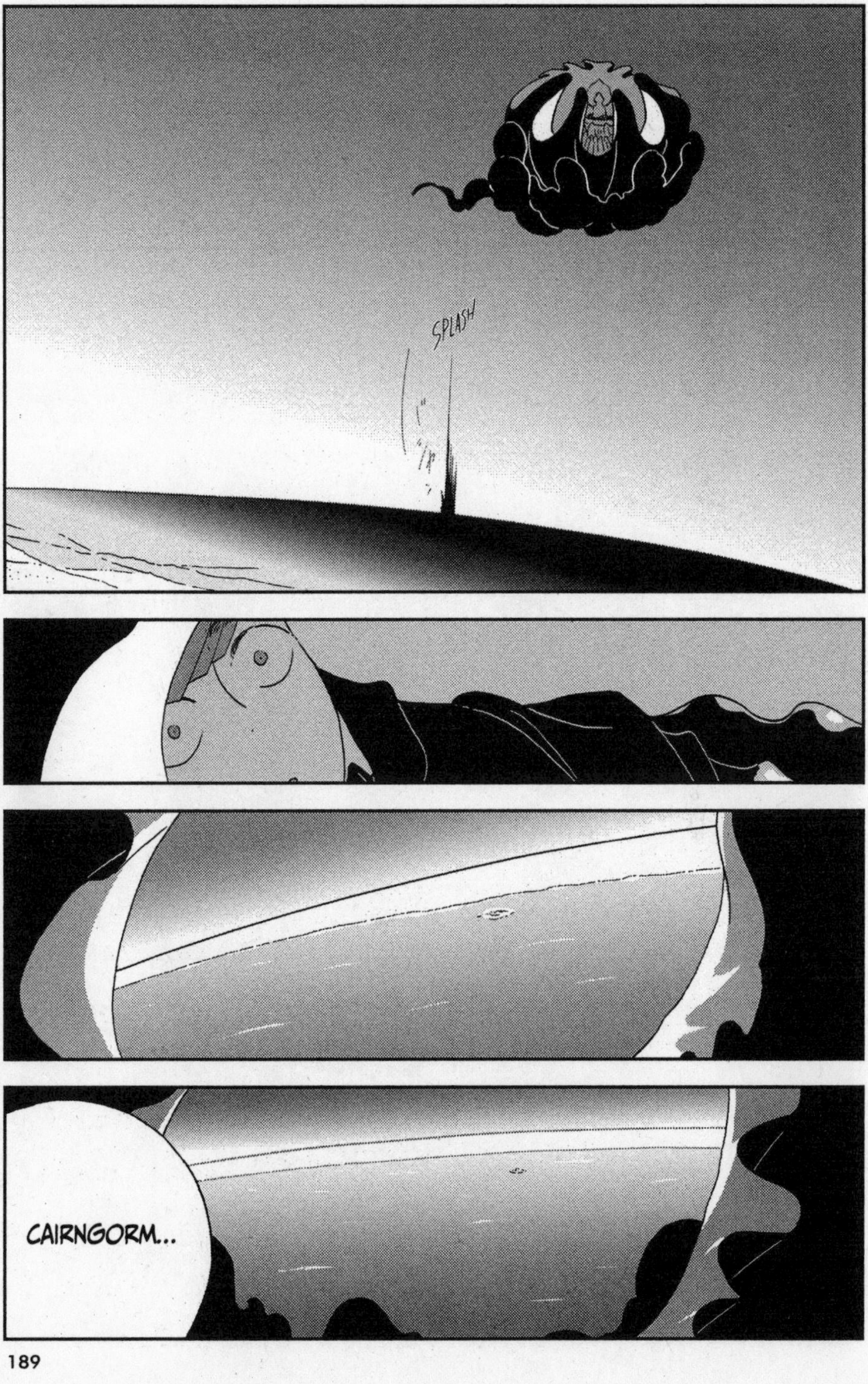
SPLASH
CAIRNGORM...

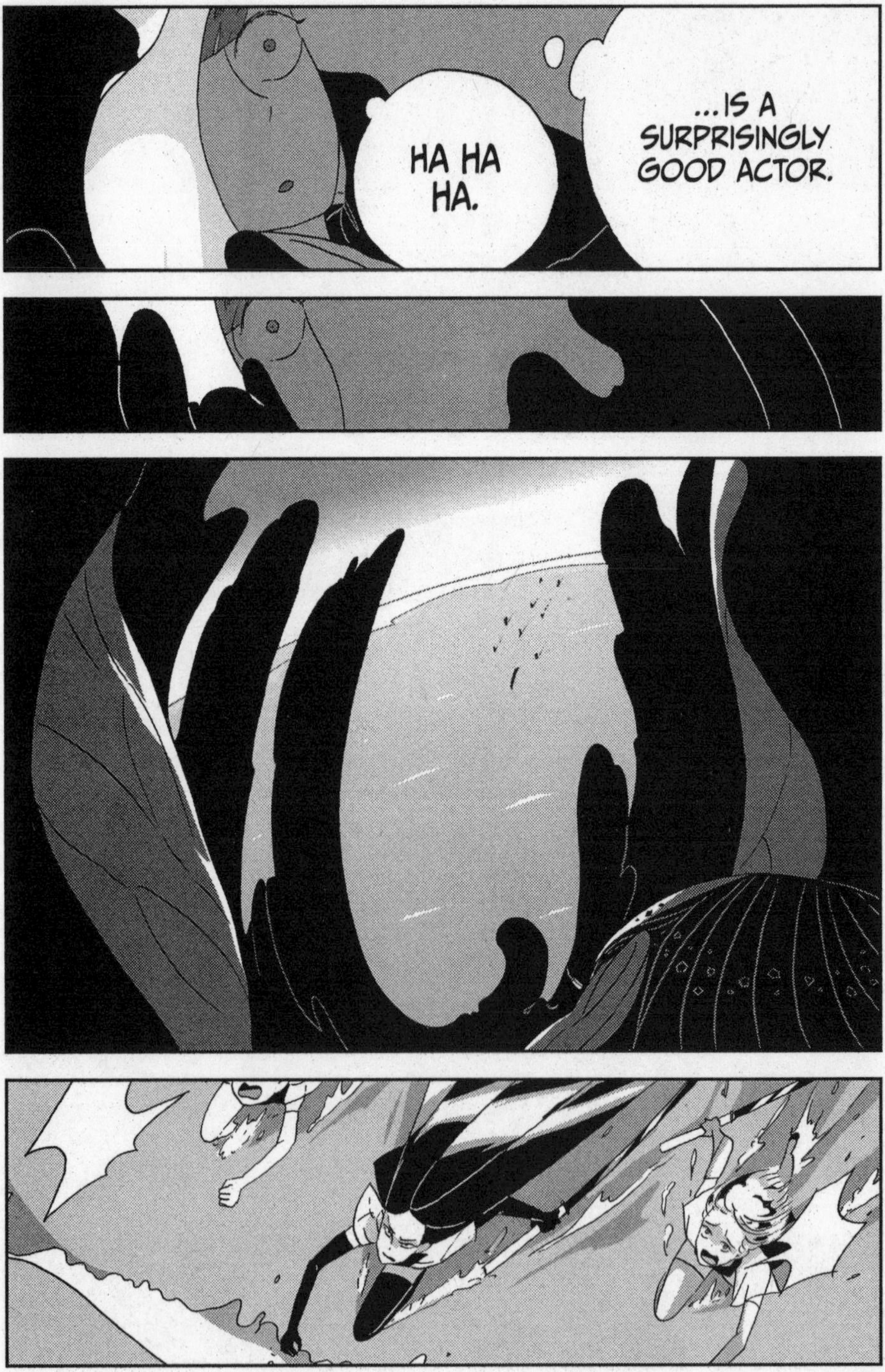
...IS A SURPRISINGLY GOOD ACTOR.
HA HA HA.

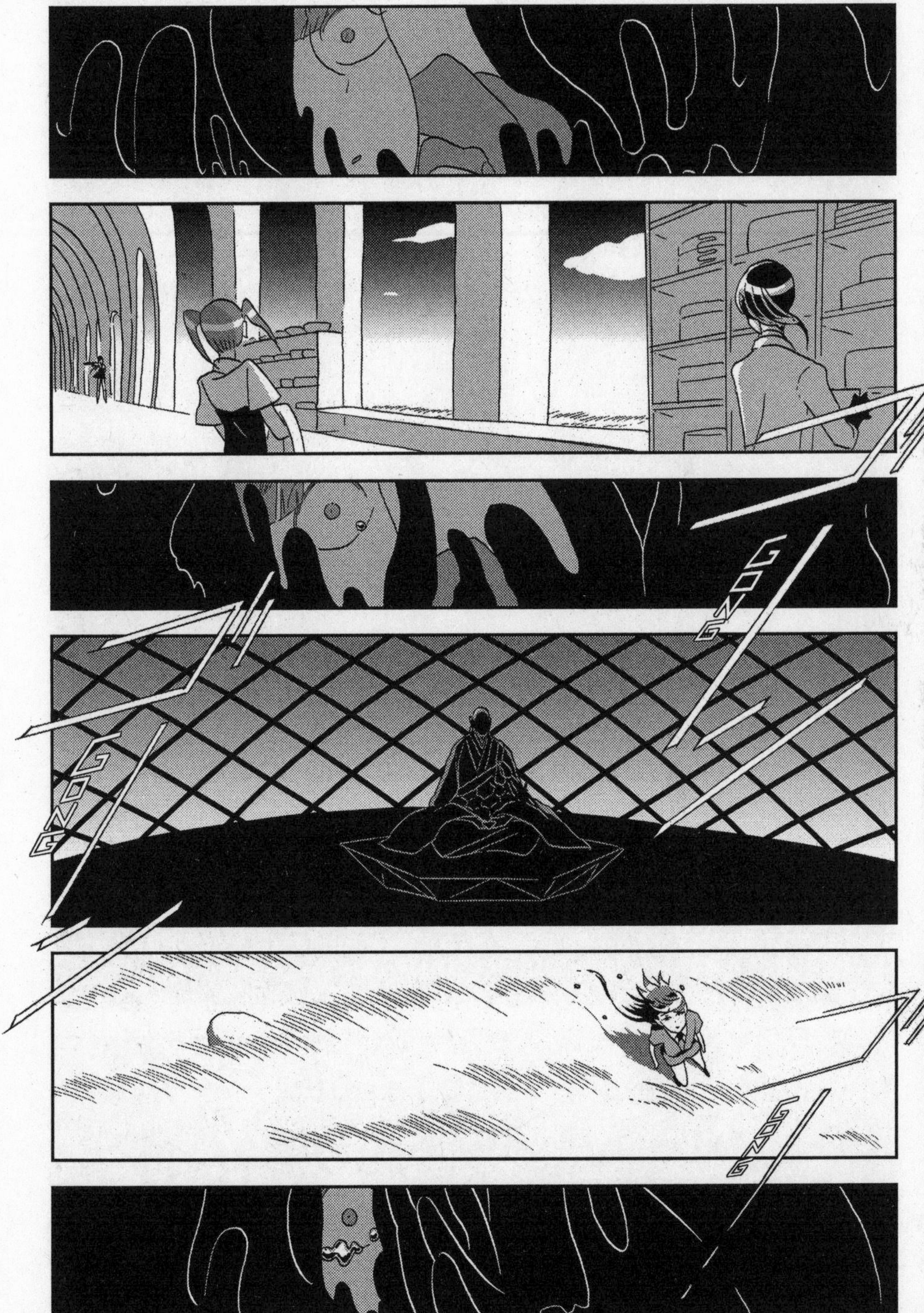
GONG
GONG
GONG

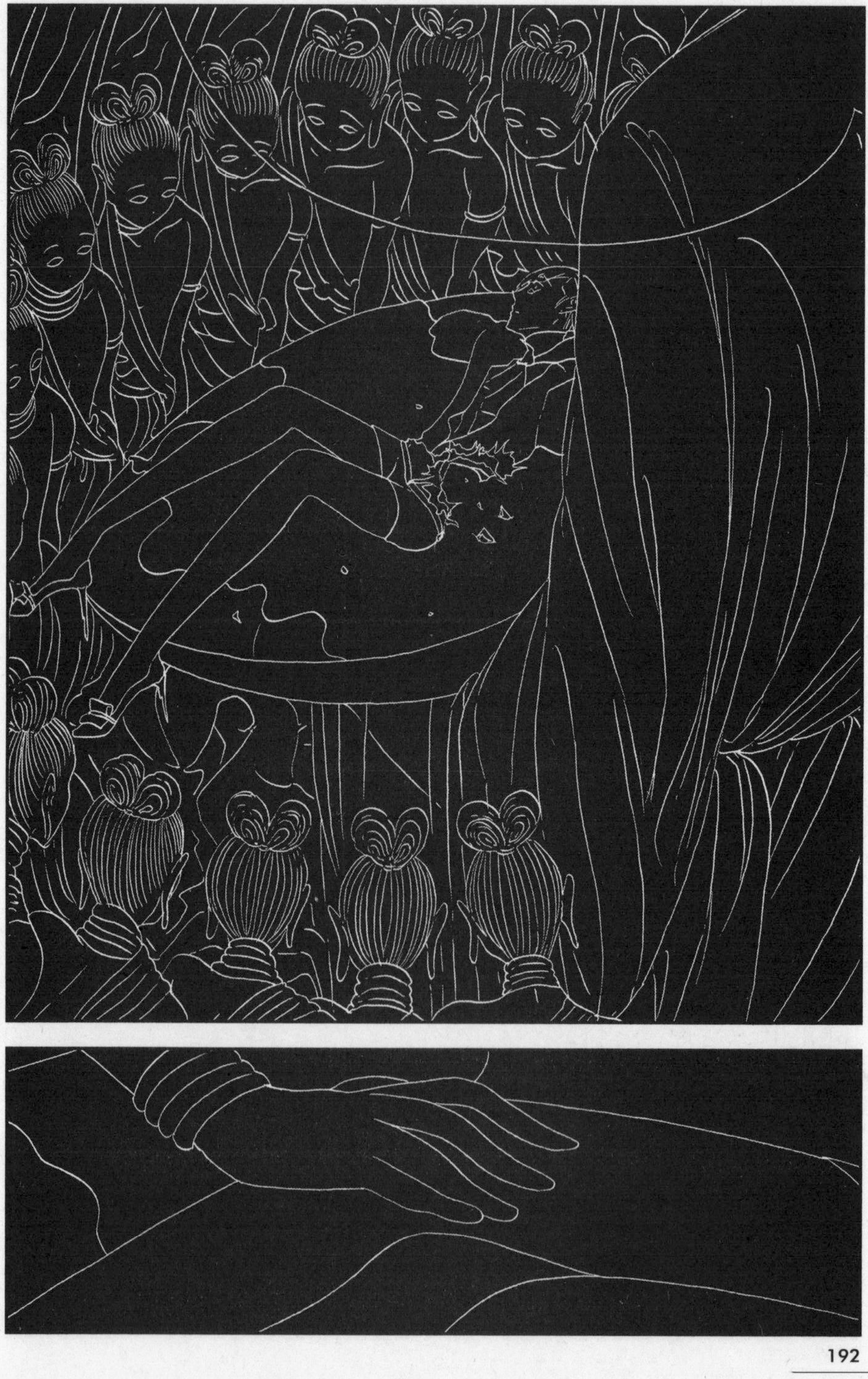

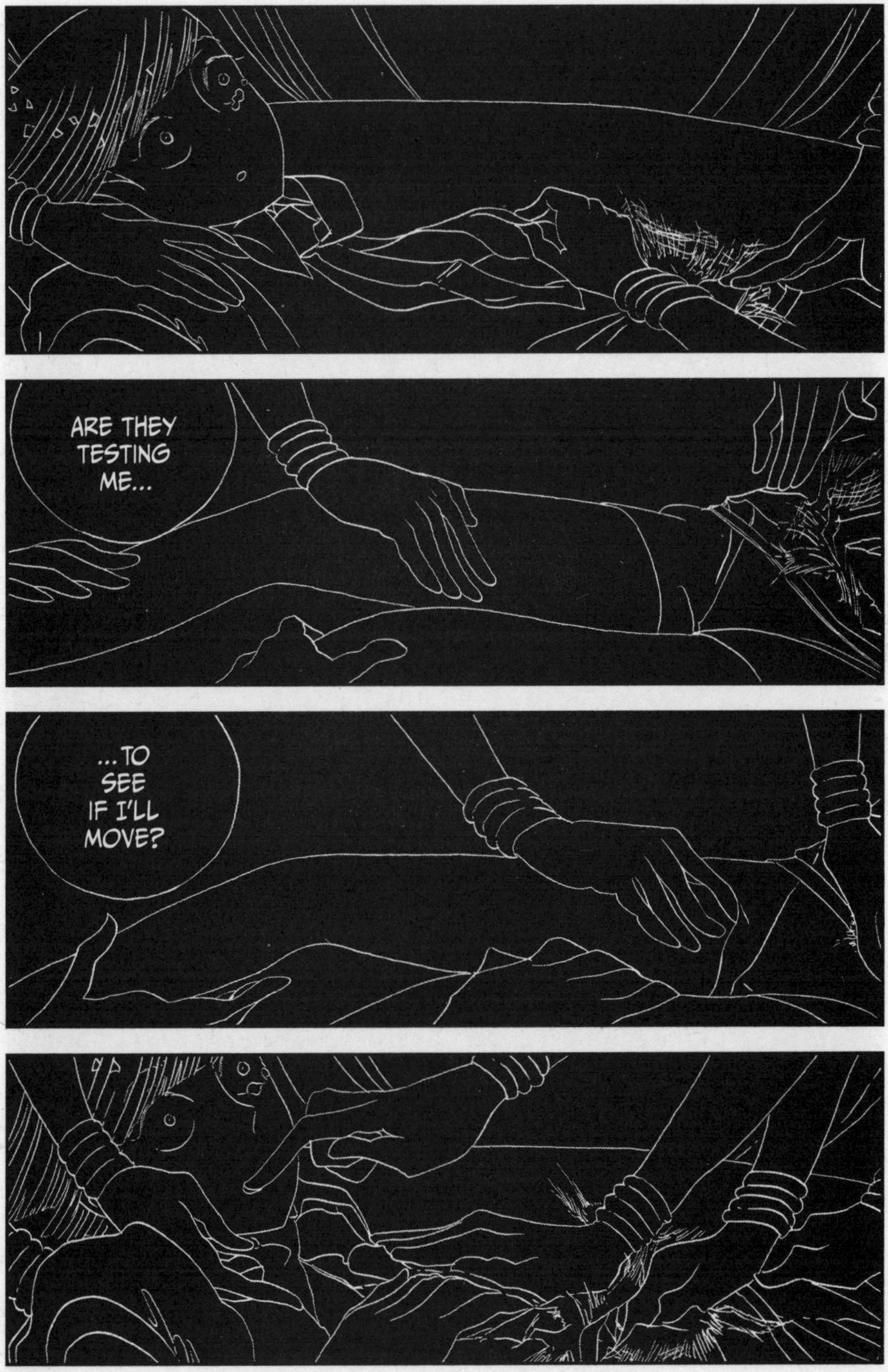
ARE THEY TESTING ME...
...TO SEE IF I'LL MOVE?

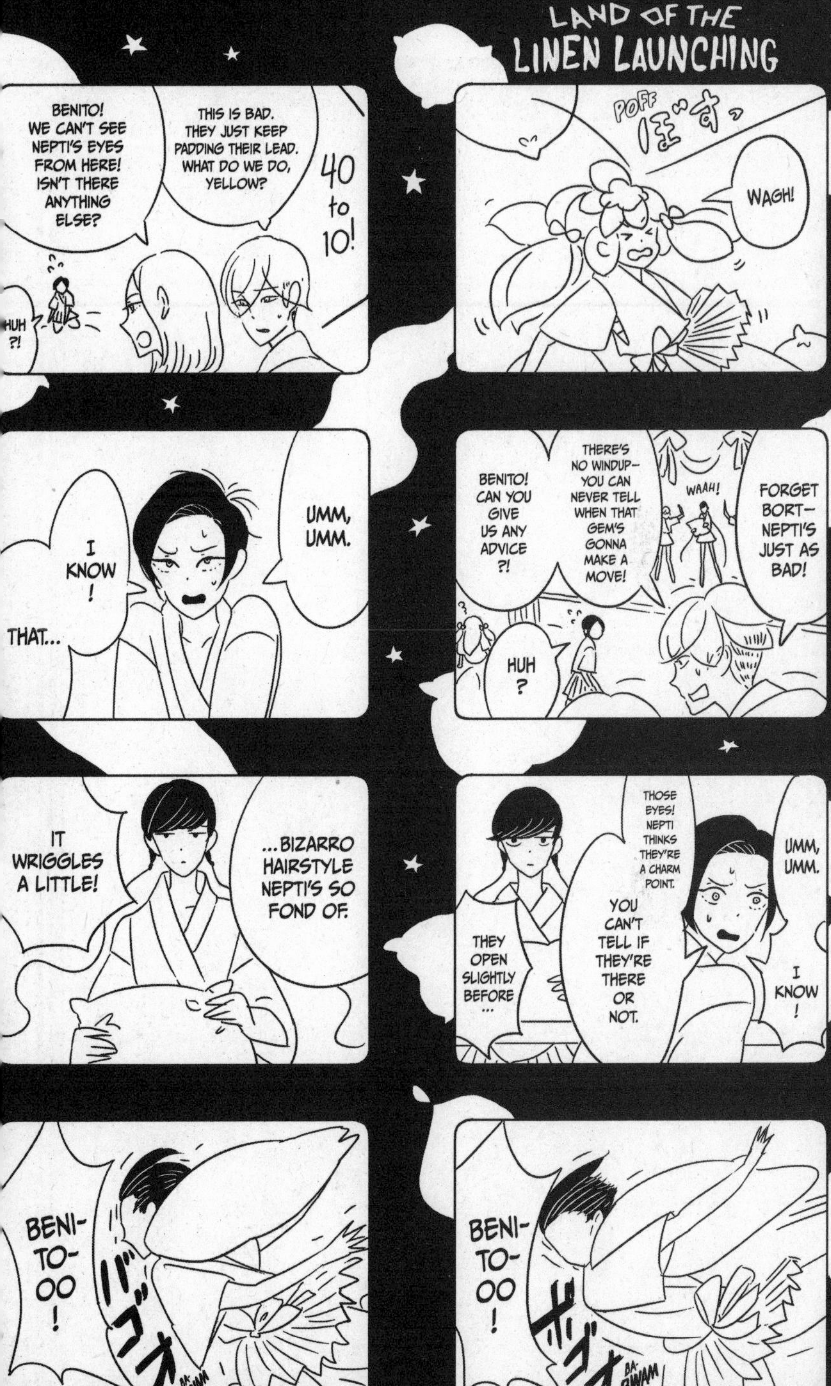
LAND OF THE LINEN LAUNCHING
POFF
ぼすっ
WAGH!
FORGET BORT— NEPTI'S JUST AS BAD!
WAAH!
THERE'S NO WINDUP— YOU CAN NEVER TELL WHEN THAT GEM'S GONNA MAKE A MOVE!
BENITO! CAN YOU GIVE US ANY ADVICE ?!
HUH ?
UMM, UMM.
THOSE EYES! NEPTI THINKS THEY'RE A CHARM POINT.
YOU CAN'T TELL IF THEY'RE THERE OR NOT.
I KNOW !
THEY OPEN SLIGHTLY BEFORE ...
BENI-TO-OO !
ボゴオ
BA-BWAM
40 to 10!
THIS IS BAD. THEY JUST KEEP PADDING THEIR LEAD. WHAT DO WE DO, YELLOW?
BENITO! WE CAN'T SEE NEPTI'S EYES FROM HERE! ISN'T THERE ANYTHING ELSE?
HUH ?!
UMM, UMM.
I KNOW !
THAT...
...BIZARRO HAIRSTYLE NEPTI'S SO FOND OF.
IT WRIGGLES A LITTLE!
BENI-TO-OO !
バゴオ
BA-BWAM

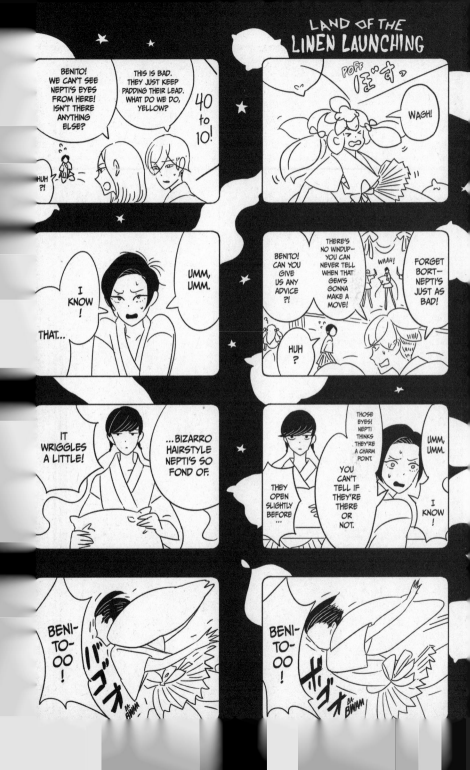

TRANSLATION NOTES

WE CAN USE MY HEAD *page 11*

As the reader may recall, Cairngorm is a form of quartz.
Agate often has layers of quartz in it, so Cairngorm is correct
in assuming that this particular material is something that
Phos's inclusions are already familiar with.

AESTIVATION *page 32*

Most of the gems hibernate, which means they sleep in the
winter. Because Cairngorm doesn't get to sleep until summer,
"hibernation" is not part of the program. What Cairngorm does
is "aestivate," which is sleeping through the summer.

DOCTOR *page 130*

Sensei calls the Lunarian *hakase*, which denotes an expert in their
field, like a professor or someone with a doctorate. Since many
experts are referred to as "doctors" in English, we went with
"doctor" over "professor."

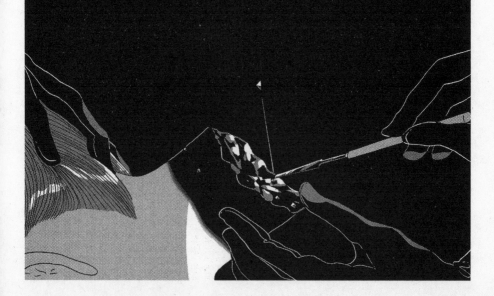

LAND OF THE LUSTROUS

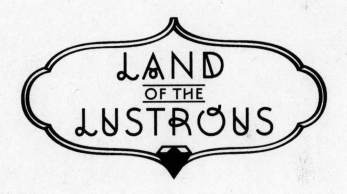

JAPANESE EDITION INSIDE COVER GALLERY
Volume 5

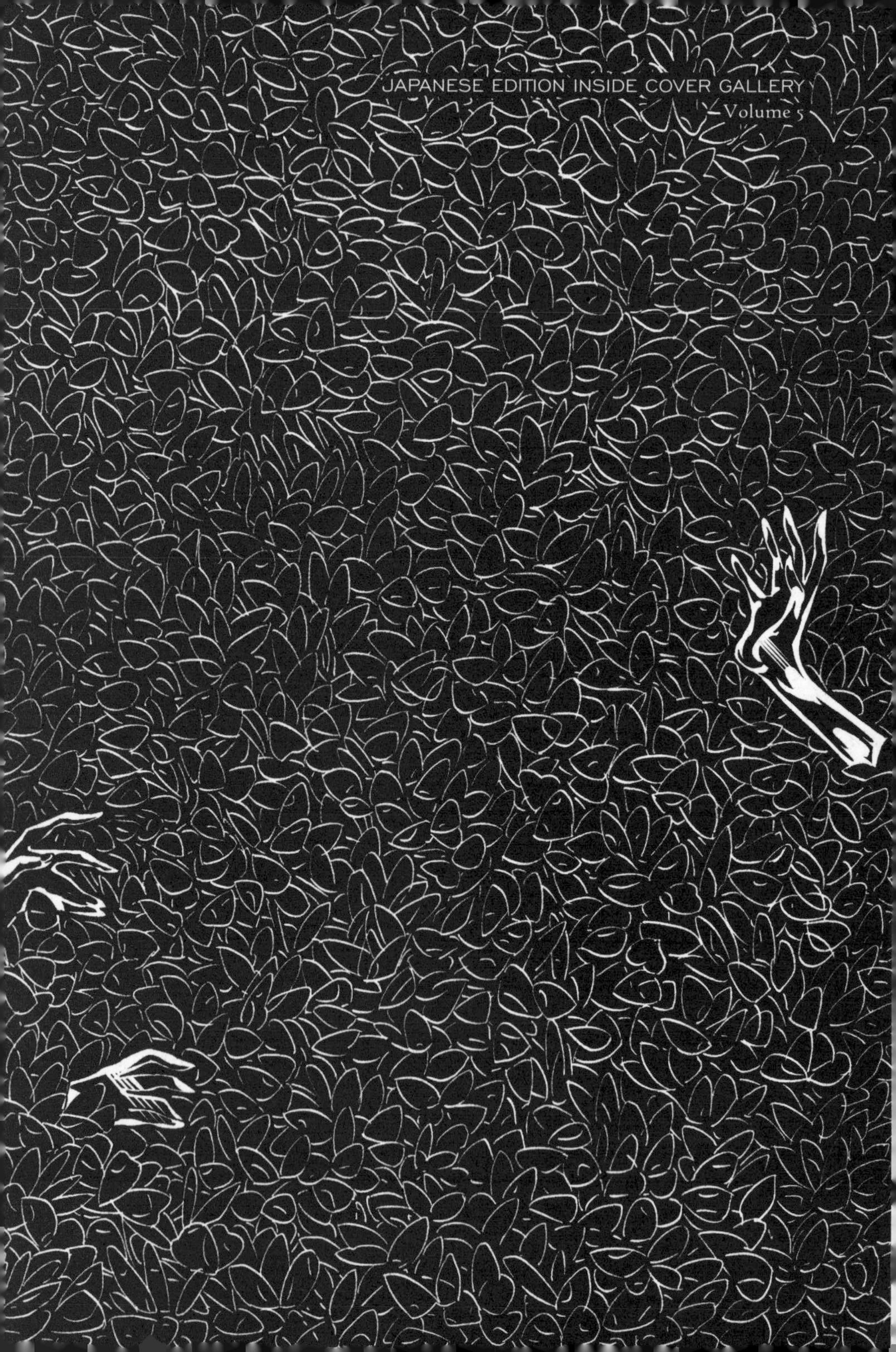

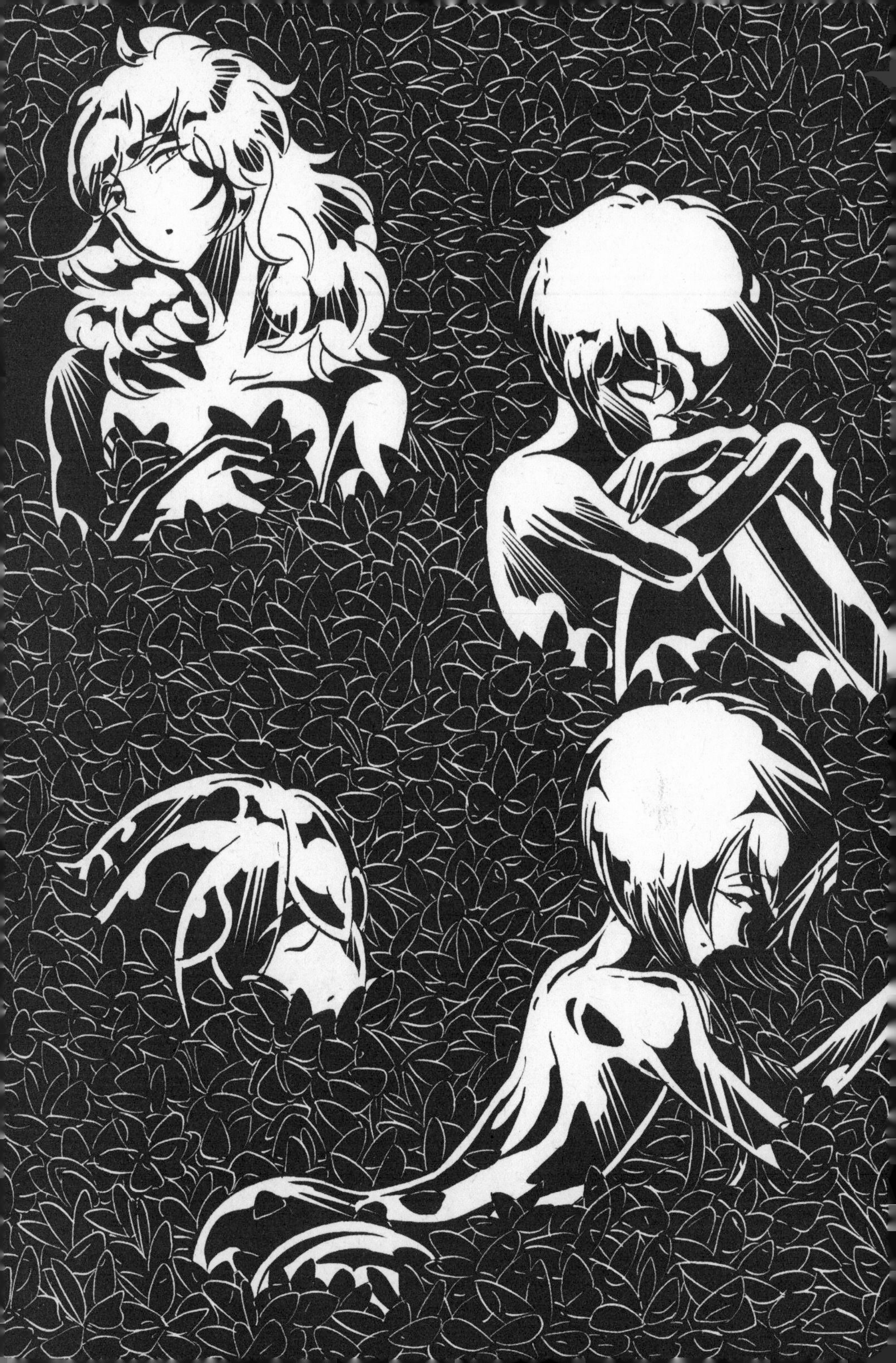

Volume 6

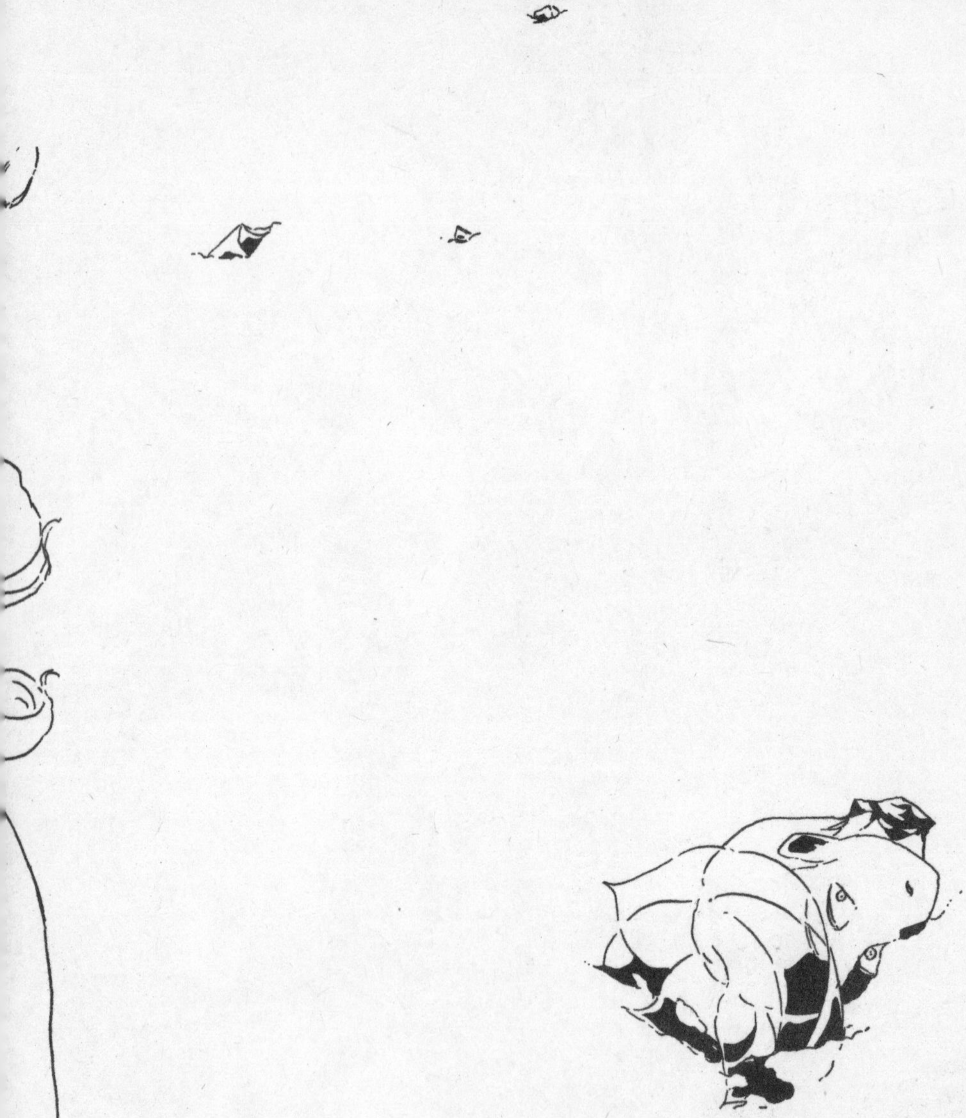

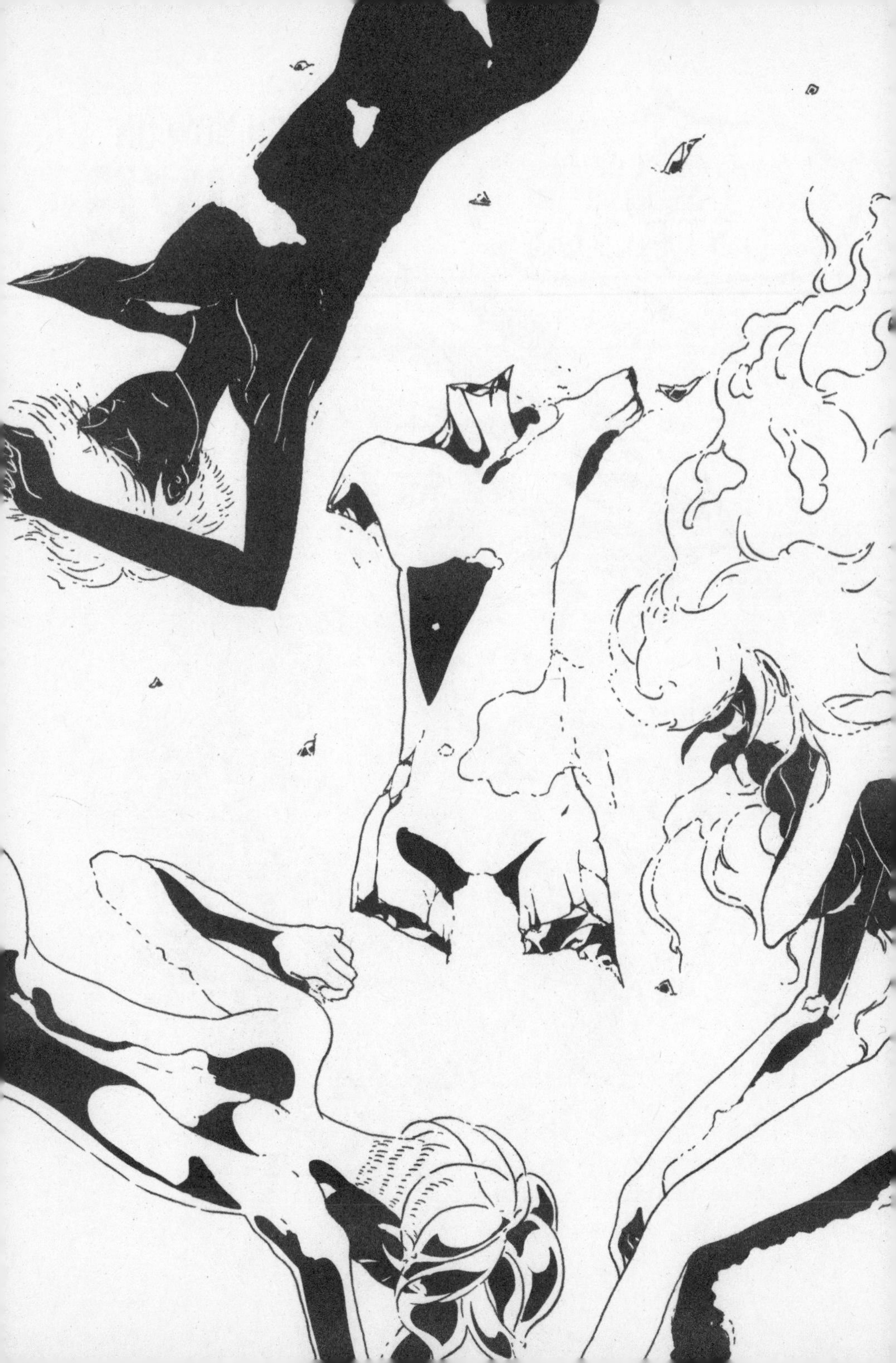

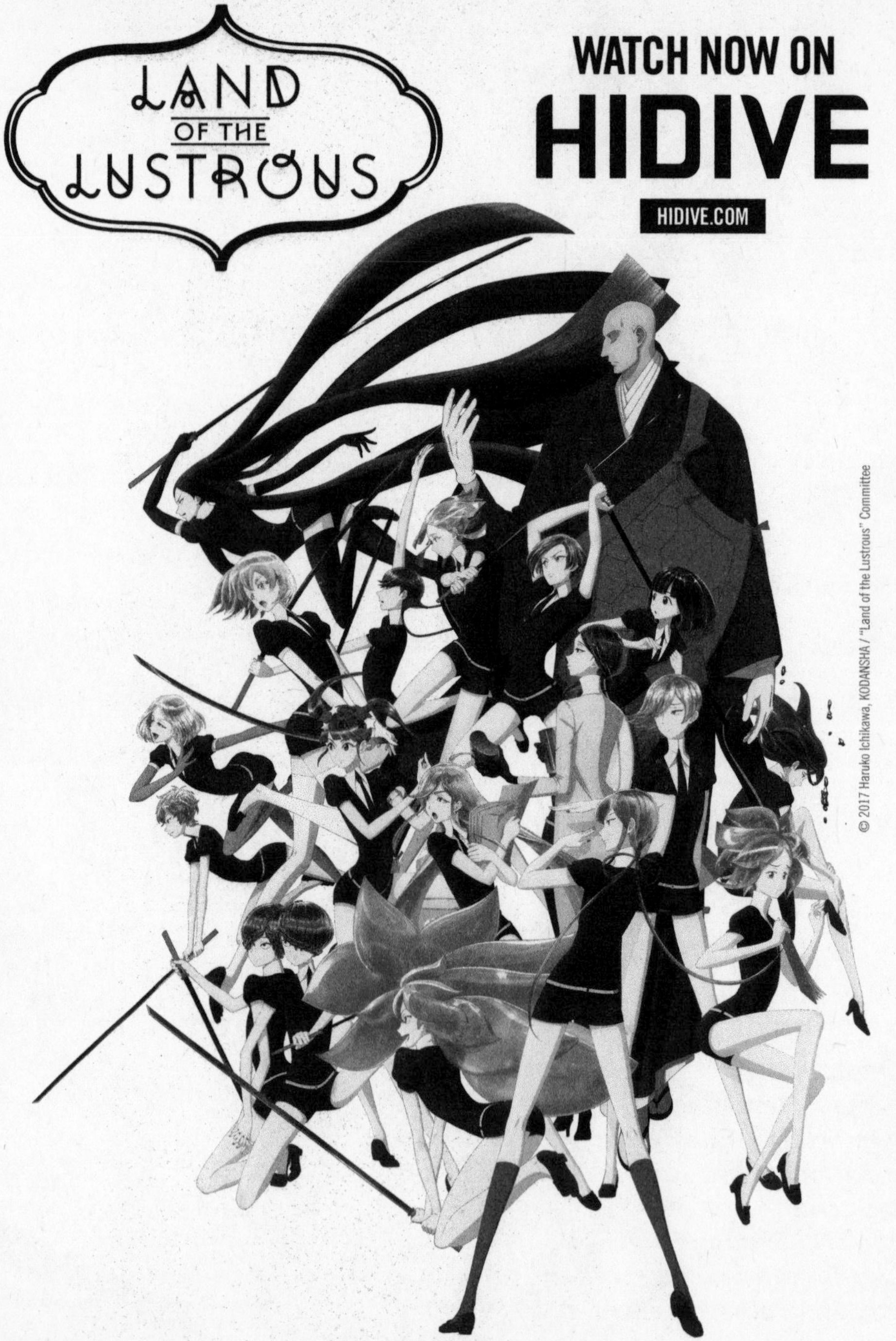
LAND OF THE LUSTROUS
WATCH NOW ON
HIDIVE
HIDIVE.COM
© 2017 Haruko Ichikawa, KODANSHA / "Land of the Lustrous" Committee

KC
KODANSHA
COMICS

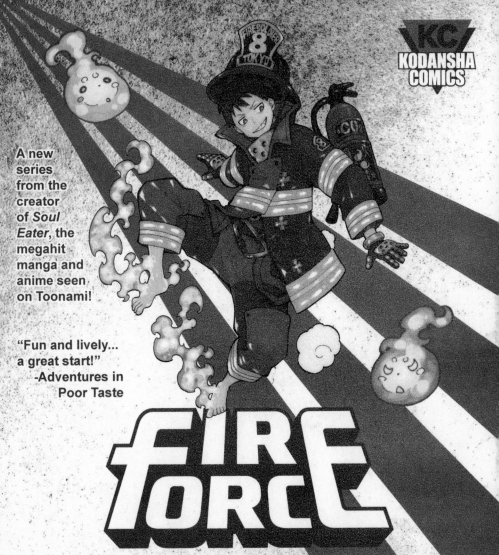

A new series from the creator of *Soul Eater*, the megahit manga and anime seen on Toonami!

"Fun and lively... a great start!"
-Adventures in Poor Taste

FIRE FORCE

By Atsushi Ohkubo

The city of Tokyo is plagued by a deadly phenomenon: spontaneous human combustion! Luckily, a special team is there to quench the inferno: The Fire Force! The fire soldiers at Special Fire Cathedral 8 are about to get a unique addition. Enter Shinra, a boy who possesses the power to run at the speed of a rocket, leaving behind the famous "devil's footprints" (and destroying his shoes in the process). Can Shinra and his colleagues discover the source of this strange epidemic before the city burns to ashes?

© Atsushi Ohkubo/Kodansha Ltd. All rights reserved.

© Hiroyuki Takei/Kodansha Ltd. All rights reserved.

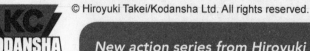

New action series from Hiroyuki Takei, creator of the classic shonen franchise Shaman King!

In medieval Japan, a bell hanging on the collar is a sign that a cat has a master. Norachiyo's bell hangs from his katana sheath, but he is nonetheless a stray — a ronin. This one-eyed cat samurai travels across a dishonest world, cutting through pretense and deception with his blade.

By
Hiroyuki Takei

"I'm pleasantly surprised to find modern shojo using cross-dressing as a dramatic device to deliver social commentary... Recommended."

-Otaku USA Magazine

The prince in his dark days

By **Hico Yamanaka**

A drunkard for a father, a household of poverty... For 17-year-old Atsuko misfortune is all she knows and believes in. Until one day, a chance encounter with Itaru–the wealthy heir of a huge corporation–changes everything. The two look identical, uncannily so. When Itaru curiously goes missing, Atsuko is roped into being his stand-in. There, in his shoes Atsuko must parade like a prince in a palace. She encounters many new experiences, but at what cost...?

© Hico Yamanaka/Kodansha Ltd. All rights reserved

KC

KODANSHA COMICS

The Black Museum The Ghost and the Lady

By Kazuhiro Fujita

Deep in Scotland Yard in London sits an evidence room dedicated to the greatest mysteries of British history. In this "Black Museum" sits a misshapen hunk of lead—two bullets fused together—the key to a wartime encounter between Florence Nightingale, the mother of modern nursing, and a supernatural Man in Grey. This story is unknown to most scholars of history, but a special guest of the museum will tell the tale of The Ghost and the Lady...

Praise for Kazuhiro Fujita's *Ushio and Tora*

'A charming revival that combines a classic look with modern depth and pacing... **Essential viewing both for curmudgeons and new fans alike.**" — Anime News Network

'**GREAT!** The first episode of Ushio and Tora captures the essence of '90s anime." — IGN

© Kazuhiro Fujita/Kodansha Ltd. All rights reserved.

"Parasyte fans should get a kick out of the chance to revisit Iwaaki's weird, violent, strangely affecting universe. Recommended." -Otaku USA Magazine

"A great anthology containing an excellent variety of genres and styles." -Manga Bookshelf

Based on the critically acclaimed classic horror manga

The first new *Parasyte* manga in over 20 years!

NEO Parasyte f

BY ASUMIKO NAKAMURA, EMA TOYAMA, MIKI RINNO, LALAKO KOJIMA, KAORI YUKI, BANKO KUZE, YUUKI OBATA, KASHIO, YUI KUROE, ASIA WATANABE, MIKIMAKI, HIKARU SURUGA, HAJIME SHINJO, RENJURO KINDAICHI, AND YURI NARUSHIMA

A collection of chilling new *Parasyte* stories from Japan's top shojo artists!

Parasites: shape-shifting aliens whose only purpose is to assimilate with and consume the human race... but do these monsters have a different side? A parasite becomes a prince to save his romance-obsessed female host from a dangerous stalker. Another hosts a cooking show, in which the real monsters are revealed. These and 13 more stories, from some of the greatest shojo manga artists alive today, together make up a chilling, funny, and entertaining tribute to one of manga's horror classics!

KC KODANSHA COMICS

© Hitoshi Iwaaki, Asumiko Nakamura, Ema Toyama, Miki Rinno, Lalako Kojima, Kaori Yuki, Banko Kuze, Yuuki Obata, Kashio, Yui Kuroe, Asia Watanabe, Mikimaki, Hikaru Suruga, Hajime Shinjo, Renjuro Kindaichi, Yuri Narushima/Kodansha Ltd. All rights reserved.

KC
KODANSHA
COMICS

Japan's most powerful spirit medium delves into the ghost world's greatest mysteries!

Story by Kyo Shirodaira, famed author of mystery fiction and creator of *Spiral*, *Blast of Tempest*, and *The Record of a Fallen Vampire*.

Both touched by spirits called yôkai, Kotoko and Kurô have gained unique superhuman powers. But to gain her powers Kotoko has given up an eye and a leg, and Kurô's personal life is in shambles. So when Kotoko suggests they team up to deal with renegades from the spirit world, Kurô doesn't have many other choices, but Kotoko might just have a few ulterior motives...

IN/SPECTRE

STORY BY KYO SHIRODAIRA
ART BY CHASHIBA KATASE

© Kyo Shirodaira/Kodansha Ltd. All rights reserved.

H·A·P·P·I·N·E·S·S

——ハピネス——

By Shuzo Oshimi

From the creator of *The Flowers of Evil*

Nothing interesting is happening in Makoto Ozaki's first year of high school. His life is a series of quiet humiliations: low-grade bullies, unreliable friends, and the constant frustration of his adolescent lust. But one night, a pale, thin girl knocks him to the ground in an alley and offers him a choice. Now everything is different. Daylight is searingly bright. Food tastes awful. And worse than anything is the terrible, consuming thirst...

Praise for Shuzo Oshimi's *The Flowers of Evil*

"A shockingly readable story that vividly—one might even say queasily—evokes the fear and confusion of discovering one's own sexuality. Recommended." —The Manga Critic

"A page-turning tale of sordid middle school blackmail." —Otaku USA Magazine

"A stunning new horror manga." —Third Eye Comics

KC
KODANSHA
COMICS

© Shuzo Oshimi/Kodansha Ltd. All rights reserved.

THE SPACE OPERA MASTERPIECE FROM MANGA LEGEND LEIJI MATSUMOTO AVAILABLE FOR THE FIRST TIME IN ENGLISH!

LEIJI MATSUMOTO'S

Queen Emeraldas

KC
KODANSHA
COMICS

"If you like space cowboys and pirates or simply want to get lost in a strange dreamlike story, Kodansha's beautiful hardcover is worth checking out."
- *Anime News Network*

"It's not so much a manga as it is a song. But you'll want to listen to it again and again."
- *A Case for Suitable Treatment*

© Leiji Matsumoto/Kodansha, Ltd. All rights reserved.

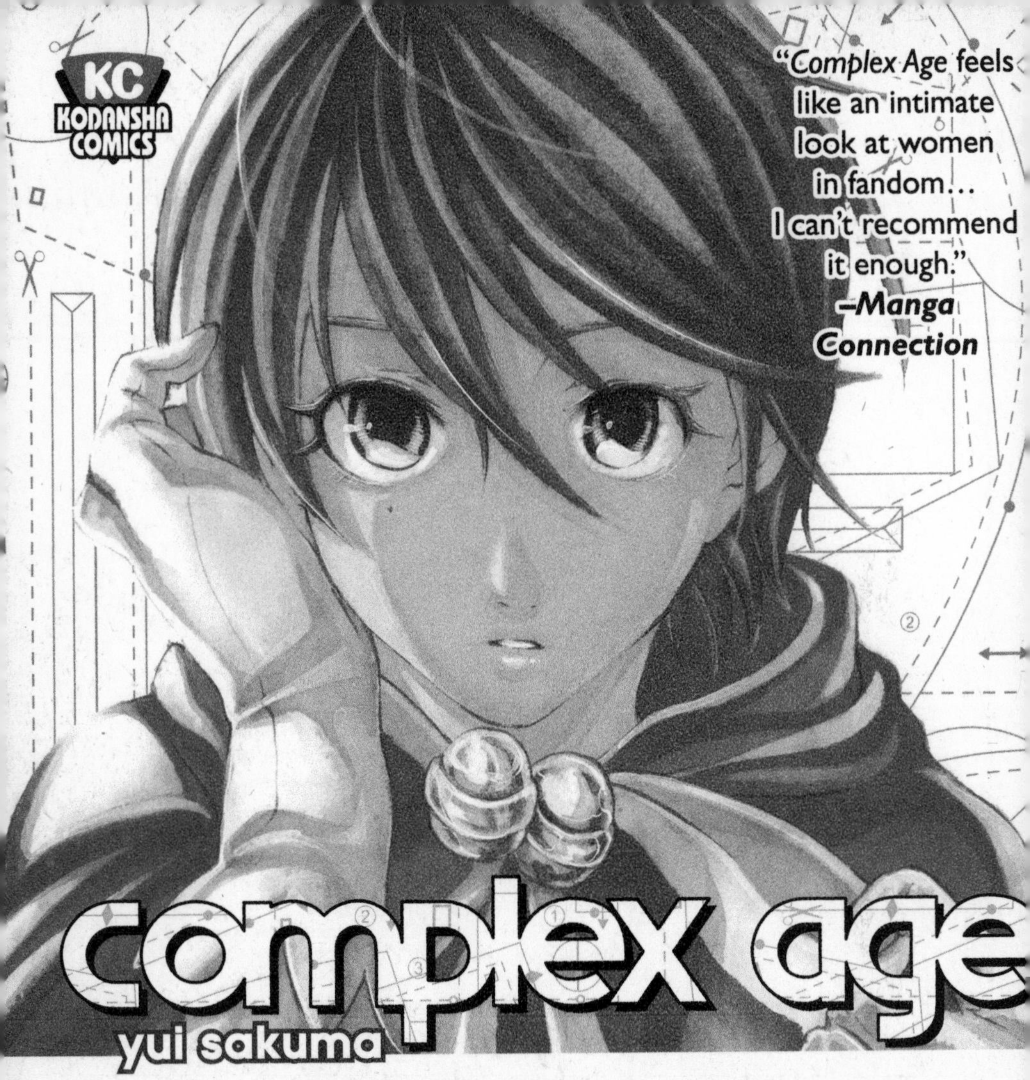
KC
KODANSHA COMICS
“Complex Age feels like an intimate look at women in fandom… I can’t recommend it enough.”
–Manga Connection
complex age
yui sakuma

26-year-old Nagisa Kataura has a secret. Transforming into her favorite anime and manga characters is her passion in life, and she’s earned great respect amongst her fellow cospayers. But to the rest of society, her hobby is a silly fantasy. As demands from both her office job and cosplaying begin to increase, she may one day have to make a tough choice—what’s more important to her, cosplay or being “normal”?

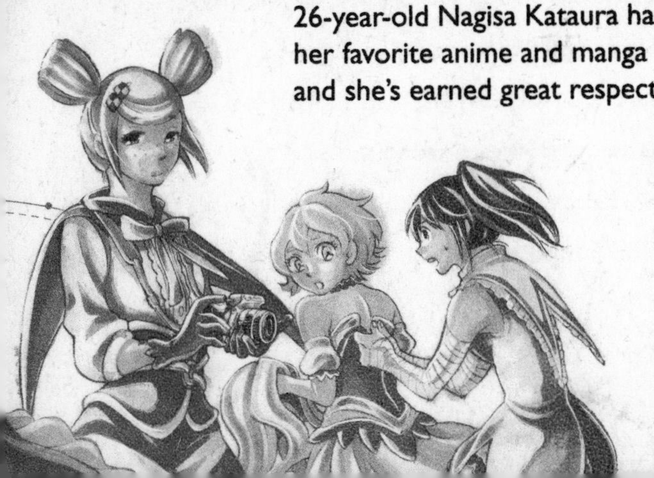

Land of the Lustrous volume 7 is a work of fiction. Names, characters, places, and incidents are the products of the author's imagination or are used fictitiously. Any resemblance to actual events, locales, or persons, living or dead, is entirely coincidental.

A Kodansha Comics Trade Paperback Original.

Land of the Lustrous volume 7 copyright © 2017 Haruko Ichikawa
English translation copyright © 2018 Haruko Ichikawa

All rights reserved.

Published in the United States by Kodansha Comics, an imprint of Kodansha USA Publishing, LLC, New York.

Publication rights for this English edition arranged through Kodansha Ltd., Tokyo.

First published in Japan in 2017 by Kodansha Ltd., Tokyo.

ISBN 978-1-63236-637-5

Printed in the United States of America.

www.kodanshacomics.com

9 8 7 6 5 4 3 2 1

Translator: Alethea Nibley & Athena Nibley
Lettering: Evan Hayden
Editing: Lauren Scanlan